Michael Warner is Seymour H. Knox Professor of English and American Studies, Yale University. He is the author of *The Trouble with Normal* and *Letters of the Republic* (both from Harvard). Jonathan VanAntwerpen is Program Officer and Research Fellow, Social Science Research Council. Craig Calhoun is University Professor of Social Science, New York University.

VARIETIES OF SECULARISM IN A SECULAR AGE

Varieties of Secularism in a Secular Age

Edited by

Michael Warner
Jonathan VanAntwerpen
Craig Calhoun

HARVARD UNIVERSITY PRESS
Cambridge, Massachusetts, and London, England   2010

Copyright © 2010 by the President and Fellows of Harvard College

ALL RIGHTS RESERVED

Printed in the United States of America

Library of Congress Cataloging-in-Publication Data

Varieties of secularism in a secular age / edited by Michael Warner,
Jonathan VanAntwerpen, Craig Calhoun.
p.   cm.
Includes bibliographical references and index.
ISBN 978-0-674-04857-7 (alk. paper)
1. Taylor, Charles, 1931—Secular age.   2. Secularism.   3. Religion and culture.
I. Warner, Michael, 1958–   II. VanAntwerpen, Jonathan, 1970–
III. Calhoun, Craig J., 1952–
BL2747.8.V37 2010
211'.6—dc22   2009032523

Contents

A Note on Citations

References to the major writings of Charles Taylor are given by an abbreviated title:

EA   *The Ethics of Authenticity* (Cambridge, Mass.: Harvard University Press, 1992)

H   *Hegel* (Cambridge: Cambridge University Press, 1975)

HMS   *Hegel and Modern Society* (Cambridge: Cambridge University Press, 1979)

MC   *Multiculturalism: Examining the Politics of Recognition* (Princeton: Princeton University Press, 1994)

MSI   *Modern Social Imaginaries* (Durham: Duke University Press, 2004)

SA   *A Secular Age* (Cambridge, Mass.: Harvard University Press, 2007)

SS   *Sources of the Self* (Cambridge, Mass.: Harvard University Press, 1989)

VR   *Varieties of Religion Today: William James Revisited* (Cambridge, Mass.: Harvard University Press, 2002)

Varieties of Secularism in a Secular Age

Editors' Introduction

MICHAEL WARNER, JONATHAN VANANTWERPEN,
AND CRAIG CALHOUN

"What does it mean to say that we live in a secular age?" asks Charles Taylor in the first sentence of *A Secular Age.* This apparently simple question opens into a massive, provocative, and complex book, exceeding even the scale of Taylor's monumental *Sources of the Self.*[1] Given its scale, the stature of its author as one of the leading thinkers of our time, and the critical importance of the topic in contemporary thought and politics, *A Secular Age* demands serious engagement. Hence the book before you; in the essays collected here, leading scholars from a variety of fields and backgrounds offer their own accounts of Taylor's work. Each charts a different conversation in which *A Secular Age* intervenes. We hope that the result, though surely not a complete or exhaustive assessment, will suggest something of the complexity

---

1 *A Secular Age* runs to 874 pages. *Sources of the Self* weighed in at a mere 593, including notes. Writing for The Immanent Frame, a Social Science Research Council blog on secularism, religion, and the public sphere, eminent sociologist Robert Bellah refers to *A Secular Age* as Taylor's "breakthrough book," calling it "one of the most important books to be written in my lifetime." See Robert Bellah, "Secularism of a New Kind," The Immanent Frame, 2007: www.ssrc.org/blogs/immanent _frame/2007/10/19/secularism-of-a-new-kind/.

of the question of secularity, the analytic density of Taylor's take on it, and the variety of discussions that *A Secular Age* opens up.

This collection benefited greatly from a conference in April 2008 at Yale University. At that event, most of the contributors presented earlier versions of these chapters for discussion. The culmination of the weekend conference was Taylor's response, which appears in revised form at the end of this volume. The book is not, however, a straightforward record of the Yale conference: papers have been revised; some that were not presented then have been added to the mix; and a few papers from the conference were unavailable for inclusion here. (The latter, regrettably, included contributions from Rajeev Bhargava, Courtney Bender, and Seyla Benhabib, all of whom made significant statements at the conference.)

A Secular Age is such a rich book that neither the conference nor this volume will be able to do it justice. But we would like to highlight a few of the challenges presented by the book. To some degree these lie not just with its content but with its form. *A Secular Age* is divided into five parts. Roughly, Parts I through IV are consecutively historical. Part I treats the early modern period, Part II the long eighteenth century, Part III the nineteenth, and Part IV the twentieth. Part V is clearly of a different order: a sustained treatment of the present condition, assessing both the problems with an exclusively nonreligious spiritual outlook and the problems besetting contemporary religiosity. But this is only a rough structuring; even the last part contains historical narratives, and the first four parts, though roughly historical, also contain some major analytic and theoretical sections (including the exposition of the idea of social imaginaries). The book does provide a liberal amount of signposting; nearly every chapter begins with a summary of what has gone before. But the historical narrative that runs through the book is not itself the structuring principle. Despite the chronological unfolding of the argument, the book is structured by its argument, and not by the consecutive narration of the past for its own sake. The fact that argument and chronology coincide more in the earlier chapters reflects in part the difference between looking at the way challenges were met in the past and the way we confront challenges in the present and still open future.

The interweaving of philosophical and historical understanding is undoubtedly crucial to Taylor's thought, and has been a conspicuous preoccupation of his long career. *A Secular Age* might even be taken as one long demonstration that the kinds of spiritual questions considered in Part V are historically conditioned. More generally, it is often hard to understand a new configuration of ideas or culture without understanding what it was developed out of or against. It is an illusion to think of intellectual history as a process of discarding false beliefs in order to shift to true ones. People work out ways of thinking in response to particular and shifting problems in their previous ideas and their larger circumstances, creating along the way a particular configuration of understandings, possibilities, and limits. Grasping any one moment in such a process requires grasping at least something of the path that led to it.[2] Taylor has analyzed a secular age as it develops within and out of Latin Christianity. The path is a crucial part of the story.

The form of *A Secular Age* is obviously related to one of its main substantive points: that questions such as those of religion and ethics, though appearing to be pressed upon us by the bare facts of existence and the universe, nevertheless get their particular form and no small part of their urgency from contexts of which we are not fully aware—unspoken premises about the kind of society we live in, the way we imagine the goods we are striving for, the practical contexts in which the questions arise, and the ways we imagine ourselves as persons. To say this is not to diminish the importance of the questions. On the contrary: for Taylor, it is to show how deep they lie in our constitution as persons and in the history of our social worlds. Historical reflection as practiced by Taylor is not relativizing, because it locates the limits of our ability to relativize.

Formally, however, it is a challenge. *A Secular Age* is neither a conventional historical narrative nor a conventional philosophical argument, and a reader who expects either is likely to be disoriented. Compounding this challenge, *A Secular Age* is also—expressly—a personal book. Taylor here speaks of questions in which he has a powerful motivating interest. Attentive readers will notice, however, that the personal voice appears only occasionally; it is generally muted. Most of the book—especially the first four parts—seems designed to function without the personal voice. Taylor has spoken of his desire to write the bulk of the book in ways that would be noncontroversial, insert-

2 See Taylor's excursis on historical explanation, *SS*, 199–207. Taylor's development of this view is informed particularly by Hans-Georg Gadamer; see *Truth and Method*, 2nd ed. (New York: Crossroad, 1989). Craig Calhoun takes up the subject in his review "Morality, Identity, and Historical Explanation: Charles Taylor on the Sources of the Self," *Sociological Theory* 9, 2 (1991): 232–263.

ing his own stance only when it is clear that other stances are possible given the surrounding description of affairs.[3]

These splits within the form and authorial stance of *A Secular Age* might help to explain why, as early reviews revealed, not everyone who reads the book immediately grasps its project. Although the book has received wide praise, several of its early reviewers seemed to have trouble describing the main themes, or sorting out the history from the argument. One notable example was a piece for the *New York Times Book Review* by intellectual historian John Patrick Diggins, who opened his review by conjuring up Taylor's "quarrel" with "secularism," defined as "the idea that as modernity, science and democracy have advanced, concern with God and spirituality has retreated to the margins of life."[4] This description, however, sounds not so much like "secularism" as like sociological theories of "secularization." Eliding the difference between the two, Diggins took Taylor to task for his ostensible opposition to both. Yet his representation of Taylor's argument was doubly misleading. While Taylor has indeed written critically about contemporary "modes of secularism"—defending one version of secularism against others in a book chapter published in the late 1990s[5]—the normative analysis of "secularism" as a political and ideological project does not figure prominently within the pages of *A Secular Age*. Likewise, although Diggins foregrounds

3 As Taylor said in a conversation about *A Secular Age*, "What I tried to do in the book . . . is to lay out a picture of the scene in which we are all involved, a scene that people could agree on even if they are coming from different positions. . . . I think everyone who is really open and honest will acknowledge that this is our scene, or our common situation, and that it has these three features that I outline in my book: great variety, great movement, and a great potential to be deeply shaken by other positions. . . . But of course this scene is lived from different positions. And I think in a book like this one should do a variety of things, both describing general features that all can agree to, and being open and honest about one's own unique position, what I describe as full disclosure, or disclosing one's particular way of looking at things." See Ronald A. Kuipers, "The New Atheism and the Spiritual Landscape of the West: A Conversation with Charles Taylor," *The Other Journal*, June 12, 2008: www .theotherjournal.com/article.php?id=375.

4 John Patrick Diggins, "The Godless Delusion," *New York Times Book Review*, December 16, 2007, 15.

5 Charles Taylor, "Modes of Secularism," in Rajeev Bhargava, ed., *Secularism and Its Critics* (Delhi: Oxford University Press, 1998), 31–53. For a helpful introduction to basic analytical distinctions among "the secular" (as an epistemic category), "secularization" (as a conceptualization of historical processes), and "secularism" (as a worldview or political ideology), see José Casanova, "Secular, Secularizations, Secularisms," The Immanent Frame, 2007: www.ssrc.org/blogs/immanent_frame /2007/10/25/secular-secularizations-secularisms/.

Taylor's supposed quarrel with what is usually called "the secularization thesis," the bulk of Taylor's book is devoted not simply to criticizing the view that modernity inevitably marginalizes religion (although he does take issue with that once paradigmatic perspective), but rather to explaining how conditions of secularity have come to shape both contemporary belief and "unbelief" alike. It is this focus on the "background" conditions of belief or the "context of understanding" in which commitments are formed—articulated clearly in the book's opening pages—that sets *A Secular Age* apart from the vast body of sociological literature on secularization that precedes it.[6] The whole point of departure of Taylor's innovative approach was entirely overlooked in Diggins's review.[7]

Some reviewers—Diggins among them—read the entire book as a personal polemic or a work of Christian apologetics, sometimes mistaking it for a brief against the secular or an argument for Catholicism.[8] Writing in the fashionable literary journal *n+1*, Bruce Robbins asserted that "Taylor has joined [Talal] Asad as a central figure in a wave of so-called 'post-secular'

6 For a critical review of the study of secularization within sociology, see Philip S. Gorski and Ateş Altınordu, "After Secularization?" *Annual Review of Sociology* 34 (2008): 55–85. As José Casanova has written, the theory of secularization "may be the only theory which was able to attain a truly paradigmatic status within the modern social sciences." Given the theory's apparently definitive standing, it went relatively unchallenged for many years and was often simply assumed. "The consensus," Casanova writes, "was such that not only did the theory remain uncontested but apparently it was not even necessary to test it, since everybody took it for granted." José Casanova, *Public Religions in the Modern World* (Chicago: University of Chicago Press, 1994), 17. The classical (and now much contested) understanding of secularization notwithstanding, "there is no single or widely accepted definition of secularization" within sociology, and the multiple sociological understandings of secularization both draw on and depart from a diverse range of "presociological" variants, as Gorski and Altınordu emphasize ("After Secularization?," 57).

7 The misunderstandings and misleading intimations in Diggins's review of *A Secular Age* are so manifold that it would be difficult to know where to begin a systematic analysis of them. We attempt no such review of the review here. Discussing the review in a conversation with Ronald A. Kuipers, Taylor himself took issue with its author's slipshod reading. "It's obvious to me," he said, "that [Diggins] simply turned to page 25 and page 375 and then closed the book. And he happened to hit a sentence that was describing some position that wasn't mine, but he attributed it to me." See "Religious Belonging in an 'Age of Authenticity': A Conversation with Charles Taylor," *The Other Journal*, June 23, 2008: www.theotherjournal.com/article.php?id=376. For critical responses to Diggins's review at The Immanent Frame, written by Harvey Cox, Colin Jager, James K. A. Smith, and Jimmy Casas Klausen, see www.ssrc.org/blogs/immanent_frame/2007/12/15/the-godless-delusion/.

8 Taylor's "main purpose," Diggins wrote, portraying the book as an apologetic attempt to "prove that God is still very much present in the world," was "to salvage religion from the corrosive effects of modern secularism" (Diggins, "The Godless Delusion").

thinking that is highly skeptical, to say the least, of democracy, liberalism, and the state, as well as of secularism."[9] It is hard to know what to make of the assertion that Taylor, of all people, is skeptical of democracy in this context; and as we will see below, Taylor's book is more accurately seen as a brief *against* the idea that we have entered a "post-secular" age.[10] *A Secular Age*, wrote Charles Larmore, citing the book's "shocking partiality" in his review for the *New Republic,* was "a book written by a Catholic for Catholics."[11] More than one reader wondered, along with Peter E. Gordon—whose long review for the *Journal of the History of Ideas* grappled admirably with book's complex historical argument—whether Taylor really did find it "inconceivable" that he might abandon his own faith.[12] A leading participant in a conference on Taylor's work at the New School doggedly and somewhat incredulously insisted that he did, flatly misreading an early passage on the optionality, revisability, and fragility of contemporary religious commitments, which Taylor sees as defining feature of a secular age. Taylor, he worried, had made an undeniably dogmatic confession of absolute and unreasonable faith.[13] Yet more often than not, such critics simply missed the point. It is difficult to clearly

9 Bruce Robbins, "Disenchanted," *n+1*, August 4, 2009: www.nplusonemag.com/disenchanted.

10 See our discussion of the "post-secular" below, pp. 21–23. Robbins inaccurately characterizes many other arguments in the book as well, including the idea of the social imaginary, which he seems to take as an activity of fantasizing that could be consciously steered. Elsewhere in the review he writes that "*A Secular Age* also presents secularism as a disguised form of Christianity, hiding theological content behind apparently secular concepts. On this reading, the disenchantment of the world never really happened." While arguments of this type have been made many times—notably by Karl Lowith, Carl Becker, and many in the neo-Schmittian school—the secular in Taylor's narrative is not a mask over hidden theology. Taylor does often point to the spiritual motives that have led to unforeseen transformations in religious traditions and their alternatives; but these are real transformations, and Taylor does not regard the resulting displacement of religious traditions as illusory.

11 Charles Larmore, "How Much Can We Stand?" *New Republic,* April 9, 2008: www.tnr.com/article/books/how-much-can-we-stand.

12 Peter E. Gordon, "The Place of the Sacred in the Absence of God: Charles Taylor's *A Secular Age,*" *Journal of the History of Ideas* 69, 4 (2008): 655.

13 In the passage in question, Taylor indicates that he wants to define and trace a change "which takes us from a society in which it was virtually impossible not to believe in God, to one in which faith, even for the staunchest believer, is one human possibility among others. I may find it inconceivable that I would abandon my faith, but there are others, including possibly some very close to me, whose way of living I cannot in all honesty just dismiss as depraved, or blind, or unworthy, who have no faith (at least not in God, or the transcendent). Belief in God is no longer axiomatic. There are alternatives. And this will also likely mean that at least in certain milieux, it may be hard to sustain one's faith. There will be people who feel bound to give it up, even though they mourn its loss"(*SA*, 3). For a brief overview of the New School conference, see José Casanova, "Secular Imaginaries: Introduction," *International Journal of Politics, Culture, and Society* 21 (2008): 1–4.

identify any passage in *A Secular Age* that might support such claims of either outright dogmatism or apologetic intent. It would be more accurate to say that the book attempts to show how stances of skepticism and faith are interwoven and mutually "fragilized."

Some have assumed that Taylor would like to return to an earlier moment in the history of Christianity, though the book repeatedly stresses reasons why this would be undesirable even if it were possible.[14] Taylor is less interested in Catholicism as a specific institutional or theological branch of Christianity opposed to Protestantism than in a series of developments in the Latin Christian tradition that have shaped both—and also helped inaugurate a secular age that opened new possibilities for reconnecting the spiritual and the material. Such reconnections would probably involve renewal of embodied ritual, changed modes of marking time, different ways of pursuing healing (*SA*, 614). They might also involve overcoming the striking tensions around sexuality that have made this such a dominant issue in Christian anxieties about the secular in recent years.

It is not slighting this huge book to say that it won't be the last word. The book has its own openings to divergent interpretations. Despite its massive size—or perhaps in part because of it—it is a less completely crafted whole than Taylor's other books, taking a number of sidetracks and frequently doubling back on itself. Like the secular age it seeks to outline, it incorporates internal tensions and even apparent contradictions. On Taylor's account, "living within" a secular age often involves being pulled in one direction or another. Those attuned to religious belief and experience, as Taylor understands it, are pulled toward openings to transcendence, while others feel the pull of "the closure of immanence." But between these two poles, as Taylor is at pains to emphasize, are a great many people who have been "cross-

14 While Taylor therefore seeks repeatedly to turn aside charges of nostalgia and to plumb the new spiritual possibilities produced by a secular age, his particular conception of Christian faith is nonetheless significantly invested in substantial engagement with earlier historical periods. Links to earlier ages, he suggests, enable both a "deepening" of the religious life and a "loosening" from "too close an identification with this age." See "Religious Belonging in an 'Age of Authenticity.'" As William Connolly aptly wrote in an earlier essay, Taylor "is not easily definable as either a secularist or devotee of lost Christendom, a defender of modernity or one who seeks to return to an enchanted world . . . Each time a philosophical or theological faction seeks to etch a division in stone, Taylor surfaces to complicate the picture." See William E. Connolly, "Catholicism and Philosophy: A Nontheistic Appreciation," in *Charles Taylor*, ed. Ruth Abbey (Cambridge: Cambridge University Press, 2004), 166.

pressured," pulled in both directions, caught up somewhere between an "open" and a "closed" perspective on the world, perhaps to different degrees in different milieus. In the midst of such pulls and pressures, with draws and demands from both sides, are individuals who are able to stand in the "open space where you can feel the winds pulling you, now to belief, now to unbelief," those rare figures who can "feel some of the force of each opposing position" (*SA*, 549). Taylor suggests that such individuals are actually quite exceptional, since for most people, most of the time, much is taken for granted and left unexamined. Yet it would not be an exaggeration to suggest that one of the great strengths of *A Secular Age* derives from Taylor's demonstrated willingness and ability to stand in the "open space" and guide his readers through the range of perspectives its vantage affords.[15]

Reading *A Secular Age*

Given the scale and complexity of *A Secular Age*, it might help readers of the present volume to restate a few of Taylor's main themes. The book begins with an important intervention—a new sense of what is meant by the historical shift to secularity, distinguished from two more familiar understandings of secularization. The first of these older models (which Taylor calls "secularity 1") is the retreat of religion from various public spaces: politics, science, art, the market. The second ("secularity 2") is more personal: the notion of declining religious belief and practice, often thought to be an inevitable consequence of modernity. With either of these two understandings of secularization in mind, people often tend to think of secularity simply as the absence of religion, not something in itself. Or they think of it mainly as a strong separation of church and state—creating again a zone of absence. These two conceptions of secularity are central to the standard sociological story of secularization and the standard public usage of the word "secular."

Taylor's book seeks to resituate the discussion and thus to recast the debate. Taylor doesn't dismiss either the decline or the compartmentalization of religion, but he suggests that the dominant discussion of each is rendered very misleading by reliance on what he calls "subtraction stories." These are

---

15 Taylor draws this understanding of the "open space" from his reading of William James. "James," he writes, "is our great philosopher of the cusp. He tells us more than anyone else about what it's like to stand in that open space and feel the winds pulling you, now here, now there" (*VR*, 59).

accounts in which authors trace the decline or compartmentalization of religion without seriously considering the transformations this entails—not just in religion but in everything else as well.[16] Taylor touches on the familiar topoi of secularization theory: urbanization, the rise of science, industrialization, and so forth. He notes that these can't be quite so autonomously and uniformly effective as has sometimes been asserted or the decline of religious practice in Europe would be matched in the United States and elsewhere. But this is not really his topic.

A Secular Age does not attempt to offer a causal account of the spread of unbelief or the writing of laws limiting public expression of religion. Taylor's explorations of the history of thinking about God, religious institutions, the natural and social order, and the person will help those undertaking to offer such explanations, especially by demonstrating how intertwined different dimensions of historical transformation have been. But Taylor's argument centers on how the development of a secular age changed both belief and unbelief, both religious and nonreligious institutions, the way human beings understood both themselves and nature. He shows secularization as a process changing dominant senses of history and time, ideas about what is open and closed in the human future, and the cross-pressures people face in struggling to understand their circumstances and live their lives.

What is secular about "a secular age," then, is not merely the dwindling of religion, or even the functional separation of Church from state, science, and aesthetics. The most searching and original—but also unsettled and unsettling—parts of Taylor's book concern what he calls "secularity 3." By this he means "a move from a society where belief in God is unchallenged and indeed, unproblematic, to one in which it is understood to be one option among others, and frequently not the easiest to embrace." Secularity is not just a net reduction in religious belief or practice, therefore, but a change in the very conditions of belief. "Secularity in this sense," Taylor writes, "is a matter of the whole context of understanding in which our moral, spiritual or religious experience and search takes place" (*SA*, 3).

In contexts that are secular in this third sense, religiosity is more and more considered a question of personal belief rather than collective ritual or

---

16 Some of the most interesting parts of Taylor's book are lengthy discussions of the ways in which ideas of personhood and subjectivity, social relations and moral obligations, material well-being and economic pursuits have been changed by both (1) changes in the ways in which religion shapes each and (2) reductions in the extent to which religion shapes each.

practice. It has also become an "option," according to which people define themselves through one orientation or another, but in either case without the kind of inevitability that would reverberate indistinctly between subjective and outward manifestations. Taylor makes it clear that in many ways this shift to secularity makes religious belief more difficult to sustain—since "even for the staunchest believer," it has become "one human possibility among others" (SA, 3)—but he doesn't see only negatives on the balance sheet. Secularization has come about alongside changes that we cannot help but value, like a deeper notion of self and subjective agency and a more egalitarian social order. Moreover, though belief may be problematic in new ways, it is also possible for it to take on new meaning.

BELIEF AND FULLNESS

Taylor really means "belief." He doesn't want to see religion as just a number of engaging practices or quasi-ethnic customs, and he is critical of suggestions that the "essence of religion" lies in the answers it offers to the "question of meaning," which he sees as an approach that absolutizes "the modern predicament" (SA, 717–718). Religion, for Taylor, entails some sort of "transcendence," especially "the sense that there is some good higher than, beyond human flourishing" (20). Yet he also seeks to steer clear of some of the common complaints against a belief-centered account of religion.[17] He does not mean belief in specific doctrines. Nor does he understand belief as an abstract intellectual commitment to the truth of a propositional statement. Rather, he devotes considerable effort to showing how that sort of narrowed "epistemological" approach is part of a package of cultural and intellectual changes that make religious belief difficult and "embattled," even while they make for advances in other domains, like science.[18]

The epistemological approach turns on a strong separation of the know-

17 Critiques of the equation of religion with belief have become numerous; one broad polemic is Rodney Needham, *Belief, Language, and Experience* (Chicago: University of Chicago Press, 1973). Similar critiques more pointedly developed in the context of religious studies include Talal Asad, *Genealogies of Religion: Discipline and Reasons of Power in Christianity and Islam* (Baltimore: Johns Hopkins University Press, 1993) and, from a different angle, Taylor's own earlier work *Varieties of Religion Today*.

18 Think by contrast of a medieval proof of the existence of God. Aquinas, for example, does not undertake such a proof from a position of epistemic neutrality, in order to see whether he can produce an argument that will convince himself or others to believe. His project is, rather, the effort of someone with faith to try to understand better what he should believe and what it means to believe.

ing mind from culture, social relations, even body and perhaps "spirit"—that is, aspects of our mental activity not readily rendered in rational-propositional terms. Taylor joins with those who have argued for the importance of other forms and dimensions of understanding, of tacit knowledge, and of the embeddedness of each of us in language and culture. As he writes near the outset of *A Secular Age,* "By 'context of understanding' here, I mean both matters that will probably have been explicitly formulated by almost everyone, such as the plurality of options, and some which form the implicit, largely unfocused background of this experience and search, its 'pre-ontology,' to use a Heideggerian term" (*SA*, 3). We are only able to engage in the kind of disembodied reason moderns value against a background of understandings we often don't recognize. Among these are some commitments that are deeper than others, more fundamentally shaping our thought and outlooks. Here Taylor builds on his argument from *Sources of the Self,* where he called these "hypergoods" (see especially 63–75). We are all committed to such higher goods, Taylor suggests, even those who claim not to be (reflecting their commitment to "objectivity" and perhaps "rationality" as principles more fundamental than some others). It is not only the religious who have some "beliefs" that go beyond the conclusions of—and indeed are orienting for—ordinary reason.

So one central move for Taylor is his attempt to change the way we think about belief. He starts out by evoking a subjective experience, what he calls "fullness." By this he means any experience of life and the world as imbued with meaning, beauty, and connection—whatever the source of the experience. Crucially, it is a subjective experience in which the fullness or satisfying intensity is understood to be objective—the way the world is, or at least can sometimes be—not merely a result of subjective attitude. Our subjective stances may afford us more or better access to fullness, but it is not merely an interior state. Indeed, it is a reflection of our individualistic, psychological orientation and also our rationalistic, epistemological criteria for knowledge that we try to grasp fullness entirely in terms of subjective states; we say we have moments of transcendent experience, thus, rather than moments when we experience the transcendent character of reality.

Fullness is not in itself a belief; it is the sense of something larger or more deeply meaningful about which we may have beliefs. Nor is the sense of fullness derived only from a perception of reality and meaning beyond this world or only interpretable in religious terms. This sense of heightened meaning and connection is always possible within humanist and naturalist frames of reference: this is the way life should be.[19] But to most moderns, this strong sense of the fullness of the world, of the wonder of it that goes beyond everyday concerns about health, material prosperity, politics, even justice, is available only occasionally. Some people may seem to have more consistent access to it, and this may be a source of their inspirational leadership, extraordinary commitments, or saintliness. But it is typically episodic, available only for moments, perhaps aided by ritual but sometimes just surprising us. And fullness is less available now than it used to be, when it seemed routinely the case that the material world was not all that there was.

Here there is an interesting twist to Taylor's argument, for he thinks this isn't all bad. A sense of fullness has become harder to achieve, but it can also be wonderful in new ways. If we can work through the various obstacles to having a sense of living amid transcendence, we can experience it in richer ways. Here Taylor's argument is loosely Hegelian (not surprisingly, since he is one of the greatest interpreters and analysts of Hegel). We start out with easy access to a sense of fullness, but don't know very well what we have. We grow in knowledge (or, as Rousseau would say, in arts and science), but in ways that cut us off from full relationships to nature, our own lives, other people, and God. Yet there is potential for returning to a sense of fullness informed by poetry and philosophy, Beethoven's late quartets, and even a deeper sense of what it means ecologically to care for the world or politically to really value other people.

IMMANENCE AND TRANSCENDENCE

Making the idea—and experience—of transcendence sensible is one of Taylor's central goals. As important as transcendence is to Taylor's account of

19 Taylor's treatment of "fullness" in *A Secular Age* has nonetheless been the subject of sustained debate, and many readers have assumed he meant to evoke a specifically religious form of experience. As he says in a recent interview, "I've used this as a generic term on the grounds that I think everybody has some sense of, and desire for, a fantastically realized life, a life realized to the full. But in talking with people and reading reviews of the book, I've found that I'm often totally misunderstood on this. They thought that fullness could only be applied to explicitly religious positions, while the whole point was that I was looking for a generic term that applied to all people, whether religious or non-religious. But fullness made people shudder, which might show that the search for a universally acceptable term might be mission impossible." See Kuipers, "The New Atheism and the Spiritual Landscape of the West." Taylor returns to the question of "fullness" in his afterword for this volume.

religion, however, most of his book is devoted to trying to understand "immanence," and in particular the historical establishment and intellectual contours of what he calls "the immanent frame." Here Taylor emphasizes the changes in the conditions of belief that he associates with secularity 3. The immanent frame, he suggests, is "not usually, or even mainly a set of *beliefs* which we entertain about our predicament," but rather "the sensed context in which we develop our beliefs" (*SA*, 549).

Reworking and substantially revising Weber's understanding of "disenchantment," Taylor suggests that "the spiritual shape of the present age" (*SA*, 539) can be characterized by the religious and secular possibilities the immanent frame allows and enables, including the possibility of unreflective unbelief introduced by the idea of a self-sufficient immanent order, a naturalist conception of the world made possible and reinforced by a range of other historical changes.[20] Yet religion and spirituality are not extinguished in this context, but have rather been refigured. We should not confuse disenchantment with the end of religion, therefore, as religious commitments and openings to "transcendence" remain possible from within the immanent frame, even as new forces push for "the closure of immanence." One way of reading much of *A Secular Age* is as leading up to Taylor's analysis of the contemporary dilemmas of the immanent frame, including the relative merits of the "closed" and "open" "spins," as he calls them: the ongoing problems of the body, particularly as manifest in sex and violence; the fate of the aspiration to transcendence; and the cross-pressuring of different perspectives.

Taylor sees the modern West as shaped deeply by the idea of a natural order that can be understood without reference to anything outside itself (unless perhaps human consciousness is understood this way, though as Taylor notes, it is often understood as one more natural phenomenon). Indeed, he suggests that this is "the great invention of the West" (*SA*, 15). It is constitutive of the frame within which one can set aside questions of divine creation, marking off a sharp boundary with the transcendent. The orderliness of the world is now impersonal, perhaps set in motion by a watchmaker God but working by means of its own laws.

A central historical phase in the movement toward this modern understanding of self and others in the world is the late seventeenth- and eigh-

---

20 "So the buffered identity of the disciplined individual moves in a constructed social space, where instrumental rationality is a key value, and time is pervasively secular. All of this makes up what I want to call 'the immanent frame'" (542).

teenth-century spread of providential deism. Taylor offers a brilliant account of how this paved the way for exclusive humanism, even though its protagonists did not understand themselves as leaving the realm of religion, and indeed understood themselves as solving problems within existing Christianity. A secular perspective grew within religion before it was taken up by the irreligious. This was already evident in Augustine, of course, but it took on new dimensions in the early modern era. Growing secularity meant at first a greater religious engagement with human relationships and other affairs of "this world." It responded to a new affirmation of the virtues of ordinary life, including not least the happiness and this-worldly nurturance of family life. It responded to a new sense of historical time, anchored partly in the self-consciousness of early moderns as inhabiting a new era in which older forms of religion might no longer suffice. But growing secularity also involved the understanding that "this world" moved according to an impersonal order of causes and effects within it. And this helped to underwrite the rise of modern science. Though at first this meant reading the word of God in nature rather than in ancient texts, it often became disengaged from religious connections to the idea of a larger, transcendent whole.

By the transcendent, Taylor generally means sources of meaning that lie beyond this world—at least as we can grasp it in either anthropocentric-humanistic or naturalistic terms. Taylor articulates three dimensions in which we go "beyond": a good higher than human flourishing (such as love in the sense of agape), a higher power (such as God), and extension of life (or even "our lives") beyond the "natural" scope between birth and death (*SA*, 20).

Taylor indicates that the God of Abraham who orients his faith is only one way to grasp this transcendent reality. He is open, thus, to the potentially equal value of grasping the transcendent in Hindu and Muslim terms (and he may mean to include Muslims when he makes reference to believing in the God of Abraham). In his afterword to this volume, likewise, he refers to his own deep sense of the power of Buddhism. He is also open to new theologies that transform the meaning of the term "God," including those that attempt to rid it of anthropocentric or patriarchal projections (though in fact theology as such doesn't figure very strongly among the many intellectual sources Taylor engages in *A Secular Age*). But Taylor's usage seems consistently focused on that which is beyond nature by virtue of the actual contemporary existence of some other or additional reality. Yet when we ask of the world as it exists "Is that all there is?" we are also asking about the future. Indeed, part of what Taylor sees as limiting in the immanent frame is a tendency toward both deterministic and instrumental approaches to human life: we are led to accept too much of what exists as the fixed character of reality, then being left to adapt ourselves to it.

Limiting or not, the immanent frame is basic to both secularism and religion as we know them today. The historical transformations that eventuated in the establishment of the immanent frame, writes Taylor, "represent profound changes in our practical self-understanding, how we fit into our world (as buffered, disciplined, instrumental agents) and into society (as responsible individuals, constituting societies designed for mutual benefit)" (*SA*, 542). We cannot make sense of the decline of religious practice (where this has occurred), the compartmentalization of religion as private, or even declarations of doctrinaire atheism without reference to these changes. The very term "supernatural" expresses something of the larger point. The "natural" is the unmarked category, and there is a sharp division from that which is outside or above it, a division ironically promoted within Latin Christendom in order to mark "the autonomy of the supernatural" (542).

Reform

At the center of Taylor's account is an epic irony: that secularity in its modern Western sense is significantly a product of the long history of reform movements within Western Christianity. Initially, reform (starting before the usual dates of the Reformation and continuing among Catholics as well as Protestants after it) was a project of producing purer religion and demanding more widespread lay adherence to high (even monastic) standards of purity. The effort to "cleanse" Christianity of folk beliefs and practices was one part of this story. So was the rise of new morality governed by self-discipline but also ever-proliferating rules, the religious counterpart to the manners prized in the civilizing process. The reform effort also helped shape the rise of an understanding of an impersonal natural order in which God intervened less frequently (if ever) and which could be the object of a purely natural science. It shaped equally a transformation of the self to create individual subjects —"buffered selves"—able to take a distanced view of everything outside the mind. This meant not only ceasing to understand the self as "porous," such that demons or God could enter it, but also gaining the ability to act instrumentally in relation to the external world and to one's own body. Reformers created a sharper division between the spiritual and the physical.

The possibility of a fully secular society is an unanticipated result of reformers' efforts to police the properly spiritual. They did so in order to "clean up" the inherited beliefs and practices of pre-Christian folk religion and focus believers' attention in a proper way on God. They sought to purge it of the magical and festive. Early modern clerical elites—notably in the era of the Reformation but on both Catholic and Protestant sides—sought to enforce among parishioners standards of piety and orthodoxy previously deemed important only for elites.[21] In doing so, they came to define the phenomenon of belief in a new way that was sharp enough to make declarations of explicit unbelief—atheism—far more prominent than in earlier times (when people might have shown little interest in religion, dissented from specific teachings, or deviated from orthodox practices without asserting an epistemic denial of God). These early modern religious elites helped set in motion a continuing purification of thought that would eventually take an antireligious turn in the Enlightenment. But it started out with efforts to get people to be better Christians.

These efforts started well before the Protestant Reformation, which has no special place of privilege in *A Secular Age*. Indeed, rather than seeing the Reformation as the beginning of modernity, Taylor more often adverts to late medieval reforms, or even to more long-standing projects in the deep history of the religions associated with the so-called axial age.[22] The secular as Taylor sees it is not a force that assaulted religion from without; it did not suddenly appear from modernity; it was not contrived by Enlightenment rationalists; and it did not entirely happen willy-nilly as the result of capitalism. Its history is at least partly—perhaps mostly—a history of spiritual motives.

The disciplinary revolution familiar to sociologists as part of a Weberian account of the rise of capitalism is also a central part of this story of religious transformation. "Training in a disciplined, sober, industrious life" helped to shape both the instrumental character of modern secular society and its pro-

---

21 Here Taylor draws upon Keith Thomas, *Religion and the Decline of Magic* (New York: Scribner's, 1971).

22 The idea of the axial age derives from Karl Jaspers; for a discussion, see Shmuel Eisenstadt, "The Axial Age: The Emergence of Transcendental Visions and the Rise of Clerics," *European Journal of Sociology* 23, 2 (1982): 294–314.

ductivity. But it also helped to produce the very sense that society and self could both be remade. It was thus an "experience on the part of élites of success in imposing the order they sought on themselves and society" (*SA*, 228). Moreover, the disciplinary revolution coincided with the civilizing process to create new kinds of sensitivities and values within secular culture.[23] If this became less violent, though, it also became oriented in new ways to a rule-governed approach to morality.

Only quite late in the process did people begin to think of themselves as standing outside Christianity or even "religion" altogether. In the world of Latin Christendom that is Taylor's focus, both modern religion and modern secularism bear the marks of this long process, which has made religion more personal, more mental, and more voluntary. Religious and antireligious people in modernity have more assumptions in common than they often realize. Taylor's secularity 3 is meant to capture this often unrecognized common condition and to show that its genealogy lies largely in the spiritual dilemmas of Latin Christendom itself. By the time the reader arrives at Part V, in which Taylor takes up the rival validity claims and ethical stances—religious and antireligious—in the present, this surface rivalry has come to be seen as the latest instantiation of dilemmas long unresolved, in some ways antedating Christianity itself. *A Secular Age* displaces the commonsense opposition between the religious and the secular with a new understanding in which this opposition appears only as a late and retrospective misrecognition.

This is a powerful and striking thesis (though, again, not so striking as to strike all of Taylor's reviewers). But Taylor is not without company here. His central point bears some resemblances to the thesis of Marcel Gauchet, in *The Disenchantment of the World* (for which Taylor wrote an introduction to the English translation), but with equally important differences.[24] Gauchet similarly argues that modern secularism extends the long history of unresolved contradictions and tensions in religion, and like Taylor he argues that Christianity has played a unique role as "the religion of the end of religion."

23 For "disciplinary revolution," see Philip Gorski, *The Disciplinary Revolution: Calvinism and the Rise of the State in Early Modern Europe* (Chicago: University of Chicago Press, 2003). The "civilizing process" is a phrase made famous by Norbert Elias, on whom Taylor draws heavily. Originally published in 1939 in German, Elias's work is best known as *The Civilizing Process, Vol. I: The History of Manners* (Oxford: Blackwell, 1969) and *Vol. II: State Formation and Civilization* (Oxford: Blackwell, 1982).

24 Marcel Gauchet, *The Disenchantment of the World: A Political History of Religion*, trans. Oscar Burge (Princeton: Princeton University Press, 1997).

Taylor follows Gauchet in linking axial age religions to the problems in the social imaginary constitutive of state societies and in insisting on the social dimensions of religious questions. Some of the same episodes in the history of Christianity figure in important ways for each. But whereas Gauchet begins by positing an anthropological axiom—that humanity is defined by its power of negation, and paradoxically required religion to negate that power of negation—Taylor refuses to see the history of religion as one long detour from mankind's original nature. And whereas Gauchet sees the history as trending unmistakably toward a post-religious future, Taylor argues that this "spin" (to use his own term) underestimates the spiritual dilemmas that motivate it.

This overarching story of the spiritual sources of the secular involves a number of subthemes, including the narrowing of the once-expected gap between the spiritual demands of ordinary people and the religious virtuosi; the rise of projects for social discipline (famously chronicled by Elias); the disembedding of what Taylor calls "the buffered self"; the long process of the "excarnation" of Christianity and, by extension, of modern life; the "eclipse of all goals beyond human flourishing" (SA, 19); the way in which the affirmation of ordinary life led to the disappearance of the need for transformation; and the attenuation of modes of ritual time, ancestral time, and higher time and their displacement by a monochronic idea of secular time.

Taylor traces the growth not just of "secularity" in the abstract but even more of a secular culture with specific content. The rise of exclusive humanism, for example, involved the notion that human flourishing defines the comprehensive good toward which human beings should be oriented. It was thus secular and limited. But it was also the source of tremendous advances in care for fellow human beings. Taylor would challenge the limitation of the good to human flourishing but not reject the advances that humanism brought. Likewise, secular culture grew with thinking about society in terms of new social imaginaries like market, democracy, and public sphere. Each was shaped by humanism, but also by notions such as the equality of human individuals aggregated in one way or another in an impersonal order. The kind of simplistic opposition of religion to "secular humanism" drawn today by some religious leaders is thus very misleading, according to Taylor. Not only would it be unfortunate to jettison the goal of human flourishing; it would impoverish rather than improve religion to try to cleanse it of engagement in the secular world.

The rise of a secular age obviously transformed attention to the temporal, material world. But it also transformed the spiritual. It brought about what Taylor calls the "excarnation," the development of the notion that the spirit was radically other than and potentially contrary to the body. We see this in the epistemological attitude, "the exaltation of disengaged reason as the royal road to knowledge, even in human affairs" (*SA*, 746). It appeared also in theology, devotions, and morality. Rather than pursuing the "enfleshment of God" (739), Taylor sees the dominant versions of modern Christianity seeking distance from the flesh. This left a large field open—initially to innovations within a Christian frame and then to those with movement outside it. Starting with deism, thus, there was new attention to "the body, history, the place of individuals, contingency, and the emotions. That is, it integrated these as essential dimensions of our understanding of human life, but it excluded them altogether from our relation to God" (288). In this Taylor sees a distancing from core Christian teachings centered on the incarnation of God in man as well as from a vital dimension of human existence.

Modern Social Imaginaries

Another major theme of *A Secular Age*—and one central to Taylor's conception of the immanent frame, though not always adequately appreciated by critics of the book—is the "implicit, largely unfocussed background" of both religious and secular thought and experience. In one main section of the book, incorporating much of his short book called *Modern Social Imaginaries*, Taylor suggests that such basic organizing frameworks as democratic nations, free markets, religious denominations, and media publics share many tacit assumptions about the social world they make possible—including that society is in its essence an aggregation of individuals acting freely in their own interest. The social imaginary, as Taylor conceives it, "is not a set of ideas" but rather "what enables, through making sense of, the practices of a society" (*MSI*, 2). Distinguishing it from "theory," which is often formulated and possessed by only a few, he shows that the imaginary has widespread moral implications—informing and informed by what he calls a "modern moral order."[25] Only against the background assumption of what makes modern society moral do many of our norms and practices make sense.

25 Taylor distinguishes the social imaginary from social theory along three dimensions. First, the

Taylor's exposition of the power of social imaginaries has made central use of examples in which ideas migrate from philosophical or legal contexts to popular practice. It has been criticized as a philosopher's account, one that does much better analyzing the writings of intellectual elites than analyzing broader popular culture or social structure (though it does have interesting and innovative things to say about each). Some have perceived Taylor's story of modern social imaginaries as a trickle-down narrative, in which the ideas of great thinkers gradually diffuse until they become so widespread as to be facts of social life. And he does claim that "it often happens that what start off as theories held by a few people come to infiltrate the social imaginary, first of elites, perhaps, and then of the whole society" (*MSI*, 24). Yet the criticism fails to fully capture the sophistication of Taylor's approach to the relationship between practice, agency, and understanding.

Taylor's rendering of social imaginaries centers on the role certain widely reproduced ways of thinking play in constituting larger ways of life. The history he relates is not simply one of the diffusion of consciously held ideas, but one in which some are able to articulate more effectively ideas that are already growing as parts of the background "pre-ontology" of an era. While Taylor focuses on philosophers, poets, and political theorists, he also discusses—much more in passing—the importance of such nontheoretical realms as fashion and sports events. These are practices that make sense only given a certain common background of understanding. This background of understanding is social, in the sense that it is reproduced in communication and interaction, and starting with language it is as much constitutive of persons as they are of it. But social imaginaries are social in a further sense. They are not merely social but about the nature of society. They project images of sociality that become part of the taken-for-granted background of modern forms of social life.

Taylor's three most frequently repeated examples of social imaginaries all turn in part on imagining social life in terms of large-scale coordination among "disembedded" individuals. Thus markets, democratic citizenship,

---

imaginary puts the focus on "the way ordinary people 'imagine' their social surroundings, and this is often not expressed in theoretical terms, but is carried in images, stories, and legends." Second, while theory "is often the possession of a small minority," the social imaginary is "shared by large groups of people, if not the whole society." And third, the social imaginary represents the "common understanding that makes possible common practices and a widely shared sense of legitimacy" (*MSI*, 23).

and the public sphere each offer a vision of social order as produced by the individual actions of strangers. In this they both reflect and reproduce crucial aspects of modern social life: the central role of understanding persons as quasi-autonomous agents, the at least notional equivalence of actors, the predominance of horizontal rather than hierarchical relations, and so forth. From Taylor's point of view, what is important is not the articulation of these views or their systematization in philosophy but the way they enable practices that make sense only with such conceptions in the background: voting, for example, or wearing home team paraphernalia, or advertising. People can live practically in the social world of such practices without noticing the idea of the social they imply, but none of these endeavors make sense without some such view of the social being available and implicit.

Such an idea poses an obvious problem for historical analysis. What would be an appropriate method for locating social imaginaries conceived in this way? The object of analysis, so defined, obviously lies well outside the comfort zone of most historiography, and Taylor has had to find ways to suggest that a shift in the basic social imaginary can be inferred from a broad range of other developments.

At the same time, the idea of background—and more specifically of the "social imaginary" as a structuring element in the background—is one of the things that motivate Taylor's historical mode of analysis, not because it is a teleological history, but because of his sense that historical conditioning lies in our background understanding.

Historical Specificity

In Taylor's work, most important questions are too historical to be understood or answered in completely abstract terms. But a corollary of this view is that history is more than a set of contingencies that we can review with disinterest. Taylor's history is in this sense closer to what is usually called genealogy (despite his well-known hostility to Nietzsche and Foucault) than it is to professional historiography. (For further discussion of the problems of history and form, see the contributions in this volume by During, Sheehan, Butler, and Jager.)

This might also help to explain why Taylor, resisting a widespread trend, does not use the term "post-secular." That term has migrated from academic contexts into the popular press and has now been embraced by such former secularists as Jürgen Habermas. In this context, the title of Taylor's book seems almost studious in its avoidance. It is not *A Post-Secular Age* but *A Secular Age*. Why?

There are no doubt many reasons, including Taylor's skepticism about other such labels for the present, including "postmodern." (Claims to have broken with the modern past, he emphasizes, are themselves very much a modern gesture. See, for example, *SA*, 716–717.) But far more important is that the "secular" in "post-secular" must be exactly that dual sense of the secular against which his book takes its point of departure. In order to believe that we are post-secular, one must have a narrow and inadequate conception of what it means to be secular. Habermas, for example, writes that "post-secular society" is that in which "religion maintains a public influence and relevance, while the secularistic certainty that religion will disappear worldwide in the course of modernisation is losing ground."[26] But this is to equate the secular with a "secularistic certainty" that was, by Habermas's own account, a mistake. This understanding of the post-secular neatly aligns with what Taylor, at the very beginning of *A Secular Age*, calls "secularity 1" and "secularity 2." The purpose of Taylor's book is to demonstrate that there is another, much more fundamental sense of the secular that is not captured by the classic sense of the secular as patterns of institutional separation and "secularistic certainty." Because this third sense of the secular comprehends precisely those forms of religiosity that are now most widely mobilized, resurgence of religion is not evidence of a new post-secular dispensation.

The idea of the post-secular is, however, much in vogue, and repeated often enough, it can persuade the unreflective that something in the world epoch has shifted. There is even a Centre for Postsecular Studies in London; but this group seems also to equate the secular with the most rigid secularist ideology. For them, "post-secular" just means such anodyne ideas (or alleged trends) as "a renewed interest in the spiritual life."[27] This conception of religiosity, in Taylor's terms, can be taken as showing just how far secularity 3 has spread.

Equally important, Taylor's attempt to hold a place for a respectable and

26 "Notes on a Post-Secular Society," *Sign and Sight,* June 18, 2008: www.signandsight.com/features/1714.html.

27 See www.jnani.org/postsecular/centre.htm; accessed June 20, 2009.

worthy religiosity is itself an expression of the secular condition of his title. As his afterword in this volume makes clear, he argues for an analysis in which the religious and the secular (or secularist), far from being in exclusive competition, coexist and are subject to both social and ethical cross-pressures. To speak of a global shift from one condition (secular) to another (post-secular) would be to miss this complex formation.

The mutual exposure of the religious and the secular is, moreover, not just an analytic observation but a rhetorical burden. More precisely, Taylor hopes by stressing the cross-pressures attending each position to induce modesty in both. Talk of the "post-secular," by comparison, suggests an unresolved mixture of triumphalism and melancholy.

The causes impelling modesty must be recognized as one of the major themes of *A Secular Age,* dominating Part V. This section of the book is devoted to a subtle exploration of what it means to say that religion, now considered as a matter of individual belief or faith or orientation, is optional—and now that the options are played out in overlapping milieus rather than in confessional societies. Taylor suggests that no matter how we might differently resolve the issues for ourselves, living in a pure immanence or orienting ourselves to some understanding of transcendent being, we still cannot escape the fact that we live with others who resolve it differently; and this fact has significance for the quality of our own convictions, no matter how securely we might think we hold them. The options, as he puts it, have been mutually "fragilized."

This is both an analytic point and a rhetorical posture. Taylor's concluding contribution to this volume should make it clear that the purpose of *A Secular Age* is not to vindicate Catholic theology—at least in its major current understandings—against "secularism." On the contrary, the major rhetorical burden of the book is to persuade us to understand this mutual fragilization more deeply, and thus to de-dramatize some of the conflicts that have been inflamed in so many ways around the world.

Of course, Taylor's effort to speak to our immediate human situation amid these challenges creates a rhetorical tension between his analytic tasks of trying to explain what has happened and is going on and his effort to reorient our less articulate perceptions. This is all the more complicated by the wide range of addressees for his argument. It is not presented simply to believers or unbelievers, nor to members of any one academic discipline alone.

SUBTRACTION STORIES

We return crucially to the reason that subtraction stories are so unsatisfactory. Many accounts of secularization treat the history of religion as the career of a mistake that can now be corrected. Taylor's polemic against "subtraction stories" is both specific to this ideology and more broadly methodological. With their implicit reference to a seemingly fixed and self-sufficient "nature," subtraction stories suggest a putatively original human condition to which we can now return (or a proper humanness to which we can aspire) once the detritus of religion is cleared away. They thus naturalize what they produce: a distinctively modern conception of social being.

Seeking to isolate one change as though it could happen without affecting the rest of social life, they distort our perception not just of what has changed but of what we imagine as continuous. The effect is multiplied when the accounts are overdetermined by what amount to ideological commitments. This is the case, for example, when people speak of religion as a prescientific attempt to explain the apparently irrational forces of the universe and the mysteries of mortal existence; or when religion is apprehended as supernaturalism, illegitimately grafted onto a self-explanatory naturalism; or when the disestablishment of state churches is thought to have left people free to determine their own religious fate without constraint, letting the marketplace of religion operate without artificial impediment. In each case, the allegedly original condition only makes sense given the history, and yet it is presented as an unexplained default rather than as a contingent achievement. People take religion to be a cognitive response to an otherwise inexplicable world only when they have very modern assumptions about epistemology and the excarnated character of religious questions. People take naturalism to be a self-sufficient stance—once it is cleared from religious supernaturalism—only when they overlook the Christian history that forced these stances into opposition, and when they overlook the very special social conditions of knowledge-making that make naturalism possible. People think of religious questions as irreducibly individual only once they have internalized the norms of modern market democracies.

Taylor's relentless criticism of subtraction stories is thus part of his attempt to show how secular modernity is both more sedimented and more creative than it takes itself to be. Secular societies are not just mankind minus the religion. They are very specific kinds of societies, imaginable only as the outcomes of long histories. They produce not unillusioned individuals who see the facts of existence nakedly, but people constituted by a distinct set of ethical goods, temporal frameworks, and practical contexts. The secular is never just the absence of religion, or its privatization, or its waning. It is a cumulatively and dialectically achieved condition, and one of its dimensions is the manifestation of religion as an optional axis of mobilization and belief.

This emphasis on the secular as having a positive social, historical, and ethical shape—rather than as the default condition denoted by the negation of religion—links Taylor to another school of contemporary critical thought about secularism, largely developed under the influence of Talal Asad. Like Taylor, Asad argues that the secular is not the taken-for-granted opposite of religion but a set of conditions in which modern ideas of religion are constructed. Like Taylor, he argues that these conditions have long and complex genealogies in Christianity. And like him, he argues that being secular involves not just skepticism or disbelief but an ethical horizon that should be understood in its own right.[28]

It is a striking fact about *A Secular Age* that this body of critical thought makes no explicit appearance. Asad is not mentioned; nor are many contemporary scholars who follow in important ways from his work, such as Saba Mahmood and Tomoko Masuzawa.[29] The same might be said also of the substantial body of critical thought in India in which many of the now widespread critiques of the secular were first articulated—by Ashis Nandy, Partha Chatterjee, Rajeev Bhargava, and many others. Taylor knows and has been in dialogue with both of these schools of thought. Indeed, his earlier essay on "modes of secularism" was published in Bhargava's landmark collection *Secularism and Its Critics*. Why, then, are they not more conspicuous as interlocutors?

28 See Talal Asad, *Formations of the Secular: Christianity, Islam, Modernity* (Stanford: Stanford University Press, 2003); and David Scott and Charles Hirschkind, eds., *Powers of the Secular Modern: Talal Asad and His Interlocutors* (Stanford: Stanford University Press, 2006). For Asad's initial response to *A Secular Age*, see "Secularism, Hegemony, and Fullness," The Immanent Frame, 2007: http://blogs .ssrc.org/tif/2007/11/17/secularism-hegemony-and-fullness/. He addresses the book in greater detail in Talal Asad, "Thinking about Religion, Belief and Politics," in *The Cambridge Companion to Religious Studies*, ed. Robert Orsi (forthcoming).

29 Saba Mahmood, *Politics of Piety: The Islamic Revival and the Feminist Subject* (Princeton: Princeton University Press, 2004); Tomoko Masuzawa, *The Invention of World Religions* (Chicago: University of Chicago Press, 2005).

The answer to this must have to do in part with Taylor's desire to intervene in the self-understanding of Western Christendom. Most of the scholars named above have concentrated on the relation between the dominant secular frameworks of modernity and those religious communities that encountered the secular primarily through colonial domination: Hindus and Muslims in India, Muslims in much of the Arab world. The validity questions that occupy Part V of *A Secular Age* lie outside the scope of these schools. And the major arena of their own analysis—the postcolonial world—lies at least partly outside the scope set by Taylor for his own book.

The absence of any explicit engagement with these other critics of the secular would seem to mark one cost attending Taylor's restricted focus on Latin Christendom. Perhaps anticipating that the objection against this focus would be couched in terms of ethnocentrism, Taylor offers a justification at the beginning of his book. It is in part simply that he couldn't do justice to such a broad topic. This is reinforced by his emphasis on secularity as part of a historically specific story of "multiple modernities" which "find rather different expression, and develop under the pressure of different demands and aspirations in different civilizations" (*SA*, 21). One may of course object that this rationale is inadequate. But more importantly, it is an answer to only one sort of criticism. Many of Taylor's interlocutors have in fact raised the question of ethnocentrism or at least inadequate breadth of coverage, asking whether secular culture doesn't follow a different pattern elsewhere. As the quoted passage suggests, he can answer "Certainly." Taylor does have strong claims about Western uniqueness. For example, "The great invention of the West was that of an immanent order in Nature, whose working could be systematically understood and explained on its own terms, leaving open the question whether this whole order had a deeper significance, and whether, if it did, we should infer a transcendent Creator beyond it" (15). Such claims can be examined on the basis of other cases and historical narratives. But this isn't the strong question. It is perfectly reasonable for Taylor not to address all cases and versions of secularity. The real question is whether he thinks about the West in too limited a way.

After all, it is not the case that Latin Christendom got to be what it is *before* it came into contact with other parts of the world, or even before its contact with those other parts had become a colonial project. As many recent scholars have shown, the colonial governance of non-Christian peoples was one of the central contexts in which Europeans developed their understandings of religion, the state, and themselves.[30] Not only that: the new ways of knowing that were developed to deal with religious difference—including our now commonsensical idea of "religion" itself—supplied the cognitive differentials that made colonialism sustainable. Missionary projects were not only a result of Western religious convictions, they were sources of transformed Western self-understandings. Colonial contact with African and New World pagans and the later subjugation of monotheistic civilizations required elaboration of new discourses about religion and belief that in turn transformed Christianity's own universalist language. It also required Europeans to identify themselves more and more with the technological progress and administrative apparatuses by which they distinguished themselves from inferiorized peoples—and which, not coincidentally, gave added meaning to what was secular about their own societies. The process by which Latin Christendom got to be secular was in large part the same as the process by which it got to be colonial. Thus it is analytically inadequate to frame the "internal" history of Latin Christendom as though this process were not internal to it. And it leaves the book oddly disengaged with the postcolonial conditions that have generated so much of the blowback against the secular. (For further discussion of this point, see the chapters in this volume by Casanova and Mahmood.)

There is, of course, much else to be said about secularity and secularism, and about the way in which struggles over religion and the secular have produced conflict around the world: the central role that colonialism has played both in shaping a certain understanding of what religion is and in spreading models of secular governance around the world; the uneven and bumpy assimilation of other religious traditions to the patterns that have emerged from Christian culture; the ongoing transformation of religiosity in the context of a now triumphally global mediatized democratic capitalism.

Other books will rightly take up other foci. Political secularism is, for example, far more varied than is often thought, ranging from American doctrines of separation of church and state within a deeply religious culture to French or Turkish versions of laïcité to efforts like that of the Indian state to

30 Asad, *Formations of the Secular;* Timothy Fitzgerald, *Discourse on Civility and Barbarity: A Critical History of Religion and Related Categories* (New York: Oxford University Press, 2007).

be equitably supportive of multiple religions. Each of these is under challenge from various directions. But grasping the contest deeply depends on going beyond a narrow emphasis on consciously held understandings and explicit institutional mechanisms. For political secularisms are all embedded in modern social imaginaries as well as in specific histories and organized against a background of generally inarticulate but powerfully constitutive understandings of people, the world, and what it means to speak of a higher good or transcendent reality. Taylor helps us see the importance of each.

The Plan of the Book

Finally, a word about the organization of this book. The authors collected here are among the most learned and creative scholars in the emerging debate over the nature of the secular, and we tried to give them free rein to respond to Taylor's book in whatever way they deemed important. Many have, in fact, written quite wide-ranging essays on original topics, some addressing Taylor more centrally than others. Rather than tediously summarizing each essay or inventing an artificial schema for them, we wish simply to note a few important clusters of emphasis and exchange. Some of these we have foregrounded by presenting the chapters in this sequence; others can easily be teased out.

The first three essays are by Robert Bellah, John Milbank, and Wendy Brown—a sociologist, a theologian, and a political theorist. Each of these essays places Taylor in relation to another intellectual tradition. Bellah usefully compares him to two other social theorists of the postwar period, Maruyama Masao and Jürgen Habermas. Milbank reads Taylor's critique of modernity in relation to long histories of Christian theology. And Brown compares Taylor's project to the historical materialism of Marx. Each writes with a mixture of polemic and appreciation; each writes as an exponent of a different intellectual tradition. Because these chapters articulate such different understandings of the contexts and conversations in which Taylor's book might be read, we think they serve well to open up the volume. Reading these three essays together gives a strong sense of the range of audiences and conversations addressed by *A Secular Age*. They also outline some alternative lines of analysis that Taylor did not pursue.

The next three essays are not primarily framed as responses to *A Secular*

Age, though each of them does have some commentary on the book. In these essays, the authors have taken Taylor's work mainly as an occasion or provocation to develop their own thought on dimensions of experience that are captured neither by secularist reductions nor by rhetorics of transcendence. Simon During, a scholar of literature and cultural studies, develops a powerful and original take on the mundane, "those forms of life and experience that are not available for our moral or political or religious or social aspirations and projects"; the mundane so conceived is a counterpressure against the spiritual hungers so emphasized by Taylor. During also works to situate the crisis of the secular in the peculiar historical moment of what he calls "endgame democratic state capitalism," in which serious alternatives have been delegitimized. William Connolly, a political philosopher, whose book *Why I Am Not a Secularist* was one of the seminal critiques of secularist ideology, similarly elaborates his own language for overcoming the antithesis of immanence and transcendence through a changed conception of nature and time, opening possibilities of "immanent naturalism" and "mundane transcendence." Stressing "an open temporal dimension exceeding human mastery," Connolly shows how an ethics of becoming must have in mind more than human flourishing as it is usually conceived, and indeed must not limit itself to the preoccupations of humanism. Akeel Bilgrami, whose work ranges from analytic philosophy to critical social theory, also engages Taylor sympathetically. Here he emphasizes how a reductive conception of nature and agency played into projects of disenchantment and colonial rule alike, but in so doing entrenched a false understanding of human agents as acting upon the world in accord with wishes and ends that are internal to the subject. In contrast, he argues that we are always called upon by the objects of our desires and actions. Our world is therefore inevitably to some degree enchanted, in this limited sense. All three of these chapters propose a deeper understanding of worldliness, beyond the various secularisms chronicled by Taylor, and without any programmatic opposition to religion.

The next group of three essays dwells on the problems of form and method. What kind of book is *A Secular Age?* What is its conception of history? Where might its narrative stand in need of correction? What challenges does it pose to the way we are accustomed to thinking about history? The first essay in this group is by Colin Jager, a literary critic. Reminding us that *A Secular Age* has "a story to tell"—and emphasizing that the book's "romantic method" produces an account that must "undergone," rather than "simply paraphrased or glossed," in order for its force to be felt—Jager identifies a "tonal ambivalence" in Taylor's work, springing from his phenomenological commitment to radical reflexivity. "Casting around for more capacious or generous ways to describe the distinct *feel* of the age," he suggests, Taylor has given us a "philosophic song," a complex and poetic narrative in which the tension between secularity and Christianity remains unresolved. The other two chapters in this cluster are by the historians Jon Butler and Jonathan Sheehan. This cluster represents a particularly vigorous debate, with considerable disagreements among the authors. To this debate can be added the opening pages of Simon During's chapter. And we have laid out our own view on the question of genre and historiography in this introduction. It will readily be seen that our own view differs in important ways from that of each of the contributors.

The final group of essays brings together the sociologists Nilüfer Göle and José Casanova and the anthropologist Saba Mahmood. Each of these contributors has written distinguished and pathbreaking work on the analysis of the secular in the present global conjuncture. Each assesses Taylor's book from the point of view of how well it allows us to analyze current developments. And each works in different ways to provincialize the Latin Christendom of Taylor's focus in relation to those other parts of the world with which it has always been engaged. In different ways, each expects the process of globalization and confrontation to continue to decenter the Euro-American understanding of secular modernity.

The concluding essay is an afterword by Charles Taylor. This is a modified version of the unscripted remarks Taylor made at the end of the Yale conference. Significantly revised, it still bears some of the marks of the earlier talk and critical exchanges of the conference. While the argument of *A Secular Age* is very difficult to summarize briefly, in this closing chapter Taylor gamely risks "the heresy of paraphrase" and offers a brief précis of his book's "master narrative of secularity."[31] Revisiting the central concept of the "social imaginary," he also responds to those who have criticized the philosophical anthropology embedded in his conception of "fullness," elaborating on this

31 For "the heresy of paraphrase," see Cleanth Brooks, *The Well-Wrought Urn: Studies in the Structure of Poetry* (New York: Harcourt Brace, 1947). For further discussion, see Colin Jager's chapter in this volume.

in greater detail here than in the original book. Building on this discussion, Taylor turns in the final pages to an explicit—and remarkably personal—account of his intentions in writing *A Secular Age*. "What we badly need," he writes, "is a conversation between a host of different positions, religious, nonreligious, antireligious, humanistic, antihumanistic, and so on, in which we eschew mutual caricature and try to understand what 'fullness' means for the other." Recalling his work with the Quebec commission on the practices of reasonable accommodation,[32] and in light of tremendous diversity and potential for conflict, Taylor imagines those who engage in such conversations as standing "like firebreaks in a forest fire." In his life and work, Taylor has dedicated himself to multiplying those firebreaks. His afterword is both a fitting conclusion to this book and an explicit call for continued conversation.

32 Taylor served as the commission's cochair. See Gérard Bouchard and Charles Taylor, *Building the Future: A Time for Reconciliation*, Abridged Report, Government of Quebec, 2008: www.accommo dements.qc.ca/index-en.html.

I
≡

Confronting Modernity:
Maruyama Masao, Jürgen Habermas, and Charles Taylor

ROBERT N. BELLAH

I have taken modernity and its challenges as the subject of my chapter, and will, perhaps overambitiously, attempt to compare Maruyama Masao's response to modernity with that of two other influential intellectuals, Jürgen Habermas and Charles Taylor, to see what we might learn from their similarities and differences.[1] I see the three of them as similarly situated in their respective societies: each of them has combined social science, rather broadly construed, with philosophy, and all of them with what Habermas has called "a practical intent." That is, each of them has been not only a scholar but an activist, and all in the service of the great modern ideal of democracy. Maruyama, from the moment he could begin to write freely after World War II, took up the argument in favor of democracy and the criticism of those aspects of Japanese culture and society that impeded democracy, and he was an active organizer of the great demonstrations against the Japanese American Security Treaty in 1960.

Maruyama was born in 1914, so he was thirty-one in 1945. Habermas was

1 This essay was originally delivered as the Maruyama Lecture at the Center for Japanese Studies, University of California, Berkeley, on April 26, 2007.

born in 1929, so he was only sixteen in 1945, and whereas Maruyama had been drafted in 1944, at the age of thirty, Habermas was drafted at the age of sixteen, only a few months before the end of the war. In the desperate situation of those days neither of them expected to return alive, but happily, both did, Maruyama because he had a desk job (though in Hiroshima at the time of the atom bomb, but far enough from ground zero to survive), Habermas because he was placed in a medical unit behind the western front as the German army was crumbling. Habermas began his higher education as an innocent, an admirer of Heidegger, and only gradually realized that most of his teachers and his admired philosopher had been Nazis. This led him to gravitate to the Frankfurt School of critical theory, and gradually to become a leading voice for democracy in postwar Germany, publishing many demanding scholarly books but also articles on issues of the day in popular magazines and newspapers. Taylor, born in 1931 in bilingual Quebec, escaped the war, but after graduating from McGill University spent ten years of advanced study at Oxford and became an active democratic socialist, publishing in such journals as the *New Left Review.* He is the only one of our three to engage as a candidate in electoral politics, having run three times for the Canadian parliament on the social democratic New Democratic Party ticket.

While all three have spent extended periods of time outside their homeland, and Habermas and Taylor and, to a somewhat lesser degree, Maruyama have been international intellectuals, Maruyama is identified with Japan and Habermas with Germany in ways that do not quite apply to Taylor. While consciously a Canadian, Taylor has taught for extended periods in Britain and the United States and writes as familiarly about these societies as about his own. I have thus chosen figures who represent two of the World War II Axis nations, Japan and Germany, and one who represents the old Anglo democracies of the North Atlantic, though with his bilingual background I think Taylor is almost as much at home in France as in Anglo-America. It is natural that these cultural locations would lead to differences in the evaluation of modernity and in the characterizations of its challenges, though what is perhaps more remarkable is the degree to which all three thinkers share fundamental features of their evaluation.

I might mention one more feature that my three figures share: they have all been prolific writers. If I had not been reading them for almost my entire adult life, I would not have dared to include them all in one essay, and even the reading I have had to do to remind myself of important topics and catch up on some things I hadn't read before has turned out to be, however deeply rewarding, quite overwhelming. Finally, I must also mention that I chose these three old men (Maruyama died in 1996, at the age of eighty-two; Habermas and Taylor are in their late seventies) because I am also an old man, born in 1927—thirteen years younger than Maruyama, two years older than Habermas, and four years older than Taylor—who shares their location in the world in aspiration, though not in influence. My work, like theirs, has always had a practical intent, most obviously in the widely read *Habits of the Heart*, which I wrote with four younger coauthors: an attempt to reinvigorate the Tocquevillian understanding of democracy in America. And not only have I shared many of my deepest concerns with these three, but they have all, to varying degrees, been my friends, Maruyama in particular. So it should be clear that I am very much identified with them and that I will be arguing with them but not in any fundamental way against them.

But what about my topic, "confronting modernity"? Isn't modernity over, aren't we beyond all that? I will argue that modernity, like history, isn't over. It is still very much with us. Sam Whimster, in his valuable recent book *Understanding Weber* (and we must remember that for Maruyama, Habermas, and Taylor, Weber's understanding of modernity was formative), argues that Weber's central preoccupations, "rationalization, disenchantment, fragmentation of value spheres . . , and the interplay of value and instrumental rationality[,] still remain center stage."[2] Needless to say, Weber's commonest way of referring to modern society, capitalism, is very much alive. Call it "late capitalism" if you wish (wish indeed), but its creative destruction is more active than Weber ever imagined. Modernity long precedes the "modernism" that "postmodernism" is supposed to replace, and will undoubtedly still be a problem for us long after "postmodernism" has been forgotten as the fad that it is.

Nonetheless Weber, an inescapable reference point for all of us, made a critical mistake, more in theory than in practice, by characterizing tradition in contrast to modernity as static, as doing things because this is how we have always done them. American modernization theory, thinking it was drawing on Weber, painted a picture of traditional, premodern society as stagnant and

2 Sam Whimster, *Understanding Weber* (New York: Routledge, 2007), 9.

unchanging, which Weber's empirical studies belie. In any case, each of my three protagonists has realized that the premodern is in important respects the essential reference point for understanding the varieties of modernity that have arisen—I think all of them would have embraced Shmuel Eisenstadt's notion of "multiple modernities"—and that each society has its own dynamics, dependent in good part on what its premodernity was like, which we must understand if we are to interpret what modernity has come to mean for them.

One way of characterizing modernity, one that helps us see it in the long-term process of human evolution, is to say that it involved a speeding up of change in a number of dimensions. That is undoubtedly true, but it is only the latest in a series of moments when things speeded up, moments that we could trace back to 2,500 years ago, 5,000 years ago, 10,000 years ago, 60,000 years ago, or 120,000 years ago, when the axial age, or the emergence of the state, or the beginning of agriculture, or the cultural explosion of the late Paleolithic, or the emergence of what evolutionary linguists call "modern language"—by which they don't mean what the Modern Language Association means, my modern language, but the fully syntactical kind of language that all humans have been speaking for over 100,000 years—emerged. Maybe that is when we have to date the beginning of modernization, except that even biologically the human species has developed extremely rapidly compared to most other species for over two million years. One must wonder if this process of ever-increasing speed of change must end in early extinction. It surely guarantees nothing like progress.

Modernity, dating from about the seventeenth century in the West, does indeed represent an increase in the speed of change in many dimensions, one that continues to accelerate today—think of technological change or the growth of scientific knowledge. But my three protagonists, though taking note of these many kinds of change, have focused on a normative understanding of modernity, have seen it as a personal, social, political, and finally an ethical project, and have tried to understand its vicissitudes as such.

I want to underscore that thinking of modernity as an ethical project puts my three protagonists in an entirely different category from what we think of as modernization theory. Although all were social scientists, none of them viewed modernity in purely value-free, positivistic, descriptive terms, as American modernization theorists claimed to do, though almost always with the hidden or not-so-hidden message that modernity would make the whole world just like us. In the case of Maruyama, this difference of perspective was brought home to me dramatically by his review of my book *Tokugawa Religion* in an issue of *Kokka Gakkai Zasshi* in 1958. This is the most extraordinary review I have ever received or ever expect to receive. It came to about fifty pages in English translation, being mainly an outline of my argument. But Maruyama's conclusion combined admiration for the rigor of my use of Weberian theory with something close to fury over my blandly optimistic modernization-theory view of Japan as a "successful modernizer." Overlooking Japan's dark side was just inexcusable to Maruyama.[3] This was the beginning of a lifelong friendship, especially when we met in person during my Fulbright year in 1960. Arguing with Maruyama was, as anyone who knew him understands, a peculiar pleasure, combining his sharp thrusts with his laughter and lightness of touch.

Rather than try to describe modernity as a whole, I will outline its social and normative aspects, because it is on these that my three figures most often reflect. I will draw from Taylor a general characterization that I think the other two would on the whole accept.[4] The seventeenth century saw, against the background of the Dutch and English revolutions, in the writings of Grotius and Locke, the first clear assertion of human autonomy, no longer embedded in a conception of the cosmos or the great chain of being but allowing humans to act freely in several spheres, most notably the economic and the political. These ideas were floated in societies still largely organized around older ideas of social and religious order. At first they floated free, as it were, not causing what would happen in the eighteenth century but influencing the interpretation of what happened.

Taylor notes the significance of the eighteenth century by looking at the beginning of the disembedding of three spheres of life that were previously

3 Maruyama Masao, review of Robert N. Bellah, *Tokugawa Religion,* translated by Arima Tatsuo, *Kokka Gakkai Zasshi* [Journal of the Association of Political and Social Sciences], 72, 4 (April 1958): 48 pp. After chastising me for using the concepts "rationalization" and "modernization" too glibly in referring to Japan, Maruyama wrote a highly ambivalent final paragraph: "Anyway, there are not many books lying around which can shake us out of our inertia, indicating the unusual talent of the author not only through his positive contributions but even through his mistaken observations. Of the many American research works on Japan which are constantly coming out, Bellah's book, more than any in a long time, has aroused my appetite and my fighting spirit."

4 In the following discussion I am relying on *MSI*.

subsumed in the hierarchical religio-political form of society inherited from the high Middle Ages, showing cracks to be sure, as in the rise of political absolutism, and even more in the Protestant Reformation, but still largely intact at the beginning of that century. In successive order the three spheres that came to operate with a degree of independence were the economy; the public sphere, in a sense that I will describe in a moment; and the sovereign people, the locus of what only in the French Revolution and more securely in the nineteenth century came to be called democracy in a favorable, not a pejorative, sense.

The idea of an economy independent of the polity is already present in germ in Locke, for whom economic life precedes the social contract, whose purpose is to a considerable degree to guarantee the pursuit of economic ends with some security. But with Adam Smith the idea of a self-regulating economy in which the invisible hand guarantees positive social outcomes even when economic actors pursue only their own interests becomes a moral ideal and a practical project. We should not, however, forget that Smith thought such an autonomous economy could operate only within an ethical and political framework organized around noneconomic motives. An economic liberal he certainly was; a neoliberal he certainly was not.

Developing only slightly later, but overlapping the disembeddedness of the economy, was the emergence of the public sphere, a realm of thought and argument independent of the state but leading to the formation of what came to be called public opinion, which politicians could ignore at their peril. Taylor draws on an early work of Habermas's, *The Structural Transformation of the Public Sphere,* to give substance to his description of this newly independent realm.[5]

The third idea, and the one that emerged only at the end of the eighteenth century, was the idea of the sovereignty of the people: that only a government that not only had the tacit consent of the governed but was elected by the citizens was legitimate. Taylor notes that this was not an idea that was conscious at the beginning of the American Revolution, when the demands of the colonies relative to the monarch were based on the notion of the rights of Englishmen, descending from time out of mind. But first in

5 Jürgen Habermas, *The Structural Transformation of the Public Sphere: An Inquiry into the Category of Bourgeois Society* (Cambridge: MIT Press, 1989).

some of the new state constitutions and then in the federal Constitution of 1789, "We the People" now supplied the basis of legitimate authority. The drafters of the Constitution did not think they were establishing a democracy, but rather a mixed constitution with monarchic, aristocratic, and democratic components, but by the time of Tocqueville's first visit, in 1830, Americans had come to believe they lived in a democracy. The autonomy here was due to the fact that the state was no longer self-legitimated or based in a cosmic-religious legitimation but depended on the ongoing exercise of the popular franchise, which could withdraw at will the authority of any elected official whenever there was an election.

These three spheres are still with us, at least as a project where they have not been fully disembedded, and even when their autonomy is endangered where they have, but the relations between them have become more than a little problematic. In fact, not only has the autonomy of one or more of these three spheres been bitterly, and frequently violently, opposed, but the tensions between them have given rise to continuous struggles. Far from being the bland unfolding of inevitable progress, the history of modernity has been one of constant strife. As Tocqueville said in 1850, once the French Revolution unleashed the forces of change, there has been a continuous revolution that shows no sign of ceasing.[6] Maruyama, living in a most unrevolutionary society, thought continuous revolution a good thing, but most of the world has found continuous revolution very hard to live with.

In current American ideology, free enterprise or the market economy is fused seamlessly with democracy as a single nonnegotiable package for the contemporary world. But already at the time of the French Revolution the tension between the rule of equality and the rule of property, characterized as the rule of egoism, became apparent, and Tocqueville in the 1830s warned that if the Americans were ever to lose their freedom, it would be because of the increasing power of the new masters of industry.[7]

---

6 See the English translation of Tocqueville's *Souvenirs: The Recollections of Alexis de Tocqueville* (Cleveland: World, 1959), 2. Tocqueville wrote *Souvenirs* in 1850, but it was published posthumously in 1893. I owe this reference to Björn Wittrock, "Modernity: One, None, or Many?" *Daedalus* 129, 1 (Winter 2000): 43.

7 On the tensions between property and equality already apparent in the French Revolution, see John Dunn, *Democracy: A History* (New York: Atlantic Monthly, 2005), especially 124ff. Dunn is a former Maruyama Lecturer. On Tocqueville's warning about the threat to democracy from concentrated economic power, see *Democracy in America,* vol. II, part II, chap. 20, entitled "How an Aristocracy May Be Created by Industry."

One early understanding of the relation between the three spheres is that the disembedded economy led to a feeling of independence among the bourgeoisie, so that, empowered by this new independence, they created the public sphere and finally ensconced themselves in power through the creation of bourgeois democracy. To the great misfortune of us all, Marx bought this picture of the disembedding of the three spheres as a single package to the extent that, once he saw the oppressive consequences of the capitalist economy, he considered the public sphere and the sovereignty of the people as integral to this economy and so rejected them rather than defending them. He had his own belief in the sovereignty of the people, but it was to be realized in a utopian socialist project where the state would wither away and there would be no need for a public sphere or a democratic politics. Alas for real existing socialism once it came into existence.

For us the important point is that our three protagonists were strong proponents of the public sphere and democracy, spending much intellectual and political energy in their defense, but none of the three has been an apologist for an unrestrained, neoliberal economy; each has shared with Marx a grave anxiety about capitalism as a threat to the full development of an autonomous citizenry. Each accepted the necessity of market mechanisms in the economy, but only in conjunction with an active government involvement that would ameliorate the consequences of purely market-oriented decisions and a vigorous public sphere that would continuously monitor both the economy and the state.

In my recent rereading of Maruyama, I was surprised at the degree to which he took a fundamentally Marxist position for granted, in spite of his harsh criticism of the Japanese Communist Party and the Soviet Union for their lack of democracy. Among those who led, or were pushed to lead, Japan into fascism in the 1930s he frequently mentioned, alongside the military and the bureaucrats, the capitalists *(zaibatsu)*. And he continued to use the term "revolution" for the moment in which an autonomous citizenry would take power, creating a democratic regime in which economic interests could be freely pursued but in which they would not dominate.

Also Maruyama's definition of fascism was very close to the Marxist understanding. Fascism was, in a word, counterrevolution, in Japan motivated in part by the paranoid fear of a nonexistent proletarian revolution but involving the denial of both the public sphere and democracy. In Japan, as elsewhere, fascism, in spite of some anticapitalist rhetoric, strengthened the power of the capitalist class by destroying the labor unions and all working-class parties. Maruyama's Marxist assumptions, though I think clearly present, can easily be overlooked, since his preoccupations on the whole lay elsewhere, in the sphere of politics and the ethics and the practice of citizenship, so that the economy was never a primary focus. Yet he was often in conversation with Marxists and he never became an anticommunist; indeed, in his famous "Letter to a Certain Liberal," he argued that anticommunism as a dominating concern was in fact a danger to the democratic possibility in Japan, not least because it was on order, so to speak, from the American authorities.[8] And Maruyama on occasion mentioned Kant and Marx in tandem as figures representing modern humanism at its noblest.

Habermas's Marxism was from the beginning filtered through the "European Marxism" of the Frankfurt School and was eventually reconstructed to the point where materialist reduction was abandoned, but a socialist he has always remained, and an ambivalent, critical supporter, but still a supporter, of the German Social Democratic Party. Taylor was early on attracted to a strongly anticapitalist but equally sternly democratic and decentralized socialism, and has remained a social democrat to this day.

So each of my three protagonists accepted the modern project insofar as it was defined by democracy, but were uneasy with capitalism as possibly dangerous to or even corrosive of that democracy. But each of them had to come to terms with the project of modernity as democracy in very different social situations; for each of them, the premodern and its understanding set the essential conditions within which a genuinely democratic transition would be possible.

For Maruyama, Japanese society was not modern, in spite of great technological and economic progress, to the extent that it was not really democratic. For him, though there were significant Japanese democrats, at least from Meiji times—Fukuzawa Yukichi being such a figure, to whom he returned time and time again—neither the Meiji Constitution nor Taisho democracy were truly democratic, since they combined some democratic forms with a lack of genuine democratic substance, that is, the rule of the people in any real sense.[9] For him the symbol of the lack of democracy was the combi-

8 Maruyama Masao, "Letter to a Certain Liberal," first published in *Sekai* (September 1950) and translated by Richard H. Minear. The "certain liberal" was Hayashi Kentarō, who became an ardent cold warrior.

9 For a sense of Maruyama's appreciation of Fukuzawa available in English, see his "Fukuzawa,

nation of the grant of universal manhood suffrage in 1925 with the passage in the same year of the Peace Preservation Law (which outlawed speech and association connected to "dangerous thought") and the large-scale arrest of subversives that followed.

Even in postwar Japan, Maruyama felt that the real substance of democracy was elusive. The dispersed and decentralized emperor systems (in the plural) were still more determinative of how Japanese society was organized than the official forms of parliamentary democracy would make one think. And his confrontation with student activists at the end of the sixties—activists who wanted to force him to sign a confession they had written and who refused to engage in open discussion with him—led him to call them "Nazis," with the full awareness of just how bitter that term would be. Habermas underwent a similar experience at about the same time in Frankfurt, though perhaps not quite so bitter.

For Maruyama, political and ethical modernity was the great unrealized project, something for Japan's future if at all. He even asked, when postmodernity became popular in Japan, how a culture that had never been modern could possibly be postmodern. But then he added that if it's not modern, it might as well be post- as premodern. He never gave up, never ceased to try to understand Japan's deep structural problems, but he was not one to celebrate income doubling or Japan's emergence as a great world economy. Discouraged and pessimistic, to be sure, but never without hope.

Habermas could not believe that Germany was not modern. What would modernity be without the great German cultural contributions? But Germany's modernity was a distorted one, a modernity that lost the way, that fell into the abyss. And although Habermas could draw on resources that Maruyama did not have, he too spoke of modernity as an "unfinished project."[10]

Habermas has spent much of his life opposing any tendency in postwar Germany to excuse the past, or to forget it, but he did not, as Maruyama did, spend a lot of time analyzing what happened. He did not experience Nazism as Maruyama did Japanese fascism; he was too young to do anything that

---

Uchimura, and Okakura: Meiji Intellectuals and Westernization," in *Modern Japan: An Interpretive Anthology*, ed. Irwin Scheiner (New York: Macmillan, 1974), 233–247.

10 "Modernity—an Unfinished Project" was the title of the speech Habermas gave in 1980 when accepting the Adorno Prize. He began the preface to *The Philosophical Discourse of Modernity* (Cambridge: MIT Press, 1987), xix, by stating that "this theme, disputed and multifaceted as it is, never lost its hold on me." It should be noted that Habermas was not thinking of Germany alone, but of modernity in general.

would have brought the Gestapo down on him as the special police arrested, released, and then harassed Maruyama for years. Nor did Habermas concern himself particularly with the German past, as Maruyama did almost obsessively with the Japanese past. Instead Habermas engaged in a large-scale effort to rethink modern society and its problems with the help of the social scientific tradition, an effort realized in the two volumes of his *Theory of Communicative Action*.[11] And he also spent a lot of energy on the normative project of creating a universalistic communicative ethic that could provide the moral context for a democratic society.[12]

What seems, and indeed was, a very different strategy from Maruyama's was motivated by the same basic concern: how to overcome particularism, how to build a democratic society with universal norms. But Habermas had the ability, which Maruyama envied, to draw on the German past in trying to construct a society that would never again fall into the abyss of fascism. He had Kant and Hegel, Marx and Weber, whose equivalents Maruyama could not find in Japan, much as he admired a figure such as Fukuzawa.

For both of them the nation remained a reference point, though for neither of them was it an end in itself. After all, where is democracy in the world today? Only in the nation-state; there is no transnational democracy. The NGOs may be harbingers of a transnational democracy; they are not models of one.

Unlike Maruyama and Habermas, Taylor did not come from an Axis nation. By birth, education, and occupation he was identified with several of the "old democracies," ones that never experienced fascism.[13] But Taylor has not spent his life celebrating how good we are, as some Americans are in the habit of doing. Rather, Taylor too has been concerned with the incompleteness of the modern project, normatively considered, even in its oldest homelands. He has been concerned, very much as Maruyama and Habermas have been, with the problem of a genuinely autonomous citizenry, and has taken

11 Jürgen Habermas, *The Theory of Communicative Action, Vol. 1: Reason and the Rationalization of Society* (Boston: Beacon, 1984), and *Vol. 2: Lifeworld and System: A Critique of Functionalist Reason* (Boston: Beacon, 1987).

12 Jürgen Habermas, *Moral Consciousness and Communicative Action* (Cambridge: MIT Press, 1990).

13 Maruyama, however, explicitly and repeatedly called McCarthyism "American fascism." See his fascinating 1952 article, "Fascism—Some Problems: A Consideration of Its Political Dynamics," in his *Thought and Behavior in Modern Japanese Politics* (New York: Oxford, 1963; rev. ed., 1969), 157–176.

to heart Tocqueville's many warnings on that score. But he has also been concerned, in a way less evident in the work of the other two, with cultural fragmentation, loss of meaning both individually and socially, and how we might respond to this problem that modernity seems everywhere to create.

Taylor has also pointed out that even in the "successful modernizers"—Britain, France, Canada, the United States—there are differences: different strengths and weaknesses, different problems that need to be addressed. (Taylor's *Modern Social Imaginaries* considers many of these differences.) He has taken very seriously the problem of multiculturalism, which as a citizen of Quebec as well as Canada he could hardly avoid, and has written incisively on the need for "recognition," in a profound sense, of cultural differences as well as the need to find ways of reasserting what we share even in our otherness *(MC)*.

Having given a brief sense of what my protagonists were about, each in the setting from which he came, let me turn to the way in which each of them situated the present in a longer-term understanding of history. Each saw that one cannot understand the modern except in terms of where it came from, except as a response to the premodern. All of them saw that much of the premodern had to be rejected: orthodoxies that denied freedom of thought and dependencies that made an autonomous citizenry impossible. But whereas Habermas and Taylor found important precursors of their ethical ideals in the religious and philosophical history of the West, and even specifically in the axial age, the first millennium BCE, when the original cultural breakthroughs occurred, Maruyama's heroes remained resolutely modern: Machiavelli and Hobbes, along with Ogyū Sorai, are among his heroes, as well as Kant, Hegel, and Marx, Fukuzawa and Uchimura Kanzō; but not Zhu Si (Chu Hsi), nor Dōgen (though he had an occasional good word to say for Shinran), nor Aquinas, nor Plato and Aristotle.

Maruyama spent a great deal of time on the premodern, probably more than on the modern. He started with Tokugawa political thought and ended with the deep structures of the Japanese past, even to the age of the gods. What was he looking for? In a word, I think, for the enemy, for that quality of Japanese thought and life that made democracy so difficult, made it almost impossible. In his work on Tokugawa thought he characterized the mainstream, against which Sorai and, in a different way, Motoori Norinaga were reacting, as "continuative," a term that foreshadows later terms such as "deep structures" and particularly *"basso ostinato."* Continuative thought, which he identified with Zhu Si Confucianism, especially in such thinkers as Yamazaki Ansai, was preoccupied with the unchanging, or the "natural," in a strong sense of the term that includes both the cosmic and the human. Continuative thought is embedded thought, the status quo thinking itself and praising itself. It had no room for the creative individual, since its chief virtues were reverence and obedience.

For Maruyama, Sorai and Norinaga were a breath of fresh air in that they saw culture as fictive, as made by human hands, and to suit the needs of the present, not some time-out-of-mind past. He did not think they were progressive in that they were preaching democracy, just that they opened the door to the possibility of someone thinking such thoughts.[14] Already in his Tokugawa book and before Herbert Norman's book on the same subject, Maruyama celebrated the "forgotten thinker," Andō Shōeki, as the only Tokugawa thinker who ever questioned the feudal regime and was rewarded for it by being almost lost altogether until his writings were rediscovered in modern times.[15] Maruyama's antipathy to the "naturalization" of thought made him hostile to natural-law thinking in the West—Aristotelian, Thomist, or whatever. My efforts to get him to see that natural-law thinking, Christian or Confucian, could sometimes be a bulwark against despotism were to no avail.

In his return to the deep things in his later years, Maruyama was not so concerned with Confucianism, or with Shinto or Buddhism either, for that matter, as with quintessential Japanese ways of being in the world. My way of putting it has been to say that Japanese culture is nonaxial.[16] Maruyama

14 Maruyama Masao, *Studies in the Intellectual History of Tokugawa Japan* (Tokyo: University of Tokyo Press, 1974). The individual essays were published separately in *Kokka Gakkai Zasshi* between 1940 and 1944, particularly parts 1 and 2.

15 Maruyama's extensive discussion of Shōeki was included in the abbreviated third of the three essays that would later be collected in *Studies in the Intellectual History of Tokugawa Japan*, 249ff. This essay, which was cut short by Maruyama's being drafted into the army in 1944 and which therefore contained only the introductory material for what was to have been a discussion of Meiji nationalism, gives no support to the idea that Maruyama was a nationalist in the pre-1945 sense, if for no other reason than by his inclusion of this extensive and very favorable discussion of the quintessential Tokugawa antinationalist, Andō Shōeki. E. Herbert Norman's book, *Ando Shoeki and the Anatomy of Japanese Feudalism,* was published in 1949 in *Transactions of the Asiatic Society of Japan*, 3d series, vol. 2.

16 See the introduction to my *Imagining Japan: The Japanese Tradition and Its Modern Interpretation* (Berkeley: University of California Press, 2003), where I argue that though cultures deriving from the axial age had entered Japan from early times, they had never replaced the givenness of the premises of Japanese society. In this regard, see also S. N. Eisenstadt, *Japanese Civilization* (Chicago: University of Chicago Press, 1997).

didn't quite say that, though he did argue that Japanese thought lacked an "axis" that Christianity, Kantianism, or Marxism might have supplied, in a sense close to what I mean by nonaxial, for he held that Japanese thought lacked any transcendent or universalistic reference point, that it was immersed in the transient moment, the forever now, and so lacked any leverage to reform the world.[17] On the other hand, Japanese thought was not static, and certainly not closed, but what he came to call its *"basso ostinato"* pointed to its capacity to maintain its own fundamental premises while absorbing all kinds of cultural imports.[18]

But if, as I think was the case, Maruyama oriented his thought to the modern alone, finding no premodern reference point that would provide sustenance for his project, why did he not commit himself to one of the modern traditions that he admired—that is, why didn't he identify himself as a Marxist, a Kantian, or even a Non-Church Christian, like his teacher Nanbara Shigeru? If he identified with anyone, it would be the rather chameleon figure of Fukuzawa Yukichi, who resolutely examined a variety of positions without committing himself to any. I think Maruyama admired Fukuzawa's ability to argue for a variety of positions while resolutely insisting on his right to do so publicly. If we can call Fukuzawa a liberal, as I think we can, he was not so in any doctrinaire form—he was not a follower of any particular figure in the history of Western liberalism. In that sense, I think Maruyama, would, if pressed, as he was at several points, identify himself as a liberal, but one

17 Maruyama Masao, "Japanese Thought," in Scheiner, *Modern Japan*, 208–215. This is a fragment from Maruyama's book of the same title, *Nihon no Shisō* (Tokyo: Iwanami, 1961).

18 Maruyama Masao, "The Structure of *Matsurigoto*: The *Basso Ostinato* of Japanese Political Life," in *Themes and Theories in Modern History*, ed. Sue Henny et al. (London: Athlone, 1988), 27–43. In the late spring of 1961 I gave three lectures at International Christian University in Tokyo on "Values and Social Change in Modern Japan," which were published in ICU's journal, *Asian Cultural Studies 3* (1963). The second and third of these lectures were included in my *Beyond Belief: Essays on Religion in a Post-Traditional World* (Berkeley: University of California Press, 1991), in which I argued that there was a tradition of "submerged transcendence" in Japan that never succeeded in institutionalizing itself because of the power of a Japanese "ground bass" that in effect "drowned out" the transcendental melodies. I have no reason to think that Maruyama's considerably later use of the term *basso ostinato* owed anything to my earlier effort. It is interesting that though Maruyama differentiates *basso ostinato* from *basso continuo*, the Encyclopedia Britannica gives "ground bass" as the translation of *basso ostinato*. There is, however, one significant difference between Maruyama's usage and mine. I used the rather crude metaphor of the ground bass "drowning out" the transcendental melodies. Maruyama uses his metaphor somewhat more subtly when he says that the *basso ostinato* altered the newly imported cultural themes when they had to harmonize with this "obstinate" (the literal translation of *ostinato*) bass. So it's not that they disappeared, but that they were "swallowed up" in the pervasive harmony of traditional Japanese culture.

who espoused the open discussion of all possible points of view, not a doctrinaire ideologist. What Maruyama feared was that when Japanese became devoted to foreign doctrines, however universalistic, under the pressure of the Japanese thought world, they almost inevitably created one more particularistic identity, even though ostensibly universalistic, as happened to both Christianity and Marxism in Japan, and, socially, one more octopus pot, his metaphor for the closed nature of Japanese ideological/religious groups. What Maruyama hated above all was particularism, and he would not commit himself to any new particularism, however universalistic its claims. He always espoused—and in this he followed Fukuzawa—a principled, ethical individualism, one devoted to public causes, but one that refused to be subsumed in one particular identity. Yet Maruyama was not in the contemporary American sense an individualist. For him, true individuals could exist only in a society of citizens, each ready to recognize each other, and, while belonging to many groups, neither defined by them nor encapsulated in them but moving in the free space of a democratic society.

Habermas and Taylor have always defended a principled individualism, for reasons similar to those of Maruyama. The normative modernity that both of them support is one that enhances principled individualism, that doesn't suppress it as premodern societies often did. But all three of them saw such an ethical individualism as possible only in a society organized in a way that supported and made such individualism possible. Such a society would have to consist not only of democratic political structures but of voluntary associations, and even certain forms of family life, that would require the active and intelligent participation of individuals, not limit it. For all of them, more or less explicitly, the bourgeois revolution—that is, the moment in which the people wrested sovereignty from the king (in England and France by executing him, in America by renouncing him) and thus rejected monarchy as the very essence of a society based on paternalistic and particularistic social forms—was a critical turning point. Since neither Germany nor Japan had had such a revolution, Habermas and Maruyama were concerned to nurture its functional equivalent.

While all three of my protagonists have viewed certain kinds of social movements as schools of democracy, they have varied in how they view their importance. I think for Maruyama it was active and thoughtful political engagement of citizens that would nurture their sense of "autonomy"—the term that I think best translates *shutaisei,* the term with which he is most closely identified, since the literal translation, "subjectivity," can have a somewhat different implication—and give them the capacity, through joining together, to resist the imposition of state power.[19]

Habermas emphasized the creation through legal and moral frameworks of the possibility of "communicative action," that is, undistorted communication in search of agreement in the formation of a public will that would ground politics in a democratic "lifeworld." The lifeworld, a term taken from Husserl, is that sphere of life in which the "steering mechanism" is speech, and it is contrasted to the systems, the economy and the administrative state, whose steering mechanisms are the nonlinguistic media of money and power. According to Habermas, only when the economy and the administrative state are "anchored" in the lifeworld—that is, when they are finally regulated by the will-formation in the public sphere of the lifeworld—is a democratic society fully realized. Without adopting Habermas's formal terminology, I think both Maruyama and Taylor would agree to something like this analysis. Both of them strongly evaluated the role of speech in the public sphere as essential to a viable democracy.

Without getting into the technicalities of Habermas's discussion of communicative ethics as the very core of his theory of normative modernity—a discussion that Maruyama never responded to, as far as I know—I need to point out that Taylor had some significant qualifications about wholly embracing Habermas's views. These have to do with the distinction between the right and the good, which in turn goes back to the difference between Kant and Hegel in their views of *Moralität* (morality) and *Sittlichkeit* (ethical life), respectively.[20] (It is hard for most of us Americans to realize how central these

19 Andrew Barshay translates *shutaisei* as "subjectivity/personal autonomy" in his *The Social Sciences in Modern Japan: The Marxian and Modernist Traditions* (Berkeley: University of California Press, 2004), 328. Barshay's chapter on Maruyama in this book, pp. 197–239, and his discussion of Maruyama at a number of points in his *State and Intellectual in Imperial Japan: The Public Man in Crisis* (Berkeley: University of California Press, 1988) and several other essays, are the best treatments of Maruyama in English.

20 For Taylor's criticism of Habermas, see *SS,* 85–88 and elsewhere. Taylor finds Habermas's "discourse ethics" an advance over pure Kantianism because of its dialogical character, but still too narrow in setting discussion of the right entirely outside the bounds of discussion of good forms of life. One might almost wonder if we have here a difference between a culturally "Protestant" way of thinking (both Kant and Habermas came from Lutheran backgrounds) and the more culturally "Catholic" way of thinking of Taylor.

two figures have been not only for the three discussed here—remember that Maruyama's education was above all in German culture—but for almost all of the leading thinkers of the past one hundred years. Taylor was going against the main current of Anglo-American philosophy when he devoted a great deal of time to a major book on Hegel [*H*], followed by a smaller one popularizing the major work [*HMS*].) For Habermas, what is essential is a universalistic morality oriented toward the right, which in practice means above all to questions of justice, a morality that applies to all human beings and transcends cultural differences, though one that in practice only becomes possible in a modern society with a rationalized lifeworld and systems that are anchored in it.

Habermas recognizes that such a universalistic morality requires a particular form of life to become effective, a form of life that will vary from society to society and that will include a variety of conceptions of the good life, but the universalistic morality of justice acts as a standard by which more contextual ethics can be judged. In this respect, Habermas is usually thought of as a Kantian, though he draws heavily from Hegel in his historical and developmental thinking: he always situates the formalism of Kantian morality in actual societies at actual moments of their history. Taylor, on the other hand, is unhappy with too rigid a distinction between the right and the good, and tends to think of a strong Kantian morality as only one understanding of the good life along with others. Nonetheless, it is hard to disagree with Habermas when he says "no one is free until we are all free" and affirms that he can give good reasons for that claim that will be valid across all cultural boundaries.[21]

While agreeing that Habermas has good reasons for his position indepen-

---

21 Actually, the passage in which this occurs is an exposition of Schelling's essay on the "Essence of Human Freedom," the subject of Habermas's doctoral dissertation. The complete passage is as follows: "No one can enjoy freedom alone, or at the cost of the freedom of another. Thus freedom may never be conceived merely negatively, as the absence of compulsion. Freedom conceived intersubjectively distinguishes itself from the arbitrary freedom of the isolated individual. No one is free until we are all free. This fact emphasizes the second aspect, the unconditional character of moral obligation, insofar as the fate of God and the world as a whole stands in balance with the good and evil that historically acting subjects mutually attribute to one another. Humanity feels the weight of the categorical Ought in the superhuman responsibility for an inverse history of salvation. Inserted as authors into such a charged world history, they must answer to world history in the form of a last judgment implacably deferred into the future." Jürgen Habermas, *Religion and Rationality: Essays on Reason, God, and Modernity* (Cambridge: MIT Press, 2002), 161.

dent of historical context, we might still argue that he is committed to a strong morality of justice, because the one thing he most fears is any regression toward particularism, above all of blood and soil, and thus the slide into the abyss. Taylor, without the experience of fascism so close at hand, is more concerned with ways of thinking of a good form of life in the midst of the collapse of all traditional forms of meaning that modernity seems to cause. Taylor is as clear as Maruyama and Habermas in affirming that modernity as an ethical project must be accepted, with its ideals of rationally defensible cognitive beliefs and normative commitments, open and participatory social structures, and autonomous personalities. Still Taylor asks the question as to whether that is enough. For Maruyama that question could hardly arise, when modernity as an ethical project seemed so difficult to attain, and for Habermas it had to be a secondary question, when the danger of losing even the beginning of that project was so great.

Let me finally return to the question of the relation between the modern and the premodern to summarize the concerns of my three figures. As we have seen, Maruyama resolutely turned away from the premodern. Even in the case of Christianity, which he did admire and whose followers Uchimura and Nanbara had a significant influence on his life, he found it too closed, both too dogmatic and too in danger of encapsulation in Japanese society. For Maruyama, even the glimmer of an ethically modern Japan was the highest aspiration.

For Habermas, the Hegelian—that is, the historicist and developmental—side of his thought brought him to think more deeply about the premodern heritage of the West and to recognize the critical importance of the Jewish, Christian, and Hellenic moments in our past, moments that laid the foundation for the ethical possibilities of modernity.[22]

Habermas has acknowledged the importance for him of Jewish religious thought in particular, going all the way back to the Hebrew scriptures. He finds in the Ten Commandments, for example, the abandonment of idolatry and the openness to interpersonal communication that foreshadows the best of modernity (one might wish that some of our evangelical brothers and sis-

---

22 The book that most fully develops Habermas's conception of the prehistory of modernity is his *Communication and the Evolution of Society* (Boston: Beacon, 1979). Here he undertakes a "reconstruction of historical materialism," in which "normative structures" are seen as the "pacemaker of social evolution" (120). See also 160, 162.

ters who want the Ten Commandments in our courthouses could discover these same things).[23] But Habermas's appreciation of the religious traditions of the West, going back to the axial age and continuing with a strong affirmation of the significance of the Protestant Reformation, seemed for a long time to end with the dawning of the Enlightenment. Once the light dawned, the prehistory of modernity could be abandoned. There are moments in volume 2 of *The Theory of Communicative Action* where he speaks of the "thawing" of the sacred, that is, its "linguistification," as though modernity requires the liquification, or, one might fear, the liquidation, of the sacred and of premodern traditions.[24]

But in recent years, though Habermas has never renounced the necessity of what he calls "methodological atheism" as essential for any philosophy that can be taken seriously, he has spoken of the continuing significance of at least some kinds of religion.[25] Whereas earlier he famously wrote that the truths of religion will probably all eventually be translated into rational discourse, when I asked him when we were together in 2005 if he still believes

23 Habermas has a remarkable commentary on the first of the ten commandments that God gave to Moses, "You shall have no gods but me": "From a philosophical point of view, the first commandment expresses that 'leap forward' on the cognitive level which granted man freedom of reflection, the strength to detach himself from vacillating immediacy, to emancipate himself from his generational shackles and the whims of mythical powers." Quoted in Sandro Magister, "The Church Is under Siege, but Habermas, the Atheist, Is Coming to Its Defense": http://chiesa.espresso.repub blica.it/articolo/20037?eng=y.) What could be more quintessentially revelation than the Ten Commandments? Yet Habermas finds the very germ of reason in the first of the ten. Further, he has also found the germ of Western individuality in the form of the encounter between God and Moses: "*You* shall have no other gods . . ." The King James version says, "Thou shalt have no other gods before me," using the archaic English second-person singular, similar to the German *du*. Yes, through Moses, the commandments are addressed to the children of Israel, and ultimately to all human beings, yet they are addressed to each Israelite or each human being individually. Not, of course, that the individual is isolated, but rather taken up and included in a defining relationship with the Lord of the universe. The utterly social and the utterly individual come together indissolubly, in the words of the great commandments.

24 Habermas, *Lifeworld and System*, 91. He does, however, on the next page, go on to say, "Something of the penetrating power of primordial sacred powers still attaches to morality; it permeates the since differentiated levels of culture, society, and personality in a way unique in modern societies." I had to make my own index of "tradition" in this book, since there was no entry for it in the index. Looking through the appearances of the term, one can detect more than a little ambivalence. At times Habermas views tradition as an indispensable reference point, but at other points it must be thawed by linguistification.

25 The use of the term "methodological atheism" is of interest, since believers can also use it— for example, Peter Berger, who is an observant Lutheran but claims methodological atheism while doing sociology.

that, he said he doesn't any longer.[26] Clearly he continues the tradition of the Frankfurt School in not demeaning religion, in recognizing at least its deep historical significance. But on the occasion of his acceptance of the Peace Prize of the German Book Trade in October 2001, he spoke of ours as a "post-secular society" in which religion continues to play a significant role, even in the midst of continuing processes of secularization—a role that we cannot presume will disappear, even an indispensable role to the degree that religion contains cultural resources that secular philosophy cannot replicate.[27] It is clear that by "post-secular" he does not mean that he expects a religious resurgence in Europe, but that the taken-for-granted idea that secularism is everywhere the wave of the future is no longer valid.[28]

For all three of my figures, modernity in its ethical form is not some inevitable wave of the future. It is a partial and precarious achievement at best, in the midst of the continuous conflict between the various tendencies of the modern age and the spiritual wasteland it threatens to create—the view from Dover Beach, as Taylor put it.[29] But while Maruyama had little hope that we can learn from premodernity and Habermas views it with respect and a degree of regret for its loss, Taylor is the only one of my three figures who clearly feels that abandoning the premodern, letting modernity obliterate our spiritual past, would be an irreparable disaster. He alone, while affirming the ethical project of modernity as strongly as the others, also affirms a premodern culture: he is a practicing Catholic.

For a long time he has referred only in passing to this side of his life, but in 1999 in his lecture "A Catholic Modernity?" he spoke clearly as a Catholic,

26 The passage in question is: "Philosophy, even in its postmetaphysical form, will be able neither to replace nor to repress religion as long as religious language is the bearer of a semantic content that is inspiring and even indispensable, for this content eludes (for the time being?) the explanatory force of philosophical language and to resist translation into reasoning discourses." Jürgen Habermas, *Postmetaphysical Thinking* (Cambridge: Polity, 1993), 51. When Eduardo Mendieta asked Habermas in an interview in 2002 about this passage and whether "for the time being?" meant that he still hoped that philosophy could completely translate religious insights, Habermas replied, "I don't know." Habermas, *Religion and Rationality*, 163.

27 See "Faith and Knowledge," in Jürgen Habermas, *The Future of Human Nature* (Cambridge: Polity, 2003), 101–115, particularly 104.

28 See Virgil Nemoianu, "The Church and the Secular Establishment: A Philosophical Dialog between Joseph Ratzinger and Jürgen Habermas," *Logos* 9, 2 (Spring 2006): 26.

29 The short book where he deals most explicitly with the "malaise of modernity" (the title of the book when first published in Canada) is *The Ethics of Authenticity*. He discusses those marooned on Dover Beach (referring to the famous Matthew Arnold poem of that title) in *A Secular Age*.

as he does, of course, in *A Secular Age*. In the 1999 lecture he even used the example of Matteo Ricci, the great Jesuit missionary to China in the late sixteenth and early seventeenth centuries, as a model for what he was trying to do. Just as Ricci sought to understand and appreciate a radically foreign culture, that of China in the late Ming dynasty, while bringing the insights of his own tradition to bear on what was to him a radically new context, so Taylor suggests that it would be well for Catholics today to try to understand and appreciate the modern Western world as, in spite of its Christian roots, radically foreign, and to consider what they might bring to it. For Taylor, however, being both modern and Catholic, standing in two worlds, involves a form of distancing from both. What he above all wants to avoid is either a root-and-branch rejection of modernity in some kind of ultramontane reaction or an uncritical embracing of modernity as though Catholicism had really been modern all along:

> Better, I would argue, after initial (and, let's face it, still continuing) bewilderment, we would gradually find our voice from within the achievements of modernity, measure the humbling degree to which some of the most impressive extensions of a gospel ethic depended on a breakaway from Christendom [earlier he mentions the modern ideal of the radical, unconditional acceptance of all people as people that conforms to gospel teaching but that Christendom did not and could not have achieved], and from within these gains try to make clearer to ourselves and others the tremendous dangers that arise in them. It is perhaps not an accident that the history of the twentieth century can be read either in a perspective of progress or in one of mounting horror. Perhaps it is not contingent that it is the century both of Auschwitz and Hiroshima and of Amnesty International and Médicins sans Frontières. As with Ricci, the gospel message to this time and society has to respond both to what in it already reflects the life of God and to the doors that have been closed against this life. And in the end, it is no easier for us than it was for Ricci to discern both correctly, even if for opposite reasons. Between us twentieth-century Catholics, we have our own variants of the

Chinese rites controversy. Let us pray that we do better this time.[30]

In *A Secular Age*, Taylor lays out the grounds on which belief is possible in modernity: "The main feature of this new [modern] context is that it puts an end to the naïve acknowledgment of the transcendent. . . . But this is quite unlike religious turnovers in the past, where one naïve horizon ends up replacing another, or the two fuse syncretistically—as with, say, the conversion of Asia Minor from Christianity to Islam in the wake of the Turkish conquest. Naïveté is now unavailable to anyone, believer or unbeliever alike" (*SA*, introduction, 21).[31]

But for Taylor, while our cultural/religious situation is different from those of all previous eras, it is not superior to them. He speaks of "the future of the religious past," which is available to us as to no earlier age. And he notes that every "advance," even the axial age and the Reformation, had a cost, the repression and marginalization of previous forms of spiritual life, which it is now possible for us to retrieve (*SA*, chap. 20). He affirms that "in God's eternity, we are contemporaries of the Neolithic tribespeople, and our prayers are heard by God together with theirs."[32]

At the end of *A Secular Age*, Taylor says that in the formidable task of giving an "account of where we are," one to which Maruyama and Habermas have also so signally contributed, we must tell "the story of how we got here," with which the present is inextricably bound. And, if I understand him rightly, he implies that recovering the past, all the way down, not uncritically but in and through criticism, may be an essential condition—one to which I think Maruyama and Habermas could be persuaded to agree—to any possibility of achieving the fragile and uncertain project of an ethical modernity.[33]

30 James L. Heft, S.M., ed., *A Catholic Modernity? Charles Taylor's Marianist Award Lecture* (New York: Oxford University Press, 1999): 37.

31 For an illuminating discussion of the "second naiveté" that replaces original naiveté, see Paul Ricoeur, *The Symbolism of Evil* (Boston: Beacon, 1969).

32 Charles Taylor, "Concluding Reflections and Comments," in Heft, *A Catholic Modernity?*, 108.

33 At the end of *A Secular Age*, Taylor quotes something I have said several times in my work on religious evolution, "Nothing is ever lost," most recently in my "What Is Axial about the Axial Age," *Archives Européennes de Sociologie 46*, 1 (2005): 69–87.

2

A Closer Walk on the Wild Side

John Milbank

A Secular Age is a magnificent, epoch-making work, the scope of whose significance has been badly grasped by most reviewers. Perhaps the casual pace, almost slangy tone, and lush detail deceive the half-attentive reader, but what we have here is nothing less than a new diagnosis of both Western triumphs and a Western malaise. We are provided indeed with almost a full-scale political, cultural, intellectual, and religious history of modern times, replete with extraordinarily balanced and yet acute judgments.

Most miraculously of all, Taylor contrives to remain serenely irenic while still putting forward a radical and even daring thesis. The confidingly indulgent tone may for some disguise the steely conceptual substance—yet the two features in the end belong conceptually together. For if the thesis is that secularization is finally attributable to the self-undoing of Latin Christendom through overobsession with "reform," then this is also a thesis whose very succinctness paradoxically allows for no very clear identification of heroes and villains. Reforming efforts that were in many ways admirable and excellent have had dire unintended consequences; secular reactions to overzealous reform are in certain ways correct; counterreactions to the preservation of the reforming impulse by secularity itself are also in certain ways correct. Any attempt to renew and deepen a Christian vision and practice must take all this into account and can only grope imaginatively toward a new sort of renewal which would not repeat the negative dialectic of the long-term reforming process.

And yet the thesis remains clear and provocative: secularization is not whiggishly on the agenda of history, but is fundamentally the result of a self-distortion of Christianity—primarily in Western Europe. It is linked with certain fatal historical turns and yet is perhaps traceable even to the beginnings of Church practice. In some ways this is a cool, detached verdict: Taylor looks at the personalist essence of Christianity as a religious practice going "beyond the law" and argues that it has in serious ways denied this essence. Yet one has here also a theological diagnosis, and toward the end of the book Taylor appears to speak with a specifically theological voice. This voice does not in any way contest credal orthodoxy—far from it—yet it contends that much Church practice and teaching has betrayed this very orthodoxy. In many ways one could attach the label "radically orthodox" to Taylor with more justification than to those, including myself, who have traded intellectually under this logo.

So one way to characterize this book is to say that it answers the "secularization debate" with a diagnosis of Western Christendom, a diagnosis that is at once historical and theological. What we are offered is a kind of large fragment of theologized ecclesiastical history—almost a modern equivalent of Augustine's or Bede's efforts in this direction. How does this arise?

Taylor's stance on secularization is basically that it is not inevitable but that it has occurred. I think that this is the right verdict, and it clearly means that he refuses any "sociological" account of this phenomenon in favor of a "total history" of a specific contingency. Comtian or Spencerian ideas of science replacing the function of religious overall explanation are refused. Durkheimian ideas of religion as, for a time, fulfilling the function of expressing social solidarity are also refused, even though a Durkheimian relationship of religion to social ecstasy is rightly retained. Equally refused is any Weberian notion of the infinitesimal vanishing of the religious impulse in the face of the dominance of instrumental rationality, formal civility, and law. And likewise rejected is any revisionary Weberian perspective that denies the fact of secularization altogether, by arguing that religion has simply mutated to a more private and expressivist form and even that in so doing it has now found its "proper" place.

No: Taylor is clear that even though these processes are not inevitable, religion in the West has gradually been excluded from the public sphere, has attracted gradually fewer avowed believers and practitioners of any kind, and has become reflexively questionable for almost all modern persons. He does indeed acknowledge that there are specifically new modern mutations of the religious impulse, yet he stresses that these mostly concern minorities or peripheral phenomena and that they are linked with more widespread but ambivalent countersecularizing trends that arose in a series of stages from the very onset of the secularizing process.

He indeed achieves a novel balance by pointing this out: not only does one have a deist and humanist critique of Christianity, one also has—starting even as far back as the seventeenth century—a proto-romantic reaction (the sublime, the unfathomable deep ruined past) to this in the name of mystery, emotion, and profounder meaning. This reaction can involve either a new style of recovery of Christian themes or else a rejection of Enlightenment rationality and discipline as being all too much a bastard offspring of Christianity itself. Here one has dark, neopagan romanticism, what Taylor calls the "immanent counter-Enlightenment." But then, he says, one gets the "nova effect" among an elite and then a "supernova" effect among all—enlightenment, light and dark romanticisms engender a vast number of strange new combinations. So all this allows Taylor to take subtle account of mutating religion and the way in which religion is not likely to go away, without going to the extreme of some sociologists in denying the reality of secularization altogether.

Secularization is a reality, but it is merely an event or a series of events, not an inexorable human destiny. This means that we cannot think of it "subtractively," as if secular belief and practice were a natural default position. To the contrary, secular ideas and cultural imaginings had to be strenuously invented in the long course of a process whose theoretical ingenuity and practical resourcefulness one cannot but admire. In particular, it had to be worked out how an immanent social order can be distilled from purely natural givens regarding human nature. And this required always some sort of new fiction about the most fundamental human essence—as freedom of choice, happiness-seeking, sympathetic, devoted to the dignity of freedom as such, heroically altruistic, and so forth. But though these are in a sense supposed to be derived from "human life" as such, they are inevitably, as Taylor says, "meta-biological" principles, scarcely susceptible to demonstration and certainly not to proof. They represent decisions as to what constitutes an immanent human transcendence—all within a further decision that only such a mode of transcendence is real or at least socially relevant.

Here, though, one should note a slight complication in Taylor's mode of presentation. By denying the automatic natural negativity of the secular humanist position, he specifically exalts, as we have just noted, its remarkable character as a positive imaginative and practical achievement. In this he is not wrong, since modernity has not only rightly insisted beyond the Middle Ages that material welfare and conspicuously free assent are important fundamental goods (although one needs to question the mode of this insistence), but has also been able to distill a new and apparently fairly stable sort of order on this minimum basis, even if the fundamental lack of justice in this order renders it more unstable than is usually imagined. However, what Taylor does not specifically say is that this ascription of positivity is a backhanded compliment, because the very logic of liberalism is bound to disguise this positivity in claiming to base itself upon a natural, neutral foundation. Once the positivity is acknowledged, within a secular perspective, then one really has to go post-humanist—either liberal rights are a pure illusion and an offense against life, or they are "absurd gestures" in the face of the void. Yet even Foucault's and Derrida's versions of this nihilist-existentialist hybrid tended to claim dubious neo-Kantian universalist foundations. More credible is Badiou's account of this combination, in which it is conceded that both affirmation of an underlying void and commitment to ideal human projects rest on pure decision. Here one has something closer to an insider admission of Taylor's crucial point that atheist positions are not usually entertained merely with sad resignation but positively embraced as attractive and heroic life stances.

In denying that secularization is a "subtraction," Taylor extends much further a view entertained already by other writers—myself, for example, and Pierre Manent.[1] Yet there is perhaps a slight unclarity in his presentation. And this focuses around the issue of "enchantment." Right at the outset of the book Taylor says that despite his going against the subtraction approach, one has to concede that there are three ways in which older circumstances

---

1 John Milbank, *Theology and Social Theory,* 2nd ed. (Oxford: Blackwell, 2006); Pierre Manent, *An Intellectual History of Liberalism,* trans. Rebecca Balinski (Princeton: Princeton University Press, 1995).

favoring religious belief have been, indeed, simply "removed." In a way these all involve "enchantment," but more specifically they are: (1) popular experience of meteorological and other natural variations as "acts of God"; (2) the assumption that the political and the religious order were inseparable; and (3) the belief that the world was full of spiritual and magical forces—the enchanted universe, specifically (*SA*, 25–26).

Now, Taylor rightly says that the rise of a scientific and historically critical outlook undermined the credibility of these three beliefs. But beyond that point he is perhaps unclear in three specific ways. First of all, if this were only a shift in popular experience as a result of elite imposition, then we are referred back to what is here the more crucial higher level of shifts in learned outlook. Yet at this level it is by no means clear that Taylor places "disenchantment" within subtraction. In fact, by the end of the book this would appear to be not the case at all. He does cite without criticism Rémi Brague, and Brague does, disappointingly, argue that disenchantment followed inevitably from the collapse of the medieval world picture—a view that ignores Renaissance and Baroque attempts from Cusa through to Bérulle to reenchant a heliocentric and infinite universe.[2] Yet Taylor *does* at certain points acknowledge this kind of possibility, and furthermore is highly alert to the fact that disenchantment perhaps primarily came about because a certain style of *theology* favored this: a style wishing to monopolize all mystery in the one God, somewhat in the way that the modern state now monopolized all coercive power at the sovereign center. One could add here that the triumph of mechanical philosophy in both Catholic and Protestant countries seems to have had more to do with a wish to eradicate any supposed "neopagan" sense of vital forces in the cosmos than with the objective natural evidence. Indeed, in the later seventeenth century, it was largely the evidence itself that forced a new recognition of occult physical forces and biological vitalism against the mechanical purity of the physics of Mersenne, Gassendi, and Descartes.[3] And Taylor himself very well narrates how an initial sense of a greater antiquity of nature at the end of the seventeenth century led to a new proto-romantic sense of cosmic time, just as a new fascination with "primitive" peoples led to a new respect for "childish" imagination and a new conception of nature itself as "poetry."

2 Rémi Brague, *La Sagesse du monde* (Paris: Fayard, 1999).

3 See Charles Webster, *From Paracelsus to Newton: Magic and the Making of Modern Science* (Cambridge: Cambridge University Press, 1982).

One could certainly concede here that certain fixed "codes" of medieval enchantment could not have really survived scientific discovery. Even though we still cover meat with spicy sauces, we can no longer honestly consider that we do this out of a need to balance the "wetness" of meat with the "fieriness" of the spice in order to encourage a balance of our humors and so of our mental state, as people did in the Middle Ages.[4] Yet it does not at all follow from this that we are obliged to abandon all notions of esoteric links between physical states and mental ones—indeed, if one believes that the latter truly exist and yet are not dualistically separated from the body, one actually *requires* some subtle mode of the pathetic fallacy, a point that the nineteenth-century Romantics often realized. Taylor himself at the end of his book implies that the medial status of the body between subjectivity and objectivity (as already recognized by Maine de Biran)[5] opens toward a more subtle, fluid, undogmatic reenchantment of the cosmos. And in Christian terms this new, subtler mode could be readily seen as a gain: the Church fathers were against fixed superstitions but still thought that the world was a cosmic temple. These two things came together in remarks scattered throughout the works of the Greek fathers about how there is an apophatic mystery of the creation as well as of the creator.

My point here is that in the bulk of the book Taylor seems to radicalize even his own initial position, implying that there may not be these three exceptions to "antisubtraction" after all. And one could further specify: the Middle Ages *did* know of speculation regarding immanent secondary causes even of exceptional natural events. Moreover, the further establishment of these in early modernity did not deny final divine causality *except* within those modes of semi-occasionalism that reduced the operation of this causality to a partially contributing "concursive" role. Amos Funkenstein has shown that these modes—curiously, it would seem—were predominantly favored by the scientific revolution.[6] Again, the Middle Ages often, as with Aquinas, *did* realize that political authority was artificially constructed, and yet it still assumed that it could not attract any legitimacy save by referral to God and by

4 I am grateful to Rebecca Harkin of Wiley-Blackwell for drawing my attention to this point of culinary history. See also, for the relations of humors to diet, Noga Arikha, *Passions and Tempers: A History of the Humors* (New York: HarperCollins, 2007).

5 Maine de Biran, *Influence de l'habitude sur la faculté de penser* (Paris: L'Harmattan, 2006).

6 Amos Funkenstein, *Theology and the Scientific Imagination: From the Middle Ages to the Seventeenth Century* (Princeton: Princeton University Press), 1986.

acknowledging participation in divine providential governance. Inversely, Carl Schmitt plausibly argued that outside this reference, political legitimacy becomes problematic in any era. Finally, the evidence suggests that where modern pressures are weak or the modern outlook is not regarded as saving all appearances and intuitions, traditional regional beliefs in fairies, demons, ghosts, and magical sympathy persist, even in areas of Western Europe today. Indeed, Taylor omits to mention how important an aspect of New Age sensibility this is. And one must remember that the fairies were initially banished from Scotland (where they have always especially thronged) not by the forces of reason but by the forces of Calvinism. Fairy belief was actually *revived* and given new intellectual support in eighteenth-century Scotland thanks to the influence of the more liberal and neoplatonically inclined theology of the "fairy minister," Robert Kirk.[7] Thus disenchantment is no more natural and inevitable than the decline of religion—and essentially Taylor affirms this.

All the same, he is not entirely consistent here. This is shown in two respects. First, consider his treatment of the newly "morbid" late medieval obsession with death. Taylor notes, after Philippe Ariès and others, that the earlier Middle Ages had sustained a time-honored human ease with death, which was for millennia so frequent an occurrence that it was seen as part of the natural cycle of life and was less an object of inveterate fear than it has become in modern times (*SA,* 65–70). But Taylor reads the shift in terms of an imposition upon the laity of a monastic fear in the face of death linked to anticipation of the Last Judgment. However, this would suggest that the most rigorous Christianity is on the side of "disenchantment" here—that it is resistant to popular ritualization and fetishization of burial grounds and the death process. Yet Taylor does not cite any evidence for this, and I would doubt that it is available. Surely the clergy, both monastic and secular, were also earlier just as at ease with death as the laity were, as indeed Ariès suggests?[8] Of course Christianity increased personal fear of final judgment, but this did not mean that it "denaturalized" biological death or removed it from the life cycle. Moreover, Christianity also increased confidence in the face of death through its promise of beatitude to the redeemed, and the doctrine of the

7 See Lizanne Henderson and Edward J. Cowan, *Scottish Fairy Belief* (East Linton: Tuckwell, 2004). It was locally believed—long into the nineteenth century—that Kirk had not died but been snatched himself to fairyland.

8 Philippe Ariès, *The Hour of Our Death,* trans. Helen Weaver (London: Allen Lane, 1981), 92.

resurrection places the individual physical body *still more* within a "natural" birth-death oscillation. Taylor ignores Jean Delumeau's conclusion at this point, despite often citing him and despite the fact that this conclusion chimes perfectly with Taylor's wider thesis.[9] This conclusion is that the late medieval and then still more the Reformation Church helped to foment an alien character and fear of death by banning the mingling of death with life celebrated by the holding of markets, festivities, and law courts (as in Brittany) within burial grounds, in communion with the ancestors. This was now disapproved of as obscenely mixing the solemnity of death with the triviality of life. So once more, as Taylor generally argues, the crucial factor is the favoring of discipline over festivity and the abstract consideration of both life and death over relational embodiment. On this reading, then, the "growing fear of death" is not the result of any Christianization of the laity but rather of that late medieval antifestive and antirelational reinterpreation of Chrisitianity spoken of by John Bossy, Delumeau, and others.

The second instance concerns Taylor's reinvocation in *A Secular Age* of the theme of the early modern "discovery of ordinary life" that was so to the fore in his *Sources of the Self.* The danger here is of subscribing to a kind of "subtraction thesis" after all. Ordinary life seems for Taylor to be just "there" once an excessive preoccupation with the otherworldly or the mentally elevated is removed. However, one could argue that what is more fundamental is a *secularization* of ordinary life in early modern times. The later Middle Ages, as Taylor mentions, saw an increasing ritualization of agriculture, manufacture, and trade—perhaps as a creative lay reaction to the increasing exclusion of laymen from the official liturgy and also to the increasingly extrinsic understanding of grace, juristic understanding of the Church, and atomistic understanding of the person encouraged by the growing dominance of Franciscan currents in theology. But this means that already in the Middle Ages, "ordinary life" was coming more to the fore. What happened in early modern times was that this process was continued in a modified way within Lutheranism (with its idea of "the vocation," etc.) and in a more drastically altered way within Calvinism. Weber had it essentially right here: Calvinism drained "the calling" and everyday life of any sacramental significance, while

9 Jean Delumeau, *Le Peché et la peur: La culpabilisation en Occident XIIIe–XVIIIe siècles* (Paris: Fayard, 1983), 48.

rendering it a kind of testing ground for the reality of election. Meanwhile the Counter-Reformation tended to clamp down on or try to control lay spontaneity and therefore negatively encouraged the rise of a more secular lay sphere.

It follows that the early modern approach to everyday life was no unproblematic discovery of a "natural" sphere but rather a questionable disenchantment that directly promoted the functionalization and massified control of human existence. Moreover, Wilhelm Roepke long ago suggested that in a certain way the eighteenth century tended to *reenchant* ordinary life—perhaps especially within the Lutheran parts of Germany or in Anglican England. The family, the house, *hausmusik,* the garden, surrounding nature, landscape painting, are increasingly seen as "means of grace."[10]

But all these suggested modifications only confirm the generally "antiwhig" thrust of Taylor's approach and the denial that secularization, even as enchantment, is in any sense inevitable.

Nevertheless, the same ambiguity regarding enchantment reemerges in Taylor's overanxiety to insist that disappearance of enchantment does not equate with decline of religion. Of course this is correct, because we have phenomena like Calvinism and Bible Belt fundamentalists, who live in a secularized space and time far more extreme than anything found in Europe. Another example is Wahabism, which has tried to remove (in a very modern fashion) all sacramental and imagistic elements from Islamic practice. However, it is central to Taylor's most crucial thesis that such phenomena in the end encourage secularization. Monotheism that allows no sacramental mediation, that renders the divine will remote and inscrutable, that sharply divides nature from supernature, itself engenders an impermeable, drained, meaningless immanence that can readily be cut off from any transcendent relation whatsoever.

Thus again and again Taylor rightly says that the overconcentration of Latin Christendom on behavioral reform tended to dampen down a popularly festive and ecstatic spirit, intimately linked to enchantment. So can he have it both ways? Is disenchantment closely linked to secularization or not?

10 Wilhelm Roepke, *The Social Crisis of Our Time,* trans. William F. Campbell (Brunswick, N.J.: Transaction, 2009), 37–82.

Fundamentally he argues that it is. With the liberal secularization of politics, first the Baroque version of Christendom and then what Taylor calls the "neo-Durkheimian" version—linking religion to nationhood and specific social movements—decline to leave behind the religion of "authenticity" that is to do with inner depth and personal quest for unique expression. However, this also involves a direct, nonsocially mediated relationship to the cosmos, and that, as I have already said, is generally linked to reenchantment. Moreover, Taylor himself points out that practices of pilgrimage and devotion to miracle-working saints returned by popular demand in the nineteenth century. Today they are reviving again, and often a new religious individualism gets combined with private visits to cathedrals to light candles by people who are by no means church-attending Christians.

So one could argue that the details of Taylor's book show that he does *not* really believe that the fate of enchantment and the fate of religion are independent of each other. Rather, he thinks that a certain mode of monotheism has tended to disenchant and that this is in the long term *fatal* for religiosity. And as I have just argued, newer, post-secular modes of religion tend to reenchant.

The third point regarding enchantment relates to the long-term effect of the axial religions, which Taylor frequently invokes during the course of his book. If, as I have argued and as he has orally concurred with, the main thesis of his book is that reform engendered secularization in the Latin West—what he calls the "reform master narrative" (RMN)—then behind this lurks a larger thesis about religion as such, which is indeed a profound and attractive one, which I find rather convincing.

What is intuitively attractive about it is that it appeals to every contemporary person's vague notion of a religious person. This is of someone who curiously "walks on the wild side" in terms of her beliefs, experiences, and practices, is generally a bit odd and extreme, and yet is also in daily life moral and disciplined, pursuing a "closer walk" with God through the example of Christ or holy people who went about doing good.

Now it seems to me that the whole of *A Secular Age* addresses this bizarre combination: religion draws on wild Dionysiac energies, it goes ecstatically beyond the constituted norms, and therefore it is often linked with sex and violence. And yet it is also most often regarded as the unique and final source of social and moral order. Here the exception does not merely prove the rule; it alone makes it—as, for example, with exceptional practices of bloody sacrifice or ritual sex.

One sees this clearly with preaxial religion, but the strange combination remains, one could argue, in all religion. Secular ethical practice can remain immanent, but it does so at the contradictory price of grounding the ethical in the preethical—"natural" happiness, freedom, and sympathy. But where the ethical is grounded in the ethical, then, necessarily, it is grounded "beyond the ethical" in the religious, which alone guarantees that the good is self-originating and not epiphenomenal. Such transcendent goodness belongs to an entire ontological reality that necessarily possesses other attributes— unity, beauty, truth, differentiation, individuation, relationality, and so forth. Hence one's "ecstatic" relationship to this reality grounds the ethical and yet exceeds the ethical. It may even be that the ultimate circumstances of one's relationship to this reality contradict the practices enjoined upon one in everyday human social existence. For example, some cultures practice human sacrifice. According to Kierkegaard in *Fear and Trembling,* even the aborted sacrifice of Isaac, taken as a metaphor, exceeds the ethical while grounding it, because death in relation to God, the source of all life, does not mean what death must mean between fragile human beings, who can only kill but cannot create or resurrect. There is therefore a religious "suspension" of the ethical that nonetheless supports every ethic not reducible to the naturalistically preethical. Taylor cites Charles Péguy's parallel hostility toward any identification of the ethical as itself the heart of Christianity. To be horrendously summary, one could say that religion, like all social reality for Péguy, begins in the mystical but ends by engendering some sort of ethical practice.

Throughout the book, Taylor repeatedly suggests that religion will collapse into the merely ethical when it ignores this mystical, ecstatic, Dionysiac root—however much monotheism must qualify a preaxial sacralization of sex and violence. And once one has the merely ethical (which quickly reduces to the amorally preethical), one has the instability (as he does not sufficiently say) of trying to ground "mutual benefit" upon basically individualistic presuppositions, which can always disturb this order through a resurgence of supposedly "natural" egoistic violence or through the latent anarchy of sovereign political power and formal economic capital. Sooner or later, a lurking nihilism within "purely ethical ethics" will emerge, conjoined with hankerings after the preaxial, which are actually far more pagan than paganism it-self, since they now seek directly to worship an indifferent, impersonal fate and discount all lesser deities. Thus one has the logical paradox that by ignor-ing the more-than-ethical one eventually gets the less-than-ethical.

It is this paradox that, I think, Taylor is most fundamentally exploring. And it is in terms of this paradox that he thinks we need a version of Chris-tianity which incorporates certain preaxial elements. Energy must not be suppressed in favor of a false, sickly version of asceticism, even though true asceticism is itself a mode of ecstatic energy, which Protestantism falsely questioned. Yet truly expressed energy can be integrated with the peaceful purposes of body and soul and so is no longer a violence to be merely "con-tained." (Taylor is authentically Pauline and Augustinian at this point.) The danger with the idea of mere "containment" is that it naturalizes violence and assumes that it is an abnormality that can be treated only therapeutically. This, as Taylor argues, fails to see the corrupted but real seed of true aspira-tion within violence and tends to give rise to the view that violence as natural can never be overcome—which engenders in turn either misanthropy or a nihilistic version of the Dionysiac.

Similarly, we need to search for a true Christian erotics—the lack of which alone perhaps kept (the finally anti-Nietzschean) D. H. Lawrence from Chris-tian belief.[11] Yet once more a full integration of sexuality and gender differ-ence into the Christian life ensures that the sexual is no longer (at least in ideal essence) an ambivalent reality to be alternately tamed and pandered to in its unbridled wildness. This is not, of course, a Freudian thesis about "re-pression." One can agree with Foucault here that it is not at all that Christian-ity has "repressed" sexuality; to the contrary, it has produced and discovered it by focusing so strongly on love and desire in every sense. But in doing so it has sequentially delivered the mixed message that this released *daimon* is ei-ther a crucial source of evil or else a crucial key to liberation if it is simply "released"—neither position being satisfactory, nor allowing that integration of sexuality within knowledge and overall character formation which Chris-tian doctrine perhaps properly suggests.

So if we need the carnivalesque, then this is perhaps (to gloss and modify Taylor) not because we are offering a sop to dark erotic and energetic forces,

---

11 See in particular the concluding passages of *The Rainbow.*

but rather because we need a comic acknowledgment of the limits of even the best-conceived sacral ritual order—and moreover because a more "general" and public sexual expression and a more intense physical engagement with each other (playfully violent, the violence of play) may be in due season an aspect of order itself. This is indeed the place of dance, an ordered interruption of order that is a figure of society itself, a regular and yet ceaselessly reimprovised formation.

As Taylor stresses, Christianity is not less but *more* pro-body than preaxial notions, because the Incarnation suggests that our entire body and sensuality can be taken up into the spiritual, so putting an end to bodily *rending,* which paganism rather encouraged. However, in saying this, he surely should not be also suggesting, as he does, that we need a kind of "balance" between the preaxial and the axial, as if Christianity as part of the axial tradition were natively too "one-sided." For *of itself,* as Taylor himself affirms, Christianity is an incarnational religion and therefore implies reciprocal festivity as well as ascetic sacrifice.

Here, it seems to me, Taylor accepts too much from Marcel Gauchet and Rémi Brague, respectively. From Gauchet he imbibes something of the view that the axial religions *implicitly* tend to disenchantment.[12] From Brague he seems to take the view that the Bible and Judaism encourage this phenomenon. But Brague misreads Philo here and ignores in a very old-fashioned, strangely Germanic way, the Hebrew Bible's interest in a sacral cosmos.[13]

As to Gauchet's claim, this is surely exactly the kind of intellectual whiggery that Taylor (and for much of the time Gauchet also) is supposed to be contesting. When one looks at the axial faiths, they all have "enchanted" and "disenchanted" variants: one has Mahayana and Theravada, Shiism and Sunnism, rabbinism and kabbalism, Catholicism and Protestantism. (This division is a grotesque caricature, of course, but serves to make a point.) The idea that the "enchanted" versions less grasp the axial essence, are less radical or more contaminated with the preaxial, is simply not defensible. If they do indeed incorporate preaxial dimensions, then this is still for integrally postaxial reasons. "Magical" powers may now be less automatically under the con-

12 Marcel Gauchet, *The Disenchantment of the World: A Political History of Religion,* trans. Oscar Burge (Princeton: Princeton University Press, 1997).

13 See Robert Murray, *The Cosmic Covenant* (London: Sheed and Ward, 1992). I hope to criticize Brague's reading of Philo in a future published writing.

trol of fate, but within a cosmos created by, or somehow related to, a personal or personally concerned power, there may be all kinds of lesser spiritual realities. Moreover, if "magic" becomes flexible and less "according to rule," it is no less magic, for Mauss long ago destroyed the "magic is automatic process" mistake.[14]

In short, Gauchet's thesis is questionable because, in the case of the monotheistic faiths, the idea of a personal god at the top may tend to depersonalize all within the creation—as, arguably, in the Quran, in which human beings are *not* said to be in the image of God (though this is massively qualified within Shiism and Sufism)—or, equally, it may tend to a semi-vitalistic near-personification of all that a personal god has created, or encourage belief in thousands of hidden angelic and spiritual forces. (And *all* of Islam allows the latter from the Quran, with its occasional tales of jinns onward).

Moreover, if anything, it is the "enchanted" version that seems truer to the profoundest logic of monotheism, and it is for this reason that monotheistic "mystics" very often ascribe to an enchanted cosmos and to "quasi-magical" notions such as the Jesus Prayer within Eastern Orthodoxy. Their correlation here with popular piety is not a lack of sophistication but the result of a sophistication greater than that of positivisitic dogmaticians.

How can this be claimed? Well, in the first place, God is one in a sense that lies beyond the contrast of the one and the many—he is not in the category "individual" any more than he is in the category "general," as Aquinas puts it. Hence the absolute transcendent is in no sort of rivalry with other, lesser spiritual powers. By contrast, the "disenchanting" version tends to reduce God to an ontic idol who *is* a supreme individual and thus tends to come into zero-sum competition with his subordinates. This "monopolization of mystery" does not really redound to God's glory, because, as Aquinas also says, that is more evidenced in the degree to which God can *communicate* his own power. The "monopolizing" God is likely to be conceived as a tyrant who usurps our proper powers because he operates on the same univocal plane of being as ourselves.[15] Hence, as Régis Debray argues, there is a demonstrable link between incidences of monotheistic religious violence and the less sacramental variants of monotheism. The desert delivers the crazed

14 Marcel Mauss, *A General Theory of Magic*, trans. Robert Brain (London: Routledge, 1972).

15 For the connection between a "monopoly God" and the growth of political absolute sovereignty, see Jean Bethke Elshtain, *Sovereignty: God, State and Self* (New York: Basic Books, 2008), 1–91.

religious enthusiast who has heard directly the literal voice of God demanding to be represented by literal words and deeds that tolerate no rivals and little glossing.[16]

Second, the naive interpersonal account of prayer supposes that we can alter the mind of God, since he is just another, if very big, individual on the same ontological plane as ourselves. But this is not compatible with monotheistic rigor, for which God's mind is eternal and unchanging. Is prayer then just consoling therapy? Here the sophisticated midpath is in some broad sense "magical," or, more satisfactorily, "theurgic."[17] By uttering certain words, adopting certain bodily postures, achieving a state of mental concentration, we "atune" ourselves to God's eternal good purposes, and thereby a divine influence *really does* flow into us, and we can take it that this is God's eternally appointed providential means of action. So, once more, the "hypersophisticated," mystically monotheistic position (whether in Judaism, Islam, or Christianity) turns out to be more in keeping with popular piety than a more woodenly abstract approach to theology, which tends to fall into a conceptual literalism. The latter kind of approach is, I think, often allied with an overly juridical mindset and so linked to an attempt to prune back popular involvements in enchantment. But surely, in the case of Christianity, the more authentically "Catholic" reality is the blend of the very sophisticated with the very popular—omitting the half-baked "bourgeois" mode of positivistic piety, prayer meetings, organizational obsession, and ill-informed, unimaginative Bible studies that waste the time one might spend having fun.

My case, then, is that Taylor's main thesis is confirmed and radicalized once one has dumped Gauchet's (lingering) whiggery. But in another way also I think that the axial moment needs to be considered a little differently, in order to give Taylor's thesis rather more of a comparativist dimension.

Basically, one needs to bring out more the difference between the Judaic and Socratic ruptures and the oriental ones. The latter are in a way actually more like Greek naturalism and sophism—Confucius was certainly more like a Sophist than he was like Socrates. His wisdom was strictly pragmatic and located within a cosmos of impersonal law that was not concerned with the "good" in a Platonic sense. Hence in the case of China, India, pre-Socratic

16 Régis Debray, *God: An Itinerary*, trans. Jeffrey Mehlman (London: Verso, 2004).

17 The agnostic Mauss often came near to good theology and implies something like this in his *On Prayer*, trans. Susan Leslie (New York: Berghahn, 2003).

Greece, and even earlier, in Babylon, one can speak of a mutation in "paganism" whereby the personal forces in the cosmos get more and more naturalized and the ultimate obscure "absolute," which had always been vaguely invoked, is more specifically identified as an impersonal power or an ultimate impersonal void. Taoism and Mahayana then tend to bring back some of the mythological magical or personal powers within this scope. But basically one could speak of a kind of "disenchantment" or even "secularization" here that is nonetheless still universally religious, unlike modern secularization, which is specifically post-Christian. (Nevertheless, this earlier sacralization all too easily coalesces with the Western one in modern Asia: already instrumentalized religion fuses with, or gives way to, instrumentalized patterns of social action; this is one reason why Europe may remain our only future hope.)

Now, the point is that whereas the other axial religions accentuate the "mythical" notion that local personal powers are subordinate to impersonal fate, Platonism and Judaism do something much more surprising. They go beyond the local only by inventing the universal itself as a "supreme locality." This is why their account of the absolute is more personal—the Bible more so than Plato, of course. But in this way they do not abandon the personal and direct aspect of the primitive—including its oral and gift-exchanging, precontractual and prelegal character—so much as generalize and universalize it. And the New Testament, by subordinating the law to the interpersonal, in a sense "reprimitivizes" all the more. As Ivan Illich pointed out, the New Testament does not say "love strangers" but "render all as kin."[18]

In a similar fashion, one could argue that the Hebrew Bible/Old Testament's rage against images is *not* the simple forbidding of imaging the one absolute God that it is so often taken to be. To the contrary, the idea that one can scarcely image this god was no novelty. Rather, the novelty of the Hebrews' outlook consisted not only in their invoking of and relating to this god, but also in their astonishingly "sublime" poetic attempts to image him remotely in both terrible-grotesque "oriental" figures (as in Ezekiel) and in "occidental" human figures (as in Daniel).[19] The rage against images is therefore a rage against the attribution to lesser gods of any independent power

18 See Ivan Illich and David Cayley, *The Rivers North of the Future: The Testament of Ivan Illich as told to David Cayley* (Toronto: Anansi, 2005).

19 Hegel was therefore perhaps wrong to think that the Hebrews required the encounter with Greece in order to achieve this synthesis, or that it begins only in the New Testament.

that might be appeased. These gods must *no longer* be imaged in merely monstrous (as opposed to terrible), sacrificial forms, but may be validly imaged in augmented, awesome, winged human form as "angels." This reconception of the gods as more benign intermediaries would appear to recall, in a more transcendent mode, a *more primitive,* preagricultural, and presacrificial sense of the sacred other as that with which one perpetually exchanges gifts. Hence the seeming dominance of the "anti-image" theme of the Hebrew scriptures is more apparent than real, as archaeological evidence has for some time been confirming. A certain imaging of the divine is actually crucial for an emergent sense of the *personal* character of the divine.

And it is just *this* aspect of the Hebrew scriptures that the (rather more "oriental") Quran of course rejects as an idolatrous corruption of the revelation once given to Abraham. This accords with the far less personal character of Allah as compared to Yahweh or the triune God. And how far may it be the case that the more literal (but I have just argued mistaken) Quranic reading of the supposed Hebrew ban on images has infected the Christian West from Byzantine iconoclasm (instigated in reaction to Islam) through to the Calvinist Reformation?

So the very personalism of Judaism and Christianity, on which Taylor frequently insists, also exhibits a special mode of continuity with the preaxial that the oriental axial religions do not have. Of course, there is also a huge shift: tribal "persons" were masked roles, as Mauss taught, but once the interpersonal has become universal, it is relatively freed from local fetishes, even if these can act as local conduits for general spiritual power. Yet all the same, Ivan Illich's crucial insight, invoked by Taylor toward the end of his book, that Christian agape operates through a network of direct relations and not through conceptual or legal imposition, is precisely equivalent to the idea that the Church, instead of founding universality on abstract right and contract, tries to found it on a kind of "universalizing" of prelegal tacit bonds of trust and gift exchange. But remarkably, Seneca in his *De Beneficiis* already conceived the cosmopolis on this model—perhaps because while you exchange gifts with friends and make contracts with everyday strangers, with more remote strangers, who share no common currency or cultural idiom, you must once more exchange gifts. And the Pauline epistles show how Paul actually tried to put such a "personalist" international network into practice.

So this comparativist perspective once more only reinforces Taylor's claims. Christianity uniquely mediates a personal—or rather interpersonal—God through interpersonal practice and not through the law.

The bulk of Taylor's book turns out retrospectively to have been about how this gets perverted through the institutionalization of charity. At the end of *A Secular Age* he generously acknowledges that there is a symmetry between this thesis and that of several theologians, including myself, according to which we can blame atheism and immanentism in the end on a justified reaction against bad theology (773–776). Taylor suggests that the most far-reaching version of this thesis may be that of "radical orthodoxy" (RO), which traces this "bad theology" back to Duns Scotus and his inauguration of a univocal ontology—combined, I should add, with an already "epistemological" theory of knowledge as representation. Part of the point here is that it is the very exigencies of Franciscan piety, especially concern for the sovereignty of God and the gratuity of revelation, that encourage a departure from a "participatory" framework seen implicitly as too pagan and Platonic. The price, though, for this was, I think, in the very long term ironically a lapse into a kind of conceptual idolatry, abandoning notions of the *via negativa* and of human deification in favor of extrinsic obedient response to revealed propositional truths. It turned out that the Christian reality precisely as Christian actually needed the pagan, since this had always been part of the mix anyway.

Now there is indeed a very exact parallel between what Taylor says and what RO says. We are saying that overpiety (Franciscan voluntarism) paradoxically undermines theology; he is saying that hyperreform of the laity paradoxically undermines belief. Taylor then asks how these two metanarratives—"the intellectual deviation story" (ID) and his own RMN, relate to each other.

As an explanation of secularization he declares that RMN is more fundamental than RO's ID. To which I would respond that he is absolutely right—of course this is the case, because the most determining processes are fusions of ideas and practices, not ideas in isolation. But actually, for this very reason, RO has never claimed that ID is *the* most fundamental account of secularization, only that it relates one intellectual thread of this tale.

I would add, however, three riders, the first relatively trivial but the second two important. First, RO writers have already tried to say some things about the wider practical setting of ID—and much of this concurs with RMN. The end of my own *Theology and Social Theory* indicates this, as does, much more extensively, Catherine Pickstock's *After Writing,* which tries to link univocity to the rise of discipline through the mediating notion of *mathesis* and which also, like Taylor, points out that the displacement of ritual courtesy by civility was a crucial aspect of the secularizing process.[20] I have also in certain places indicated that I think the Hildebrandine reform was highly ambivalent—too much removing the laity from Church affairs, too much imposing on them a quasi-monastic and clerical discipline.

I only say this to reinforce a fundamental agreement between RO and Taylor. He has taken the "ambivalence of reform" thesis considerably further by linking it up with the wild/taming paradox of religion and also by connecting it with disenchantment. The more that discipline involves self-discipline, which forgets the surprisingness of grace, then the more it gets Stoicized, as Taylor argues, and the more it links with the idea of a "buffered self" impervious to the impact of spiritual forces—and remarkably attractive just for that reason. (This is one of Taylor's really crucial theses.)

It also gives rise to "totalizing" political disciplinary programs as described by Foucault. Taylor succeeds in showing just how these programs are intimately linked to secularizing immanence. Crucial here, as he says, was Justus Lipsius's Stoicizing ethics, its later fusion with Calvinism, and its influence on the birth of liberalism with Grotius (*SA*, 119ff.).

My second rider concerns a greater RO stress than with Taylor on the sinister *political* aspect of secularization. One can begin by elaborating Taylor here in saying that what one has with Lipsius is a specifically post-Christian neo-Stoicism that perverts the unlimited hopefulness of the Augustinian reform program. In the case of pagan Stoicism there is a resignation to disciplining the passions by a drastically reserved inner withdrawal from their sway. In the case of Augustine, by contrast, as expressed in Book XIX of the *Civitas Dei,* there is a hope for the entire redirection of the passions toward love of God and the neighbor. Here "perfectionism" is located in the "festive" space of the human "between" which both Illich and Taylor wish to celebrate. But in the case of Justus Lipsius one has a novel and most regrettable hybrid: the Augustinian hope for "total reform" is no longer located in the entire redirection of passion but in an impossible "total control" or even "to-

20 Milbank, *Theology and Social Theory,* 440–442; Catherine Pickstock, *After Writing* (Oxford: Blackwell, 1998), 121–166.

tal repression" of the passions that is no longer simply an inner withdrawal. Indeed, it is as if the absolute "inward" aspect of ancient Stoic ethics has now invaded the "outward" aspect, which had originally been to do with a relational fulfilling of respective social "offices." (The possible different emphases one can give to Stoic ethics provide a somewhat unconsidered continuum from antiquity through the Middle Ages—when Cicero was much deployed —right up to the eighteenth century.)

Moreover, the modern perfectionism that perverts the Christian reform drive is dangerously *utopian* in a way that the latter is not. This is because "perfecting" for the Augustinian vision belongs in a social space which exceeds that of the political. Therefore, mere political "limiting" of the bad passions remains inescapable in time, yet at the same time "something more than this," something driven by a logic that is content with nothing less than perfect peace and harmony, is "already begun," to however small a degree, within the *ecclesia*. By contrast, the modern post-Christian neo-Stoic project pursues a quasi-Christian perfectionism within first strictly political, statist terms and then within politico-economic terms. This means that it is at once dangerously optimistic (in hoping to achieve perfect discipline before the *eschaton*) and yet *not hopeful enough,* insofar as an interpersonal peace and harmony based on perfected passion and complete mutual reconciliation is a far greater ideal than modernity is prepared to countenance or espouse.

Modernity therefore tends to replace the Church with the state, and for this reason the state assumes an odor of sanctity and requires ever-increased obeisance. This is a theme that Taylor indeed intimates but perhaps does not make enough of. For if this is the case, then one has to see secularization as involving a semideliberate power strategy on the part of the state and not simply as a relatively benign working out of how one can establish an order based on the mutual recognition of individual freedom.

Here, also, more might have been said about the tension within this mutuality between assented-to contract based on self-interest on the one hand and the spontaneous operation of sympathy on the other, so constantly spoken of by the Scottish Enlightenment (whether or not that is a projection onto the other of self-interest or an intuitive reaching beyond the self). In neither case is "mutuality" really an organic order based on collectively shared goals and horizontal and vertical placements of "offices," which in theory and practice informed medieval order. Yet arguably, *any* human society has in reality to be held together in this "medieval" way, as the ordo-liberal Wilhelm Roepke argued, such that modern thought and practice is a kind of semi-impossible denaturing of the social as such which has already led to extreme violence in the twentieth century and may do so again.[21]

However, Taylor is near to grasping this issue when he speaks about Rousseau (*SA*, 201–206). For Rousseau, rather like Adam Ferguson in this respect (or more likely the other way around), realized that liberalism, if it is to be a complete political philosophy, has to believe that self-interest and mutual sympathy without mimetic rivalry (the false amour propre consequent upon property) can together spontaneously generate a politico-economic order. What is more, as Taylor points out, Rousseau realized that the usual Anglo-Saxon contractualism and political representationalism could not resolve the "biopolitical" dilemma (involving tension between "nature" and artifice) of an always imperfect coincidence of individual and state interest—always threatening, respectively, anarchy and tyranny. Accordingly, he tried to think of the "general will": the perfect Leibnizian coordination of each and every will with every other will and with the interests of the whole.[22] This could come about through a social contract in which the exercise of the individual right of freedom was paradoxically most shown through an entire surrendering of this right to the social totality. (One can see how Kant tried to offer an atemporal ethical equivalent.)

By doing this, Rousseau at once produced the most modern, because most ultraliberal, of all political theories (from which most socialisms have been born!) *and* produced the liberal theory that most of all echoes both ancient virtue politics and the politics of Saint Augustine (a curious combination that republican France itself surely reflects to this day). Thus for Rousseau one can only pursue self-interest through political participation in the state, seen as an echo of the ancient polis. Also, the general will is supposed to produce a harmonious and peaceful coexistence of all with all that echoes Augustine's "City of God" rather than any pagan polity. (Just as Rousseau's *Confessions* solipsistically echo the view of Augustine's *Confessions* that discovery of truth and the narrative formation of character are one and the same thing.) But in the absence of any teleology save the self-referring promotion

21 Roepke, *The Social Crisis*, 37–82.

22 For the demonstration of Rousseau's Leibnizianism, see Alexis Philonenko, *Jean-Jacques Rousseau et la pensée du malheur* (Paris: Vrin, 1984).

of negative freedom, nothing in this formal scheme suggests how coordination of real interests can arise, nor any ontological ground for its possibility.

Sympathy (added to the benign asocial *amour de soi-même*) is not enough, for two reasons. First of all, the human being is a social being who thinks and desires as someone speaking a shared language. There *is* no innocent desire prior to mimesis and the distribution of shares (in every sense), even if this desire need not necessarily, as Rousseau taught, be corrupted. (The older Augustinian sense of corruption was at once less dogmatic and socially gloomy, if alternatively insistent on its natural pervasiveness, which was not, all the same, until Luther, a "total depravity.") Hence sympathy cannot be for the naturally given in the other, but we must always *judge* as to what is deserving of our sympathy—and if we *imagine* ourselves in the position of the other, then this should be insofar as we conceive our shared but various participation, along with the other, in the objective good. Therefore sympathy is not "foundational," as the eighteenth-century theory of moral sentiments requires.

But for a second reason also it cannot be foundational. This is the fact that we do *not* naturally sympathize in undiluted fashion with another's misfortune where it is to our advantage. Schadenfreude is far from rare. Nor do we naturally sympathize in undiluted fashion with another's joy when a share in this joy seems to be denied us—given that there can be *no* society prior to the distribution of shares in some sense, contra Rousseau's naturalism. Hypocritical congratulations through clenched teeth are far from rare either. Hence while the exercise of moral sympathy is indeed morally crucial (as the Cambridge Platonists and Shaftesbury already taught in a more subtle way), it is not spontaneously right, and it can only be rightly guided by the imagination through the desiring judgment of a right order of distribution. Plato and Augustine already saw that eros is crucial in the discernment of justice, but they did not deny the crucial role here of reason, nor seek to displace distributive justice as the transcendent foundation of social order with sympathy as an immanent foundation.

Indeed, the latter foundation remains strictly impossible to build upon. Without shared goals in an interlocking hierarchy, there are no real horizontal or vertical relational bonds (an entire web of such bonds, rather than a linking of human beings only through Rousseau's sovereign center) that would weave together a social peace. Accordingly, Rousseau's ideas suggest either the impossibility of Proudhon's anarchy or else the terroristic imposition of those claiming to speak "as" the general will—which of course came to pass during the Jacobin era. In either case one sees the consummation of the idea that a merely immanent human civil society, and not the Church, is pursuing the originally Christian "project of perfection," which is now pursued in a diluted and parodied manner—either too merely pragmatic or else too unrealistically utopian (or both at once).

So on this reading, it is not just that "excessive reform" has destroyed religiosity in the West. It is also the case that it has produced the idolization of the state. This would further mean, as Taylor does not quite consider, that the secular state and economy are not simply projects of immanent order but can exist at all only as a "quasi Church" operating a "quasi economy of salvation." In this respect, "civil religion" (in contrast to simply "nationalistic religion" in the nineteenth century) would appear to be a more abiding constituent of secularity than Taylor perhaps allows. However much we may be forced to conclude that in a pluralistic world we have to establish some sort of liberal order, critical rigor should still allow us to entertain a secular pessimism that would acknowledge that the problematic of liberalism as exposed by Rousseau is not resolvable save at the expense of deeming all personal liberty (including both permission rights and entitlement rights, which are thereby held in balance at the political center) to be participation in the political state, which thereby becomes the "sacred" source of our very humanity. This is exactly the "republican" rather then merely "liberal" conclusion arrived at by Luc Ferry and Alain Renaut.[23] But it is surely unacceptably statist—especially for liberals.

Within the Rousseauesque liberal order, as we have seen, one finally gets the self who cannot really be ecstatically connected to other people through a web of specific relationships (but only through the political center, like a windowless monad with other monads) and that ultra-Cartesian "coldness" that palpably afflicts aspects of French culture to this day. This was best summed up in Lacan's deduction in Seminar XX that in a disenchanted universe where there are no occult links between body and body and mind and

23 Luc Ferry and Alain Renaut, *From the Rights of Man to the Republican Idea*, trans. Franklin Philip (Chicago: Chicago University Press, 1992).

body, "sexual intercourse" is impossible.[24] With total Cartesian rigor, he reasons that if knowledge is not metaphorical sexuality, then there can be no knowledge in actual sexuality. One suspects that Taylor would rightly add that surely Lacan preferred it that way—it is not that in the face of loss of enchantment we must accept loss of even human relationship; it is rather that we prefer the citadel of the solipsistic and secure self to the disturbances of both alien hatred and alien love.

The third rider is equally crucial. It is actually not the case that RMN concerns popular processes while ID concerns elite ones. RMN concerns indeed much more *mass* processes, but these processes were all imposed from above by elites—on Taylor's own account. So one could argue that a *still more* adequate account of secularization would have to bring together RMN and ID in terms of exactly how scholastic theology related to disciplinary, pastoral, and legal practice.

And perhaps rather uncomfortable questions might have to be asked here about the contrast between different procedures in different aspects and movements of the Church. Is it, for example, an accident that it was the Dominican Eckhart who tried to offer to the laity not clerical behavior but rather mystical participation in Christ as something they could know without any "way" in the midst of their ordinary, everyday lives? Is it an accident that it was the layperson Dante who tried to impart doctrine in the lay poetic vernacular? By contrast, for all the glory of Saint Francis, is there not something ambivalent about an attempt to be a too literal *alter Christus,* or at least about the interpretation of Francis's significance in this manner by his followers?[25] Is this connected with the representational realism of Franciscan-inspired painting like that of Giotto, whereas the Dominican or Dominican-influenced painters (Fra Angelico, etc.) tended to use perspective rather to reinforce the traditionally iconic as a participating passage between our world and the beyond? Is there, as David Aers has argued in writing about *Piers Plowman,* a danger recognized in that text of a Franciscan focus on the discipline

24 See Jacques Lacan, *Encore: The Seminars of Jacques Lacan, Book XX,* trans. Bruce Fink (New York: Norton, 1998).

25 The reverse side of this is a Franciscan tendency in effect to see Christ as Francis and so to produce semi-Nestorian Christologies that push the reality of Christ's human nature in the direction of a human "personal" independence. I am indebted to conversations with Aaron Riches here.

of poverty rather than the fulfillment of agape?[26] And does not that line up with the way in which Franciscan writers tended, as Pierre Rousselot long ago showed, to stress love as a one-way, disinterested ecstasy where Aquinas rather saw it as reciprocal friendship?[27] And that in turn connects with a Franciscan tendency to separate will from intellect, rendering the former more force than bond and the latter more a conceptuality taken apart from true desiring? This circumstance might then finally be linked to a tendency only to accept the univocally graspable or the representable.

I believe that these questions have to be answered in the affirmative. But whether or not this specific thesis is true, its elaboration would be one example of how one might begin to link up theological belief with disciplinary and pastoral procedure—and so ID with RMN. (Actually, Taylor does this more with philosophy beginning in the seventeenth century than he does with earlier theology.)

And this would only be to take further an enterprise that Charles Taylor has inaugurated. It must be said that Taylor has, with *A Secular Age,* consummated his invention of a new intellectual genre—a kind of historicized existentialism, in which the philosopher seeks to disinter the assumed "mood" or Wittgensteinian "picture" that causes people, often unconsciously, to take up the positions that they do, far more fundamentally than any mere conceptual reasoning. Thereby he engages in a kind of historical metaphilosophy, somewhat reminiscent of R. G. Collingwood. But he does not stop at any mere historicism: rather, he seeks to adjudicate between our inherited options by pointing out the observed or likely practical consequences of different positions, as, for example, with his handling of the implications of religious and nonreligious attitudes to violence, as described above. This is a subtle sort of apologetic: again exampled when he argues that only a religious outlook can hope for an unlimited human and cosmic reciprocity and that such a hope is likely to achieve at least some real extension of reciprocity, as opposed to the cultivation of lone absurdist gestures toward a social good that we know can never arrive, à la Derrida.

But to be able to espouse such an outlook requires, as Taylor says, a leap

---

26 David Aers, *Sanctifying Signs: Making Christian Tradition in Late Medieval England* (Durham: Duke University Press, 2004).

27 Pierre Rousselot, *The Problem of Love in the Middle Ages: A Historical Contribution,* trans. Alan Vincelette (Milwaukee: Marquette University Press, 2001).

of faith—even if humanisms and nihilisms involve also their own leaps. And so finally he offers us a reading of Latin Christian history in terms of this faith—a theological reading, as I said at the beginning.

According to this reading, with which I largely concur, the Church has failed in practice to be *orthodox enough*, because it has failed to be really true to the Incarnation—and in the end has perversely produced excarnation and an impersonal order where we can negotiate "safely" (for a while) with strangers and where we all face a sovereign center in a fantasized simultaneous space rather than seeking to relate directly to each other. Almost from the outset Christianity has excarnated by failing (with insufficient fidelity to Jewish roots) to allow that the way of marriage is of at least equal dignity with that of celibacy and by failing to integrate sexual joy into the path of deification. This failure has often connected with a belief in eternal damnation—refusing the (perfectly orthodox) universalist option of Saint Paul (arguably), Origen, and Gregory of Nyssa. The late Middle Ages, instead, saw a newly accentuated focus on sexual and bodily sins at the expense of interpersonal ones (as John Bossy has shown), and this again went along with accentuated attention to the horrors of death in fearful anticipation of the perils of hell, as described by Delumeau and others.

Without question this consideration allows us once again to link up RMN with ID, because the idea that God has arbitrarily predestined some to damnation (found, sadly, even in Aquinas) undoubtedly encouraged the gradual obsession with God's reserved "absolute power" and the slide toward voluntarism. This then surely shares a root in nonuniversalism with the tendency to rule the laity through fear rather than through love.

And the converse of this would be that the anticipation of universal cosmic redemption, as Péguy believed, would far more encourage the notion that we begin to attain to salvation through festive practices of conviviality (to echo the language of Illich) that anticipate in some measure eschatological joy. This indeed sustains *methexis,* just as belief in *methexis* sustains social "participation." But belief in the ultimacy of hell works to destroy participation in both the social and the metaphysical sense. Lonely in the face of arbitrary terror, we imbibe the prescribed private remedies and undertake and internalize the disciplines that the central powers ordain for our benefit— eternal for now, but soon in the course of time to become purely temporal.

Perhaps the really big question that remains from all this, though, is the following: How do we acknowledge the truth of Illich's insights while still saluting the uniquely *practical* bent of Latin Christianity? How do we allow that some procedure and institutionalization is required without destroying the interpersonal? This is an especially relevant question today because arguably, as Taylor fails to mention, the age of religious "authenticity" is mutating into a *further* era of newly imagined and constructed religious global networks, which once again are playing a major social and political role in the face of the evident bankruptcy of quasi-religious secular ideologies—including neoliberalism.

Perhaps we need here to say that despite the over-clericalization of the Church, despite the overfocus on hell, despite the denigration of sexuality (all of which helped to foment secular enlightenment, as Taylor says), it still remains the case that before the late medieval corruption, the early to high Middle Ages witnessed a certain proliferation of the "voluntary association" which to some degree managed to fuse the personal with the constitutional —as, for example, in the emergence of the notion of "personal" political representation itself, which was not as yet conceived on the model of epistemological or pictorial representation and so left the "representative" figure answerable to God and justice as well as to the people he represented. Given the wider medieval distribution of political power and the lack as yet of an absolute sovereign center, hierarchical rule was more of a personal handing-on of the power to rule, and different bodies had to negotiate with each other as "corporate personalities."[28]

Perhaps along these sorts of lines one can qualify Illich and start to render his intuitions more practicable. But one must, with Taylor, not lose sight of the sense that there is no past golden age to go back to and that the history of Christianity is, unsurprisingly, the history of the failure to live up to the radicalism of "incarnation" from the very outset.

This is just why, as Taylor stresses, we still remain correctly in a "romantic" moment—in the moment of a romantic reimagination of Christianity. (Could one also almost say that we need to "re-Augustinize" Rousseau, as opposed to espousing a merely "classical" rejection of Rousseau?) This reimagining itself newly stresses the imagination, and for two reasons. First of all,

---

28 See my "The Gift of Ruling," in *The Radical Orthodoxy Reader*, ed. Simon Oliver (London: Routledge, 2009), 338–362.

we now see that even patristic and medieval thought was overrational. The end of the line of trying to rely on reason alone is nominalism, which makes us see clearly how the theological participatory cosmos is not in any way "obvious." Hence we now return reflexively to the older tradition, knowing indeed that we must reinvent it with Shelley's "subtler language," as invoked by Taylor, and that the deeper, more erotic power of reason is itself a creative power which continues the blind creative thrust of nature herself, already intimated in the Augustinian doctrine of seminal reasons. Hence, as Taylor says, it is literary geniuses such as Péguy, Claudel, Bernanos, Chesterton, Eliot, Auden, and Flannery O'Connor who have virtually reinvented a vibrant Christian belief and practice in modern times.

But the second and deeper reason is that we now see, with Kierkegaard, that we can respond to the ungraspable mystery of incarnation only indirectly—through our own bodily, imagined performances, which seek, however faintly, nonidentically to repeat this mystery. These new imaginings have to be interpersonal and political as well as artistic. Charles Taylor has enormously helped and encouraged us in bringing these to birth.

But there remains one final ambivalence in *A Secular Age*. It *could* be read as declaring that we have reached "the end of religious history." First, this is insofar as *all* positions, religious and secular, after a history of religious questioning, have become reflexively debatable. Second, this is insofar as we must assume an irreducible religious pluralism stretching into the long-term future. A concomitant of the second is that Taylor might suggest a modification (in terms of respecting the group rights of religions and their role in civil society) of the displacement of *ecclesia* by state and market, but would not in any sense suggest a serious questioning of this displacement. In this crucial sense he projects a continuation of "a secular age."

The first conclusion seems to be unquestionably right. However, is the second conclusion, for all its seeming sanity, entirely consistent with the deep ground bass of the whole book—that is to say, the RMN? I would suggest that it is not. For if Christian catholicity collapsed because of an entirely contingent deconvivialization of its character in the Latin West (the Illich thesis), then how can one be sure a recovery of conviviality does not have the power to restore a lost universalism of Christian belief and practice? Nothing in Taylor's radical insistence on the historical rule of contingency would seem to preclude this.

And this apparently unrealistic question gains in plausibility if one addresses, as Taylor really does not, the question discussed by some recent *atheists,* especially Alain Badiou, namely that Christianity may be a peculiarly universal religion precisely because it first invented a both "enlightened" and "romantic" grammar of universality in terms of the imaging of God in humanity as such, the deliverance of humanity by true humanity rather than by law or alienating *cultus,* and the availability of this deliverance to all by virtue of the wisdom of love alone.

And then when one reflects upon the uniquely increasing global spread of Christianity (particularly in China) in our own day, which is unlikely in the long run to be outstripped by Islam (with its greater cultural specificity), the apparent unrealism of the question of a possible return of Christendom fades from sight almost entirely.

Within this perspective, what Taylor's reflections however suggest is that no continued distorted version of Christianity, neglecting the festive in favor of discipline, overshadowing the joy of salvific release with the fear of hell, would be likely ever again to command universal human assent. The same RMN mechanisms of the reduction of the religious to the ethical because the religious came to be seen as both redundant and horrific would once more take effect. One could therefore optimistically conclude that only a more benign, more festive Christianity could ever hope to reestablish a new and now global Christendom.

Hence the deepest, if latent and unacknowledged, implication of *A Secular Age* is that a festive Christianity, in the face of the political *aporias* of secular liberalism that I have outlined, could still in the future stake its claim to be the true enlightenment and the true romance. Equivalently, the *ecclesia* could stake its claim to be the true site of a general will based on a charitable and just distribution. Thus it might steer through the seas of time and space between and beyond secular utilitarianism and secular utopia, like a zigzagging caravel double-rigged at once for a manipulated straight course and for receiving the influence of the winds from whatever quarter they might chance to blow.[29]

29 I owe this image to my son Sebastian Milbank, who points out that the ship in C. S. Lewis's *The Voyage of the Dawn Treader* was of such a kind.

3

The Sacred, the Secular, and the Profane:
Charles Taylor and Karl Marx

WENDY BROWN

Religion fused with and inspiriting political movements and political power is having a global renaissance today. This renaissance interrupts a common tale in which the secularization of public life defining Western modernity was secure and was also presumed to herald the future for all the globe. Even in the United States, overt professions and practices of faith have become mandatory among politicians, religious schooling has become routine in Jewish families that spurned it for generations, Islamic youth have taken up religious signs and rituals that their elders shed years ago. So widespread has been the relegitimation of religion that even those not captured by recognizably religious sentiment have become, if not resigned to the human "need" for religion, deeply appreciative of its contemporary power to inspire and incite as well as soothe. It was in this vein that the rise of the Bush regime from an evangelical Christian base produced calls among liberals for the development of a "spiritual left" to match the neocons' political mobilization of religious affect and grounding for values—a development intended simultaneously to rebut the right's tarring of political liberalism with amorality, decadence, and vacuity of soul and to affirm our own investment in matters of spirit and not only hardheaded reason or interest.

This said, there appears to remain a sustained left presumption that religious *zeal,* particularly in the United States, remains the purview of conservatives, reactionaries, and perhaps even the uneducated—the magical thinkers who refuse reason, science, Darwin, the facts of global warming produced by carbon emissions, and the humility and thoughtfulness appropriate to an aging and inept superpower. This presumption was intensified by post-9/11 foreign policy, when G. W. Bush initially framed the war on Afghanistan and Iraq as a "crusade" and identified a father "higher than his own" as the one he consulted for the rightness of his foreign policy undertakings. But at the very moment of this intensification, the tables also begin to tilt. Ironically, it was Samuel Huntington's infamous "clash of civilizations" thesis that formally punctured the conceit of pure reason at the heart of the West (and lent credibility to Bush's crusade), insofar as it identified the West not primarily with rationality and science but rather with "Judeo-Christian values."[1] At the same time, among young secular educated Muslims new affirmations of religious orthodoxy upended a historiographic schema of progress that presumed a development from religious primitivism to secular sophistication.[2] Thus, the idea that religious zeal belongs to the primitive, solidaristic, or uneducated, while nonbelief or quiet, private belief, as Charles Taylor would have it, belongs to the more advanced, enlightened, and cosmopolitan—an idea that has underpinned European modernity for at least two centuries—is today being challenged from all sides. This is not to say that the idea is finished and even zealots continue to propagate it. The "secularizing Islam" project of the Bush-Cheney administration, the widespread belief in the civilizing effect of free trade, the conviction that We are tolerant and They are not—all these and more produce an odd mix today of religious zealotry and opposition to it in one and the same political project or formation.

Nothing, however, made more palpable the left's own availability to religious fervor than the emergence in early 2008 of the Obama phenomenon. Obama's capacity to counter despair with hope was, of course, the signature of his presidential campaign. But the salient terms here exceeded the posting of hope, possibility, and change against resignation, impossibility, and inertia.

1 Samuel Huntington, *The Clash of Civilizations and the Remaking of the World Order* (New York: Simon and Schuster, 1996), 312.

2 See Christine Helliwell and Barry Hindess, "The Temporalizing of Difference," *Ethnicities* 5, 3 (2005): 414–418.

What Obama incited during the primary season, as any of his wild enthusi-asts could attest, was the countering of cynicism with belief—a form of be-lief as religious as anything ever touted by the Christian evangelicals, just as strikingly contrasted to earthly realities and pragmatics, just as intentionally aimed at the desperation for relief from such realities. ("I never knew change was so easy," one Obama supporter remarked in early 2008, confirming that change itself had become a religious ideal, a matter of converting to a belief in it and worshipping at its altar.) The belief Obama stirred was not belief in particular projects, possibilities, or trajectories. Rather, his gift to progres-sives was belief itself—belief in belief, hence belief that uplifts, belief that in-spires, belief that reawakens and excites us after so many years of no belief, no excitement, no faith in the future. Thus, while Obama is certainly one of the most talented politicians in recent history, what was striking about the Obama phenomenon was what it revealed about us—how much American liberals and leftists yearn for this belief, this renewal of hope, this excitement of political desire . . . even if it is without content or aim. Nor is it incidentally but, rather, necessarily empty: its religiosity is contoured by this very empti-ness, and its religiosity is the heart of the matter. (Of course, no little bit of the religiosity devolves to the miracle of the phenomenon: could a black man of vaguely Muslim heritage, whose middle name is Hussein, truly become president of the United States in 2008? This was surely a miracle, especially from the vantage point of the political climate and possibilities a mere five, let alone forty, years ago.)

In this regard, the crucial link between Obama and John F. Kennedy lies not in the fact that Obama is another young, beautiful, charismatic leader whose oratory is vastly to the left of his politics and record. Nor is the cru-cial link that each appeared on the scene heralding the end of an exception-ally dark stretch in American politics and political culture. Rather, it is that Obama's unique talents and unlikely rise strike a crucial redemption of hope and futurity themselves at this moment, just as Kennedy's did following the grim Hoover-McCarthy years.

Obama's "Yes we can" was a yes to our own nay-saying, our own unre-lenting cynicism and surrender of belief in a promising future—for America and for the world. The adversary, the "no" implicitly figured by "Yes we can," was not an external enemy but the no within, the absolute (rather than deter-minate) negation of belief and will. This is why it was so easy to mock Hillary Clinton's attempt to defang Obama with the charge that he was generating "false hopes." The hope he promulgated is not false or true—for that, there would have to be content. Clinton's attack boomeranged because it amounted to telling the born-again to go back to their lost-in-the-dark ways, to return to ennui, rudderlessness, even nihilism in the face of absent compass points for a future.

So much for Al Gore's *Assault on Reason,* his 2007 book on the Bush years, in which he argued that the Democrats must and would take back the White House based on their superior commitment to rationality, facticity, science, and norms justified by reasons.[3] Religion is now being met with religion; indeed, America appears to be headed for its own odd kind of religious war. And since we have all accepted the human "need" for religion, it is difficult to know what would avert this war. Faith against faith, religious principle against religious principle. Our hopes versus their hopes, our Messiah versus theirs.

If today we are strangely accepting of the enduring human "need" for religion, this was not the case for the nineteenth-century German left. What Feuerbach, Marx, and others then engaged in the critique of religion struggled to understand was precisely when and why human beings generated phantasmatic powers and actors in the cosmos in lieu of affirming and articulating their own agency, freedom, and spirit. Not satisfied to regard us as creatures who in some generic or Dostoyevskian fashion required illusions, these critics sought to theorize the precise relation between particular earthly orders of existence and the human production of religion. This theoretical aim differs from debunking religion, on the one hand, and casting it as an eternal human need, on the other. Rather, they asked, what human conditions generate religious illusion? What precisely does religion satisfy, and how is what it provides different from other kinds of illusion or indirect need satisfaction, such as that provided by philosophy, ideology, or fetishism?

For all the now discarded conceits about the possibility of directly apprehending human existence entailed in these critiques, there is insight available from revisiting them, especially given contemporary Western political theory's own impoverished understanding of religion and religious need. Marx and Feuerbach really wanted to know what generated religious consciousness, what particular forms of this consciousness symptomized about lived

---

3 Al Gore, *The Assault on Reason* (New York: Penguin, 2007).

human existence, and what yearnings for a different existence these forms carried and expressed. It was their appreciation of religion as a historically specific projection of human experience, alienated powers, and thwarted desires that made religion such an important target of critique— even the foundation of all critique, where critique is understood not as rejection or rebuttal but a critical dissection of a phenomenon that simultaneously illuminates both what its internal contradictions are and what meaning and world it generates.

It is Charles Taylor who returned me to thinking about Marx and Feuerbach on religion. In *A Secular Age,* Taylor invites us to think of secularism not as a system of beliefs, principles, or mode of organizing state and society, though it certainly comprises these things (or, perhaps better, these become some of secularism's effects), but instead as a matter of human experience in the most profound sense. Taylor wants readers to appreciate modern Western secularism as a peculiar way of being, knowing, inhabiting the world —indeed, as a condition of being, knowing, and inhabiting the world in a particular way, one that is as nonoptional in the contemporary West as a polytheist worldview was for the ancient Greeks. He gives us, in short, the first erudite phenomenology of secularism through a remarkably erudite and detailed story of the historical construction of secular subjectivity.

Taylor's story and the historiography underpinning it aim not only to displace liberal shibboleths about secularism that equate it with value pluralism, church-state separation, and state protection of conscience. They aim as well to challenge what he identifies as materialist accounts of the process of secularization in the West with one that centers on a history of ideas and beliefs. Taylor's only explicit discussion of his approach to studying secularism occurs in Chapter 5, "The Spectre of Idealism." Especially compared with the rest of the work, the chapter is an odd one, not only in its brevity but in its striking defensiveness against the charge of idealism and in its caricature of its putative opposition through a markedly thin and mostly unrecognizable version of materialism.[4] Let us see how this goes.

---

4 This discussion even undermines the richness of Taylor's particular genre of idealism in certain ways, a richness achieved by eschewing a progressive unfolding of ideas or consciousness and by dispensing completely with the dialectic. Taylor's idealism is informed by Foucault and Weber and has a strong genealogical cast, aiming at a history of the present by way of a story that features not only industrialization and political revolutions but accidents and surprises in ideational development, rather than steady progress toward an inevitable and positive conclusion.

To begin with, Taylor identifies materialism with a theory of humans as driven by economic motivations, an identification that converts materialist analysis from attempting to explain what generates historical conditions to what psychologically animates human action (*SA,* 212–213). These represent very different problematics of historiography and historical change. One need not subscribe to the idea that human beings are driven by economic or material motives to be a historical materialist; the whole point of a substantive materialism could be said to lie in differentiating human motives or aims from the conditions through which they are shaped, constrained, and enacted. There is, in other words, a crucial difference between reducing humanity to *Homo economicus* (ironically, it is contemporary neoliberal rationality that performs such a radical reduction) and an account of historical change in which modes of production are a main stage upon which a plethora of human aspirations and capacities are played out. When Marx argues in "The Eighteenth Brumaire" that "men make their own history but they do not make it just as they please . . . under circumstances chosen by themselves," he is plying precisely this distinction, arguing that whatever our motives, our actions and possibilities are conditioned by forces beyond our control, and even our cognition.[5] So a materialist account of historical possibility is interested not in motives for action but in the conditions that produce and contour such motives, the conditions in which our actions are iterated, and the conditions with which our actions interact to produce certain effects. In fact, it is already an idealist move to misread materialism as a matter of motives, desires, interests, or aims, all of which can be ideationally figured.

Reducing materialism to action motivated by economic interests is only one aspect of Taylor's odd representation of historical materialism. He also speaks of it in terms of "efficient causal relations" (*SA,* 213). But again, a materialist understanding of history does not imply that economic imperatives "cause" or directly "determine" human existence; rather, within a certain order of economic and attendant social relations, there are many possibilities for belief and action. But there are *not infinite possibilities.* Thus, for example, unbridled capitalism cannot cohabit in the long run with certain kinds of traditional values, as Mennonites in America know well, which is precisely why

---

5 "The Eighteenth Brumaire of Louis Bonaparte," in *The Marx-Engels Reader,* ed. Robert C. Tucker, 2nd ed. (New York: Norton, 1976), 595. Hereafter cited in the text as Tucker. All Marx citations except those from *Capital* are drawn from *The Marx-Engels Reader.*

they insulate themselves as much as they can from contemporary capitalist forces and commodities.

Still another plank of Taylor's objection to materialism is folded into his more general critique of what he calls "subtraction arguments" (*SA*, 22). This critique, with which I am generally sympathetic, is leveled against any Enlightenment account, not only materialist ones, of the inherent convergence or necessary mutual entailment of (1) the emergence of the individual, (2) the reign of reason and transparent truth, and (3) the throwing off of custom, prejudice, mystery, religion. Taylor's critique of the subtraction argument, like Foucault's critique of the "repressive hypothesis" (and seemingly informed by that critique in some respects), challenges not only the essentialism but the presumed neutrality and aperspectivalism, and hence the uninterrogated normativity, at the heart of what such argument intends to explain. In the case of secularism, Taylor's critique of the subtraction argument challenges the commonplace that minus religion and blind adherence to custom, the secular subject experiences and knows the world more clearly or truly than its predecessors. Taylor replaces this conceit with an appreciation of historical difference rather than truth, Weltanschauung rather than objectivity or neutrality, a constructed rather than an essential human experience, a hermeneutic rather than transparent self. As Taylor puts it, "Each stage of the process [of becoming secular] has involved *new* constructions of identity, social imaginary, institutions and practices" (Chap 14.10 in MS, 530).

But how is the secular subject to be grasped and articulated, how is its history to be traced, what are the most relevant conditions of its emergence, and what kind of consciousness is secular religious consciousness? This is where we critics of the subtraction argument are bound to differ. Taylor's answer to these questions derives from a complexly accounted story of the metamorphoses of Latin Christian ideas and practices. As I have suggested, this answer diminishes the importance of (without fully eschewing) historical *forces* conditioning and contouring secularism that do not take shape primarily as ideas or explicit human aims. It is this diminution that this chapter aims, in part, to address. It does so through reconsideration of the complex materialism in Marx's critique of religion, although there are other thinkers, especially Weber, who would contribute to this project as well.

One caveat before proceeding: Marx's critique of religion is indisputably flawed, limited, and even crude in places. His materialism is also easy to criticize. My aim is not to redeem or accept his thinking in wholesale fashion but to consider what insight into our contemporary condition we lose by virtue of Taylor's quick dismissal of Marx and materialism in his study of secularism.

Feuerbach

Marx appropriates a good deal of Ludwig Feuerbach's critique of religion—the idea that religion is fundamentally an expression of human alienation, a fanciful projection of human needs, capacities, and powers, as well as a confession of human desires for sovereignty, freedom, and union with others. However, Marx does not share Feuerbach's relatively easy route to casting off religion. For Feuerbach, "he who no longer has any supernatural wishes, has no longer any supernatural beings either."[6] But for Marx, religion is generated by and expresses specific social arrangements of unfreedom. Feuerbach's materialism is historically vaguer and shallower, and religion is for him a more direct effect of the phenomenon of consciousness itself, hence more easily resolved by a shift in consciousness.[7]

What generates religion for Feuerbach? On the one hand, it issues from a distinctly human capacity for consciousness that exceeds existence, which Feuerbach says permits man to be conscious of himself as a species—to reflect on human nature and possibilities.[8] This very capacity is what occasions the invention of God. For Feuerbach, God is consciousness of our species nature and species powers projected onto an imaginary figure. He is our divine nature—our capacity for reason, love, and goodness and above all our infinitude as a species—imaginatively conferred elsewhere. Not only can humans alone conceive infinitude, we alone have infinite capacities as a species. By contrast, a dog can only think and be her own particular dogness. In our unique powers of being and consciousness, however, humans are also uniquely capable of making what Feuerbach conceives as the mistake of reli-

---

6 Ludwig Feuerbach, *Essence of Religion*, trans. A. Loos (Amherst, N.Y.: Prometheus, 2004), 55.

7 Feuerbach is clear that religious consciousness will evaporate as this alienation is resolved: "He who no longer has any supernatural wishes, has no longer any supernatural beings either." *Essence of Religion*, 71.

8 Ibid., chap. 1.

gion. Dogs do not make dog gods, and hence do not "disunite themselves" and project their capacities and powers elsewhere.[9]

If, for Feuerbach, one source of religion is the direct effect of our capacity for consciousness in excess of our own experience, "the feeling of dependence in man" is identified as a second source.[10] In particular, the original experience of dependence on nature makes man feel small and impotent. And (it is hard not to think of Freud here) we resolve this unbearable dependence by inventing an anthropomorphic being to whom we attribute the creation of nature—we place a figure of ourselves behind the scene of our unbearable dependence and subordination, thereby indirectly resurrecting our potency and sovereignty.

Now Marx is in wholesale agreement with Feuerbach's treatment of religion as projection, alienation, subordination through dependence, and a sign of humanity's unfulfilled possibilities and wishes. But for Marx, Feuerbach's materialism is insufficiently historical, and the history he does reference is too focused on superstructure—political formations and epochs. The unsatisfying result, in Marx's view, is that consciousness in Feuerbach's treatment remains relatively independent of historically specific social arrangements. Put another way, in Marx's view, Feuerbach cannot make good on his insight that religion reflects man's material life projected and inverted, because his materialism is so crude and unhistorical, comprising transcendent needs and desires rather than historically produced and organized ones (Tucker, 143–145).

So while Marx takes over Feuerbach's formulation of religion as an inversion and projection of human experience, needs, and powers; while he adopts Feuerbach's materialist challenge to Hegelian idealism; and while he appropriates many other Feuerbachian themes—from Feuerbach's subject-predicate critique to his notion of species being—he revises Feuerbach's insights in a way that makes the project of overcoming religion and shedding religious consciousness much more difficult. Indeed, the depth and intimacy of the relation Marx posits between material existence and religious consciousness, closely attended, can even be seen to produce a challenge to con-

9 Ibid., 33. This paragraph is a précis of chaps. 1 and 2.
10 Ibid., 1–2.

ventional readings of Marx's own materialism (insofar as religious conscious-ness is not only an effect of material life but an element in its reproduction), and to produce an aporia in Marx's anticipation of the recognized need for revolutionary transformation. We turn now to Marx's texts to see how this goes.

Marx

Marx is usually thought to argue that the secular subject, birthed by cap-italism but only completed by communism, is also the True subject, and one who grasps the Truth, one who sees the world truly and conceives human rather than divine powers as making the world. Certainly this is the reading that permits Taylor's relegation of Marxism to the order of "subtraction ar-guments." But does Marx in fact tell a story of capitalism's steady seculariza-tion and desacralization, its unmasking or revealing of the true nature of world and subject?[11] Does he tender a subtraction argument, in which false or religious consciousness is shed in favor of true and rational apperception of the world? Certainly this is implied by Marx's infamous remark that "religion is the opium of the people," along with sentences from the *Economic and Phil-osophic Manuscripts of 1844* such as "The more man puts into God, the less he retains in himself" (Tucker, 72). More generally, it is easy to regard Marx's ar-gument that relations of capital tear asunder all formerly sanctified or senti-mentalized relations as an argument that capital delivers its truth in a secular and transparent form or that its secularization of the world reveals the truth of human history and human existence. The verbs Marx uses in the opening pages of the *Manifesto*—"the bourgeoisie *has stripped* of its halo every occupa-tion hitherto honoured," "*has torn away* from the family its sentimental veil," "*pitilessly tears asunder* the motley feudal ties" and "*drownes* the most heavenly

---

11 Taylor distinguishes secularism from desacralization in his deliberate focus in *A Secular Age* on what he calls "secularism 3." This is secularism not in the sense of a state constituted "above religion" ("secularism 1") or in the sense of the decline of religious belief ("secularism 2") but only in the sense of the existence of a subject who can have religious faith without expecting others to share it. This definition analytically separates secularism from concerns with the prevalence of religion and religi-osity and from the phenomenon of desacralization. That said, Taylor's story of secularism is one in which the world is very much desacralized even as individuals may cling strongly to notions of the sacred. I take this desacralization to be very much what he means by the loss of "embeddedness" in a world of spirits, demons, and moral forces.

ecstasies of religious fervor"—contribute to this view (475). Or consider the famous passage from the *Manifesto,* "All fixed, fast-frozen relations, with their train of ancient and venerable prejudices and opinions, are swept away; all new formed ones become antiquated before they can ossify. All that is solid melts into air, all that is holy is profaned, and man is at last compelled to face with sober senses, his real conditions of life, and his relations with his kind" (476). Again, at first blush this passage would seem to narrate the subtraction of everything that interferes with the ontological and epistemological transparency of man, indeed to account the elimination by the force of capital all prejudice, religion, and other modes of mystification to leave man standing naked before himself and others, and to lay bare political economy as the fundamental human relation.

While such a narrative of desacralization of world and man is indisputably present in Marx, even this passage can be made to resist it and tell a more complex story. First, Marx does not argue that man has arrived at an ontological truth, but a historical one: the truth of his condition is revealed by conditions beyond his control, and in particular by the force of capital. What "compels" man to face "his real conditions . . . and relations" is something outside himself, just as these conditions and relations are themselves a product of something outside man. Man and world have not been stripped down to their secular essence by capital but have been profaned— violated, defiled—by capital. What is holy is not revealed but *profaned,* violated, and not therefore rendered in its true form. All that capitalist relations lay bare is the *violence* of the order and of its values, its single god of profit. Again:

> The bourgeoisie has stripped of its halo every occupation . . . it has converted the physician, the lawyer, the priest, the poet, the man of science, into its paid wage-laborers . . . it has torn away from the family its sentimental veil, and has reduced the family relation to a mere money relation. (Tucker, 476)

> The bourgeoisie . . . has put an end to all feudal, patriarchal, idyllic relations. It has pitilessly torn asunder the motley feudal ties that bound man to his "natural superiors" and has left remaining no other nexus between man and man than naked self-interest,

than callous "cash payment." It has drowned the most heavenly
ecstasies of religious fervour, of chivalrous enthusiasm, of philis-
tine sentimentalism, in the icy water of egotistical calculation . . .
In one word, for exploitation, veiled by religious and political illusions, it has substituted naked, shameless, direct, brutal exploitation. (475)

These are often read as passages in which Marx either applauds the desenti-
mentalization of vocations, family relations, and other associations or formulates these as nothing more than economic functions heretofore veiled by religion, but the accent marks can be placed differently. Marx is identifying the
violence that capital does to human things and relations—vocations, associations, etc.—the value of which is ineffable and hence cannot be placed on a
"cash nexus" and survive. Capitalist relations do not ontologically or episte-
mologically *reveal* these vocations and associations but rather defile and even
destroy them. In short, what is at stake here is not exposure but violence, not
transparency but defamation, possibly even deformation.

The Thus my second point, that Marx is far from celebrating this "profaning
of the world" or equating it with the truth about man or his possibilities. This
is no subtraction argument. While stripping human relations of their "veiled
religious and political illusions" is an inevitable dimension of the historical
process he is accounting, and a fundamental feature of capitalism, what capital lays bare is not humanity but itself, and even this is a curious baring. As
it makes man and world in the image of itself, capital exercises a religious
power, one that supplants man's own sovereignty and displaces man's own
essential nature as a species being and as a creative being. What is laid bare is
the most extreme subjection of all existence to the most intensified form of
class antagonism; what is revealed is not man or truth but capital's violence
toward both man and the sacred.

There is thus an entwining of violences in Marx's use of profanation to
describe capital's effects, a dehumanization and a desacralization but, again,
not therefore an emergent truth. Rather, the movement of capital violates
both the creation of man (species being) *and* human capacity and creativity
(making what we will of ourselves)—it violates holiness and humanism at
once. Capital's profaning power blasphemes human divinity and inverts the
proper order of things, reducing us to its effects. "In one word," Marx de-

clares in the *Manifesto,* the bourgeoisie "creates a world after its own image," thereby blaspheming the original creation of the world after the image of God. Or, to quote more precisely from Genesis, blaspheming "the creation of man in God's image" (Genesis 12:7).

Borrowing from scripture as it does, this line paradoxically imputes a religious power of creation to a profaning force and at the same time figures capital itself as a profaning force. This perverse conjoining of capital's godlike power with profanation (or even desacralization) introduces another matter requiring our attention, which is that if Marx in the *Communist Manifesto* renders capital as that which strips bare what "religious and political illusions" have hitherto covered, namely, the class basis of all societies prior to communism, the exploitation of labor, and the discrepancy between ideology and material reality, he elsewhere suggests that capital itself *entails* and *requires* its own religiosity. Hinted at in the line just considered, this suggestion is more fully elaborated in "On the Jewish Question," in the little essay on money in the *Economic and Philosophic Manuscripts of 1844,* and also in *Capital.* Let us turn briefly to each of these.

"On the Jewish Question"

The discussion of Judaism in part 2 of "On the Jewish Question" makes most contemporary Marx aficionados cringe. There Marx declares the "profane" or "everyday" basis of Judaism to be "huckstering" and its "worldly god" to be money, and this to argue that Judaism is the "practical spirit" of Christian nations and that "Jews have emancipated themselves in so far as the Christians have become Jews," i.e., money makers (Tucker, 48, 49). Judaism, Marx continues, articulates the spirit of civil society, both mirroring and consecrating it. Thus, he concludes, religious emancipation will be complete only when money, "the jealous god of Israel, beside which no other god may exist . . . [and which] has . . . deprived . . . both the human world and nature of their proper value," is no longer the "universal and self-sufficient value of all things" (50).

The anti-Semitic stereotypes in these passages are obvious enough. But this should not prevent us from considering the formulation Marx is struggling to develop about the religious dimension of capital—the need of capital for religion, the operation of capital *as* religion, and the religious organization of capitalist society. Marx argues that Christianity and Judaism have been secularized and in this way preserved and disseminated in capitalist society, and also structure the contemporary order. That is, even when secularized, religious consciousness is essential to class-stratified orders; more than the "opium of the people" or a legitimating gloss, religious consciousness is a condition of the existence of such orders.

The precise form of this argument in part I of the essay "On the Jewish Question" is well known. There Marx claims that Judaism constitutes the spirit of civil society while Christianity constitutes the spirit of the state. Civil society is the domain of self-interest, "practical need," egoism, and above all the place where private property acts as a social power even after it has been abolished as a "political qualification" for officeholders or citizens (Tucker, 50). But in what sense is the secular state a Christian state? Here Marx's argument is severalfold. First, the constitutional state is Christian insofar as it represents itself as the site of freedom, or, in Hegelian terms, as the realization of the Idea of freedom. This representation Marx calls religious, or more precisely Christian, because a distinctly human experience and practice—freedom—is attributed to a distant and sovereign power, the state. Similarly, the sovereignty of man is derived from the sovereignty of the state, and at the same time a distinctly human thing—sovereignty—is imputed to an imaginary being, God. Borrowing fairly directly from Feuerbach's critique of religion, Marx elaborates, "Religion is simply the recognition of man in a roundabout fashion; that is, through an intermediary. The state is the intermediary between man and human liberty. Just as Christ is the intermediary to whom man attributes all his own divinity and all his religious bonds, so the state is the intermediary to which man confides all his non-divinity and all his human freedom" (32). Marx is not arguing that attributions of divinity to God and of freedom to the state are ideological, hence false, but that these attributions ("projections," in Feuerbach's terms) are an expression of a specific form of our unfreedom *and* a particularly Christian rendering of this unfreedom.

This becomes clearer if we consider a second manner in which Marx analyzes the Christianity of the bourgeois state in this essay, namely through its division of human existence and representation into two orders, political and civil, or state and economy (which he identifies as "celestial" and "terrestrial"). Following his account of what he calls the abstract and limited way in which man is "emancipated" from stratifying social powers such as property and education when the state declares its own indifference to these powers to treat us as equals, Marx argues that this move reveals the political state even at its most secularized to be Christian. That is, the bourgeois state's representation of liberty, equality, and fraternity represents an ideal as opposed to actual human experience in capitalist society, just as we are all equal in the eyes of God though unequal on earth. The state figures a Christian political imaginary that abstracts from our everyday lives: in contrast to its ideals of liberty, equality, and fraternity, actual life in civil society is unfree, unequal, and atomistic. Thus, Marx concludes,

> where the political state has attained to its full development, man leads, not only in thought, in consciousness, but in reality, in life, a double existence—celestial and terrestrial. The political state, in relation to civil society, is just as spiritual as is heaven in relation to earth. . . . Man, in his most intimate reality, in civil society, is a profane being. Here, where he appears both to himself and to others as a real individual he is an illusory phenomenon. In the state, on the contrary . . . man is the imaginary member of an imaginary sovereignty, divested of his real, individual life, and infused with an unreal universality. (Tucker, 34)

Again, Marx's argument here is severalfold. In a liberal constitutional state conjoined with a capitalist economy, subjects' relationship to the state is Christian insofar as their freedom, equality, and unity is understood to be conferred by the state and is also unreal in relationship to actual life, life in civil society. He is also arguing that the state itself iterates a Christian structure of religiosity in ordering life and consciousness; and that the state legitimates itself through a belief structure that depends on constituting itself as the source of sovereignty, freedom, and equality—as being that which makes us free and equal (as opposed to that which iterates our subjection and inequality). In short, Marx offers a political theology of the constitutional state *avant la lettre* (where Carl Schmitt is the letter).[12]

A third way in which Marx argues for the Christianity of the secular constitutional state extends the analysis of our divided existence—"celestial and

---

12 Carl Schmitt, *Political Theology: Four Chapters on the Concept of Sovereignty*, trans G. Schwab (Chicago: University of Chicago Press, 2005).

terrestrial," "imaginary and real"—by exploring the fictional status of sovereignty in both domains:

> The members of the political state are religious because of the dualism between individual life and species-life, between the life of civil society and political life. They are religious in the sense that man treats political life, which is remote from his own individual existence, as if it were his true life; and in the sense that religion is here the spirit of civil society, and expresses the separation and withdrawal of man from man. Political democracy is Christian in the sense that man, not merely one man but every man, is there considered a sovereign being, a supreme being. (Tucker, 39)

In this passage, Marx identifies the sovereign individuality (Taylor's "disembedded self") articulated by political democracy as both fictional and isolating. Every man is an imaginary king, an imaginary sovereign, god of himself—a depiction that isolates every man from every other man and from cosmological relatedness. In this respect, Marx identifies both state and individual sovereignty as resting on a religious formulation of sovereignty. Again, it would seem that for Marx, political democracy is literally founded in a Christian theological stance toward the real and the imaginary in which freedom and sovereignty are posited in an ideal way against their material negation.

"THE POWER OF MONEY IN BOURGEOIS SOCIETY"

In the little fragment on money in the *1844 Manuscripts,* Marx, borrowing from Shakespeare, depicts money as the "visible divinity" which "transforms all human and natural properties into their contraries . . . [performing] the universal confounding and overturning of things" and making "brothers of impossibilities." He also describes money as the "alienated ability of mankind" in giving man the means to do what his "essential powers" proscribe (Tucker, 104). Money's properties and powers at once substitute for those man lacks and confer upon him qualities and powers he does not have. Consider: "I am ugly but I can buy for myself the most beautiful of women. Therefore I am not ugly. I . . . am lame, but money furnishes me with twenty-four feet. Therefore I am not lame. I am bad, dishonest, unscrupulous, stupid; but money is honoured, and therefore so is its possessor" (103).

Money, Marx concludes, is the great "overturning power," transforming "fidelity into infidelity, love into hate, hate into love, virtue into vice, vice into virtue, servant into master, master into servant, idiocy into intelligence and intelligence into idiocy" (Tucker, 105). Money "confounds" and "compounds" all "natural and human qualities" and thus turns the world upside-down, making beloved, beautiful, brave, and honored those who are not. Marx contrasts this condition to one in which love, trust, art, and ability are authentically attained or recognized, or, perhaps comporting more easily with contemporary skepticism about authenticity, one in which these things are unmediated by exchange value. Most interesting for our purposes, Marx regards the powers of inversion, conversion, compounding, and fraternizing of impossibilities as money's *divine* aspect. "The overturning and confounding of all human and natural qualities, the fraternization of impossibilities—the *divine* power of money—lies in its *character* as men's estranged, alienating and self-disposing *species-nature*" (104). Indeed, in this essay Marx not only wages a critique of money as an intermediary or corrupting force, and as the alienated power and ability of man, but figures money itself as a force simultaneously profaning, desacralizing, and divine. Money profanes and desacralizes insofar as it destroys ineffable goods and qualities such as love, intelligence, beauty, bravery, and honesty *by* making them purchasable. Different from the commodification or fetishism processes he accounts elsewhere, here Marx insists that money transforms "the real essential powers of man and nature" into "abstract conceits, imperfections and chimeras" and, conversely, "transforms real imperfections and chimeras—essential powers which are really impotent, which exist only in the imagination of the individual—into real powers and faculties" (105). So money is not only worshipped as a god (and, like a god, represents the alienation of man's own powers), it also has godly powers in market societies—"money is the truly creative power" Marx says, the "almighty being" (104). But what makes money unique is that it is a profaning God, it mimics God's power and origin yet inverts the natural or proper order of things—making the ugly beautiful, the unlovable loved, the bad good . . . Donald Trump or Paris Hilton worthy of public interest.

In short, for Marx, money, like all deities, is man's own power alienated and projected, a power that then becomes sovereign over man. But more than being merely worshipped, money actively destroys the sacredness and truth of the world. Money is at once a deity that displaces and replaces man's natural powers and capacities and a profaning force that destroys what is most sacred about man and world.

CAPITAL

Which is most crucial in generating and sustaining capitalism, the production of a proletariat that has nothing to sell but its labor power or the fetishism of commodities (including the commodity, labor power) and an ideological and hence false figuration of fairness and freedom in the realm of exchange? In *Capital*, Marx makes clear that the processes are intricately linked and that only by grasping their connection can we bring the secret of capital clearly into view. These two processes together facilitate, stabilize, and legitimize capitalism. Thus while the extraction of labor power in the production of commodities is the actual source of capital, the fetishism of commodities, including the commodity labor power, Marx says, is "inseparable from the production of commodities."[13] So a "physical" and an "intellectual" process, neither of which can operate without the other.

Let us remember how this works. Marx's remark that understanding the fetishism of commodities requires "recourse to the mist-enveloped regions of the religious world" is among the most frequently quoted passages of *Capital*. But what is Marx really saying here? Here is the full passage:

> A commodity is . . . a mysterious thing, simply because in it the social character of men's labour appears to them as an objective character stamped upon the product of that labor. . . . That is the reason why the products of labour become commodities, social things whose qualities are at the same time perceptible and imperceptible by the senses. In the same way the light from an object is perceived by us not as the subjective excitation of our optic nerve, but as the objective form of something outside the eye itself. But, in the act of seeing, there is at all events, an actual passage of light from one thing to another, from the external object

13 Karl Marx, *Capital*, vol. I, ed. Frederick Engels, trans. S. Moore and E. Aveling (New York: International, 1967), 72.

to the eye. There is a physical relation between physical things. But it is different with commodities. There, the existence of the things *qua* commodities . . . have absolutely no connexion with their physical properties and with the material relations arising therefrom. There it is a definite social relation between men, that assumes, in their eyes, the fantastic form of a relation between things. In order, therefore to find an analogy, we must have recourse to the mist-enveloped regions of the religious world. In that world, the productions of the human brain appear as independent beings endowed with life, and entering into relation both with one another and the human race. So it is in the world of commodities with the products of men's hands. This I call Fetishism which attaches itself to the products of labour, so soon as they are produced as commodities, and which is therefore *inseparable* from the production of commodities.[14]

Just as divinities, as products of our imagination, come to appear and act as real powers, world-making powers, so commodities, the products of our hands, come to life.[15] Thus two different sites of human production—brain and body—bear in common the capacity to produce things that are endowed with life and bear enormous power. We are, in this regard, extraordinary creators, capable of endowing our mental and physical productions with autonomy, generativity, even sovereignty. Both commodities and gods are human creations, expressions of human relations, that assume the form of sovereign powers. This is why fetishism and religion are so proximate for Marx and why commodity fetishism requires "recourse to the mist-enveloped regions of the religious world."

"A commodity is . . . a mysterious thing, simply because in it the social character of men's labour appears to them as an objective character stamped upon the product of that labor . . . a social relation between men . . . assumes . . . in their eyes, the fantastic form of a relation between things."

14 Ibid.

15 Here, as elsewhere in Marx's writing, he expresses a fascination with the workings of the human eye, and relates these workings to questions about the perceptibility and imperceptibility of power. This aspect of Marx's thought is worthy of extended consideration but cannot be undertaken here.

Again, this fetishistic or religious orientation is an indispensable aspect of capital in Marx's view. Thus while capitalism profanes, it does not do away with religious consciousness or religious objects—it is not secular in that sense—nor is it incompatible with religious belief. Just as the generation of surplus value in the domain of production is obscured by the fiction that profit is generated in the realm of exchange (a fiction itself incited by commodification), and the generation of the value of commodities by labor is obscured by the belief in their intrinsic value or "life," the generation of class society through private property is obscured by the fiction that our equality and liberty are secured through rights protected by the state. Linking the production of these fictions is a misattribution of powers generated by human activity, mystification of the process by which this misattribution occurs, and the sacrifice of human freedom that this misattribution entails. What links them as well is their origin in a history that is not yet human, that is, history orchestrated by forces humanly generated but not apprehended as such and not humanly controlled.

In sum, Marx's materialist critique of religion and religiosity does not equate commodification, profanation, or state proclamations of secularism with the demise of religion or religiosity, with disbelief, with disenchantment, or even with the arrival of an order that has ceased to be inhabited by "spirits, forces or powers . . . recognized as being in some sense higher" (SA, 147). Rather, as capitalism profanes the world, it generates and draws upon a broadly disseminated religious orientation to the world. The secular state, too, draws upon and reproduces a "religious attitude" (Tucker, 36). The profaning of all relations by capital—capital's laying bare of its own values and effects—is convergent with the fetishism of commodities and with the mystified nature of the production of value. And Marx identifies the power of money in bourgeois society as a religious power, an overturning power, a profaning power, a creative power, though not yet a human power. Profanation and fetishism are at once the peculiar power of capital and the seat of capital's own religious bearing. This is *some* materialism, one that could not be further from a simple reduction of human history to economic motives or processes, a world of casual efficiency, or an account that equates secularism with the displacement of mysterious forces by transparent ones. And this is *some* secularism, one that neither involves a subtraction story in which the true world or true self is revealed as capitalism shreds the veil of religion nor equates secularism itself with ontological or epistemological truth.

Conclusion

Of what contemporary value is Marx's complex account of the profaning power of capitalism combined with its religious structuration, form, and generation of religious consciousness? Perhaps it helps us understand why the evaporation of serious challenges or alternatives to capitalism over the past two decades has been accompanied by an intensification and relegitimation of religious consciousness and expression. If capitalism has lost a global outside, both in practice and in imagination, then it has lost the place from which its religiosity and religious power would be challenged. Today, not only the value of capitalism but its global sovereignty—its supersession of other powers, including those of nation-states—is generally taken as given, even praised as salvation for a troubled political globe. More than the zenith of freedom that Milton Friedman and Friedrich von Hayek once took capitalism to be, free markets are formulated by neoliberals today as the consummate civilizing force, capable of attenuating violent conflicts and bringing insurgents to heel as no mere state or even multilateral political actors can.[16]

When capital becomes sovereign, undermining and displacing the sovereignty of nation-states, it obtains a religious quality from yet another source. Sovereignty, Schmitt reminds us, is not only conceptually theological in its origins; it maintains a religious status insofar as it is above and beyond the law, deciding and decisive for human existence, and is a power that bows to no other—what Hobbes called an "over-awing power" likened to God. When capital radically escapes both its container and its limits in the nation-state, when it becomes a genuinely global power, it acquires many of the specifically religious trappings of sovereignty—absolute, enduring, supreme, decisive about life and death, beyond human control, and above all beyond accountability to law or morality. Thus three distinct yet convergent pressures

16 Thus is capital simultaneously heralded by neoconservatives as (the only true) religion and as a secularizing force that softens and eventually eliminates religious and ethnic conflict, just as neoconservatives often manage a twin identity as secular and Christian imperialists.

overdetermine the intensification of religiosity inherent within and in response to capitalism today: external challenges and alternatives to capitalism have receded, capital itself has eroded the political limits of the nation-state, and a historically specific form of normative social and political reason, neoliberalism, fashions market rationality into a complete worldview with a totalizing reach.

There are, of course, various fringe opposition movements to capitalism and especially to its neoliberal variant, but from Al Gore to Barack Obama, free trade is praised for its world-building and problem-solving capacities. Even French "socialists" and Scandinavian workers' representatives have become neoliberals, and here we need to remember that as a governing rationality that extends well beyond the market to configure both the state and the individual subject, neoliberalism openhandedly makes a religion of capital, and features its own religious structure, to a degree Marx never dreamed of. Within a neoliberal rationality, every endeavor and enterprise—indeed, every human being—is enjoined to shape itself in capital's image, surviving or thriving through appreciation of its value, declining or dying through value depreciation, judged at heaven's gate by its capacities for entrepreneurial autonomy and ingenuity.[17]

17 See "Neoliberalism and the End of Liberal Democracy," in my *Edgework: Critical Essays on Knowledge and Politics* (Princeton: Princeton University Press, 2005), 37–59, and my "American Nightmare: Neoconservatism, Neoliberalism, and De-Democratization," *Political Theory* (December 2006): 690–714.

4

Completing Secularism:
The Mundane in the Neoliberal Era

Simon During

I want here to extend a brief critical reading of Charles Taylor's *A Secular Age* into a consideration of the "mundane" as a philosophical and historical concept. In effect, I will be sketching an alternative account of the contemporary moment to that which Taylor presents to us, but which nonetheless engages his by taking on board certain of his choices of method. It is impossible to broach this task except from a specific disciplinary location: mine is literary criticism as it is currently fertilized by European philosophy, intellectual history, and political theory. There are many reasons to feel skeptical about this mix, but the mundane is exactly the kind of topic it suits. That's because it enables literary close reading to combine with (in this case) philosophic history in the interests of uncovering some of contemporary experience's qualities.

A Secular Age is a remarkable achievement, an erudite, generous-minded, path-breaking book. And it marks the culmination of a life's work. As far as I'm aware, Charles Taylor's argument first took shape in an essay he wrote forty years ago for the volume *From Culture to Revolution* as a member of the Catholic New Left. At the time he was committed to a non-Marxist "radical socialism" that was programmatically opposed to capitalism—a system he understood (à la Western Marxism) to cause alienation and domination by its constant appeal to means-end rationality. For Taylor at the time, Marxism was an enlightened humanism that failed to understand that each human being must "reach beyond himself and renew contact with the non-human, and . . . the more than human." This means that alienation under capitalism cannot be annealed through any social movement that fails to understand that man and his works "can never have the transparency of pure project, thrown in front of him into the future."[1] So the restitution that Taylor encouraged against capitalism was not a transcendentalizing resacralization or an (impossible) encounter with the real as much as an acknowledgment that the world we inhabit is a gift from God. Such an acknowledgment can inspire forms of community based on receiving from and giving to others, that is, on Christian agape. From within what Iris Murdoch in the fifties had called the "new house of theory," community can be figured as a form of donation, of worship, and of imitation of divine charity and love in terms that ground participatory socialism and restored "public meaning."

A Secular Age is less politically engaged than this. Now Taylor argues that the West has indeed undergone secularization, but not because science has disproved religion or because religious interests and institutions have been separated from politics and state government. Rather it's because over centuries, Latin Christianity, partly through its many internal reformist movements, became committed to the Aristotelian project of general human flourishing. During the Enlightenment, central elements of the Christian faith were transformed into a humanism whose ethical and conceptual framework and purposes were fundamentally immanent. In the process a cultural "nova" appeared in which new knowledges, faiths, orientations, styles of life, and identities proliferated. At the same time, governmental apparatuses developed autonomous privatized "buffered selves" capable of making choices between competing faiths and identities.

For Taylor, there is no renouncing either the humanist focus on happiness and health or Western modernity's cultural nova. But what has been weakened through and in both is a "higher," "fuller" orientation toward the sacred and transcendent based on tradition, although admittedly, "tradition"

---

1 Charles Taylor, "From Marxism to the Dialogue Society," in *From Culture to Revolution: The Slant Symposium 1967*, ed. Terry Eagleton and Brian Wicker (London: Sheed and Ward, 1968), 154.

is not a concept that Taylor emphasizes (but see *SA,* 719). Actually, there appear to be two versions of the sacredness that modernity weakens: according to the first, stronger version, what is in jeopardy is a "higher" perspective in which this world is ordinarily positioned in a (subordinate) relation to a divine order; the second, weaker version of what is in jeopardy is fullness or depth, that is, the loss of what we might call hierarchized existentialist value through which some experiences and moments are fundamentally more meaningful, and so to say more spiritually enriching, than others. His argument's sweeping ambit partly relies on its ambiguation of these two spiritual drives, an ambiguity that Taylor accepts, I suspect, because he assumes (in my view mistakenly) that the first entails the second as a matter of anthropological fact.

At any rate, Taylor claims that what he calls "spiritual hunger" is integral to human beings: it constitutes (to rephrase Simone Weil) a theoretical limit to acceptable social transformations.[2] In effect, (and to rephrase a point Jonathan Sheehan made in his post to the Immanent Frame blog),[3] his argument is based on an existentialized/theophanized moral anthropology. It is as if it accepts David Hartley's eighteenth-century argument that even beginning from a Lockean, enlightened genetic psychology that refuses concepts like grace and innate ideas, it is possible to show that theophany is natural and essential to man.

So for Taylor, orientation to the transcendent may take secular as well as religious forms, but either way it is occluded by modernity. (Of course, societies can also develop supernaturalisms that don't bear any relation either to the transcendent as "higher" in Taylor's sense or to hierarchized existential value, but he is not concerned with these.) To restore the sacred, he now looks not to participatory socialism but to a somewhat less collective "conversion into fullness" and "openness to transcendence," which takes practical form in concrete, individualized "itineraries towards faith" (*SA,* 745). This individualization is important: for Taylor, following Ivan Illich, spiritual hunger is most purely felt *personally.* Its institutionalization always threatens to petrify it into norms, rules, and habits, which in turn, he contends, leads to spiritual elitism and conformism and ultimately to the dangerous identification of

2 See *SA,* 679; Simone Weil, *Oppression and Liberty,* trans. Arthur Wills and John Petrie (London: Routledge, 2006), 53.

3 http://blogs.ssrc.org/tif/2008/01/14/framing-the-middle/.

faith with civilization (737–744). This surprisingly Protestant account of faith exists in a certain tension to Taylor's impeccably Catholic/sociological insistence that individual consciousness is formed through larger social imaginaries. But what is in effect a Protestant methodological individualism would seem to be required if the openness to the transcendental is to be saved from its modern wreckage, just because modern Western society contains no institutions capable of collectivizing "conversion into fullness" on a grand scale.

One of *A Secular Age*'s most distinctive features is its genre. Taylor is the only intellectual I know who hearkened to the New Left call for theory by revivifying a genre known in the eighteenth century as "philosophical" or "conjectural" history ("conjectural" because it did not depend on known facts). Speculative books like Adam Ferguson's *Essay on the History of Civil Society* (1767) and John Millar's *The Origin of the Distinction of Ranks* (1771) and their heirs, Hegel's *Phenomenology of Spirit* (1807) and Comte's *Course of Positive Philosophy* (1830), were monuments of emergent secularism, even if recent scholarship (like Taylor's, indeed) asks us to consider their connection to what Gerald Radner has called "Christian reform," namely, those modes of Christian practice that found soteriological promise in civil engagement and improvement.[4] The philosophical historians' stadial theory, along with their capacity to classify historical formations and tendencies into units and moments that instantiate discrete abstract categories, were important in generating the command over the past required by progressivism and were also important in reconciling readers to the historical record by sidelining conflict and violence. Ironically, if *A Secular Age* has forebears, those are they. Taylor himself, I suspect, comes to the genre through his engagement with Hegel, and in particular in the wake of his historicization of *The Phenomenology of Spirit*'s deployment of immanent critique in his influential first book on Hegel.[5]

Taylor too uses stadial theory and a historiography reliant on more or less discrete categorical classifications. Like his forebears, he has a liking for dividing history into the triplets that Barthold Niebuhr in his 1811 *History of Rome* (a devastating critique of philosophic history and a milestone in Bib-

4 Gerald Radner, *The Idea of Reform* (Cambridge: Cambridge University Press, 1959).

5 *SA*, 218, 347. Also see John Milbank, *Theology and Social Theory*, 2nd ed. (Oxford: Blackwell, 2006), 157.

lical criticism) thought characteristic of mythic narration. However, where the secularizing philosophic historians looked to a progressive extension of liberty and rationality able to retain civic humanist virtues (courage, independence, manliness, and so on), Taylor, of course, tentatively hopes for the containment of Aristotelian humanist flourishing (i.e., eudaimonia) whose merely worldly norms have come to marginalize and corrupt a sense of the sacred.

Despite its capacity to claim mastery over the past, philosophic history is rarely written these days, in part because it can't well account for historical causality. Ultimately it is interested not in historical cause but in telos. And it seems that Taylor neglects important underlying material causes (most obviously capitalism and urbanization), not so much because the channels through which such causes operate in all their materiality remain largely hidden from us, but because he believes that to engage such causes is to risk embracing a reductive form of immanence, namely materialism.

It has to be said, however, that if Taylor believes that the secular world has lost a fullness available only through the transcendent, the secularist may feel an equivalent emptiness in Taylor's own analysis, since its attempts to explain how history happened, and how it happened differently in different places in the way that it did, are so abstracted and distanced from the events to which they ultimately refer. Admittedly, Taylor has a complex account of how "social imaginaries" change: piecemeal shifts in social practices gradually come to require holistic ideological transformations in which the intelligibility and value of social phenomena may themselves be radically altered. (This account is rather reminiscent of Tawney's description of the collapse of the medieval Catholic worldview in *Religion and the Rise of Capitalism* [1926]). In this way, history's paths and circles are simplified into an ultimately unaccounted-for displacement of a transcendental orientation by the pursuit of merely worldly well-being. Why, given Taylor's commitment to an existentialized/theophanized moral anthropology, did this displacement happen? Why did modern man betray his own integral nature? At this point, there exists an absence at the center of Taylor's narrative: it is not as if he can simply accept as natural that, to put it very crudely, so many Europeans came to prefer security, reason, and money to God. But if we regard the various forms of spiritual hunger and its satisfaction not as givens but as contingent social functions, then, like it or not, we can concede that societies may successfully do without them, and there is no historiographical problem about their loss.

Taylor is, in effect and despite himself, writing a philosophic history that has turned conservative in what remains, just, a recognizably Burkean mode.[6] In summary terms, Burke's own most lasting contribution to theory was to revalue tradition and cultivation by joining Western religious orthodoxy, court-Whig constitutionalism, and Adam Smith's political economy in the face of the French Revolution's threat to oligarchic mixed government and Church property.[7] But for Burke, orthodoxy and its institutions (the Anglican and Roman Catholic churches) had produced a secular, gentlemanly culture bound to classical learning, chivalry, and honor. Without the churches and the social hierarchy that they underpinned, the new theories being disseminated by the *philosophes,* harnessed to the professional bourgeoisie's resentful drive to power, would lead not just to the chaos of democracy but to a collapse of, as Burke famously put it, "conscious dignity, a noble pride, a generous sense of glory and emulation."[8]

For all its efforts to avoid conservative melancholy and to resist appeals for the reanimation of past social forms, Taylor's argument is based on nostalgia for a lost fullness and coherence. This means that it is Burkean in structure, if not in content. Unlike Burke, Taylor has, as we have seen, accepted the ideals of democracy, liberty, and equality, and unlike Burke he has little faith that a worldly alliance between orthodoxy, tradition, and secular dignity might resist materialism and immanence. Only personalized spiritual practices, here detached from ecclesiology, can do that. In this regard, Taylor stands closer to another romantic conservative: the Jena school's Fried-

6 My understanding of the history of intellectual conservatism owes something to Anthony Quinton, *The Politics of Imperfection: The Religious and Secular Traditions of Conservative Thought in England from Hooker to Oakeshott* (London: Faber and Faber, 1978).

7 The claim that Burke accepts Adam Smith's political economy may ring hollow to some. The relation between each corpus is complicated and uneven; see Emma Rothschild, *Economic Sentiments: Adam Smith, Condorcet and the Enlightenment* (Cambridge, Mass.: Harvard University Press, 2001), p. 61ff for a good discussion of this. My own reading of the *Reflections* is somewhat different from Rothschild's in this regard: it seems to me that Burke becomes the first (conservative) *cultural* critic in part just because he accepts Smith's model of market autonomy along with the rights of private property, and does so even though some of Smith's enemies are his friends in the *Reflections.*

8 Edmund Burke, *Reflections on the Revolution in France* (New Haven: Yale University Press, 2003), 48.

rich von Hardenberg (Novalis) who, arguably, inaugurates the application of a transcendental/immanent distinction to counterrevolution in Burkean terms. That is to say, Novalis attempts to buttress social organicism against rationalism by a religio-metaphysical concept (transcendence) inaugurated by Clement of Alexandria in the second century CE and whose great vehicle, in the West, became the pre-Reformation church. For Novalis, the modernity that the French Revolution inaugurates threatens not just Christian faith and Church power but, more sweepingly, our sense of an ontological otherness, hedged by mystery, in which the poetry of the ideal takes form.

But it is only right to receive a book as rich as *A Secular Age* on its own terms. And if, for me, it is not finally persuasive, that's not simply because of its genre or religio-Burkean conservatism but because of a series of interlinked problems, many of which have been rehearsed by its commentators, and of which I will mention three, relevant to my purpose.

First, it is important to Taylor's argument that he discounts the fact that Christianity is a revealed religion, most of whose central claims are, under modern truth regimes, false, unverifiable, or unproven, since, although his concepts of the sacred and fullness extend beyond any particular religion, his central historical case remains limited to Latin Christendom. Believing or not believing Christian doctrine is not a choice for those living "in the true" of rational, probabilistic knowledge, nor is it necessarily an expression of a preference for organized eudaimonia. It is impelled upon them in approximately the same way that they are impelled to know that Barack Obama is (at the time of writing) president of the United States. Of course, when Christianity stops being true in fact—a "true truth"—it may still be true as feeling, as morality, as tradition, as a disposition, as myth—an "untrue truth." I will return to this.

As to my second point, it is clear that Taylor can elide the question of Christian revelation's untruth just because his final interest seems to be in an ontological distinction between the transcendent and the immanent rather than in religion as such. But as soon as you deontologize transcendence and immanence, you don't have to choose between them and can find other ways of avoiding Taylor's narrative of enchantment's loss. Taylor himself, of course, points to forms of "immanent transcendence," thinking mainly of the existential spiritualizing of death as "a gathering point for life," which he believes continues the old spiritual hunger on new terms (*SA,* 726). However, more flexible forms of (post-Spinozist) immanent transcendence that allow history and imagination to play a more complex role than they do in existentialism also become available.

Let me offer a rather obscure literary example. In his Epicurean 1861 country-house satire, *Gryll Grange,* Thomas Love Peacock described a Mr. Falconer, who, although irreligious, surrounds himself with the iconography of the famous fourth-century martyr and patron saint of philosophers and theologians, Saint Catherine of Alexandria. A friend warns Falconer against "becoming the dupe of your own mystification," to which he replies:

> I have no fear of that. I think I can clearly distinguish devotion to ideal beauty from superstitious belief. I feel the necessity of some such devotion to fill up the void which the world, as it is, leaves in my mind. I wish to believe in the presence of some local spiritual influence; genius or nymph; linking us by a medium of something like human feeling, but more pure and more exalted, to the all-pervading, creative, and preservative spirit of the universe; but I cannot realize it from things as they are. Everything is too deeply tinged with sordid vulgarity . . . the intellectual life of the material world is dead. Imagination cannot replace it. But the intercession of saints still forms a link between the visible and invisible. In their symbols I can imagine their presence. Each in the recess of our own thought we may preserve their symbols from the intrusion of the world. And the saint whom I have chosen presents to my mind the most perfect ideality of physical, moral, and intellectual beauty.[9]

In terms of cultural history, this remarkable passage, which clearly draws on the Spinozism of its time, articulates a way between Tractarian and ritualist revivalism on the one side and William Beckford's transgressive, isolationist, aesthetic Catholic atheism on the other. What's remarkable about it is not its existential sense of the void, or its assumption that modernity and modern truth have barred human feeling from the universe's creative spirit, or even that the local itself has lost a spiritual power that it retained, for instance, as

9 Thomas Love Peacock, *Gryll Grange* (Harmondsworth: Penguin, 1947), 58, 59.

recently as Wordsworth and Coleridge's *Lyrical Ballads* (1798), but that spiritual practices are based on a conscious will to believe, and then, that the individual imagination cannot itself replace the losses that such a will invents, and by implication, nor can aestheticism.

For Falconer, literary subjectivity is helpless to overcome deadly modern materialism. What is required is an immersion in the products of a particular, historical *institution,* namely the orthodox Church, but without granting the Church's doctrines any credence, since of course for him as an enlightened gentleman, they are false. Here a fictionalization of orthodoxy, a true untruth around which a practice of life can form, does the work of supplementation and retrieval required by Novalis's iteration of cultural Burkeanism, although, as Peacock is aware, it does so only in impossible isolation from the demands of sexuality and sociability. At any rate, Falconer's is the privatization of orthodoxy not in the direction of Protestantism, not by displacing the long Pelagian tradition of Christian reform, but in the direction of aesthetic fiction as an ethos, to use a term that the Tractarians themselves donated to the English language.[10]

But—and this leads to my main point—what about those who neither feel the spiritual emptiness of modernity nor embrace secular reformism's promise? It's a question that, although it does not concern Taylor, arises with some force in this context, since the secular as a concept is positioned not just against the religious but also, if less visibly, against the mundane. That's because ever since the Enlightenment, the secular has denoted not so much what lies beyond religion's interest and grasp but what contributes to its intermittent diminution, corruption, marginalization, and undoing. The mundane is the philosophical concept that names what stands outside that division between the secular and the religious. Taylor does not take it seriously just because he believes that to be properly human is to be possessed by spiritual hunger. The mundane, however, consists of those forms of life and experience that are not available for our moral or political or philosophical or religious or social aspirations and projects.

That is one of the ways in which it differs even from neighboring categories like "common sense" and "everyday life" and the "ordinary," which may

---

10 For the Tractarians and "ethos," see Peter Nockles, *The Oxford Movement in Context: Anglican High Churchmanship, 1760–1857* (Cambridge: Cambridge University Press, 1997), 6.

contain promise of epistemic or social benefit and indeed even soteriological promise, as they do indeed for Taylor, who thinks of the ordinary as the domain in which "depth and fullness" is ultimately encountered (*SA*, 711). This is not to say that philosophy has had no use for the mundane. It rises into view in categories such as the Greek *adiophora;* Calvin's realm of indifference; Hegel's bad infinity (the serial order of things governed by chance, which knows hierarchy or substantial difference); and in Heidegger's concept of *Alltäglichkeit,* or everydayness, in which "everything is one and the same" but is so within a fundamentally instrumental and immediate relation between individuals and individuals and things. But these terms tend to come clearly negatively coded against the spiritually and culturally enriched, whereas the mundane is external to the system (the various social imaginaries, if you like) in which such coding is intelligible. The mundane also falls out of academic knowledge: after all, the modern university system is sanctioned by the social utilities it produces. For all that, some philosophical ethics in particular can enjoin us to mundanity from afar. There may be a strain of Nietzsche's thought, for instance—the strain that resists metaphysical groundedness, ethical appeals to eternity, progress, and salvation as well as any form of Kantian or utilitarian rationalism—which, in standing outside both the secular and the religious, asks us to be strong enough to live mundanely.

Once in the grip of that fundamentally philosophical understanding of history which treats modernity as a contest between enchantment and disenchantment, between religion and the secular, between the transcendent and the material, we postulate the mundane as a category outside the fray; then another kind of philosophic history rises to view. This history does not begin in superstition and tyranny and end, like Hegel's and Comte's, in freedom and the full human development of human capacities. Nor does it begin in a unified and coherent universe and end in an incoherent society. Rather, it moves from mundanity through progress and back again to mundanity. Admittedly, this narrative is, as far as I know, not anywhere articulated in quite those terms by philosophic historians, but it is implicit in a strain of European philosophy, especially during the mid-twentieth-century period of emergent European unification.

Take the first step in this history, the leap from mundanity to incipient progressive rationality. That's a concern of Edmund Husserl in his famous

1935 Vienna lecture "Philosophy and the Crisis of European Man," where he isolates this transformative moment in the sixth-century BCE Greek discovery of *theoria*. *Theoria*, for Husserl, is a disinterested and critical attitude toward the world ("critical" in that it is not determined by the empirical). Before theory, the Greeks, like everyone else hitherto, lived inside their beliefs, true or false; inside an endless cycle of transitory events and passages, a mundane world marked by its indifference to infinity and its internal indistinction. There, all achievements are "identical in sense and in value."[11] Both Plato and Aristotle claimed that what ended the dominion of this mundane order was *thaumazein*, wonder, as triggered by the childlike but primordially metaphysical question "Why is there something rather than nothing?" and a consequent reorientation from the finite to the infinite. As soon as that reorientation established a new vocation and new forms of solidarity, as soon as it produced the small, elite group that named themselves philosophers, then the history of progress, led by critical European science and philosophy, was on its way.

Let's bypass the more familiar history-of-progress segment of the world-historical passage from mundanity to mundanity, to turn to the question of what life might be once progress has been completed. And here a problem arises, because emancipatory secularism with all its conceptual baggage will necessarily wither away once rationality is known to have been fully socially implemented or, to state this in another vocabulary, once a maximum of goodness has been socially achieved. At that moment, by definition, there would be no possibility of social restructuring or political revolution. There would be no politics in the classic sense: no hard contests over power's distribution across interests and identities, let alone over what kind of social system should be in place. Presumably, policy debate would involve endless reformist, and fundamentally minor, fine-tuning of relations between the sociopolitical system's component parts in the interests of economic productivity and agreed-upon principles of political justice. Certainly there would be no world-historical hope: all traces of the "political Joachimist" eschatological tradition would have imploded.[12] From a philosophic-historical point

11 Edmund Husserl, *Phenomenology and the Crisis of Philosophy*, trans. Quentin Lauer (New York: Harper & Row, 1965), 161.

12 For "political Joachism," see Marjorie Reeves, *The Influence of Prophecy in the Later Middle Ages: A Study in Joachism* (Oxford: Oxford University Press, 1969), 75.

of view, humanity would return to a condition of *geistlich* indistinction and indifference remarkably similar to that which Husserl imagined as existing prior to the Greek invention of philosophical life.

This apparently improbable scenario was of real philosophical concern for a few midcentury continental philosophers who, either under the spell of a promised European unity or of Old World communism, or dreaming of a postwar, post-Fascist European social-democratic union, began, like Hegel himself, seriously to anticipate history's end.

Thus, for instance, Theodor Adorno, pondering the strengths and weaknesses of Hegelian dialectics in 1946, began to imagine what living in a "society rid of its fetters" might look like. And he described it like this: *"Rien faire comme une bête,* lying on water and looking peacefully at the sky, 'being, nothing else, without any further definition and fulfillment,' might take the place of process, act, satisfaction, and so truly keep the promise of dialectical logic that it would culminate in its origin."[13]

Another example: the Heideggerian and Stalinist Hegelian, Alexandre Kojève, spent most of his working life as a senior French diplomat, playing a major role in the implementation of key elements in our epoch's legal and economic infrastructure—the Marshall Plan, the European Community, and GATT. Able to imagine the completion of historical progress, he argued that it would reveal the species' existential dilemma in its purity, precisely because atheism would then triumph and progressive hope become otiose. At the end of his lectures on Hegel's *Phenomenology of Spirit,* delivered in 1937 and 1938, he noted that history cannot banish human mortality, but that this unsurpassable finitude actually provides for the continuation of freedom in terms that bear no relation to historical rationality. Only death releases man from the Calvinist sentence by which one's fate is determined in advance of one's birth.[14] Because man dies and can choose to die or "escape from Being," he can exit from whatever history delivers to him, and that possibility belongs to each of us precisely as individuals.[15] Otherwise put: it is death that preserves a sense of serial time—of incomplete life after incomplete life after incomplete

13 Theodor Adorno, *Minima Moralia: Reflections on a Damaged Life* (New York: Verso, 1974), 156–157.

14 Alexandre Kojève, *Introduction to the Reading of Hegel: Lectures on the Phenomenology of Spirit,* trans. James H. Nichols, Jr. (New York: Basic Books, 1969), 249.

15 Ibid., 248.

life—but at the same time releases man from the mundane indistinction that threatens us once progress is completed.[16]

Here is Kojève: "If, in truly homogeneous humanity, realized as State at the end of History, *human* existences become really interchangeable, in the sense that the action . . . of each man is also the action of all, death will necessarily oppose each one to all the others and will particularize him in his empirical existence, so that universal action will also be particular action (or action liable to failure where another succeeds), and therefore *Individual.*"[17] Kojève's reading of the *Phenomenology* ends at this rather unsatisfactory point —unsatisfactory since it still isn't clear exactly how the *posthistoire* collective commitment to action in which individuation is granted only via death would in fact differ from something like Husserl's prephilosophic mundanity. It sounds like another attempt to buttress social solidarity by a metaphysical (this time existential) concept, even if one that is neither, in traditional terms, religious nor secular.

This issue was addressed by Joachim Ritter, a postwar German philosopher who was interested in dissociating Hegel from statist Prussianism and showing, ecumenically, that Hegel's philosophy continues both the French revolutionary project and Adam Smith's discovery of the market's autonomy and regularity.[18] Ritter effectively recognized the abstract possibility that *posthistoire* will mark the triumph of the mundane, but he argued that this is forestalled by the Hegelian dialectic.[19] For him, conventionally enough, Hegelian modernity involves a division between those structures of the state/civil society nexus that will deliver emancipation and those that will extend "romantic" withdrawn interiority like Mr. Falconer's irreligious cultivation of religious icons. Conventional enlightened rationality dismisses romantic subjectivity, with (as I'd contend) its roots in Pauline/Lutheran doctrine of passive obedience, as irrelevant to the struggle for freedom and justice. For

16 As John Milbank, leaning on Jean-François Lyotard, has pointed out, this process of indifferentiation is embedded in capitalism's tendency to view a variety of needs, products, and values as basically the same. See Milbank, *Theology and Social Theory*, 194.

17 Kojève, *Introduction to the Reading of Hegel*, 252, translation modified.

18 For a full account of Hegel's relation to the Scottish School in terms rather different from Ritter's but relevant to this paper, see Laurence Dickey, *Hegel: Religion, Economics, and the Politics of the Spirit, 1770–1807* (Cambridge: Cambridge University Press, 1989), 186–205.

19 Joachim Ritter, *Hegel and the French Revolution: Essays on the Philosophy of Right*, trans. Richard Dien Winfield (Cambridge: MIT Press, 1982), 78.

Ritter's Hegel, indeed, freedom cannot be realized through any form of individualism at all but only within rationally legitimated institutions. Nonetheless, this dismissal of individuality risks an outcome in which substantial notions of justice and freedom are lost precisely at the point when practical emancipation is achieved. Only interiorized spiritual longing and a personal relation to the tradition can maintain the spirit of the emancipation project after civil society has delivered substantial justice and freedom to all, in the sense that without them, our will to emancipation will vanish as such, just because it is universal and knows no other. Therefore Hegel dialectically preserves what we can call a privatized Burkeanism within the Absolute State that is history's terminus.

So at history's end, old-style cultivated, emancipation-driven interiority and the religio-cultural tradition live on as energizing reminders of history's now completed drive forward. And because of this, Ritter's version of Hegel, though resolutely antiliberal, remains open to Carl Schmitt's critique of liberalism. Schmitt argues that once the friend/enemy distinction is lost to politics (as it must be in both liberalism and Hegelian posthistory), then social and individual risk and meaning vanish, and domains of life that were once touched by national identity politics of aggression are effectively transformed into "a world without seriousness"—into what he calls mere "entertainment," which, in the terms of the philosophic history I have been engaging, we recognize as the mundane.[20]

It seems to me that with Schmitt's formulation we approach the social system that we actually inhabit. I will think of that system as marked by the unprecedented degree to which the media, the state's disciplinary, educational, and welfarist apparatuses, its techniques of monitoring and surveillance, its formal political processes, along with (in the United States especially) religion, the military apparatus, finance capital, the forces of material, intellectual, and cultural production, and the market, have become technologically and ideologically integrated. Since about 1968, this integration has become so thorough as to delegitimize any imagination of, let alone any widely endorsed work toward, an alternative system: we live under what

20 This account of and the quotes from Schmitt come from Heinrich Meier, *The Lessons of Carl Schmitt: Four Chapters on the Distinction between Political Theology and Political Philosophy* (Chicago: Chicago University Press, 1998), 113.

Sheldon Wolin has called "superpower."[21] Endgame democratic state capitalism, as we can name it, has indeed become the final horizon of global society, and, bar paranoia, today is seriously threatened only by blind nature.[22] This is not to say that it marks the end of history as progressivism imagined it. Certainly it cannot be understood as an instantiation of perfection (it's better thought of as its overturning). But it does mark an end of historical hope.

By the same stroke, there are signs that it makes a return to the philosophers' mundane. One such sign of particular relevance to academics is that endgame democratic state capitalism's integrative machinery has appeared with an abridged theoretical legitimacy. It has been metonymically legitimated in the sense that only those aspects of the whole apparatus that make appeal to various elements of universal rationality in old progressivist enlightenment/revolutionary terms (e.g., democracy, liberty, human rights) can be philosophically sanctioned.[23] But now those legitimations are required to carry out the work of sanctioning the whole. More than that, endgame capitalism is "unmappable," since it provides no possibility of an external or Archimedean position for an objective totalizing conspectus. Such a self-knowledge deficit is, as almost goes without saying, a condition of mundanity more generally.

Where should we look if we wish to consider more intimately what is at stake in endgame capitalism's putative mundanity? In the end, not to theory, I think. Nor to sociology. Nor to cultural studies. After all, the mundane does not primarily inhere, pace Kojève, in collective action or individual behavior but rather in discourse and most of all (to invoke a rather problematic con-

---

21 Sheldon Wolin, *Politics and Vision: Continuity and Innovation in Western Political Thought*, 2nd ed. (Princeton: Princeton University Press, 2004), 591ff.

22 These claims clearly require an essay, or rather a library, to themselves. But there's a sense, too, in which they belong to a conventional wisdom which reaches back about a century, and which is variously articulated in, for instance, Carl Schmitt's concept of "neutralization," Adorno's "late capitalism," and Raymond Williams's "managed capitalism." In *Transcending Capitalism: Visions of a New Society in Modern American Thought* (Ithaca: Cornell University Press, 2006), Howard Brick's historicization of the twentieth-century "postcapitalism," as he calls it, and his argument that much social thought from both the left and the right in the short twentieth century (c. 1914–c. 1970) failed to address capitalism's embeddedness in Western society, are also to the point here.

23 For one such attempt, which accommodates itself to contemporary religion's political agency, see Jürgen Habermas, "The Secular Liberal State and Religion," in *Political Theologies: Public Religions in a Post-Secular World*, ed. Hent de Vries and Lawrence E. Sullivan (New York: Fordham University Press, 2007), 251–261.

cept, which I don't propose to elucidate further here) in experience, which we can think of under Henry James's definition as "our apprehension and our measure of what happens to us as social creatures."[24] At this point we strike a barrier, since other peoples' interior experiences are hardly available to true truth. Where they are so available, they are best available through untrue truth (which in this case is also a virtual truth), and especially, for the past two centuries or so, through literary fiction, which has, coincidently, become increasingly dependent on representations of what Henry James called "finely aware" feeling, or what the Bloomsbury circle thought of as the "inner life."[25] Precisely because it is not a form of true truth, literary fiction is able to imagine and represent such inner life and thence the age's most revealing experiential forms.

In carrying out this task, literary fiction not just reveals deep interiority's complexity and interest for modernity but, by the same stroke, characteristically presents the subtleties, surprises, and intensities of modern experience as a reward for continuous struggle and suffering. Modern serious fiction, in its virtuality, has the capability both to report what it is like to live now across a range of situations, identities, and types—to feel, think, share, love, hate, dream, hope, despair, drift—while essaying unrealized experiential possibilities by binding characters and their interiorities to situations within new forms of language and narrative organization. Which is to say that if, in a philosophic-historical sense, mundanity is the chord struck by the contemporary flow of no longer quite "serious" political, religious, self-transformative, aesthetic, etc. experiences and discourses, then that chord is most likely to be explored imaginatively via fictional characters.

Technically, that possibility is a consequence of authors' absolute power over their characters. Imagined characters possess no privacy in relation to their creators, and novelists don't need to respect their rights and moral dignity. And, of course, not being real people, they are not restricted to actual social conditions. Yet because literary fictions are necessarily finite and ordered, characters and their experiences are fixed in their bounded fictions forever. Frozen and transparent, endlessly open to interpretation, fictional

24 Henry James, *The Princess Casamassima* (Harmondsworth: Penguin, 1977), 11.

25 Ibid., 9. Henry James's preface to *The Princess Casamassima* is a manifesto for the importance of descriptions of self-perceptive consciousness to the art novel.

characters are available to reveal anything, even truth and experience's potentiality.

So it is that the quality of experience under endgame capitalism is a compelling theme for contemporary art novelists. And few have explored it more subtly than Alan Hollinghurst in *The Line of Beauty* (2004). The novel is set in London during Thatcherism's heyday (1983–1987), a crucial moment in the neoliberal fine-tuning of the contemporary democratic state capitalist machine.[26] Its central character, a young gay man, Nick Guest, has just come down from Cambridge. Nick is witty, intelligent, charming, and a knowledgeable aesthete in the tradition that Schiller inaugurated out of Burkeanism. While living close to Thatcherism's center, he is writing a dissertation on Henry James. He boards with the family of Gerald Fedden, a Thatcherite MP and businessman, and for much of the novel he works for his rich Lebanese lover, Wani Ouradi, whose father is a major Tory Party donor. He's an apolitical Thatcherite himself.

The novel describes the tensions between Nick's increasingly promiscuous sex life and his proximity to a neoliberalism that has ditched both progressivist secularism and Christianity and is instead committed to the reformist extension of property ownership, economic privatization and deregulation, risk-taking entrepreneurialism, and a virtue ethics based on self-reliance (which is itself, admittedly, grounded in old English Dissent). But at the same time Thatcherism promulgates a homophobic and xenophobic moral order based on family values. Nick deals with the tension between these two aspects of Thatcherism by never developing any kind of social conscience, nor an interest in self-transformation, nor any of the deep interiority and reflective sympathy to which most serious modern novels are committed, those of Henry James not least. Although a literary scholar, he does not even develop a romantic interiority à la Hegel. Against a backdrop of endless media events, self-serving political intrigues, and market cycles, he wholeheartedly engages a mundanity of *luxe* consumption, cultivation of aesthetic tastes, "idle" daydreams, sexual and narcotic pleasure, and moral disengagement.

The novel reveals its full power in its last paragraph, which describes Nick

---

26 My knowledge of Thatcherism owes much to E. H. H. Green, *Thatcher* (London: Hodder and Stoughton, 2006). See also Richard Vinen, *Thatcher's Britain: The Politics and Social Upheaval of the Thatcher Era* (London: Simon and Schuster, 2009), and Peter Jenkins, *Mrs. Thatcher's Revolution: The Ending of the Socialist Era* (London: Cape, 1987).

packing his things after being evicted from the Feddens' grand Notting Hill house for having brought scandal down upon the family. More ominously, he is privately awaiting the results of a test for the HIV virus, which he believes, and for good reason, will be positive.

> The words that were said every day to others would be said to him, in that quiet consulting room whose desk and carpet and square modern armchair would share indissolubly in the moment. . . . What would he do once he left the room? He dawdled on, rather breathless, seeing visions in the middle of the day. He tried to rationalize the fear, but its pull was too strong and original. It was inside himself, but the world around him, the parked cars, the cruising taxi, the church spire among the trees, had also been changed. They had been revealed. It was like a drug sensation, but without the awareness of play. . . . None of his friends could save him. The time came, and they learned the news in the room they were in, at a certain moment in their planned and continuing day. They woke the next morning, and after a while it came back to them. Nick searched their faces as they explored their feelings. He seemed to fade pretty quickly. He found himself yearning to know of their affairs, their successes, the novels and the new ideas that the few who remembered him might say he never knew, had never lived to find out. It was the morning's vision of the empty street, but projected far forward into afternoons like this one decades hence, in the absent hum of their own business. The emotion was startling. It was a sort of terror, made up of emotions from every stage of his short life, weaning, homesickness, envy and self-pity; but he felt that the self-pity belonged to a larger pity. It was a love of the world that was shockingly unconditional. He stared back at the house, and then turned and drifted on. He looked in bewilderment at number 24, the final house with its regalia of stucco swags and bows. It wasn't just this street corner but the fact of a street corner at all that seemed, in the light of the moment, so beautiful.[27]

27 Alan Hollinghurst, *The Line of Beauty* (London: Picador, 2004), 500–501.

This is an immensely rich passage, in which Nick finds within himself the quasi-Nietzschean courage to face death and the incompletion of his life from within a carefully described mundanity (see *SA*, 722–726). It is in effect exploring across a range of registers how spiritual longing and consolation may survive in, and be reconciled to, the mundane social order.

First: time. After his death, Nick thinks, the world will go on serially, barely remembering him. He has not lived the kind of secular, reflective, "full and productive" life that would secure him a place in others' memories: his friends will wake up mornings thinking of other things. His failure to insure his future memory may indeed owe something to his foreseeing himself a victim of a virus that is, of itself, a contingent force of nature outside any human will, and that therefore cannot grant his death any Kojèvean individuality or bind it to any progressive, secular concept of history or to any Christian notion of transcendentally oriented sacrifice as the dark and bloody motivating force of collectivization (as theorized in the nineteenth century by Pierre-Simon Ballanche, for instance). Lucidly and (in the end) almost impersonally, he adjusts himself to the termination of purposive individual self-realization and self-knowledge, as well as, of course, eternal life. Facing death, he acknowledges his life's mundanity: this moment is not going to change what remains of his life. It's no conversion to fullness.

Second: his attention to the Feddens' house's stucco exterior of "swags and bows" in the penultimate sentence is symbolically resonant, not least because it exemplifies the line of beauty that gives the novel its title. *The line of beauty* has told a story of Nick's gradual recognition that he himself, as a gay aesthete, is at best merely decorative with regard to Thatcher's England's social infrastructure. Indeed, the beauty that Nick's taste so strongly inclines toward is neither (in a complex pun) straight nor weight-bearing—it's found in stucco, after all—precisely because today beauty can only be ornamental to the social machine. But this means, paradoxically, that his outsider status can become socially representative: there's an important sense in which *all* individual lives are largely extraneous to democratic state capitalism's economic/political processes and cycles. So his aesthetic experience here, his realization that what is beautiful is not this street corner of rich people's stuccoed houses but the simple "fact of a street corner," more ontologically secure than any line of beauty, marks a letting-go of the straight versus not-straight criterion of beauty. It is an aesthetics of indistinction and indifference that twists the Greek experience of wonder. The sheer existence of material things becomes not a puzzle or a limit or a medium but an amazement, and an amazement that opens up from within Nick's experience of mundanity, and in its indistinction is expressive of it.

"Amazement" is too loose a word, of course. It is "a shockingly unconditional love of the world"—shocking because, coming from nowhere, it is wild, a word that here peeps through "bewilderment," which is another term used to describe his experience. And it's shocking and bewildering not so much because it is surprising or transgressive but in the sense that to forgo discrimination, to abandon private qualifications and conditions in one's judgments, to find oneself deindividuated in that way, is, on the part of individuals themselves as they lose themselves, to experience shock. Yet Nick's experience is also felt as shocking and bewildering because his relation to the world has until now been so conditional, in two senses. He has been, as his name suggests, a guest in the world, holding it at bay, taking it on only conditionally, not fully seriously. He has lived a conditioned life too, doing just what society, in its messed-up way, conditions him to do. His having lived so conditionally helps to explain why this irruption of the unconditional is shadowed by abyssal terror. And yet, as an unqualified acceptance of the world, beyond resentment, beyond finite and human pity, beyond even terror, this experience—a "love of the world"—is a form of Christian agape, even if it lacks orthodox agape's promise of binding communities together around mutual love and charity. Nick's aestheticised, gracelike experience falls outside theological virtue, since he directs it to indifferent things rather than to people. That's another sign of its mundanity.

Here, then, faced with the severest of spiritual/existential personal challenges, endgame capitalism does produce from within mundanity an experience that bears the weight of two great, but less than compatible, Western traditions, orthodox Christianity and aestheticism, and, pace Schmitt, seriously enough. It does so outside of any transcendent/immanent distinction and outside the thematics of cosmic abandonment of meaning which that distinction so often carries. No doubt it is for all that a deeply conservative ending, since it changes nothing and aims to change nothing. Indeed, it leads us to understand that all *posthistoire* translations of experience into politics belong to conservatism, just because historical hope has vanished. This means that the passage also hints that at the end of historical hope, cultural conservativism need no longer be contained by its counterrevolutionary pasts nor attached, for instance, to any transcendently directed spiritual hunger, and instead may be able to generate complex, weight-bearing, posthistorical forms of living in the mundane.

To summarize this line of thought, Nick's experience presents a strong rebuke to Taylor's argument. As we have seen, Taylor's philosophic history supposes (1) that lived fullness and richness requires an orientation to the transcendental, and (2) that a disposition toward (or even a longing for) richness and fullness is integral to moral anthropology. But Nick's apprehension of the streetscape, which, I take it, is "full" and "rich" by any persuasively ecumenical spiritual standard, lacks any transcendental dimension whatsoever. Indeed, its fullness and richness (if that is the vocabulary we wish to bring to bear upon it, rather than, say, one of intensity) cannot be separated from its sheer worldedness, from the self-undoing, dislocating shock of the here and now. It's a dislocating experience, which, as I say, comes to a young man placed at particular location at a particular historical moment, which is also a moment in the progress of a specific epidemic, and our accession and assessment of Nick's experience, in all its virtuality, depends on the novel's own detailed invocation and critique of that actual historical moment—of Thatcherism. So what *The Line of Beauty* is telling us is that today, spiritual gravity may inhere in the self-emptying contingencies through which we are concretely placed in history, nature, and place, and for that reason needs no other home than the immediate and the mundane. In fact, I think it's probably telling us more: that if spiritual intensity and realization have another home than the mundane, then that intensity and that realization are compromised.

5

Belief, Spirituality, and Time

William E. Connolly

No one has asked me to direct a film. That is understand-able, since I lack the skill to do so. But still, it is frustrating. There are activi-ties that need to be seen, or at least visualized, for us to appreciate and in-ternalize them. Recent work in neuroscience, for instance, suggests that visualization of an activity in the right mood is effective at installing it on the lower-frequency registers of affective-cognitive life.[1] Mystics have known this for centuries, but the neuroscience evidence is nice to have too. Anyway, after watching *The Da Vinci Code,* a film I attended with high hopes, I again felt the urge to direct a film. For the theopolitics forming the ostensible object of this film faltered.

So let's imagine a sequel, one to visualize as we proceed. It stars Angelina Jolie and George Clooney. After a steamy scene reenacting the passion that threw Jesus and Mary Magdelene together for the first time, the adventurers

---

1 See, for example, the symposium on the mind-body relation organized by Antonio Damasio, published in *Daedalus* in the summer of 2006. The essays by the Damasios and Gerald Edelman are particularly relevant, with the first discussing the implications of the discovery of "mirror neurons" for understanding how the sociality of experience precedes language and the second suggesting that consciousness is an afterglow rather than an antecedent to action. My essay in that symposium seeks to connect themes in neuroscience to an understanding of how micropolitics works on the visceral register of cultural life. It is entitled "Experience and Experiment," pp. 67–75.

ponder again the diverse forms Christianity has assumed. They ask not only how variable it was during that long, bumpy period between the sayings of Jesus and the late 380s, when the priority of the crucifixion, resurrection, and Trinity were set in stone by the Church and Emperor Theodosius; they also ponder what it might become during a time when several world religions again intensify conflict within and across territorial regimes. They sense that a plurality of creeds will always bloom in a world of becoming, unless several are crushed. And they are impressed with how the acceleration of pace in several zones of life today exacerbates these tendencies.

They sense, with Charles Taylor, that the secular conception of homogeneous time in which that first adventure was set formed part of the problem. So they read and recite sections from Bergson and Proust to each other at night, allowing Bergson to teach them the importance of dwelling occasionally in pregnant moments in which layers of the past and future anticipation reverberate back and forth, and allowing Proust to provide hints about how to prime themselves to sink into such moments if and when they start of their own accord. (It is an art-house film.) One night they ponder the life of Jesus before going to bed.

As Sophie dreams that night about the world of her putative grandfather and grandmother to the nth degree, the screen flashes to Jesus, standing in the midst of an unruly crowd. This dissident rabbi sometimes calls himself "the son of man"—almost as if any man whatever could have sired him. He communes with the restive crowd in words translated into English from the earliest written version of the gospel: "'Rabbi, this woman was caught in adultery, in the very act. Moses, in the Law demanded us to stone such women to death, what do you say?' But Jesus stooped down and with his finger wrote on the ground. And as they continued to question him, he stood up and said to them, 'Let whoever of you is sinless be the first to throw a stone at her.' And again he stooped down and wrote on the ground."[2]

The judgment is distinctive. Perhaps even more notable is how it arrives. As Jesus stoops and draws dreamily on the ground with his finger, he may allow the indignity of his earthy conception, the shame of being born of an unwed mother, the plight of his people under the yoke of empire, the danger

2 Stephen Mitchell, ed., *The Gospel According to Jesus* (New York: Harper, 1991), 123–124.

of the vengeful crowd, the Mosaic code he and they have absorbed, the acute danger facing the accused woman before him, and his own unconventional relation to Mary Magdalene to mingle together in a crystal of time. A new maxim crystallizes as these layers of memory, pressure, and concern reverberate together in a new situation. Care for the world, informed by exquisite sensitivity to an unpredictable moment, merely sets conditions of possibility for it.

The sequel presents further adventures by the sensitive couple. But we must remain content with this clip for now.

Such a creative moment in the life of Jesus does not mesh neatly with those modern doctrines of time, secularism, and exclusive humanism reviewed by Charles Taylor. It does not because it focuses on a fecund moment of dwelling in duration that punctuates the secular time of everyday perception, judgment, and action. During such a moment multiple layers of the past and elements unfolding in the current situation reverberate back and forth, sometimes issuing in something new as if it came from nowhere. The new is ushered into being through a process that exceeds rational calculation and/or the derivation of practical implications from a universal principle. It remains to be seen whether such a process can be as well understood through an immanent philosophy of becoming as through a theology of transcendence.

The event could be endowed with transcendent meaning. Many read it that way. But I think it can also be folded into the tradition of immanent naturalism Taylor characterizes, as long as that tradition is protected from the reading of Nietzsche that Taylor brings to it. I have reviewed differences between his reading of Nietzsche and mine elsewhere, and will not rehearse them here.[3]

Instead, I draw upon a wider band of immanent naturalists who find time to be composed of multiple force fields periodically interacting in an open universe without divine transcendence. When Taylor contrasts a philosophy of pure immanence to one that goes through immanence to transcendence,

---

3 William Connolly, "Catholicism and Philosophy: A Nontheistic Appreciation," in *Charles Taylor*, ed. Ruth Abbey (Cambridge: Cambridge University Press, 2004), 166–186.

he often distinguishes between them by calling the first open and the second closed.[4] There are immanent naturalists who fit that description, contending that in principle everything is perfectly explicable through universal laws. But I am interested in that version of immanent naturalism which projects an open temporal horizon exceeding human mastery that is irreducible to both closed naturalism and radical transcendence. I also pay attention to those who hear a whisper of transcendence in the uncanny experience of duration, as they too advance an image of time as becoming. I engage both to draw out the version of immanent naturalism, duration, periodic interruption, and becoming I confess, testing its power against Taylor's account of exclusive humanism and placing it in contestation with the vision of transcendence he confesses.

So two groups. The first, the immanent naturalists, includes (to varying degrees) thinkers such as Democritus, Epicurus, Lucretius, Spinoza, Thoreau, Gilles Deleuze, Ilya Prigogine, and Michel Foucault. The second, philosophers of immanence in a world of becoming with a trace of transcendence, includes Henri Bergson, William James, Alfred North Whitehead, and perhaps Marcel Proust. Both groups emphasize the importance of dwelling in fecund moments of duration, as sustained sensitivity to resonances between a new event and layers of the past sometimes helps to usher a new idea, maxim, concept, faith, or intervention into being. All the modern thinkers on both lists are philosophers of time as becoming, posing a world in which time is not circular, linear, or purposive. It periodically folds the new into being in a universe that is intrinsically open to an uncertain degree.

In a world of becoming, emergent formations are often irreducible to patterns of efficient causality or simple probability, and they never conform to an intrinsic purpose or long cycles of recurrence. Becoming occurs in part through periodic intersections between different force fields, as neural, viral, bacterial, geological, climatic, species, and civilizational force fields set on different tiers of chrono-time infect (or disrupt, charge, invade, etc.) each other, in part through the periodic emergence of new and surprising capacities for autopoeisis when such collisions occur, and in part through the patterns of reverberation back and forth between these collisions and capacities for autopoeisis during fateful periods of accelerated disequilibrium. I mean here

4 See chap. 15, "The Immanent Frame," *SA*, especially pages 544–550.

to distinguish chrono- or clock-time—the difference measured by a clock between, say, the length of a human life and that of a hurricane—from durational time, as those (often) short periods of phase transition when reverberations back and forth between two force fields set on different tiers of clock-time change something profoundly. Some biologists think that the momentous phase transition from nonlife to life was rather short in clock-time but intense in what I am calling durational time.[5] For our species, these can be particularly pregnant moments in which to dwell, as Jesus reveals so forcefully. For a world of becoming is not only *open* to an uncertain degree, but each temporal force field in it periodically encounters an *outside* that affects it profoundly. Devotees of radical immanence, indeed, transfigure a radical notion of transcendence into the idea of the outside.

There are periods of relative stability and equilibrium in each zone or force field: a human life endures, a geological formation persists, a climate pattern stays, a civilization retains a relatively high degree of stability, a biological species survives, a faith evolves slowly. But particularly when one mode of endurance is touched, infected, electrically charged, or battered by those on other tiers of chrono-time, a more dramatic change may be in the cards: as when an asteroid shower destroys dinosaurs and sets the stage for the rapid evolution of human beings, as when a period of capitalist growth accelerates climate change that then recoils back on the self-sustaining capacity of capitalism, as when a powerful new virus jumps from birds or pigs to human beings, as when a group of devout Christians encounter Buddhism and find themselves tipping toward conversion, and so on.

The thinkers listed above also find it important to cultivate and amplify gratitude for being in the world of becoming. Such modes of cultivation are important both for the effects they have on ourselves and for the positive ethical energies they generate as we respond to new circumstances for which old moral principles, codes, rules, and habits are not adequately prepared.

As already indicated, some philosophers of duration and becoming affirm a world of immanence, a world in which the new periodically surges into being without the aid, obstruction, or protection of a divine force. Others focus on duration and becoming as they confess a *limited* God—a God

---

5 See Stuart A. Kauffman, *Reinventing the Sacred: A New View of Science, Reason and Religion* (New York: Basic Books, 2008).

who is both real and exceeded by the vicissitudes of time. Each tradition is equipped to honor Jesus by offering a distinctive interpretation of his calling and mode of inspiration. In doing so, each emphasizes the importance of sensibility, spirituality, and collective ethos to identity, faith, art, culture, economic life, and politics.

Charles Taylor would absorb the first set of thinkers characterized above into a tradition of immanent materialism, a tradition that contrasts with the tradition of transcendence he admires most.[6] That is okay by me, though I prefer the phrase "immanent naturalism" to play up the absence of divinity and play down obstinate assumptions that keep attaching themselves to the word "matter" following the long debate between Christian transcendence and mechanical materialism.

Consider two senses of the word "transcendence." By *radical* transcendence I mean a God who creates, informs, governs, or inspires activity in the mundane world while also exceeding the awareness of its participants. By *mundane* transcendence I mean any activity outside conscious awareness that crosses into actuality, making a difference to what the latter becomes or interacting with it in fecund ways, again without being susceptible to full representation. I do not confess radical transcendence, though I have not disproved it. I confess radical immanence replete with fugitive encounters with mundane transcendence. Now a specific field of immanence periodically encounters an outside that makes a difference to it.

You can be a devotee of radical transcendence without adopting a providential image of history. You can even embrace the idea of time as becoming. Both William James and Henri Bergson adopt the latter combination. Each embraces a limited God who participates in a world of becoming without creating or governing it. Each seeks, at key moments, to dwell in mystical experience in order to enhance his ability to be a vehicle through which something new and noble is brought into the world.

Can those who confess immanence with mundane transcendence also

---

6 Taylor's discussions of immanent materialism can be found in *SA*, 360–368, 398–401, 541–550, and 595–598.

dwell productively in the experience of duration? Yes. You dwell in a fecund moment to see whether something new and pertinent blooms forth through you, particularly when you encounter suffering or difficulties for which established codes of divinity, rights, morality, and identity have not adequately prepared us. If, as the layered past communicates with a new encounter, you help to usher something new into the world, it will be filtered through the experience of duration; it will be touched by the sensibility you bring to the moment of dwelling; and it will later be influenced by the intelligence you and others bring to bear as you refine it in relation to established codes, principles, understandings, and creeds.

To an immanent naturalist such experiments sometimes involve complex passages through which that which has heretofore been unthought—not quite shaped like thought—bumps or surges into an ongoing pattern of thought under the pressure of need, altering or energizing thinking in this way or that. That which undergoes such a passage cannot be known or represented before it appears, because it did not possess the shape of the representable before the passage began. It was at first merely *sensed* and later an *emergent* idea or theme, confounding those who demand that all passages be smooth. Such a crossing may even be comparable to the passage of carbon from nonlife to life, with the latter also being irreducible to that from which it emerged.

Such a set of views is what I mean by the philosophy/faith of radical immanence. It advances an image of mundane transcendence, encouraging movement back and forth between the virtual and the actual during periods of accentuated disequilibrium in this or that domain. In a world of becoming (as construed through this lens), each tier of chrono-time—the specific clock-time of a single circuit through the body-brain network, of species evolution, of the evolution of a civilization, or of a child's growth into an adult—oscillates between periods of relative equilibrium and accelerated disequilibrium, with the latter sometimes triggered by moments of collision with and/or infusion by force fields set on other tiers of chrono-time. Sometimes a seer dwells creatively during such a crossing, as when the Son of man or God drew in the sand and issued that noble maxim, as when Epicurus conceived the idea of atoms that swerve, as when Spinoza conceived of body and mind as two dimensions of the same substance, as when Zarathustra first dreamed of eternal return as the return of the fecundity of difference and then affirmed a world so defined, as when Gilles Deleuze first drew something magical from the encounters between experimental film and the desolate landscapes of post–World War II Europe and then helped to usher into being a concept of causation through resonance that scrambles the classical distinction between social science and interpretive cultural theory. None of these guys is transfixed by violence—as Taylor sometimes suggests immanent naturalists who follow in the wake of Nietzsche are. Nor are they tempted profoundly by it, though there are devotees of mundane transcendence in a world of immanence who are. All transcend the experience of homogeneous time from time to time, even as they recognize, with Henri Bergson, that the operational requirements of action-oriented perception solicit such a linear conception. That is, all distinguish between mundane time and durational time. And all evince a care for this world that resonates with the sensibility of Charles Taylor without embracing the final source from which he draws inspiration. Are he and they ripe candidates to enter into noble relations of agonistic respect?

Consider a couple of nonhuman examples of mundane transcendence in a world of immanence. When the first bits of DNA broke loose from the host cell and "invaded" another cell, the host cell usually died. But as these barrages continued over time, a few invaded cells were spurred into a new activity of *self-organization*. Out of the movement back and forth between the invasion and the creative response, the first nucleated cell emerged. It provided a basis from which biological evolution proceeded. That phase transition is called *symbiogenesis*. Ilya Prigogine, Brian Goodwin, and Lynn Margulis think that such creative movements periodically occur in several aspects of nature; they are incompatible both with efficient causation and with a conception of science based on the reduction of complex wholes to simple elements. Each also denies that an ideal observer in the vicinity when the first invasion occurred could have predicted the creative response. The invasion response fomented real creativity in the world. We immanent naturalists find such events to be as wondrous as others find the divine creation of the world from nothing to be. Similarly, when a human being takes a slow, aimless walk during a fraught situation, allowing layered reverberations between past and present to course through him in the hopes that a new idea, judgment, or strategy will emerge for consideration, that can also be wondrous. For us, such events repeat at a higher level that fecund process of symbiogenesis by which the first nucleated cell emerged. The latter possibility evolved from the former passage.

The two processes are not identical, for the first involves a mode of auto-poeisis that does not include a crossing from the unthought to thought, while during the second, the case of human dwelling, something passes from the immanent field of the unthought—that which is not entirely shaped like thought—into an established intersubjective matrix of thought. To rework modestly an invaluable insight Taylor advanced several years ago, such a crossing *expresses* but does not *represent* that which precedes and enables it. His sources are ambiguous and wondrous because they move you as they are carried into the world even as they are not fully articulable in themselves (*SS*, 74, 96). Ours are ambiguous, and sometimes wondrous, as they cross from one phase state to another. They hence infuse articulation without being representable in themselves. Again, the antecedent was not shaped like thought; or, in other cases, it was at most an incipient thought replete with pluripotentiality. It has one shape before the crossing and another after, something like the early crossing from the nonnucleated to the nucleated cell.

The articulation of a new idea, judgment, maxim, or concept both changes in some way our sense of the source from which it draws and alters the cultural net it enters in a small or large way. This is another version of the double process of articulation beautifully described by Taylor in *Sources of the Self.*

Deep pluralism cannot gain a secure foothold in predominately Christian states until confessions of Jesus by Jews, Muslims, Buddhists, and immanent naturalists are allowed to compete legitimately with Christian confessions of him as a divine savior. From the point of view of the last philosophy, mechanical naturalism degrades human beings and values analysis over dwelling too much. And many—though not all—theophilosophies of radical transcendence render humanity so unique that its connections and affinities to other parts of nature are obscured. Doing so, they risk disparaging our essential connections to nonhuman nature. The funny thing is that exclusive humanism displays a similar tendency. It also pulls humanity too far above the rest of nature, with results for those to see who have eyes to see.

It is one thing to *believe* in a world of becoming; something additional is needed to *affirm* that world. To come to affirm such a world, it is needful to work on ourselves by multiple means to overcome resentment of the world for not possessing either providence or ready susceptibility to human mastery. Taylor is dubious about our creed, though he acknowledges that he cannot give knockdown arguments against it. So in a second movement he recoils back upon his initial judgment, calling on himself and others to enter into what I would call a relation of agonistic respect with the bearers of such a creed. That is the nobility of Charles Taylor.

The minor tradition I embrace is replete with difficulties, puzzles, and problems amid its glowing promise. It pursues a conception of ethics anchored first and foremost in appreciation of our modest participation in larger processes of creation, in presumptive care for the diversity of life and for the fecundity of the earth. This ethic infuses mundane human interests, identities, tasks, and understandings rather than expressing an unconditioned law or divine inspiration above them. It is impure, essentially. Its advocates pursue strategies to come to terms, without existential resentment, with the obdurate fact of death as oblivion, in a world without an afterlife. We also acknowledge tragic potential in a world without either divine providence or a strong susceptibility to human mastery. Moreover, we seek to replace the quest to discover transcendent meaning with a readiness to *invest* selected activities with meaning. To the extent we succeed in affirming the world as we confess it to be, those investments will express a modicum of care for diversity, the future, and the earth. Further, we seek to challenge the vexed tradition of free will (in which the will is deeply divided against itself after the fall) with a notion of freedom bound to the process of thinking, particularly when you dwell creatively in fecund moments. Freedom is not entirely the property of agents, then; it is a strange process in which we participate.

Because we adopt an image of time as becoming, we do acknowledge a specific kind of division that periodically emerges within ourselves when pressures from the past (habits, emotions, principles, assumptions) encounter new circumstances for which they are unprepared. We transfigure the themes of primordial guilt and an intrinsically divided will into a more prosaic appreciation of the struggles that must ensue when old habits and new turns in time arise. Such dissonant conjunctions can be difficult, even agonizing. They can also on occasion foment creative thinking, as you dwell in duration to help usher something new into being, something that, you may decide retrospectively, deserves to be refined, modified, and cultivated further.

Finally, we relocate the element of mystery projected into radical transcendence into several natural and cultural processes themselves, as they find expressions in our experiences of time, causality, duration, and freedom. We know that times arise when we live forward into mystery.

From our point of view, the division between theological philosophies with mystery and naturalist philosophies that dissolve it "in principle" provides an insufficient list of credible perspectives. That is one reason that immanent naturalism is irreducible to either eliminative or mechanical materialism. For the immanent naturalist there is no guarantee that the capacities of human knowledge in an undesigned world will ever mesh entirely with the crooked way of the world itself. So we join theologians in supporting a place for mystery against the hubris of some kinds of materialism; and we join some materialists in suggesting that a theological recognition of mystery invests no set of priests with legitimate authority over everyone. Above all, we seek to cultivate existential affirmation of the world as we confess it to be, so that the insidious force of ressentiment does not seep into the inner core of our being, dividing us too profoundly against ourselves. In that, we make contact with theists such as Charles Taylor, Karl Jaspers, Catherine Keller, and Martin Buber, who advance similar pursuits from their side. A refined ethical sensibility involves care for the world, a presumptive respect for established principles, the cultivation of sensitivity to new circumstances, and attempts to craft new and timely precepts if and when it seems propitious to do so.

Our agenda is not free of paradox and uncertainty, then. In that respect we replicate in our way the elements of paradox, mystery, and division encountered in other traditions.

From the vantage point of a philosophy of immanence set in a sensibility of care for this world, a pressing need today is to negotiate deep, multidimensional pluralism within and across territorial regimes. That is, as I receive him, important to Taylor too, though he is inspired by a different fundamental source in the first instance. By deep pluralism I mean the readiness to defend your creed in public while acknowledging that it so far lacks the power to confirm itself so authoritatively that all reasonable people must embrace it. By multidimensional pluralism I mean a political culture in which differences of creed, ethnicity, first language, gender practice, and sensual affiliation find expression in a productive ethos of political engagement between participants. Deep pluralism and multidimensional pluralism set conditions of possibility for each other today, the first because it expresses presumptive care for the fundamental sources pursued by others, and the second because it helps to ventilate the internal discourses of church and secular associations.

What is most noble about Jesus, to us, is his method of teaching and his capacity to dwell with care and creativity in protean moments from time to time. He cultivates exquisite sensitivity to movements of world. My sense, again, is that deep, multidimensional pluralism in the Western world in which Christendom has prevailed will arrive when a wide array of voices can articulate publicly their readings of the word of Jesus without drawing rebuke for treading on ground outside their purview. As others periodically confess their Jesus to us for consideration, we bring ours to them for critical response. As they present their accounts of Epicurus, Lucretius, Spinoza, Nietzsche, and Deleuze to us, we reply. When Christians, Jews, humanists, Muslims, Buddhists, and nontheists can participate publicly and legitimately in such exchanges, deep pluralism will be on the way. It is not that such exchanges must be constantly in play, but that they must find expression during periods when they are pertinent to a major issue of the day. Some, of course, see such an ideal of pluralism as a mere projection from the academy to the larger cultural world. Fair enough. I see it as the most promising response to the late-modern condition in which a veritable minoritization of the world is taking place at more rapid pace than heretofore before our very eyes.

The issue is critical because with the accentuated globalization of capital, media, travel, and population movement today, the world is not simply becoming more homogenized, as many love to say. It is rapidly becoming a world of multiple minorities, who will either find ways to coexist on the same territories or confront each other in increasingly bellicose struggles for hegemony. We inhabit a world in which each territorial regime is increasingly populated by minorities of multiple kinds, and in which every putative majority said to make up the center of "the nation" is more a symbol of what many wish were the case than what is the case. In such a world, the productive ethos of engagement already negotiated today between Catholics, Jews, and Protestants, when each is at its best, needs to be extended in several directions. In such a world, immanent naturalism will be one minority creed among others.

If I understand Taylor correctly, he concurs in advance with much of what I have said, though the starting points of faith are very different.

Here I need to test another point of difference or concurrence between us—and another point of strife within myself. Taylor is admirable in pointing to the predicaments inside a variety of modern traditions. But what living forces help to determine whether those predicaments are explored by devotees as they seek relations of agonistic respect with other traditions or are repressed as they demonize those traditions? We concur that the latter politics is dangerous and often hovers on the edge of possibility. We also concur, I think, that the outcome of such a struggle could be fateful for the late-modern era. But what are its cultural sources? And how should they be engaged?

Class, age, race, ethnic, gender, and creedal "positions" do not suffice to explain political stances, and not only because of the cross-cutting affiliations that sociologists study. Another source is the different existential sensibilities among people who share a formal creed, racial identification, class position, or linguistic tradition. The existential or spiritual dimension is so critical that its cultural variations deserve to be schematized. In forming such a matrix, I do not suggest that belief and spirituality are fully separate. I suggest, rather, that affect and belief are always interinvolved, with neither being entirely reducible to the other—as when a belief is shared with others but held with a different degree of intensity, or when we differ in belief but evince an affinity of spirituality across that difference, or when you feel a surprising thud in the gut when a belief previously hidden in this nook or cranny has just been challenged.

In the "matrix" I have in mind there is no place called "unbelief." Every existential stance is infused with belief, though often punctuated by doubt, etc. Moreover, different existential dispositions can be attached to the same formal creed. So this matrix places an array of creedal *beliefs* across its horizontal axis and an array of existential *sensibilities* across its vertical axis. The distribution of belief flows from faith in a singular God on the right side to belief in the eternality of becoming on the left, with several stances in between, such as belief in a limited god, or a spiritual power without personal traits, or a mechanical world without transcendence. On the vertical axis are differences in existential sensibility, with love of this world forming the end point at the top and existential resentment at the bottom.

On the upper right side of this matrix are saints who embrace God and love of this world; on the upper left side are seers who embrace the immanence of becoming and love of this world; on the lower right we find those who mix existential resentment into belief in an omnipotent God; on the lower left, those who deeply resent the world of becoming as they themselves confess it to be. There are, of course, numerous points on the vertical axis too, with most of us being inhabited by a degree of ambivalence, or inclining in one direction at some points in life and another at others. It is easy to locate my earthy rendering of Jesus on the upper left and the transcendent reading of him adopted by many on the upper right. But what about the Christ of the Book of Revelation? Until someone teaches me things I have yet to discern, I locate this figure at the lower right end of the matrix.

It is also relatively easy to locate Lucretius, Augustine, Spinoza, Arendt, Kant, and Taylor on this schema. After an exhaustive, symptomatic reading of his writings, for instance, I would locate Taylor in the upper right box, inclined toward the high end on the vertical scale of love of this world and about a quarter of the way down the right-to-left axis between transcendence and immanence.

The point of such a schema is to suggest how important it is for individuals *and* constituencies to cultivate strategies to overcome resentment of the most fundamental way of the world, as they themselves confess it to be, or even as parts of themselves suspect it to be below the level of explicit belief. For the self is a complex social structure. Some theists may secretly resent the world because they suspect it in fact deviates from the belief they explicitly confess, or because the God they confess demands too much of them. Some nontheists may do so because part of them believes the God they deny will condemn them, or because another part wishes they could believe in a salvational God. Numerous other possibilities subsist as well. But today it is a fundamental responsibility of individuals and constituencies to seek to affirm the most fundamental way of the world as they themselves confess it to be as they come to terms without deep resentment with the profound contestability of that vision in the eyes of others. The struggle between minoritization and fundamentalization depends upon it.

How to do this? That is the difficult question. You might seek to shift your doctrine to find a better comfort zone through which to respond with presumptive care to new minorities whose very presence disturbs you. Or you might work artfully on your dispositions to deepen care for the future of the earth and the diversity of being. Difficulties will be encountered.

There are powerful theological and psychological pressures against admitting a feeling of resentment about the terms of existence as you officially embrace them. Under such a regime, existential resentment is apt to find expression in the bellicosity and exclusionary character of the political stances you adopt. That's why Nietzsche, for instance, found it important to read behavioral *symptoms* as well as doctrinal *confessions,* with Jesus faring well on the first scale and Paul less so. It is why Augustine was pressed to do so too, in his engagements with potential heretics. Either might have been too confident or faulty in the symptomatic readings he presented. But my point is to suggest that however we might wish to avoid such readings, the current historical juncture makes it politically and ethically incumbent to explore them in reflective ways. Commentators who purport to avoid such judgments indirectly express them anyway in the terms of art they use and the modes of description they offer, for ordinary language regularly folds moral appraisals into terms of description.

Today, in the United States and to varying degrees elsewhere too, one salient line of political division is between those who infuse a large quotient of care for the future of this world into their desires, identities, creeds, consumption practices, political loyalties, and economic doctrines and those who infuse a drive to revenge against difference and the weight the future imposes on the present. Today one set of capitalist elites and resentful secular males enter into alliance with a subset of evangelical Christians. The connection between them is intense. Each constituency suppresses its differences of belief from the others to accentuate the affinities of spirituality between them.

Egged on by the media, they form a veritable resonance machine, in which the creedally inflected spirituality of one constituency augments and amplifies that of the others. What they share is a disposition toward existence that deflates care for the diversity of being and for the future of the earth. The right edge of the capitalist class vindicates it by pretending that the free market takes care of itself even as it heightens the income curve, engenders financial crises, creates self-defeating modes of consumption, and intensifies global warming. The extreme edge of the evangelical right looks to a second coming in which the future of the earth as we now know it becomes unimportant. Check out the Left Behind series, which has sold 60 million copies as well as a huge number of DVDs. Both sides deflate the importance of global warming, resist pluralization, and support bellicose military policies. To some, the Iraq war will hasten the desired event; to others, concern for the future would disrupt demands for special entitlement now. Yet others are tempted by the constellation of ressentiment as they face a series of demeaning economic and social experiences.

Each spiritual constituency amplifies dispositions in the other, until a resonance machine emerges that is larger and more intense than the sum of its parts. Some who are now ensconced inside the evangelical-capitalist resonance machine might be encouraged to flee from it if more of us paid close public attention to the role that the contagion of spirituality plays in keeping it alive.[7] Indeed, there is ample evidence today that many young members of this machine are being drawn away from it as they experience its results and develop a more vivid sense of the shameful spiritual drives that have shaped it.

It may be said that these dicey issues can be bypassed by addressing differences in belief and policy alone. The assumption that this is so reflects those brands of intellectualism supported by some branches of secularism and exclusive humanism. I used to adopt one such position myself.[8] Today I doubt, along with Bergson, James, and Nietzsche, that it suffices. Thus, it is often said that the need is to improve the economic circumstances of those who

---

7 I explore these issues in *Capitalism and Christianity, American Style* (Durham: Duke University Press, 2008). Things now look a bit less bleak than they did when that book was started, immediately after the reelection of George W. Bush in 2004.

8 I worked critically on that earlier self-orientation in *Why I Am Not a Secularist* (Minneapolis: University of Minnesota Press, 1999).

are most vulnerable to such messages. This is pertinent but incomplete. Supporters of the ethos of existential resentment are distributed across class positions and creedal stances. Have you listened to publicists such as Sean Hannity and Glenn Beck on Fox News? Or representatives from the American Enterprise Institute? Or to Paul Wolfowitz, who has moved from being an architect of the Iraq war to being the head of the World Bank to taking a position at the Nitze School of Advanced International Studies at Johns Hopkins? It is insufficient to say that they seek to manipulate others. A bellicose spirituality infuses their performances, and they seek to communicate that spirituality to a wider audience.

Many privileged elites participate in the evangelical-capitalist resonance machine, working to amplify it. That is why attention to economic self-interest, elite manipulation, and so on are insufficient to the issue. The point is not that the distribution of existential resentment and attachment lacks familial, social, economic, and political sites of expression. It is, rather, that spiritual disposition has a degree of partial autonomy even as it finds variable expression in different social positions. This degree of partial separation also promotes the possibility of a new resonance machine, composed of multiple constituencies who have positive affinities of spirituality across those differences.

Since existential resentment is not a disposition that many confess, it is most apt to find indirect expression in actions taken. Producing, owning, driving, and militantly opposing state regulation of SUVs provided one manifestation of this tendency, at least until the recent fuel crisis and financial meltdown. People from a variety of social positions converged to protect and enlarge this market, even though everybody could have known for years, if they had wanted to, the dangers, fuel costs, resource effects, and results for global warming these vehicles represent. But auto producers, cowboy capitalists, a section of the white middle class, and an angry branch of evangelicals militantly blocked regulation of these vehicles. Interconstituency support for SUVs displays a lack of concern for the collective future. Similar things could be said about intense support for capital punishment, eager embrace of reckless wars, happy support of ruthless politicians, easy tolerance of state torture, casual acceptance of sharp inequality, and demonization of many who confess neither Christianity nor unfettered capitalism.

The substance of the positions on these issues is not the most critical issue, since there are real debates on some of them. It is, rather, the bellicosity with which the position is supported, the dogmatism with which the rationale on its behalf is embraced, the burning desire to stoke scandals about those who oppose you, and the easy willingness to make the most optimistic assumption about the future cost of the thing you most want now. An existential disposition has two dimensions: its fundamental orientation toward this world and the intensity with which it is expressed. And again, affinities of spirituality can bind constituencies together who diverge in this or that way on economic and religious belief.

I agree that it is risky to think and say these things. You run the risk of replicating the very stances you resist, particularly if you think, as I do, that opponents of the evangelical-capitalist resonance machine must ratchet up their own levels of intensity today. Nonetheless, it seems to me that those who prize democracy, deep pluralism, egalitarianism, and the future of the earth must now run these risks as reflectively as possible. There is no risk-free way to proceed in the current historical conjuncture. You might even say that the secular tendency to maintain a disjunction between private religious belief and public deliberation has kept too many of us out of touch with this dimension of politics for too long. It has discouraged many outside official religious constellations from addressing the spiritual dimension of political and economic life.

One way to dramatize the situation we are in is to say that the difference between the Nixon era and the Bush era is Fox News and the battalion of right-wing think tanks it draws upon to stoke the juices of ressentiment. The two eras display similar tendencies, but the amplification machine forged by the Fox News/think-tank/evangelical-capital right is more entrenched and dangerous than that forged by Nixon and his henchmen.

We must interpret publicly the existential symptoms of the most bellicose movements, as we recoil upon ourselves to resist becoming a version of the thing we oppose. One way to reduce that risk is to bear in mind that *no single social category, including a creedal community, corresponds neatly to the existential disposition you seek to expose, resist, or overcome.* A second is to probe points, places, and constituencies on the margins of the assemblage you oppose to draw some factions away from the machine. A third is to engage ourselves on this front from time to time, particularly when reading others symptomatically, to insure that we do not become what we seek to overcome. And a fourth is to spend more time stoking the positive assemblage than dwelling on the negative spiritualities.

Today it is urgent to forge a counterresonance machine composed of several constituencies who diverge along lines of creedal faith, class position, ethnic affiliation, sexual affiliation, and gender practice. It is to enlarge the cohort that gives priority to the earth, however they themselves interpret the most fundamental terms of existence. It is to work on ourselves and others to insure that we do not resent the way of the world as we ourselves grasp it. That involves affirming a world in which the creed you embrace regularly brushes up against alternatives that challenge, disturb, and disrupt its claim to universality.

If I read Taylor correctly, he concurs, not with the existential creed advanced here, but with the ethico-political need to amplify positive spiritualities attached to several creeds. He also concurs with the need to forge a new assemblage—cutting across differences of class, gender, sensuality, age, and creed—to foster pluralism, egalitarianism, and care for the future. Where we differ, perhaps, is in the hesitancy Taylor displays to read social movements symptomatically—though he does so with some—and the urgency I display in doing so. I am unsure how deep this latter difference goes or who is right about it. I know I am divided against myself at this point, while now giving a degree of priority to one side of that division.

6

What Is Enchantment?

Akeel Bilgrami

Modern life is beset with distinctive anxieties. This is something on which philosophers as diverse as Rousseau and Marx and Gandhi are wholly agreed. And, if true, it suggests that the early modern period of history (and intellectual history) of the West is the appropriate focus for a *genealogical* diagnosis of the conditions in which and with which we now live and cope. Charles Taylor's remarkable new book provides a learned and illuminating diagnosis of just this sort. Abstracting from its many details, let me fasten on two hypotheses that are, by his own lights, central to his argument. The first is that we have come not just to have secular *doctrinal* commitments and secular *political* arrangements (to the extent we have) but to live in a secular *age,* by which is meant that we live in an age that possesses the conceptual preconditions that make possible such changes in doctrine and in the polity (wherever they occur), by making merely optional the belief in God and religion and its relevance to public life. The second hypothesis is that these preconditions came into being not by a mere process of subtraction of "transcendental" elements from a previous conceptual framework in order to produce an intellectual commitment to "immanence," but rather by a positive philosophical construction of a new set of interconnected ideas about the nature of the human subject and agency and a new ethical order within which human happiness is to be conceived. This order is elaborated in assertively individualistic terms, invoking new notions of responsibility and value. How this ideological story of addition and construction (rather than mere subtraction) occurred, from its early modern beginnings in providential deism, provides the genealogical diagnosis I just mentioned. And if I read Taylor correctly, there is a normative point being made by the claim that we have come to be in a secular age not by *losing* a sense of transcendence but rather by *developing an ideological conceptual system* which had its beginnings in early modernity. That normative point is to put into question the apparent innocence of the widespread claim that the modern West, by arriving at such an exclusively humanistic secular age, has achieved an advance in rationality.

In the passage of my argument, I will say something about the doubtful philosophical coherence at the heart of the ideological construction, but let me begin by saying something about how stressing the diagnostic account in *early* modernity, as Taylor does, reveals far more of the thick textures that go into the notion of rationality that we so triumphantly claim for our own times and our own part of the world (if I may speak in that proprietary way of the part of the world that is my place of current domicile) than other works which, as Taylor says, present this ideal of rationality either as having no genealogy at all or as the normatively drawn end point toward which we are supposed to have cumulatively progressed and converged. So, for instance, the seemingly endless stream of books published these days[1] about how impressive is the exclusively humanistic rationality at which we have arrived, and by which we eschew such unscientific beliefs as that the world was created in six days a few thousand years ago, all present that rationality as merely a commitment to making claims on the basis of the sort of evidence that science will allow. They present it as an end point of a hard-won sequence of struggle against obscurantism and chide the tendencies to obscurantism in our own time as a continuing, infantile dependence on a father whose death was pronounced over a century ago, in late modernity.

What goes entirely missing in this simplistic picture is the intellectual as well as cultural and political prehistory of the demise of such an authority figure. Well before his demise, brought about partly (but only partly, as Taylor points out) by this scientific outlook, which we all now rightly admire and

---

1 See for instance, Richard Dawkins, *The God Delusion* (Boston: Houghton Mifflin, 2006); Daniel Dennett, *Breaking the Spell: Religion as a Natural Phenomenon* (New York: Penguin, 2007).

which is recommended by the authors of these tedious tomes, it was science itself, and nothing less than science, that proposed in the late seventeenth century a quite different kind of fate for the father: a form of *migration,* an exile into inaccessibility from the visions of ordinary people to a place outside the universe, from where, in the now familiar image of the clock-winder, he first set and then kept an inert universe in motion. It is worth expounding in some detail on this deracination of God from the world of matter and nature and human community and perception, so as to understand its large and abiding effects not just on theology but on politics and political economy.

There is no Latin expression such as *deus deracinus* to express the thought that needs expounding. The closest we have is *deus absconditus,* which, though it is meant to convey the inaccessibility of God, conveys to the English speaker a fugitive fleeing. Rather, what needs expressing is the idea that it is from the roots of nature and ordinary experience that God was removed. *Racine,* or roots, is the right description of his immanence in a conception of a sacralized universe, from which he was torn away as a result of being exiled by the metaphysical outlook of early modern science (aligned with thoroughly mundane interests).

But although my (somewhat grotesque) neologism *deus deracinus* in some respects better captures what I want to express, in another respect the expression we have, *deus absconditus,* suggests something of what I want to ask. The phrase, quite apart from standing for the inaccessibility of God that was insisted upon by the late seventeenth-century ideologues of the Royal Society, conveys a certain anxiety that I think lay behind their insistence. *Conditus* means "put away for *safeguarding,*" with the *abs-* in some uses reinforcing the "awayness" of where God is safely placed. What I want to ask is, why should the authority figure need safeguarding in an inaccessibility; what dangers lay in his immanence, in his availability to the visionary temperaments and capacities of all those who inhabit his world? And why should the scientific establishment of early modernity seek this safekeeping in exile for a father whom late, more mature modernity would properly describe as "dead"? That question is crucial, not merely because the answers we give to it will show that humanistic rationality did not emerge whole all at once but also because it reveals that even if we allow it to be a gradual outcome of a triumphantly progressive intellectual history, to focus, as Dawkins and Dennett and others do, on the end point of that history as an ideal toward which we have sequentially progressed and converged is to give oneself an air of spurious innocence. The *accretions,* which are central to the notion of what makes up humanistic rationality, are most visible in the early modern *origins* of our modernity, and in one sense I think the chapter on providential deism, in which some of these origins are discussed, is the most revealing part of Taylor's book.

It is in that chapter that we get hints as to why a scientific establishment of early modernity would have found it convenient to put away the father in safekeeping, away from the visionary temperaments of ordinary people. In my own writing on Gandhi, given Gandhi's more straightforwardly political interests, which were centered on British colonial rule in India, I have stressed perhaps more than Taylor does two explicitly political features that were salient to Gandhi's understanding of the Enlightenment[2] and its origins in the early modern West, though they are both quite continuous with the argument to be found in Taylor's book.

First, the removal of God to a place of exile definitively converted an ancient and spiritually conceived conception of nature into something brute and desacralized. This did not happen easily—much vocal freethinking dissent by other scientists (then called "natural philosophers," of course) had to be silenced by the growing metaphysical orthodoxy around the new science in the Royal Society. These dissenters, such as John Toland[3] in England and a number of others on the continent, influenced by Spinoza's pantheism, rightly argued that the Newtonian laws were perfectly compatible with a conception of nature in which God was not put away in some external place, giving the universe a push from the outside to put it in motion, but present in nature itself and therefore providing an *inner* source of dynamism that was responsible for motion. The orthodoxy won out over this dissenting view, not because of any scientific superiority, as conceived then or, for that matter, as we conceive it now—after all, by our thoroughly modern lights, it is no improvement to think that motion is due to an external divine intervention rather than an inner divine source of dynamism. The former view won out because the ideologues of the Royal Society, around the Boyle lectures started

---

2 Gandhi's writing on these subjects is most sustained in his book *Hind Swaraj* (Cambridge: Cambridge University Press, 1997), but it is also scattered in an overwhelmingly large collection of short dispatches to young India and in any number of interviews and letters.

3 In a number of works, including *Christianity Not Mysterious* (1696) and *Pantheisticon* (1704).

by Samuel Clarke, forged an alliance with commercial and mercantile interests that were keen to view nature in predatory terms for profit and gain. If God was not everywhere in nature, a sustained metaphysical obstacle to viewing nature as a source of extraction in the form of deforestation, mining, and plantation agriculture (what we today call agribusiness) was removed. Weber made familiar the claim of the rise of capitalism in the new attitudes of Protestant Christianity toward the notion of work. But the removal of this obstacle was just as important to its rise. The point is not that no one ever took from nature before a certain metaphysics grew around the Newtonian laws. But in many a social world, such taking as was done was accompanied by communitywide rituals of reciprocation, which in general showed an attitude of respect and restoration toward nature—rituals performed before cycles of planting, and even hunting. The exile of God to an external place made all these qualms and compensations unnecessary. With no metaphysical obstacles remaining, the scale of taking from nature's bounty could be pursued with unthinking and unconstrained zeal. Nature, being brute, could not make demands or put constraints on us. Because it was brute, we did not need to respond to it on *its* terms. All the term-making came from *us,* and the terms we would summon were increasingly the terms of utility and gain, converting the very idea of nature—without remainder—to the idea of natural *resources.*

The second crucial consequence of the forced inaccessibility of God was more political than economic, not that these can be strictly separated. So, for instance, in England, the ideologues of the Royal Society added to their alliance with commercial interests a key further alliance with Anglican interests. For all three sets of interests, the unrest of the pre-Restoration period was to be avoided at all costs, and one source of the unrest was that the radical sectaries of that period, such as the Diggers, the Levellers, and various other groups, generated their "enthusiasm" to turn "the world upside down" on the grounds that the most ordinary of people may be inspired by the "leveling purpose" (to use Gerrard Winstanley's term) of a "God present in all things and all bodies."[4] Such accessibility of God had the potential for remarkable effects of democratization. The exile of "the father" implied that a

---

4 See George Sabine, ed., *The Works of Gerrard Winstanley* (Ithaca, N.Y.: Cornell University Press, 1941).

trained priestcraft, with its learned scriptural judgment, alone could pronounce on a God made thus inaccessible. A God perceptible in the experiences of ordinary people made the university-trained divines and their learning arcane and irrelevant, and this democratization was not by any means restricted to matters of religion, even if it was the original source of the political inspiration ordinary people could claim. What the alliance between the Royal Society and the Anglicans succeeded in doing by silencing dissent was to create much more than just a religious elite. That is to say, the form of cognitive elitism bestowed by this metaphysics on an Anglican priestcraft was generalized to a cognitive elitism much more broadly in matters of law and political governance (a statecraft to match the priestcraft), by the broad analogy that a monarch and his courtly entourage of propertied elites ruling over a brute populace was just a mundane version of the ideal of an external God ruling over a brute universe.

The dissenters were prescient about this form of preemption of the possibilities of a democratic culture and in their dissent explicitly invoked the ideas of the radical sectaries of some fifty years earlier, who had actually claimed on the basis of God's accessibility not only the irrelevance of a cognitively elevated priestly class, but also the elimination of tithes, the elimination of feed lawyers in matters of law, the elimination of the high costs of medicine and the canonical status of the College of Physicians, and quite generally the elimination of elitist control of the cognitive dimensions of power and political governance. It was these elements in society, they argued, that thwarted the local form of egalitarian community that the radical sects had wished to establish.

The dissenting position should not be confused with the cliché about how the Protestant Reformation allowed for an individual's relation to God to undermine popery and its powerful priestly surround, since it was the *Protestant* establishment in England and its counterparts abroad that were in the forefront of the elitist turn made possible by the early modern metaphysical orthodoxy around the new science. Its eventual effect was therefore much deeper and more pervasive, given the deep and pervasive entrenchment of the Protestant establishment that was to follow. This thwarting of a democratized cognitive basis for political power was evident in the emphasis placed on ideals of courtly civility. I would add to Taylor's interesting discussion of "politesse," along with others, such as Norbert Elias and Peter Burke, who have also written illuminatingly on the notion of early modern civility, the following functional point. What such civility provided was a screen that hid from the early modern courts the cruelty of *their own perpetration,* so that they recognized only the cruelties in the behavior and lifestyles of a brute populace lacking such civilities, and this is what morphed in somewhat later modernity, with the codifications of the Enlightenment, into rights and constitutions. For all the great good they have done and are deservedly admired for, these continue to have the function of screening from metropolitan Western societies the cruelties they themselves have perpetrated on distant lands, so they see only those cruelties that exist in societies lacking these codifications and commitments to rights and constitutions.

The effects of this ruthless elitist control of the cognitive and commercial source of power are everywhere with us—effects seen not merely in the seemingly ineradicable inequalities of our times, but in the cultural detritus and the psychological desolation they have wrought—and I bring no news in saying so, except to insist on their provenance in an early modern metaphysics that generated a thick notion of rationality through unblushingly formed alliances of worldly forces. Hence, in stressing the political and religious and economic alliances that shaped this metaphysics, I want to stress just how thick the accretions around the notions of rationality were. One manifest symptom of this thick texture of rationality can be found in the fact that it provided the justifications for the rapacious conquest of distant lands, not merely on the grounds that they were just more stretches of brute nature to be mastered for profit and gain, but because the inhabitants of those lands were infantilized as people who lacked precisely this rationality, lacked the right attitudes toward nature (which made it possible to take this predatory attitude toward it). The point of colonial rule was partly the pedagogical project of making them more rational in these terms.

I have brought out more explicitly than Taylor the economic and political side of what followed on the theology and metaphysics of a certain dominant strand of deism to show just how specific and thick the accretions around what Taylor calls "humanistic" rationality were, which Dawkins and Dennett present unadorned, in *innocently thin* terms, as merely the tenets that demand scientific evidence for all answers to scientific questions. One does not have to deny that scientific questions should get answers in terms that respect the tenets of scientific evidence to see that what these writers present is conveniently thin and shallow. But what I have said in presenting these thick accretions is entirely continuous with Taylor's elaborations of the genealogy, which are really the deeper and more underlying *ethical* constructions of new individualistic notions of agency and responsibility and the new form of impersonal ethical order that they generated.

The continuities are not hard to see. What Taylor calls the "buffered self" is a self that is not open to normative demands from any site external to itself, an inevitable consequence of the fact that a world conceived as brute does not, in any case, contain anything that *could* make those demands. If we are the source and makers of all value, then all talk of our moral behavior as something responsive to callings from some source outside ourselves was at best sheer projection and at worst irrational, an abdication of human agency and the rigors of individual responsibility. It is not that this purely human source of value had to be seen in mere utilitarian terms, though that form of objectification of value certainly emerged later from the version of humanism that Taylor describes. Notions of sympathy and benevolence might well transcend utility, but even so, they did not transcend the boundaries of *our own making.* Sympathy, and moral sentiments generally, were merely human dispositions, just more causal tendencies in nature, our nature, and value *had no other source* but these tendencies, with which we were endowed. This is not to deny that sympathy may (as Smith elaborates the idea)[5] get refined by the social contexts in which we find ourselves; nor is it to reduce the view to some debased notion of self-interest. The point, rather, is that sympathy was not, on this view, to be seen as *responsiveness* to any *external source of value,* which demanded in a normative sense the exercise of our dispositions to sympathy in our practical agency. There was no other site of value but what resided in our own dispositions, and human happiness lay in the satisfaction of these human desires and dispositions.[6] It no longer lay in conceptions of an unalienated life, by which I mean a life of *harmony* between the demands of an *external* source of value and our dispositional responses to its demands. To stress human flourishing was precisely to leave out the external source. These points in Taylor are the deeper and more underlying considerations, because the specific political accretions around rationality I have stressed

5 Adam Smith, *The Theory of Moral Sentiments* (Cambridge: Cambridge University Press, 2002).
6 See David Hume, *An Enquiry Concerning the Principles of Morals* (Oxford: Clarendon, 1998).

(Taylor, of course, stresses other political accretions) *presuppose* these points about value emerging entirely out of our own desires and dispositions.

Let me explicitly raise the issue about whether this underlying construction of self, agency, and a new form of ethical order that Taylor finds in the radical shift in the early modern period, of which he is, of course, implicitly highly critical, even so much as makes coherent internal sense. I think it is arguable on more or less strictly philosophical grounds that there can be *no* notion of agency when one has a conception of value as residing entirely in our desires and moral sentiments rather than as external callings that make demands on us, to which our desires and moral sentiments are responses.

Agency consists in the presence and exercise of a certain point of view. Consider the fact that one cannot both *intend* to do something and *predict* that one will do it at the same time. Why not? Because when one predicts that one will do something, one steps outside oneself and looks at oneself in a detached way, as an object of causal and motivational histories; that is, one looks at oneself as another might look at one, and so we might call this the third-person point of view. But when one intends to do something, one has *not* got a detached observer's angle on oneself; one is rather asking as an *agent*, "What should I do?" or "What ought I to do?" One is in the first-person point of view. We can occupy both points of view, but we cannot occupy both points of view *at once*. That is to say, one cannot be both an agent and a detached observer of oneself at the same time. If I look at myself and say, "I predict that I will. . . ," the second use of "I" in that assertion is an *object* of my detached gaze, it is not the *subject* of agency. By contrast, in the expression "I intend that I will . . . ," both uses of "I" are fully agentive and the assertion is made fully within the first-person point of view. The second "I" there marks a subject or agent, unlike the object of a third-person, detached observation, explanation, or prediction, which is not an agent.

With this distinction in place, something important comes to light about the view of agency that emerges out of the ethical construction that Taylor elaborates as having its origins in the early modern period. Such a view of agency sees it entirely in terms of the pursuit of the gratification of one's desires and moral sentiments. On the face of it, this might seem to be a perfectly coherent conception of agency: in being agents, we are active in the world, and our activity may be viewed as our efforts to gratify our desires and moral sentiments. I want to raise a fundamental question about such a picture of agency, a question about the relationship between our desires and our agency. To do this, let me say just a word first about the nature of self-knowledge.

The philosopher Gareth Evans, in a brilliant passing remark on self-knowledge, pointed out that if someone asked him, "Do you believe that it is raining?" he wouldn't scan his mind to see if it contains the belief that it is raining.[7] He would simply look outside to *see* if it is raining. So it turns out that the questions "Is it raining?" and "Do you believe it's raining?" prompt the *same* response from the person asked: looking outside to see whether it is raining. Self-knowledge (that is, knowledge of one's own beliefs) is not—at least not in the standard and unproblematic cases—to be prized apart radically from knowledge of the world, such that it becomes the product of a detached observation and study of one's interiority. Now, I want to extend this brilliant point made about self-knowledge of the objects of one's beliefs to the objects of one's desires. If someone asks me, "Do you desire *x*?" I don't scan my interior to see if it contains a certain desire; I look at *x* (or try to imagine *x*) to see if *x* is desirable. If this is right, then it follows that the objects of our desire are experienced by us as desir*able* rather than as desir*ed* by us. This should in fact not be surprising at all. If the objects of our desires were experienced by us as desired rather than as desirable, we would be stepping outside ourselves and observing our desires in a detached way and thereby precisely ceasing to be agents. It strictly follows, then, that it is only when the objects of our desires are experienced by us as desirable that we are related to our desires as agents. Consider my assertion "X is desired by me." That is a report on my desires from a third-person, detached perspective. Consider by contrast my assertion "X is desirable." That is not a report at all; it is the expression of a desire, made from the first-person point of view of agency. So it is only because the world itself contains desirab*ilities* (or values) that we perceive that our agency really gets triggered or activated. The very possibility of agency, therefore, assumes an evaluatively enchanted world.

It is because philosophers tend not to ask the question I have posed about desires and their relation to agency that they don't see the incoherence in the idea that our agency consists in the pursuit of desires and moral sentiments, conceived in this self-standing form, which leaves out the *external* calling of

7 Gareth Evans, *Varieties of Reference* (Oxford: Oxford University Press, 1983), 225.

value from the world. So disenchantment—the exclusion of all external callings that Taylor identifies in the new ethical construction of buffered selfhood and agency emerging from the early modern period—would have the effect of putting into doubt whether *any* notion of agency has been constructed at all. Disenchantment does not merely produce alienation in the loose sense of that term (as a depression, or a loss of interest in things, sometimes does), it produces an alienation in the quite strict sense of an absence of agency, reducing us to mere receptacles for our desires and their satisfaction. I will return to this question of the link between agency and alienation, but let me first pursue something more immediately linked to Taylor's different conception of transcendence.

I have been arguing that the world from which God was exiled—no longer, as result of that exile, an *anima mundi*—was then assiduously argued also to be no longer something to which we were answerable in our moral agency. All value came instead from us; it owed to nothing but our utilities and gain, and even when there was an acknowledgment of our capacity for sympathy and moral sentiments, this was seen not as our responsiveness to the normative demands of a world laden with value but as something that we *projected* onto the world (a metaphor, as I said earlier, that is explicit in Hume and Adam Smith) and that, as the idea was developed in the tradition that followed, we kept under the control of the demands of efficiency and consequence and utility. Why, one might ask, should the fact of the father's exile to an external place as a clock-winder have led to an understanding of the universe as wholly brute and altogether devoid of value? Why was it not possible to retain a world suffused with values that was intelligible to all who inhabited it, despite the unintelligibility and inaccessibility of the figure of the father? Why must value require a sacralized site for its station, without which it must be relegated to proxy, but hardly proximate, notions of desire or utility and gain?

I will not deny that these questions are anachronistic, suited only to what Taylor calls our secular age, where belief in God and religion is merely an option and where we might conceivably (though perhaps not with much optimism) seek *secular* forms of reenchanting the world. One cannot put them coherently to a period in which value was so pervasively considered to have a sacred source. There is no gainsaying this. But what it allows us to do is to read a sustained and interesting ambiguity in Taylor's implicit ideals.

On the one hand there is the positive construction of a new ethical order and notions of freedom or agency, which leaves out any external calling that makes normative demands on us. If this is disenchantment, we may claim reenchantment in a secular age by finding such external callings in a quite different conception of value than is found in the constructions of modernity— something like the very interesting neo-Aristotelianism of John McDowell,[8] for which I have tried to give a very specific argument via the notion of how we must view the objects of our desires in order to even put in place the idea of our agency. If agency requires us to think of our desires as formed in the perceptions of desirabilities or values in the world external to us, we have a version of enchantment, since this stands opposed to (pretty much) every important feature of the early modern construction that Taylor elaborates. It insists that there is more to agency than the newly emergent notion of freedom in the wake of providential deism. It requires something quite external to the sympathy and moral sentiments with which we are endowed, thereby denying a self-standing benevolent ethical order. It finds quite inadequate the idea that the ethical is exhausted by human flourishing and the satisfaction of desires and values entirely of our own endowment or choosing. And because it *so pervasively* sees values as making an *external* calling upon our agency and sympathy, it necessarily sees the world as containing features that are not capable of being investigated by the impersonal and disengaged methods of study emerging in early modernity, thereby not just leaving the resistance to those methods as "occasional punctuations" (as Taylor describes miracles as we moderns conceive of them) but a thoroughgoing resistance, a systematic exposure of the limitations to the coverage of nature and the world by those impersonal methods.

On the other hand, it is also true that what I have argued for does not commit itself to the external callings being *transcendental,* since the callings come from a conception of value as something that is laden in the world. But even so, I insist that it makes *external* demands on us and is not of our own making in any interesting sense of the idea of "making." I don't deny that it does presuppose human perceptual sensitivity to the value elements that enchant the world independent of us, and it presupposes too human agency

8 John McDowell, "Values and Secondary Qualities" in *Meaning, Knowledge, and Reality* (Cambridge, Mass.: Harvard University Press, 1998).

(the first-person point of view, as I put it earlier) that responds to their normative demands. Creatures that lack agency would find darkness in the world where we perceived value and responded to its demands. But these do not in the slightest suggest anything like the early modern construction's claim that all human flourishing consists in the satisfaction of human desires and moral sentiments of sympathy and benevolence. Rather, it claims something quite other: that human flourishing lies in the unalienated life in the very specific sense that comes from a certain *harmony* with the demands of external callings, from the response to demands that are not merely of human making. It would be a crass confusion (or, at any rate, conflation) to think that the idea that human agency is a requisite for one even to perceive the evaluatively enchanted elements in the world external to us really shows those elements to be not external at all but rather of our own making, as in the constructions of early modernity. The point is this: the ambiguity I find in the notion of "enchantment" is equally there in the notion of "transcendental." To the extent that immanence is characterized in terms of the constructions of early modernity, these callings, being external to human desires and moral sentiments of sympathy and benevolence, are to that extent *transcendental*. They do *not* see flourishing in the terms of that form of exclusively humanist construction. Of course, they are not transcendental in the sense of having a sacred source, but that is just the second meaning of "transcendental" in the ambiguity I am trying to identify.

Taylor is perfectly aware that an ambiguity of this sort looms in recurring passages in the book where he speaks of an anti-Enlightenment tradition that also stands opposed to the construction he elaborates from early modernity. But there is something deflecting about the repeated appeal to Nietzsche whenever he cites that tradition. Nietzsche, for all his brilliance in resisting the construction of early modernity, and resisting much else besides, had no real understanding of or sensitivity to the points I have made about value, desire, and agency and their scope for undermining the construction of early modernity and placing in its stead a form of evaluative enchantment external to our making. The one place where Nietzsche figures less prominently in these passages is a reference to the views of a school of historians of science and culture from Edinburgh, with the self-description "deep ecology," but I think here too there is a certain marginalization and circumscription of the points I am stressing by the narrowing and restrictive term "ecology." The point is not that *nature* in some *self-standing* sense is to be understood as enchanted, but rather that the world, understood as *nature in its relations with its inhabitants, and a tradition and history that grows out of these relations,* comprises the external evaluative enchantment. This Heideggerian conception of "the world," which provides the external evaluative callings to our agency, would only be reductively described if it were described with the label "ecology," however deep ecology is supposed to reach.

So the ambiguity I am identifying lies in the fact that if the notions of "disenchantment" and "immanent" are given in terms of the construction of early modernity, one may oppose them with notions of "enchantment" and "transcendental" that are in a quite different sense *not* enchanted or transcendental at all, because it is not a sacred or supernatural form of transcendence and enchantment. (I will resist the temptation to say that the notions of "sacred" and "supernatural" too are ambiguous in the way I am insisting applies to the terms "enchantment" and "transcendental," because we must, after all, at the end of it, find some vocabulary to capture the second part of the ambiguous ideal.)

Having said that, I want to make very clear that I point to this ambiguity not *at all* to suggest that Taylor has no right to his view that we can conceivably be open to transcendental callings in his intended sense of "transcendental." Though I will declare myself an atheist, I in fact think that he is quite right to insist that nothing in the constructions of modernity, not even *late* modernity, have shown definitively that we cannot be open to it or that it would be irrational to be open to it. This needs careful statement, since it might seem to suggest that I should declare something less than atheism, if it is allowed that one may be open to this possibility of Taylor's ideal of transcendence. But a proper understanding of what is at stake in allowing it should make the suggestion of agnosticism here quite unnecessary.

I think Taylor's claims for the "transcendental," in his more religious sense of that term than mine, are made with a very special kind of philosophical scruple that is worth making explicit. Let me present it in my own terms and vocabulary. I have displayed my own sense of the idea of enchantment in terms that are "immanent," in one sense of that term, even though it has (pretty much) all the important features that oppose the claims of the ethical construction of the immanent framework since early modernity. This makes things easier for me in one sense. The notion of enchantment as *I* have it merely finds value to be in the world external to human desire and benevolence, without there being any sacred source for value. Should someone say that I am being unscientific in claiming that the world, including nature, contains something like values, on the grounds that natural science cannot study such evaluative properties of the world and nature, I can reply that it is not unscientific to claim that not all properties in the world and in nature are within the purview of natural science. It is not a proposition in any science that science has full coverage of nature and of the world, so it cannot be unscientific to deny such a proposition. The idea that nothing exists in nature and the world that is not countenanced by natural science is an idea that only philosophers—and scientists playing at being philosophers, like Richard Dawkins—have asserted. One can find it to be bad philosophy, as I do, and cannot, for the reason I gave, be accused of doing bad science in return, since it is a dispute within philosophy, not science.

Taylor, it might seem, cannot so easily make this reply. For him, the calling is transcendental in a quite different sense of that term, something that someone who subscribed to enchantment and transcendence in my more minimal sense could (if he were dogmatic and missing the scruple that I think Taylor is careful to imply) dismiss as adding a gratuitous further element of transcendence that really *is* unscientific. How might such a dogmatic objection be articulated? Roughly, like this: the idea of values being in nature and the world may not amount to anything unscientific, it will be said, but the claim to a supernatural, sacred source of values cannot claim for itself a compatibility with the evidentiary demands of scientific rationality. It cannot hide behind *my* defense, which says that value is merely a subject outside science's purview and not a violation of the tenets that define that purview. A supernatural, transcendent God *is* an affront to the constraints laid down by the demands of scientific evidence, since it is necessarily making claims to address *science's* questions, not stand aside from their reach. Thus, for instance, Dawkins's insistent complaint—surely correct—that creationism, intelligent design, etc., address unscientifically a scientific question about the origins of the universe. No claim to a supernaturally transcendent source can avoid addressing questions of that kind.

It is precisely Taylor's scruple, I think, that he is not inclined to present the transcendental in such terms, as addressing questions of that kind. It is rather addressing the possibilities of the transcendental, which, like my more immanent and secular version of that ideal, are defined entirely in terms of contrast with the narrowing exclusive humanism that begins to take incipient shape in early modernity. Taylor's ideal of "transcendence" happens not to coincide with the more minimal transcendence that I have urged, but there is no decisive reason to favor my sparer version—we are, after all, not required to be wielding any Occam's razor in this region of thought. It would be quite arbitrary to wield it, since some may experience callings that make normative demands on their agency in terms that are more richly religious than anything I have described in the enchantment I have briefly argued for. If these callings do not address scientific questions and therefore do not violate any rules of scientific evidence—any more than the presence of values does in my version of enchantment—the religious overlay reflects only the fact of the experienced callings to which one's moral agency responds; and we cannot simply excise those facts on the grounds that Occam's razor requires a more minimal description of the callings. To do so would be to deny the facts, the facts *as taken in from within someone's first-person point of view of agency and to which that agency responds.* Occam's razor is not supposed to shave off facts, only gratuitous ontology.

But now: this means that we must go back to the insight about how intention crowds out prediction and notice one of its large implications. It implies a disjointing failure of fit between first-personal facts and facts perceived from a detached third-person point of view, thereby putting into question *all* of the widely held forms of dependence that are proposed between evaluative facts and the facts of nature as studied by the natural sciences—nomological corelation of one with another, contingent identity of one with the other . . . Indeed, it follows from the insight that even the weakest form of dependence sometimes proposed, called "supervenience," is questionable. Supervenience is the thesis that two worlds in which there are identical material facts must both also contain identical evaluative facts; otherwise evaluative facts would have a quite arbitrary status. To almost all philosophers I know, including John McDowell, whom I invoked earlier with admiration, this sort of dependency relations seems harmless, indeed sensibly avowed. I want to be careful to say, as I think Taylor would too, that in questioning the dependency, one is not *disavowing* or *denying* something like supervenience. If, as I have argued, value is always given to our first-person point of view in the apprehension of the world, to assert *or* deny the thesis of supervenience would be to pretend that we can meaningfully assess the claim that facts given in a first-person point of view are in some at least globally systematic way dependent on facts given in a point of view that *is not visible* when one is in the first-person point of view. So it is not that I am denying supervenience. It is not deniable, any more than it is assertable. An analogy may be useful here, up to a point. Consider Wittgenstein's familiar duck-rabbit image. It sets us up for perspectival defections from which we may perceive a duck or a rabbit in turn, but not both at once. As with intention and prediction, which is to say, as with the first-person and third-person point of view, the duck perception crowds out the rabbit perception. In each case, therefore, the claim that facts given in the one perspective should be systematically dependent on facts given in the other is not something to affirm or deny. It is not an assessable claim. True, in the Wittgenstein example, *both* duck facts *and* rabbit facts are dependent (supervenient) on certain *other* sorts of facts—the lines on the page that contains the image of the duck-rabbit. But that is what takes us beyond the limited analogy I am drawing with Wittgenstein, because that is just the element *missing* in the contrast between the first- and third-person point of view—there is simply no richer perspective than the first- and third-person point of view to which one can go; one is always either in one or the other. If one is in neither, one is likely to be asleep, not in some elevated, richer cognitive state that subsumes both.

Nothing in what I have said regarding this failure of fit between two points of view requires one to say that the agential, first-person point of view cannot make a causal difference to what happens in the material world, including our own bodies. The idea is not to claim a dualism of *substance,* since bodies and the world itself, as I said, are shot through with value, so there is nothing Cartesian about the failure of fit between the two points of view.[9] When I switch from seeing someone with very low caloric count to seeing him as being in need, I have switched from seeing him from a detached third-person point of view to seeing him from a first-person point of view, calling on my moral engagement and agency. When I see a glass of water as an op-

9 For a more detailed discussion of these issues, see chap. 5 of my *Self-Knowledge and Resentment* (Cambridge, Mass.: Harvard University Press, 2006). For McDowell's resistance to the idea that supervenience is not an assessable doctrine because it is neither assertable nor deniable, see John McDowell, "Reply to Bilgrami," in *McDowell and His Critics,* ed. Cynthia McDonald and Graeme McDonald (Oxford: Blackwell, 2007).

portunity to quench my thirst, I am seeing something *material*—but from a first-person point of view, so it is not brutishly or merely material. But it is material. It is not in the realm of some other, ethereal Cartesian substance. That is one kind of relations between the world and us, from the world to our first-personal agency. That happens in *perception* of value. But when a perceived value engages us and prompts our agency to *action*, the relations go the other way too, from our first-personal agency to the difference our action makes in the material world. What is true is that though our agency in this way uncontroversially makes a causal difference to the world around us, it does not make that difference by *causing* things *in the sense of "causality" that is subsumed under natural scientific laws*, since those causes fall within the purview of a *third*-person understanding. In a real sense, then, there is a deep ambiguity in the notion of "cause" itself, even if there is no dualism of substance; but Taylor implies this in his pioneering early work on the explanation of human action.

I have strayed into large and abstract questions that are implied by the modesty of my claims to secular forms of enchantment that fall short of Taylor's ideals. That modesty consisted in saying that to embrace, as I do, only one half of the ambiguous notion of "transcendence" (and enchantment) is not by any means to have shown that Taylor's more religiously formulated other half of that ambiguous notion is gratuitous or unscientific. These abstract points about first- and third-personal points of view are meant to make clear that what is needed in order to be able to say that there is nothing unscientific entailed by his more religious formulations of transcendence is to see them as not positing anything that addresses scientific questions. In the past (in Kierkegaard, for instance), the idea that one could avoid addressing scientific questions by one's religious beliefs was asserted in the claim that religion was a matter of faith rather than of evidence. But that response is too underdescribed, too indifferent to the variety of things that Taylor has outlined in the ethical constructions of secularity since early modernity that enchantment, in either my more minimal or Taylor's richer, more religious sense of that ambiguous term, seeks to repudiate. By contrast, the abstract points I have been making are meant to show that the religiously formulated notion of transcendence can avoid the charge of positing something unscientific because, properly understood, it need not posit anything that figures at all in the facts traversed within the boundaries of a detached, third-personal understanding of the world. And I am claiming that this can only be shown, if one denied any intelligibility to the idea that the first-personal facts from within which such transcendence might be given to some, stand in some systematic dependence, on the facts that go into a detached, impersonal, third-personal understanding of the world. And because there is no intelligibility to the idea of such systematic dependency relation, my granting that we should be open to the religiously richer transcendental facts does not mean that I am declaring myself to be something less than an atheist (an agnostic, say) if my own first-personal point of view apprehends no such "transcendental" callings in Taylor's sense of that term. Agnosticism is a thesis about how experience *qua* evidence underdetermines the existence or nonexistence of transcendental phenomena, in Taylor's sense. But questions about evidence are questions within a detached third-personal understanding of the world that I am discounting as irrelevant.

So much for how to characterize and *not* to characterize such *differences* as there might be in the ways that Taylor and I have responded to the disenchantment of the world. What is *common* to his richer and my more minimal notion of "transcendence" is that in stressing a responsiveness of human agency to external callings of one kind or another, they propose a notion of a life of harmony between the experience of agency and the world in which one lives—*merely lives,* not masters or conquers—and thereby flourishes at the cost of becoming merely a passive receptacle of desires and their fulfillment, and at the cost therefore of the perpetual possibility of alienation. In an argument that I gave earlier in this chapter, invoking a remark of Gareth Evans's, I insisted that this amounts to saying something as basic and deep as the following: our responsiveness to *external* callings of one kind or another makes possible what it is to be an agent at all and therefore makes possible the most abstract condition for living an unalienated life. The abstraction with which I presented my argument makes this point seem more remote than it is. Its exemplifications are in fact concrete, quotidian, and ubiquitous.

The abstractly made argument spelled out the implications of the idea that we may perceive the world itself as containing not just properties to be studied from a third-personal, detached explanatory perspective on it, but values that we perceive from the first-person point of view. The chief implication was that when we perceive the world in this latter way, *in doing so* we also experience *ourselves* as agents—that is, experience ourselves as *subjects* and not as objects who possess desires observed from the outside with detachment. So in the very moment and act of perceiving values *without*, we also perceive ourselves *within*, as subjects rather than as objects. The experience of value without and agency within are not two different and independent experiences. This happens at every turn in everyday life. So, for instance, a glass of water perceived by one when one is thirsty is something quite other than what it is taken to be when observed from a detached third-person point of view. It is an opportunity to quench our thirst, and no natural science studies such things as opportunities. We may, of course, from the detached third-person point of view, perceive the water as H_2O, but when we perceive it from the first-person point of view as an opportunity to quench our thirst, chemistry is not to the point.[10] And the point I am now making is that when, from this first-person point of view, we perceive these opportunities *in the world*, we experience *ourselves* in these perceptions as agents, as subjects with a capacity to act on the world and satisfy our desires, our thirst. So also we may see a certain population from the detached, third-person point of view as having a certain average daily caloric count, but we may also see them from another perspective, which engages our practical agency, and describe the very same people as having needs to which our agency responds in one way or another—by sending funds, by joining political movements to improve the conditions of the poor, and so on. In other words, in *perceiving the world* not just in terms of *populations* and *caloric counts* but in terms of *people* and their *needs*, we experience *ourselves* as agents, experience ourselves *as generous or compassionate*. Perception of the external and experience of our own subjectivity therefore go hand in hand in what Taylor calls the nonbuffered self, who is responding to a world enchanted with value elements (that is, a

---

10 In my essay "The Broader Significance of Anti-Naturalism," in *Naturalism and Normativity*, ed. Mario De Caro and David Macarthur (New York: Columbia University Press, 2009), I show how one cannot stop at saying that opportunities inhabit the world but must go on to add that values inhabit it. If one stopped with opportunities, one would get a scientistic version of the social sciences, in which the world contains things (opportunities) which are desire-satisfying properties we apprehend, but there is no more to value than a sophistication of the notion of human desire and moral sentiments. On this picture of value, the world itself does not contain any values or desir*abilities*. Such a picture is merely an extension of scientism to the social sciences. Because the world contains such things as opportunities, it cannot be comprehensively explained by the *natural* sciences, but the social sciences, conceived of in this scientistic way, would account for it. Nothing short of values suffusing the world counters scientistic naturalism.

world described in value terms rather than in terms such as "population," "caloric counts," etc.).

This twin and simultaneous way of experiencing the world and ourselves is what gives substantial meaning to the cliché that to be unalienated is to be *at home in the world*. It is the first and the most abstract metaphysical condition for the possibility of an unalienated life. Marx, especially in his early writing, made central to his doctrine such an idea of the unalienated life, and when he did so, he formulated other, more sophisticated conditions for it. But without this first and most abstract condition in place, those other, further conditions cannot even be so much as formulated. And since this initial and more basic condition essentially involves a certain experiential subjectivity, his term "materialism" cannot quite capture the significance of what he was after when he said that it is social, or, more broadly, *externally* constituted experiences of one's *self* and one's *agency*, such as these, that make for an unalienated life. The terms and the examples with which I have formulated the thought here are too individualistic to fully capture what he was after. It has to be writ large on a social canvas before we can view the deepest philosophical gains that are aspired to in notions of enchantment. Some of that larger canvas is superbly traversed in *A Secular Age,* as is the whole intellectual history—what I called the "genealogical diagnosis"—of the religious and social changes by which we philosophized our way out of the conditions that would make possible such an aspiration of an unalienated life.

7

This Detail, This History:
Charles Taylor's Romanticism

COLIN JAGER

Poetry is the breath and finer spirit of all knowledge.

—William Wordsworth

The poems are finding words for us.

—Charles Taylor

One notable feature of the current debate about secularism is the manner in which something called "Romanticism" circulates within it.[1] As Mark Lilla tells it in *The Stillborn God*, at the center of our current predicament is Romanticism's problematic reaction to the Hobbesian/Enlightenment separation of religion and politics. In Lilla's story, the "children of Hobbes" have been battling it out with the "children of Rousseau," and Rous-

1 The epigraphs are from William Wordsworth, "Preface to *Lyrical Ballads*" [1802], in *William Wordsworth: The Major Works*, ed. Stephen Gill (Oxford: Oxford University Press, 1984), 606; and *SA*, 353. I am grateful to Craig Calhoun, Akeel Bilgrami, William Connolly, and John Milbank for comments on the version of this paper presented at the "Varieties of Secularism" gathering at Yale University.

seau's admirable but finally naive and weak legacy has inspired the counterdevelopment of modern political theologies: nationalism, communism, facism, fundamentalism. Lilla wants to call us away from this Romantic tradition and back to a Hobbesian/Enlightenment secularism less sanguine regarding human possibility. "If our experiment is to work," he writes in the book's final sentence, "we must rely on our own lucidity."[2]

While Lilla hesitates between blaming Romanticism for political theology and simply claiming that Romanticism cannot handle the messianic passions that such theologies unleash, Ayaan Hirsi Ali has no such reservations. In an essay in the *New York Times Book Review*, Hirsi Ali indicts Islamic fundamentalism in passing but saves her real critique for the "enemies of reason within the West: religion and the Romantic movement." On her reading, Romanticism encourages us not to fight the battle of ideas: "Moral and cultural relativism (and their popular manifestation, multiculturalism) are the hallmarks of the Romantics. . . . Thus, it is not reason that accommodates and encourages the persistent segregation and tribalism of immigrant Muslim populations in the West. It is Romanticism."[3] Apparently there are lots of fundamentalists ready to shake off their tribal identities and join us on the path of individualism and enlightenment, but we can't see this because we've all been reading too much Wordsworth and Hölderlin.

This is by some measure a less subtle analysis than Lilla's, but its picture of Romanticism is very similar. For both Lilla and Hirsi Ali, Romanticism represents a failure of nerve, an inability to follow through on enlightenment, reason, and lucidity. By the same token, it is too much like "religion." In fact, Romanticism is doubly pernicious, for historically it helped to invent the very movements that it is now (in the form of "relativism and multiculturalism") apologizing for.

In this chapter I claim Charles Taylor as a Romantic thinker.[4] In a general way, this is not a surprising claim. In many of his books, including *A Secu-*

2 Mark Lilla, *The Stillborn God: Religion, Politics, and the Modern West* (New York: Knopf, 2007), 309.

3 Ayaan Hirsi Ali, "Blind Faiths," review of Lee Harris, *The Suicide of Reason: Radical Islam's Threat to the West, New York Times Book Review,* January 6, 2008, 14–15.

4 "Romanticism" is a notoriously slippery notion; what I mean by it is fairly close to what Taylor means by the "expressivist turn." However, I wish here to distinguish between two common readings of romanticism. In one, romanticism seeks to undo the enlightenment in the name of a nostalgic desire for the past; in the other, romanticism is understood as a "critique of critique"—that is, as dedi-

lar Age, Taylor puts considerable emphasis on what he calls the "expressivist turn," a movement of the late eighteenth and early nineteenth centuries that encompasses the Romantic period. And he is an authority on Hegel, among other things. So to say that Taylor is influenced by Romanticism seems unobjectionable.

But my claim is that romanticism runs deeper in Taylor, and that it shapes and colors the picture of secularity drawn in *A Secular Age.* (From here on I will refer to "romanticism" with a small *r,* in order to distinguish between a big-R "movement" and a small-*r* attitude or disposition that is more widely distributed.) To get at Taylor's romanticism, I will propose a reading of *A Secular Age* inspired by the thought that the book speaks in more than one voice. In effect, this treats the book as if it were a literary text—a move itself licensed by the fact that a recognizably modern notion of literariness, as something simultaneously distinct from Christianity and yet remarkably proximate to it, emerges for the first time during the Romantic era. Taylor takes such "literariness" for granted but doesn't analyze it in the book, and in my reading, this aspect of romanticism's genealogy contributes to the ambivalence of Taylor's engagement with secularism.

Taylor's romanticism is not the Romanticism indicted by Lilla and Hirsi Ali. At least, not always. For them, a simplistic opposition between Enlightenment and Romanticism does a great deal of heavy lifting. Some of the weaker moments in *A Secular Age* are the moments when Taylor appears to be telling a similar story, largely derived, in his case, from treatments of literary romanticism prevalent in the 1960s and 1970s. Here I want to criticize Taylor for those moments when he tells an "Enlightenment versus Romanticism" story, for that story not only betrays his best insights but also helps to institutionalize a kind of secularism he would do well to question. But I also want to uncover a different, rather more shadowy romanticism in Taylor's account, one that, far from cementing the "Enlightenment versus Romanticism" opposi-

---

cated to asking how the enlightenment's critical project might be carried forward differently. Whether defined historically or conceptually, romanticism of course contains both movements. In this chapter I am interested in the second, in a romanticism in dialectical conversation with an enlightenment that is its condition of possibility. If we understand romanticism in this way, then we cannot conceive of it as something that merely arises chronologically after the Enlightenment. Later I criticize Taylor's idea that the "immanent counter-Enlightenment" arises only after the Enlightenment. I'll be proposing a different kind of historical thinking, one less tied to sequential chronology—one that I will argue is actually closer to what Taylor wants, despite what he sometimes writes.

tion, in fact elucidates literary romanticism's ability to trouble and frustrate the kind of thinking that gives rise to such oppositions in the first place.

My aim, then, is threefold: first, to explain why Taylor's book takes the form that it does; second, to illuminate an influential, romantic history of the relationship between the secular and the literary; and finally to outline an alternative to that history that is also rooted in romanticism.

Disenchantment and Reflexivity

One important strand of Taylor's argument involves the relationship between disenchantment and what he calls the "buffered self." In the enchanted world of premodernity, human beings thought of themselves as "open and porous and vulnerable to a world of spirits and powers" (*SA*, 38). There was a continuity between the mundane world and the spirit world; the two impinged on each other, intersected in numerous ways. And thus, in that world, you couldn't just rely on yourself, your own thoughts or powers, to keep darkness and evil at bay. You depended on, you *needed,* to line yourself up with a higher power—not the Christian God, necessarily, but some power capable of securing you. But now, in the disenchanted world, we don't think in such terms. We draw the boundaries between ourselves and everything else in a very different way. Thus the disenchanted world is "a world in which the only locus of thoughts, feelings, spiritual élan is what we call minds; the only minds in the cosmos are those of humans; and minds are bounded, so that these thoughts, feelings, etc. are situated 'inside' them. This space within is constituted by the possibility of introspective self-awareness. . . . The 'inward' in this sense is constituted by what I have called 'radical reflexivity'" (30). Taylor's reference here is to a moment in *Sources of the Self* where he distinguishes between reflexivity and "radical reflexivity." While simple reflexivity involves a focus on the self, in the stance of radical reflexivity we adopt a first-person view of the world, becoming "aware of our own awareness." Our own experience becomes the object of our attention: there is "something that it is like to be an experiencing agent," as Taylor puts it (*SS*, 130). In *Sources of the Self,* Augustine is a principal source of the turn toward radical reflexivity; in *A Secular Age,* though, Taylor argues that this turn is not generalized until the early modern period, and he links radical reflexivity much more explicitly to the disenchantment that is the chief background condition of secularity. Radical reflexivity characterizes what Taylor calls the phenomenology of the secular. It gives to modern religiosity a distinct feel. All of us—religious and irreligious alike—live in the disenchanted world, live with the buffered self. In this sense, secularity is simply a condition of life as we know it.

Habermas and Reflexivity

Contrast Taylor's meditations on reflexivity and religious subjectivity to those of Jürgen Habermas. In an essay entitled "Religion in the Public Sphere," Habermas too has recourse to the concept of reflexivity in order to explain what it means to be religious today. He claims that there has been a "change in religious consciousness" since the advent of modernity, driven by pluralism, modern science, and the spread of "profane morality," and with this Taylor would surely agree.[5] Yet there is a normative difference between their accounts that will help us see why Taylor's book takes the form that it does.

To begin with, Habermas describes the tensions between religion and modernity as epistemological challenges *for* religion. Religious citizens, he writes, must "develop an epistemic attitude toward other religions and world views," "develop an epistemic stance toward the independence of secular from sacred knowledge," and "develop an epistemic stance toward the priority that secular reasons enjoy in the political arena."[6] This suggests that Habermas understands religious adherence as a matter of being convinced that certain beliefs are worth holding even within the context of the various challenges to such beliefs posed by modernity.[7] Once religion has been "epistemologized" in this manner, the naturalness of religious reflexivity can be invoked without argument: "Every [religious] citizen must know and accept

5 Jürgen Habermas, "Religion in the Public Sphere," *European Journal of Philosophy* 14, 1 (2006): 1–25.

6 Ibid., 14.

7 This presupposition puts Habermas at odds with some of the more powerful analyses of secularism offered in recent years, which despite their variety find common ground in a shared commitment to a historical understanding of secularism and its relationship to religion. See, as representative examples, Peter Harrison, *"Religion" and the Religions in the English Enlightenment* (Cambridge: Cambridge University Press, 1990); William Connolly, *Why I Am Not a Secularist* (Minneapolis: University of Minnesota Press, 1999); Talal Asad, *Formations of the Secular: Christianity, Islam, Modernity* (Stanford: Stanford University Press, 2003); John Milbank, *Theology and Social Theory: Beyond Secular Reason,* 2nd ed. (Oxford: Blackwell, 2006).

that only secular reasons count beyond the institutional threshold that divides the informal public sphere from parliaments, courts, ministries and administrations. But all that is required here is the epistemic ability to consider one's own faith reflexively from the outside and to relate it to secular views."[8]

The casualness of that last sentence ("*all that is required* is the epistemic ability to consider one's own faith reflexively") springs from the manner in which Habermas moves silently from a historical observation to a normative claim. It may in fact be the case that we are all reflexive about our beliefs, whether we like it or not, but it does not *necessarily* follow that this is the inevitable state of affairs. Or, rather, it only follows if we think that the task at hand is the strictly analytical one of sorting out the relevant confusions, difficulties, and tensions entailed by the relationship between "religion" and the "public sphere," and that thought is in turn based on a tendency to treat historically contingent definitions of religion (as centered on belief and epistemology) as the truth of "religion" per se. Once we set that supposition aside, other sorts of questions suddenly emerge. How, for example, did the relevant question come to be that of the relationship between religion and the public sphere? Why do we find ourselves thinking in *these* terms and not some others? *Do* we all think in these terms? Are there alternatives? Do they matter?

Such questions, which tend toward the historical and genealogical, are barred from Habermas's analytic methodology. This is certainly not to dismiss his formulation. Indeed, it is worth remembering how much he thinks he is giving up when he turns his attention to the cognitive burdens faced by religious persons within the context of modernity.[9] It is, however, to observe that Habermas—together with most analysts and commentators, academic and otherwise—takes as his starting point the very things that Taylor is trying to historicize in his book. Why, then, does Taylor think it is so important to historicize them?

A Story to Tell

"The change I want to define and trace," writes Taylor, "is one which takes us from a society in which it was virtually impossible not to believe in God to

---

8 Habermas, "Religion in the Public Sphere," 9–10.

9 A point made by Craig Calhoun during a discussion of this essay at the "Varieties of Secularism" colloquium sponsored by the SSRC, May 12, 2007, New York, N.Y.

one in which faith, even for the staunchest believer, is one human possibility among others" (*SA*, 3). How does one tell a story so big and complex, so multifaceted, in such constant motion? Here is one answer:

> It is a crucial fact of our present spiritual predicament that it is historical; that is, our understanding of ourselves and where we stand is partly defined by our sense of having come to where we are, of having overcome a previous condition. . . . In other words, our sense of where we are is crucially defined in part by a story of how we got there. . . . Our past is sedimented in our present, and we are doomed to misidentify ourselves, so long as we can't do justice to where we come from. This is why the narrative is not an optional extra, and why I believe I have a story to tell here. (29)

This passage comes quite early in Taylor's book, while he is still assembling the pieces of the "story" that he will tell over its almost 900 pages. The passage is perhaps most easily read as a defense of the sheer length of the book. Stories, at least good stories, are full of details that demand time and space in a narrative. They are worth it, though, because they make narratives more like real life: good stories are thick and messy rather than thin and sterile. They take surprising twists and turns, double back on themselves, try things out from another angle.

What is the other option? According to Taylor, it is bare conceptual analysis: "But why tell a story? Why not just extract the analytic contrast, state what things were like then, and how they are now, and let the linking narrative go? Who needs all this detail, this history?" (*SA*, 28). Taylor's answer is that "this detail, this history" is not an optional extra, not just a set of examples or illustrations. Rather, details are where we live, because details are where history lives, and we are historical creatures. The way we know this is that we tell stories to ourselves about who we are and how we got here.[10] To focus strictly on content and ignore how that content is embedded would miss the heart of the matter.

---

10 Of course, Taylor is not *only* telling historical stories. As he notes shortly, "the whole discussion has to tack back and forth between the analytical and the historical" (29). Yet on the methodological level the book's emphasis clearly falls on the latter.

Many years ago the literary critic Cleanth Brooks called this "the heresy of paraphrase."[11] The heresy here is against literary language itself, which cannot be summarized but must be experienced. This has been an article of faith for literary critics of all stripes and persuasions, and it is an article of faith for Taylor as well. Put differently, this is the difference between saying, with Habermas, that "all that is required" is that the faithful consider their faith reflexively, and trying, with Taylor, to capture *what it feels like* to adopt that reflexive posture. Where Habermas aligns reflexivity with a perspective "from the outside," Taylor describes *radical* reflexivity as the moment when *my own* experience becomes my object—in this case, my experience of the reflexivity that characterizes modern life. Radical reflexivity in the context of the secular age is a fraught business, then, because it seems to demand not simply that one adopt a third-person perspective on one's own commitments (which might be hard enough) but that one actually work the movement between first- and third-person perspectives into one's understanding of what the first person entails. My experience may be of the world as it is *for me,* but part and parcel of that experience is my acknowledgment that the world as it is for me is not the world as it is for other people.

If this is right, then Taylor's question—namely, "What does secularity feel like from the inside?"—is the sort of question that can be asked only *after* a certain kind of secular age, associated with Enlightenment reflexivity vis-à-vis belief, has run its course. The characteristic questions of that age have to be understood as important but limited, and one has to begin casting around for more historically generous ways to describe the distinct *feel* of the age. So Taylor's method is "literary" not simply because it is committed to both the first and the third person, but because of how it seeks to convey the passage of time. When Taylor says he has a story to tell, he means that his account must be undergone, not simply paraphrased or glossed.

Here we are already partway to understanding the ambivalence of *A Secular Age.* Consider again the contrast with Habermas. Both men put reflexivity at the center of their account, but Habermas is comfortable with the third person; he never allows reflexivity to become *radical* reflexivity. A good deal of the tonal ambivalence in *A Secular Age* springs from Taylor's methodologi-

---

11 Cleanth Brooks, *The Well-Wrought Urn: Studies in the Structure of Poetry* (New York: Harcourt Brace, 1947).

cal commitment to radical reflexivity and consequently to phenomenological, first-person description. But what do those methods, influentially laid out
in *Sources of the Self* and put to use so evocatively in *A Secular Age,* commit him
to? While the Taylor of *Sources of the Self* may defend the legitimacy of the
modern age, the Taylor of *A Secular Age* keeps his distance. He is positioned
as it were *after* reflexivity, which is to say after enlightenment, which is to say
within romanticism.

The Expressivist Turn

The background condition for the idea of "story" as embedded content is
what Taylor calls "the expressivist turn," a broad intellectual movement that
begins with such eighteenth-century figures as Rousseau and Herder, passes
through the various romanticisms, and culminates with Hegel. It is not much
of an exaggeration to say that most of Taylor's career has been an attempt to
measure the impact of this "turn." In books large and small, he has returned
again and again to the tension between universalism and historicism, between mimetic and expressivist models of selfhood, between "tolerance" and
"recognition"—in short, between the Enlightenment and what came after it.
Putting it so schematically, of course, doesn't do justice to the nuances of
Taylor's narration. Yet it remains the case that the thinkers and problems of
the expressivist turn do a particular and unique kind of intellectual work in
his texts. Herder, in particular, offers a sophisticated and influential version of
the dominant themes of the historical "story" that Taylor wants to tell in *A
Secular Age:* an intimate, first-person theory of historical method, and a notion of literary language as something unique and unparaphrasable.[12]

Herder's crucial innovation was the link between language and the human as such. If I express my anger, it could mean just that the anger was inside me and that I "express" it by yelling; that would be an "Enlightenment"
or mimetic theory, in which the thing is thought to exist before its expression.
But in the stronger sense of expression that Taylor draws from Herder, my
yelling is a *part* of my anger—in some way it actually brings that anger into
being. As Taylor puts it in *Sources of the Self,* "[a] human life is seen as mani-

---

12 *Herder: Philosophical Writings,* trans. and ed. Michael N. Forster (Cambridge: Cambridge University Press, 2002).

festing a potential which is also being shaped by this manifestation; it is not just a matter of copying an external model or carrying out an already determinate formulation" (375). As Herder suggests in the *Treatise on the Origin of Language* (1772), this means that the "content" of an utterance cannot be understood apart from its context, form, and situation.

Famously, Herder extends this notion from individuals to groups, and to nations.[13] In each case, there is no external or "objective" model against which either individual or group can be evaluated; rather, each is to be evaluated according to its own terms: "Moreover, their relationships are so national, so much according to the peculiar manner of thinking and seeing of that people, of that inventor, in that land, in that time, in those circumstances, that they are infinitely difficult for a Northerner and Westerner to get right, and must suffer infinitely in long, cold, paraphrases."[14] To what kind of historical method might the northerner and westerner appeal in order to avoid such cold paraphrases? This is the problem that Taylor confronts most explicitly in his discussion of the "nova effect": the proliferating spiritual options that characterize the secular age and the lack of an objective hierarchy against which to adjudicate them. Comprehending that nova will take a new kind of historical methodology, which Herder formulates as *Einfühlung,* or "feeling one's way in": "*The whole nature* of the soul, which *rules* through everything, which *models* all other inclinations and forces of the soul *in accordance with itself,* and in addition *colors* even the most indifferent actions—in order to share in feeling this . . . go into the age, into the clime, the whole history, feel yourself into everything."[15] As an alternative to the magisterial survey of Enlightenment historiography, the historian must "go into" the particular age in question—but if such empathy isn't just to cancel difference and thus return us to enlightenment universalism, the gulf between now and then, between us and them, has to be worked formally into the interpretive process itself, so that the act of interpretive understanding is always also marked by the fact of

13 His thought is thus the origin of modern notions of both culture and nation, as well as of contemporary multiculturalism. In view of some of the criticisms Herder has received on this score, it is important to distinguish his picture of cultural difference from the racist implications of Enlightenment-era theories that postulated a geographic determinism. Indeed, Herder saved some of his bitterest irony for this view (which he associated with Voltaire, among others).

14 *Treatise on the Origin of Language* (1772), in *Herder: Philosophical Writings,* 114.

15 *This Too a Philosophy of History for the Formation of Humanity* (1774), in *Herder: Philosophical Writings,* 292.

cultural and historical difference. We need, in other words, a radically reflex-ive method that allows us to recognize our ancestors *as* ancestors and simul-taneously helps us feel their absolute historical distance and difference.

And so, where Habermas refers in passing to what "sociologists have de-scribed [as] 'modernization of religious consciousness,'"[16] Taylor's evocation of the changes in background conditions that have brought about modern reflexivity lends itself to something much more intimate: an attempt to find a way around the "cold paraphrase" and describe what it feels like, in the first person, to live in a secular age. "I want to talk about belief and unbelief, not as rival *theories,* that is, ways that people account for existence, or morality," Taylor writes. "Rather, what I want to do is focus attention on the different kinds of lived experience involved in understanding your life in one way or the other, on *what it's like* to live as a believer or an unbeliever" (*SA,* 4–5; my emphasis).

Einfühlung has its own problems, though—most obviously because if our knowledge and self-understanding are historical, then this must apply to the historical storyteller as well: the storyteller himself must be situated, and un-derstand himself as situated. And this leads to a tension that *A Secular Age* never resolves but rather comes increasingly to exemplify. For at one and the same time, the book can be viewed as too secular *and* as too religious. Too secular, because it is of course radical reflexivity that is the crucial part of the story of secularity that Taylor himself is telling. The experience of the secu-lar age, on his account, *just is* the experience of shifting back and forth be-tween the first and the third person. Simply by virtue of living in the secular age, we find ourselves feeling our way deeply into peoples and places that are not our own; this is "the new context in which all search and questioning about the moral and the spiritual must proceed" (*SA,* 20). From this angle, the experience of reading *A Secular Age* becomes a working-through at the meth-odological level of the secular reflexivity whose historical genesis the book narrates.

At the very same time, however, the book's methodological emphasis on the phenomenological feel of radical reflexivity can be read as a subtle tilting of the playing field in favor of Christianity. For when it comes to his descrip-tion of the phenomenology of the secular, Taylor's emphasis falls most upon

---

16 Habermas, "Religion in the Public Sphere," 13.

those who wish to identify themselves as members of a religious tradition. In other words, the phenomenology in which Taylor is most interested is the phenomenology of a Christian in a secular age—the person who must live with the knowledge that his or her faith is an option. This comes directly from Taylor's interest in the first-person perspective and the way he narrates its historical genesis as part of the expressivist turn. For if the only way to do history is to tell a story, and the only way to tell a story is to feel one's way in, then from a certain perspective the only story that can be told is one's own story—but if one tells it right, it will also be the story of one's difference from every historical and cultural other, and so it is their story too.[17] From this angle, the book seems to argue that Christianity is the best way to grasp the secular. To be sure, this is partly a historical thesis, for the official argument of the book is that Christianity "caused" the secular (in a very complicated and paradoxical way). But it is more than just a historical thesis: unofficially, as it were, Taylor seems to argue for the existential validity of Christianity as the best response to the secular age.

This tension between the book's secularity and its Christianity remains unresolved. Indeed, the latter sections of *A Secular Age* are best read as a series of experiments in how one might best express, rather than resolve, this tension. And in this search, literature begins to do a considerable amount of work.

Literature

In *Sources of the Self,* Taylor describes and defends an "affirmation of ordinary life" as fundamental to modern selfhood. In *A Secular Age* he extends this theme, noting that the affirmation of ordinary life "put the center of gravity of goodness in ordinary living, production and the family. It belongs to this spiritual outlook that our first concern ought to be to increase life, relieve suffering, foster prosperity" (370). He traces the sources of this affirmation back to a variety of impulses, from the late medieval nominalist revolution to the Reformation to the humanist critique of religion that carried Western cul-

17 For versions of the argument that one cannot legitimately route multicultural evenhandedness through a Christian phenomenology, see Jonathan Sheehan, "Framing the Middle," and Stathis Gourgouris, "A Case of Heteronomous Thinking," both at *The Immanent Frame:* www.ssrc.org/blogs/immanent_frame/category/secular_age/.

ture across the threshold into a truly immanent frame. On Taylor's telling, such affirmation of ordinary life provokes a counter-Enlightenment response that seeks to return to traditional hierarchies, but it also inspires what Taylor calls an "immanent counter-Enlightenment" that revolts against a secular religion of life but remains on a worldly plane. The immanent counter-Enlightenment has two sources: first, a "continuing spiritual concern with the transcendent, which could never accept that flourishing human life was all there is, and bridled at the reduction" (371–372); and second, an aristocratic ethos, which "protested against the leveling effects of the culture of equality and benevolence" (372). Thus by the nineteenth century we have two different strands of the immanent counter-Enlightenment, one of which is Romantic, the other Nietzschean. Such reactions and counterreactions are what Taylor means when he talks about a "nova effect."

As Taylor tracks the multiplying possibilities of the nova in the second half of his book, it becomes clear that the Nietzschean strand (which he links to such latter-day figures as Bataille, Foucault, and Derrida) will not be asked to do much work; it seems to interest him mostly as a symptom of the nova. By contrast, it is clear that Taylor is taken with the Romantic strand—which, he writes, is "linked with a primacy of the aesthetic. Even where it rejects the category . . . it remains centrally concerned with art, and especially modern, post-Romantic art. Its big battalions within the modern academy are found in literature departments" (372). Whether or not this is empirically accurate,[18] it highlights the increasing weight that literature will bear in Taylor's account. This includes not just literary examples themselves (though from Wordsworth to Mrs. Humphry Ward to Hopkins, there are plenty of those), but also ways of putting things that can be traced back to literary forms of expression (Taylor's archetypal example of fullness, for example, taken from Bede Griffiths, is unimaginable without Wordsworth's "spots of time") and finally theories of literature, from Schiller's "play" to Shelley's "subtler lan-

18 It would take an entire book to analyze why Taylor perceives literature departments as the primary carriers of such values as phenomenology, *Einfühlung*, historicism, and storytelling. Perhaps it will suffice to say for the moment that his appeal is made possible by the historical transformations that he is analyzing. That is, literature comes to be understood as a distinctive area of human endeavor during the period that Taylor calls the expressivist turn. Useful—though somewhat hostile—accounts of this transformation are to be found in Clifford Siskin, *The Work of Writing: Literature and Social Change in Britain, 1700–1830* (Baltimore: Johns Hopkins University Press, 1998), and John Guillory, *Cultural Capital: The Problem of Literary Canon Formation* (Chicago: University of Chicago Press, 1993).

guage." In sum, "the literary," in all its forms, emerges in the latter half of *A Secular Age* as a privileged window—perhaps *the* privileged window—into the inner workings of the varieties of secularism.

Most importantly for my argument here, the sense of difference that characterizes this nineteenth-century nova becomes lodged in the literary. Recall Herder's worry that comparing disparate ways of life commits us to "cold paraphrase." What drops out of a paraphrase, of course, is the poetry. Here the nation and its self-realization in the form of its characteristic linguistic expression comes under the wider banner of an emergent ideal of literature that simultaneously expresses the unique characteristics of a people and offers a "way in" to those characteristics for those who are outside. We can feel what it is like to be a member of a particular culture or nation if we can get past paraphrase to poetry.

In *The Spirit of Hebrew Poetry* (1782), Herder makes this case most dramatically. Explictly indebted to the Englishman Robert Lowth's claim that the Old Testament should be read as sublimely inspired poetry, Herder's text also criticizes Lowth for not taking his ideas far enough.[19] Like an enlightened northern European, Lowth paid too much attention to the letter; a proper understanding of the *spirit* of Hebrew poetry, Herder declared, would allow people to understand "the Hebrews" as if they were Hebrews themselves. Through poetry they could "feel their way in" to the lives of these quintessential *Volk*.[20] In this text literature read just the right away emerges as the primary conduit of the empathetic historical understanding that was Herder's lifelong aim, and the idea of reading the Bible as a literary work powerfully transforms both what counts as "literature" and what counts as "religion."

Famously, Herder called attention to Hebrew's lack of written vowels. In his account, the space between consonants, heard but not seen, becomes a window into the childhood of the human race. In the *Treatise* he refers to this as "writing the inessential and omitting the essential"; the essential song and poetry of the language is contained in the "breath" and "spirit" of the unseen

---

19 See Robert Lowth, *De Sacra Poesi Hebraeorum* (1753), trans. 1787 by G. Gregory as *Lectures on the Sacred Poetry of the Hebrews,* 4th ed. (New York: J. Leavitt, 1829); J. G. Herder, *The Spirit of Hebrew Poetry,* trans. James Marsh (Burlington, Vt.: Edward Smith, 1833).

20 See Maurice Olender, *The Languages of Paradise,* trans. Arthur Goldhammer (New York: Other Press, 2002), 37–39.

vowels.[21] Closer to nature, Hebrew is also closer to divinity: carried by breath and spirit, the vowels become a channel to the mysterious, ineffable manifestation of God. Blessedly caught in a time before abstraction, before scholarly systematization, Hebrew connects the modern reader to effects that cannot be precisely pointed to but only felt and experienced. In trying to describe this effect, Herder turns continually to the language of "breath," "spirit," and "soul." This is the spirit of Hebrew poetry, indeed "the very breath of the soul,"[22] in which the true spirit of a people allows itself to be heard. Poetry is spirit, and spirit is the "way in" to history.

At such moments poetry, scripture, and historical understanding become one.[23] By 1800 Wordsworth is declaring in the "Preface" to *Lyrical Ballads* that "poetry is the breath and finer spirit of all knowledge." (Wordsworth was a close reader of Lowth; he got his Herder indirectly, from Coleridge, via Michaelis and Eichhorn.) If Herder turns scripture into the literature of a specific folk, Wordsworth will make the language of the folk ("the language really used by men," he calls it in the "Preface") into the secret, hidden scripture of humanity itself.

If this gesture has an appeal for Wordsworth and Herder, it also has an appeal for Charles Taylor. And the appeal is once again third-person *and* first-person: the new spiritualization of literature is an example of the expressivist turn, but it is also a "way in" to that turn. In *Sources of the Self,* Taylor refers to several places where the lines between scripture and literature fade: Coleridge's famous definition of imagination from Chapter 13 of the *Biographia Literaria,* Schlegel's and Coleridge's definitions of the symbol, Schiller's notion of play. Summing up these ideas and developments, Taylor follows Shelley and calls them "subtler languages," languages that had to be developed poetically over the course of the expressivist turn in order to capture the new sensibility of an age in which the old, objective verities were losing their hold. Taylor gets the idea of the "subtler language" from the literary critic Earl Wasserman; he quotes the following passage from Wasserman's 1968 book of

---

21 Herder, *Treatise on the Origin of Language,* 70.

22 Herder, *The Spirit of Hebrew Poetry,* 35.

23 See Jonathan Sheehan, *The Enlightenment Bible: Translation, Scholarship, Culture* (Princeton: Princeton University Press, 2005). Sheehan's book, especially its sixth chapter, provides a rich historical setting for the changes over the course of the eighteenth century that I am gesturing at all too briefly in my discussion of Herder.

that title: "Until the end of the eighteenth century . . . men accepted . . . the Christian interpretation of history, the sacramentalism of nature, the Great Chain of Being, the analogy of the various planes of creation. . . . By the nineteenth century these world-pictures had passed from consciousness. . . . Now . . . an additional formulative act was required of the poet. . . . Within itself the modern poem must both formulate its cosmic syntax and shape the autonomous poetic reality that the cosmic syntax permits."[24] And here is Taylor's gloss: "The Romantic poet has to articulate an original vision of the cosmos. . . . [Wordsworth and Hölderlin] make us aware of something through nature of which there are as yet no adequate words. The poems themselves are finding the words for us" (SS, 381).

In *A Secular Age*, Taylor quotes this very same passage from Wasserman, and he quotes his own gloss from *Sources of the Self* almost verbatim. But in the later book, the subtler languages emerge in the context of a discussion of "how the development of modern poetics . . . has enabled people to explore . . . meanings with their ontological commitments as it were in suspense" (SA, 351). These languages, Taylor continues, have "opened a space in which people can wander," created a "neutral zone" or "free space" (352) aligned with Schiller's notion of play (358), and in so doing they "offer a place to go for modern unbelief" (356).

What has happened here? Whereas the subtler languages became in *Sources of the Self* a crucial site of the modernity that the book largely defends, in *A Secular Age* Taylor seems to recognize in those languages a sensibility about which he is more ambivalent. In the form of aesthetic "neutrality," or "freedom," romanticism's subtler languages, unhooked from ontological commitments, begin to look a lot like secularism, and the fact that "the poems are finding words for us," as Taylor now phrases it, takes on a darker tone.

Genealogies

Taylor's differently inflected discussion of romantic literature in *A Secular Age* implies a methodological shift from "genetic" to "genealogical" history. The

---

24 Earl Wasserman, *The Subtler Language* (Baltimore: Johns Hopkins University Press, 1968), 10–11.

former method comes once again from Herder—the *Fragments* (1767) this time—who had influentially recommended two principles of interpretation to the historian. First, an action or creation must be seen as the product of a specific time and place; second, we must understand such things from within their own moment and according to their own internal rules. For any reader of Herder, or any student of the expressivist turn in general, these will seem familiar points, and they can certainly be folded back into the kind of phenomenological empathy that Taylor recommends. The method of *Sources of the Self* is genetic insofar as it seeks a historically sensitive explanation of modernity; though it eschews universals, it implicitly functions as a defense of modernity's "affirmation of ordinary life." But genetic history can also be radicalized, so that the historian's empathy is directed not only at understanding how the world was in its own terms, but also at how those terms render other possibilities irrelevant and thereby continue to set the frame for our thinking in the present day. Indeed, the method *was* radicalized in just this way, by Nietzsche and again by Foucault, thinkers today associated with "genealogical history." For them, history is not in the service of present life but in fact serves to put present life—its ways and habits of thought—at risk.

Now it is totally characteristic of Herder to be ambivalent about the implications of his genetic method, for history of the kind he recommends is pulled in two directions: toward a humanism whose apotheosis seems inevitably to be some version of Western (post-) Christian humanism, *and* toward a genealogical critique whose aim is to separate itself from exactly that kind of destiny. I hope it is clear by now that this is precisely the tension that I have been tracking in *A Secular Age*. On the one hand, the dominant strand in this book is the humanist one; on the other, when Taylor revisits his own earlier analysis of the subtler languages, he implicitly suggests something less genetic than genealogical.

The possibility of such a critique is muffled, however, by the way Taylor construes the intellectual terrain. As we've seen, to the modern affirmation of ordinary life—work, family, production, charity—he opposes the varied forces of the immanent counter-Enlightenment: a romantic "concern with the transcendent, which could never accept that flourishing human life was all there is," and a Nietzschean aristocratic contempt for ordinary human flourishing. On my reading, this distinction is the methodological crux of the book. Taylor has never had much use for Nietzschean antihumanism, yet it is precisely that tradition's interest in genealogy that would sharpen his analysis; without it, his sometime impulse to criticize the secular age is deprived of a methodological foundation. By the same token, the romantic humanist strand that Taylor clearly loves, and to which he turns both for examples and for intellectual sustenance, is perhaps less friendly to the book's argument than it may appear, for deprived of any genealogical edge, the romantic critique of enlightened secularity becomes simply a nostalgic desire for something more, some "spirit" of poetry that will open our mundane earthly lives toward the transcendent.

What, then, would a genealogical reading of Taylor's romantic humanism look like? It might begin simply by following the logic of Herder's insistence that cultures and nations are to be evaluated according to their own time and place and by their own lights, and his importation of the spirit of poetry as a magical connector between the interpreter and the nation he would interpret. On the far side of this development, we might note, is a rendering of the spirit of German Protestantism as a universal religion, the true inheritor and developer of a heritage stretching back to the Hebrews—an idea already implicit in Herder and developed fully by those who followed in his wake, from Eichhorn to the Schlegels to, preeminently, Schleiermacher.[25] Yet because Protestant Christianity is thereby transformed into a universal religion, it is also *not really religion* any longer. It is simply, as Herder writes, a *"subtle* spirit, '*a deism of human friendship,'* . . . [a] *philosophy* of *heaven* that, precisely because of its loftiness and its unearthly purity, could embrace the whole earth."[26] The metaphors Herder goes on to use are telling: Christianity is the yeast that mixes with the dough of a particular nation or culture; it is the "subtle vapor" mixed with earthly materials. Or as Wordsworth would put it in a related context, Christian fellow-feeling is the "secret spirit of humanity."

The point to emphasize here is how *secular* these various spiritualizations are. Whatever overt intentions motivated this simultaneous spiritualization and nationalization of scripture, its effect was to replace the Bible as source

25 For Herder, see Olender, *The Languages of Paradise*, 39; for Schleiermacher, see Colin Jager, "After the Secular: The Subject of Romanticism," *Public Culture* 18, 2 (2006): 301–322.

26 Herder, *This Too a Philosophy of History*, 304.

of revelation with the Bible as a repository of "culture" and of poetic "resources."[27] When Schiller's "play" and Coleridge's symbol find their institutional home in departments of national literatures, a hugely influential variety of secularism is institutionalized under the guise of the literary. From this genealogical perspective—which I am arguing is one that from time to time emerges in *A Secular Age* itself, a kind of counterspirit to its dominant spirit—simply taking the methodology of the expressivist turn on board is a secular move, even or perhaps especially when this is done *in the name of respecting religion.*

We are now in a position to understand at a deeper level why *A Secular Age* seems both too Christian and too secular. It is certainly the case that aspects of the book seem biased in favor of Christianity. Taylor's expressivist turn may acknowledge the space of unbelief, the criticism goes, but it functions chiefly as an expression of yearning for some enchanted other world—and therefore implies that unbelief, no matter how poetic, is missing out on something. From the genealogical perspective I have just been outlining, however, some of the very same passages that seem to reflect a normative Christianity might also be understood to reflect a normative *secularity,* insofar as their turn to literature instantiates a particular transformation of scripture and poetry into a spirit whose fulfillment seems always just around the bend. That some readers may find the account too secular and others too Christian, then, is not simply a matter of different readers having different perspectives. It is, rather, a reflection of Christianity's specific relation to secularism *as that relationship is taken up and transformed* by the secret spirit of poetry.

Charles Taylor's Philosophic Song; or, Telling the Story Properly

My argument has been that the romantic method of *A Secular Age* both narrates the arrival of a modern "formation of the secular" and, read properly, provides the tools for its genealogical critique. This becomes clear, I have sug-

---

27 For elaborations of this argument, see Talal Asad's reading of Clifford Geertz in *Genealogies of Religion: Discipline and Reasons of Power in Christianity and Islam* (Baltimore: Johns Hopkins University Press, 1993), 27–54; and Saba Mahmood, "Secularism, Hermeneutics, and Empire: The Politics of Islamic Reformation," *Public Culture* 18, 2 (2006): 323–347. See also Asad's reminder that "if the Bible is read as art . . . that is because a complicated historical development of disciplines and sensibilities has made it possible to do so." *Formations of the Secular,* 9.

gested, if we pay attention to the mutual constitutions and reconstitutions surrounding such terms as "literature," "poetry," and "spirit." If I am right about this, then Taylor's discussions of literature recapitulate the basic tension of the book. Just as *A Secular Age* is both "too secular" and "too Christian," so literature sometimes seems a secular form of *Einfühlung*, sometimes a substitute religion. As Stephen Prickett nicely phrases it, such confusions have left literary critics with an embarrassed sense that "they are somehow still in the salvation business."[28] To be sure, Taylor's book can be read as an oblique acknowledgment of the "salvation business" in which the spirit of poetry trades. But there is another way to read the book, too—at once sterner and more utopian—which draws upon a different romanticism.

Consider Taylor's discussion of disenchantment: "We are widely aware of living in a 'disenchanted' universe; and our use of this word bespeaks our sense that it was once enchanted. More, we are not only aware that it used to be so, but also that it was a struggle and an achievement to get to where we are; and that in some respects this achievement is fragile. We know this because each one of us as we grew up has had to take on the disciplines of disenchantment, and we regularly reproach each other for our failings in this regard" (*SA*, 28–29). At first glace, this account is in real tension with Taylor's professed desire to avoid "subtraction" accounts of modernity. How would we tell a story of disenchantment that is not also a subtraction story? The term itself seems to point precisely in that direction. Taylor's answer to this apparent dilemma is quite clever.

We are aware of living in a disenchanted universe, he writes, because that is one of the stories we like to tell about ourselves, and just because we *do* tell ourselves that story, it describes the truth of our modern condition. Stories, that is, bring a certain state of affairs into existence—they have a "performative" truth. This should not be confused with empirical truth. Consider this version of a disenchantment story: "People once believed in gods and demons, but modern science made that belief unnecessary." Somewhere in the background imaginary of *that* story is the thought that if we had a fancy enough fMRI machine, we could snap a picture of the place in the brain that used to hold the belief in gods and demons but that now acknowledges the

---

28 Stephen Prickett, *Words and The Word: Language, Poetics, and Biblical Interpretation* (Cambridge: Cambridge University Press, 1986), 198.

truth of science. And if we could do that, disenchantment would be an empirical matter: we would know whether the story was true or false. In contrast to this scientistic form of truth, Taylor remains interested in what I just called performative truth: if we tell that story about demons and science to ourselves, then it becomes a part of our self-understanding, and thus becomes true as a description of how we think about ourselves.

Now, it would be possible to describe the difference between enlightenment and romantic historicism in terms of this contrast between empirical truth and performative truth. Hume and the *philosophes* didn't think they were telling stories; they thought they had discovered a basic fact about the way the mind works, and they developed techniques to explain it (the *philosophes* called it "priestcraft," Hume called it the "natural history of religion"— these were the fMRI machines of their day). The picture here is of stripping away illusion to reveal truth.

If, by contrast, we consider disenchantment performatively rather than empirically, we would view the very prevalence of disenchantment stories as offering an important window into a culture's self-understanding. Rather than the cultural universalism presupposed by the fMRI model, such an approach invites us to ask about the kind of work that disenchantment stories do within their "local" cultures. Who tells such stories, and to what ends? Of course, this means we still have to take disenchantment seriously—but it dispenses with the fMRI picture and substitutes a historicist one.

Historicism of this sort always courts conceptual relativism, but Taylor is after something else. "Just because we describe where we are in relating the journey," he writes, "we can misdescribe it grievously by misidentifying the itinerary. That is what the 'subtraction' accounts of modernity have in fact done. To get straight where we are, we have to go back and tell the story properly" (*SA*, 29). To say this is to imagine, at least for a moment, that the situation can be changed, that we can weaken the power of the subtraction story and thereby alter how we understand ourselves, if we change the story *in the right way.*

The question is *how* one goes about changing the story—and it is just here that Taylor falls back on a relatively weak notion of romanticism as an attempt to reintroduce transcendence in the aftermath of the early modern scientific revolution. I call it a "weak notion" because this way of telling the story accepts that the terms of the debate have been set by an early modern consensus that rigorously separated the natural from the supernatural, the immanent from the transcendent, the rational from the irrational, and the scientific from the religious. Yet it is exactly the seeming naturalness of these distinctions that going back and "telling the story properly" would dislodge. Telling the proper story, here, doesn't mean telling a more accurate story; it means finding the essential thing that got lost or sidetracked the first time and highlighting *that,* and thereby telling a different story, with a different ending. This is a more radical rendering of the historicism that characterizes the expressivist turn. And, I'd like to suggest, it's the meaning lurking in the shadows when Taylor writes that we have to go back and get the story right.

Recent revisionist work by Akeel Bilgrami, Michael Saler, and others suggests how we might tell a different story about enchantment. Saler reminds us that modern disenchantment has always been a relatively elite discourse, with limited appeal beyond certain enclaves—there is no reason to conclude that the modern world *is* especially disenchanted, notwithstanding all the voices telling us so. Bilgrami, meanwhile, develops a reading of enchantment as a critique of enlightened modernity that sprung up within modernity itself.[29] Focusing in particular on the development toward the end of the seventeenth century of a resistance to "scientific rationality," he highlights the deists, pantheists, and radical immanentists who dissented from Royal Society orthodoxy. Like Taylor, Bilgrami notes the profound irony that it was largely mainstream Christians who, for good pious reasons, removed magic from the world and installed it in a divine source understood as definitively outside the natural world, thereby stripping the world of meaning and delivering us into a disenchanted modern cosmos. Unlike Taylor, however, he finds resistance to this trend arising from *within* it, rather than retrospectively and in reaction to it. While Taylor interprets deism, for example, as part of the general trend toward disenchantment, Bilgrami understands it as a counternarrative to a developing scientific orthodoxy. The deistic dissenters were every bit as *scientific* as Newton and Boyle; what they objected to was "the official metaphysical picture that was growing around the new science," according to which matter was brute and inert.[30] The attitudes, the habits of mind, the forms of

29 Michael Saler, "Modernity and Enchantment: A Historiographic Review," *American Historical Review* 111, 3 (June 2006): 692–716; Akeel Bilgrami, "Occidentalism, the Very Idea: An Essay on Enlightenment and Enchantment," *Critical Inquiry* 32 (2006): 381–411.

30 Bilgrami, "Occidentalism, the Very Idea," 396.

rationality celebrated by this official metaphysical doctrine have real cultural effect, and the disenchantment that trails behind them can be devastating. On Bilgrami's reading, the anti-Newtonians glimpsed this future—and that makes them, despite their theologically heterodox opinions, better allies for contemporary religious persons than the mainstream Royal Society Christians who sought to preserve Christianity and wound up making it irrelevant.

Bilgrami here models a reading practice that looks simultaneously forward and backward, that recommends we return to an early modern moment in order to see how its dissenters may have anticipated us.[31] Taylor, by contrast, tends to describe intellectual movements sequentially, so that the immanent counter-Enlightenment can appear only *after* and in response to the Enlightenment. "For many people, then as now," he writes, deism "has seemed to be a gratuitous reduction of human scope. There is a long train of thinkers, *from the Romantic period on,* who have reacted against this excision of the heroic dimension from human life" (*SA,* 231; my emphasis). Interestingly, and symptomatically, Taylor's syntax takes a reaction that seems at first to be located in the early modern period itself ("then") and refits it as a reaction of "the Romantic period." Bilgrami, by contrast, thinks that the reaction *is part and parcel* of the early modern period.

This distinction between Bilgrami's method and Taylor's is consequential for the notion of going back and telling the story properly. For on Taylor's own testimony, a great deal rides on what story we go back and tell. It matters whether the counternarrative to our secular age takes shape in the late eighteenth century rather than the late seventeenth century. This is not, or not only, because a lot happened during those one hundred years. More crucially, it is because by missing or downplaying the immanent counter-Enlightenment *at the moment of its inception* in the seventeenth century and only picking it up in its later form, Taylor has in effect preordained that it will appear only as romantic nostalgia or Nietzschean antihumanism. Yet that very distinction, which is so crucial for Taylor's account, is from the perspective of the seventeenth century an artificial one. In the past decade Jonathan

---

31 For a spirited defense of anachronistic romantic history, see Jerome Christensen, *Romanticism at the End of History* (Baltimore: Johns Hopkins University Press, 2000).

Israel has done more than anyone else to excavate a Spinozist/pantheist tradition of the "radical enlightenment" running through the seventeenth and eighteenth centuries.[32] Israel's book allows us to start placing romanticism, and romantic Spinozism in particular, within a wider culture of radical thought stretching from Spinoza and deism through the French Revolution. We might, further, extend that line into a nineteenth-century tradition that includes both Wordsworth *and* Nietzsche (and Blake, Hölderlin, and Bataille)[33]—not, this time, as representatives of alternative "reactions" to the Enlightenment but rather as joint participants in a radical intellectual tradition whose target is the official metaphysics of a mainstream consensus stretching from Locke and Newton forward to the official guardians of order, security, and the market in our own day. This countertradition, in all its variety, is the one especially attuned to the costs—metaphysical, spiritual, psychological—of modernity. It doesn't simply fight disenchantment with reenchantment but diagnoses the felt need for both as a product of specific historical events, circumstances, and decisions *that might have been otherwise.* This gives a different inflection to the command to "go back and tell the story properly." It becomes more radical—and more romantic in the sense I am trying to isolate here.

How would we tell such a story? In *The Prelude,* Wordsworth tells of his wish to write "some philosophic song / Of Truth that cherishes our daily life" (Book 1, 229–230). Perhaps such a "philosophic song" would refuse to distinguish between poetry and philosophy; it is not merely philosophy in verse but a specific kind of thinking that can take place only in poetry. One consequence of disenchantment, that is to say, might be a rigorous distinction between metaphysics and poetry that writes off cultural devastation and economic exploitation as of merely "poetic" interest (to be addressed by the new discourses of sympathy and charity, and also by prisons and madhouses) rather than as part and parcel of the very metaphysics of disenchantment itself. Poetic thinking or "philosophic song" would be a way to resist this development by resisting its motivating distinction.

---

32 Jonathan I. Israel, *Radical Enlightenment: Philosophy and the Making of Modernity, 1650–1750* (Oxford: Oxford University Press, 2001).

33 On Spinoza and Wordsworth, see Marjorie Levinson, "A Motion and a Spirit: Romancing Spinoza," *Studies in Romanticism* 46 (2007): 367–408.

Simon Jarvis, who has recently made a forceful claim for the distinctiveness of just this kind of poetic thinking, notes that Wordsworth was keen to demonstrate the extent to which disenchantment and enchantment remained bound together despite the official metaphysical picture of the early modern period. Idol-breaking, for example, understood in the early modern period as both a scientific and a religious imperative, is bizarrely susceptible to a reversal whereby the idol-breaking activity of reason can itself become an idol and the imperatives of disenchantment can become their own forms of enchantment. In making this case Jarvis turns to a passage in which Robert Boyle speculates on the origin of idolatry: "The looking upon merely corporeal and oftentimes inanimate beings as if they were endowed with life, sense and understanding, and the ascribing to nature and some other beings (whether real or imaginary) things that belong but to God, have been some (if not the chief) of the grand causes of the polytheism and idolatry of the Gentiles."[34] This is a classic example of what Taylor means by disenchantment: by identifying the mistake through which people "ascribe to nature . . . things that belong to God," Boyle strips meaning from the world and lodges it in a God who is safely *out* of the world. On Boyle's reading, idolatry is not only a mistake, it is a specifically *literary* kind of mistake that hinges on misunderstanding the relationship between literal language and figures of speech. It may be fine for poets to look on dead matter "as if" it were alive, but the natural philosopher recognizes such things for the illusions that they are—and may need to smash those illusions in order to keep disenchantment on its proper course.

As Jarvis reads him, Wordsworth's philosophic song offers a strong rebuke to this kind of effort to definitively distinguish between science and poetry, disenchantment and enchantment. In *The Prelude,* Wordsworth criticizes those for whom

> truth is not a motion or a shape
> Instinct with vital functions, but a block
> Or waxen image which yourselves have made,
> And ye adore. (Book 8, 431–436)

34 Robert Boyle, *A Free Enquiry into the Vulgarly Received Notion of Nature* (1686), quoted in Simon Jarvis, *Wordsworth's Philosophic Song* (Cambridge: Cambridge University Press, 2006), 67.

According to Boyle, nature is inanimate; looking upon it as if it were endowed with life is the mistake characteristic of polytheists and idolators; the new science is the best defense against such a mistake because it has the courage of its literalism: it sees inanimate matter for what it is. According to Wordsworth, though, attitudes like Boyle's are actually *examples* of idolatrous thinking. To begin with the assumption that the world is meaningless or dead, and therefore that any meaning to be found there is a projection (to be rigorously policed by referring to it as merely a figure of speech), simultaneously "invents" the very possibility of idolatry and occludes other possible modes of experience by blocking the "vital functions" with which the world is shot through. To be a literalist about the world, to insist on calling things according to what they are, is not to be disenchanted but rather to make an idol of one's own supposedly disenchanted reason.

But what is *poetic* about this way of thinking? The notion that reason and illusion emerge together, Jarvis writes, is not "merely an opinion held by Wordsworth. It is undergone at the level of technique. It is central to the revolution in Wordsworth's way of writing poetry and thinking about poetry which takes place in the late 1790s."[35] Or, to put this in Taylor's idiom, one cannot simply extract the analytic content from the story; the story has to be told, experienced, undergone, in order for its force to be felt. So philosophic song is not something to be mined for what its content might tell us about the spirit of the age. Rather, philosophic song is a mode of critical thought because it forces its readers to undergo the very thing it is describing.

This, I submit, is the secret spirit of *A Secular Age*. Officially, Taylor is a defender of humanism and of modernity's affirmation of ordinary life. He is ambivalent, however, about the secularity that is central to those developments. We may have gained much, but we have also lost something, and Taylor looks to romanticism and the expressivist turn in order to find language for what we have lost. Accordingly, he treats the literary texts to which he refers not as philosophic songs but rather as philosophy in verse, whose analytic content can be extracted. But secretly, in the shadows as it were, Taylor is looking for readers willing to undergo modernity with him, looking for readers who will experience the book as a form of poetic thinking, a story that

35 Ibid., 37.

needs to be retold properly. In those shadows such a reader might catch a glimpse of a different world, one in which Robert Boyle would be talking nonsense rather than common sense. A different world, mounted on the strength of some alternative and anachronistic history in which things had somehow turned out otherwise. This secret desire is Charles Taylor's romanticism.

8

Disquieted History in *A Secular Age*

Jon Butler

Charles Taylor's *A Secular Age* teems with history. Yet Taylor's long historical exposition from the Middle Ages to 1800, which consumes the first half of *A Secular Age,* drew little interest from the book's first reviewers. Most focused on the end product of Taylor's historical analysis—his critique of modern secularism's intellectual and moral failures—and on Taylor's philosophical commitment to an affective religious belief, especially his stress on tolerance, openness, and what Taylor terms "fullness," beliefs that for Taylor are epitomized in his public Catholic commitment. Most speakers at the 2008 Yale conference on *A Secular Age* likewise eschewed history; they too focused on the substance, insight, and problems of Taylor's critique of modern secularity. Similarly, the many Catholic laypeople who bulged the audience hearing Taylor's closing talk clearly hoped to comprehend Taylor's vision of religion's potential to address the modern condition. Taylor's version of history in the collapse of near-ubiquitous Christian belief before 1500 and its subsequent descent into modern secularism may be the foundation of the critique of modernity, but, like many foundations, it is one easily stepped over.

A Secular Age teems with history precisely because it places so much emphasis on modern secularism's origins from the fifteenth through the eighteenth century. Taylor argues that these centuries created the principal openings for the secularity that triumphed in the nineteenth, twentieth, and now twenty-first century. Of course, many books assess religion and culture between about 1500 and 1800. But *A Secular Age* employs its history principally to shape an understanding of modern secularism's roots and, in turn, its character and limits. This is not history for historians, meaning history meant to uncover the past for its own sake (for better or worse) or for the sake of other historians (mainly for worse). Rather, it is history for argument about modernity, the cause of the modern condition, and its possible cure. It is a history of lament and failure intended to propel readers toward a history of meaning and fulfillment.

A Secular Age is not Taylor's first go at this subject. That is found most obviously in *Modern Social Imaginaries*, published in 2004. Like *A Secular Age*, *Modern Social Imaginaries* reaches back before the nineteenth century. But its 200 pages scarcely compete with the 874 pages of text and endnotes in *A Secular Age*, which weighs two pounds plus on a bathroom scale. *A Secular Age* expands on the historical context of secularity, its origins, and its problems in *Modern Social Imaginaries*, principally through its exceptional and historically detailed account of religion and belief from the Middle Ages through the eighteenth century.

The vast historical sweep of *A Secular Age* simultaneously attracts and deflates. Reviewers concentrating on Taylor's critique of twentieth- and twenty-first-century secularity acknowledge Taylor's awesome tour through the sixteenth, seventeenth, and eighteenth centuries but quickly skip to the present, sometimes because they find Taylor's history confusing, no matter its seeming erudition. Christopher Insole's long lead review in the *Times Literary Supplement* complains that "the reader is bombarded with rises, falls, spectres, shifts, dilemmas, cross-pressures, frames, and ages" and that "overall, the book evokes the same sort of awe and bewilderment that we might feel about a map of the world that was the same size as the world." Then Insole jumps from Middle Ages "voluntarism" to modern secularity, spending few words on the history in between. Stuart Jeffries, writing in the *Guardian,* touches on Taylor's argument about the route from the Reformation to the Enlightenment and modern science and highlights the importance of deism in fomenting secularism. But Jeffries concludes, as he begins, with the relevance of Taylor's book to the question of modern secularism, not the accuracy of Taylor's history. Even the historian John Patrick Diggins, writing in the *New York*

Times, refers to Taylor's historical argument only obliquely and instead focuses on Taylor's argument "that God is still very much present in the [present] world, if we only look at the right places." In the end, Diggins rejects Taylor's conviction, concluding that "there are many reasons to read the profound meditations in *A Secular Age,* but waiting for God to show up is not one of them."[1]

The history elucidated in *A Secular Age* seems strongly guided by a distinction Taylor poses, in his introduction, among three kinds of secularity, of which he intends to focus on the third. What he calls "secularity 1" centers on the divorce of religion from politics: "public spaces . . . have been allegedly emptied of God, or of any reference to ultimate reality" (*SA,* 2). "Secularity 2" involves "the falling off of religious belief and practice, in people turning away from God, and no longer going to church" (2). "Secularity 3," which is Taylor's principal interest in *A Secular Age,* "focus[es] on the condition of belief . . . of a move from a society where belief in God is unchallenged and indeed, unproblematic, to one in which it is understood to be one option among others, and frequently not the easiest to embrace" (3).

All three of Taylor's "secularities" are problematic and probably wrong. It would be hard to tell that the divorce of religion from politics in secularity 1 reigns throughout the United States, many if not all parts of Europe, and most of the Middle East, Africa, South Asia, and Latin America. Public places in all these societies are more than full of "God," whether the God of Christianity, Islam, or Judaism, or the gods or transcendent forces of so many other religions, all visible and many the source of immense political conflict and violence. Some might wonder if Taylor has been observing modern world politics since 1990, and others might feel that the world would be safer if, indeed, secularization 1 triumphed.

Secularity 2 has most relevance to modern Protestant and Catholic Europe as well as to modern China (meaning straying from traditional Chinese

1 Christopher J. Insole, "Informed Tolerance: How to Deal with Disagreements about Truth in an Age of Fragmented Realities," *Times Literary Supplement,* February 1, 2008, 3–5; John Patrick Diggins, "The Godless Delusion," *New York Times,* December 16, 2007 (Michael Warner argues in the introduction to this volume that Diggins "misstates [Taylor's] arguments"); Stuart Jeffries, "Is That All There Is?" *Guardian,* December 8, 2007. As of May 2009, I could locate only two reviews in history journals: Peter E. Gordon, "The Place of the Sacred in the Absence of God: Charles Taylor's *A Secular Age," Journal of the History of Ideas* 69, 4 (2008): 647–673, and Martin Jay, "Faith-Based History," *History and Theory* 48 (February 2009): 76–84.

Buddhism, obviously not from the Church). But it is not clear that decline in "belief and practice" after 1800 typifies the United States and Latin America or the Middle East or South Asia, even if substantial readjustments among religious groups have undoubtedly occurred, such as the rise of conservative Protestantism at the expense of "mainline" denominations in the United States or the rise of Pentecostalism in Latin America at the expense, and irritation, of traditional Catholicism.

Finally, Taylor handles the discussion of "conditions of belief" for secularity 3 as a largely philosophical issue without asking for whom the conditions pertain—a critical question if one assumes, as Taylor seems to do, that the conditions of belief must pertain to everyone—in religious terms, the laity in all its variety—not just intellectuals. It is not clear that belief was as "axiomatic" in the West before 1500 as Taylor claims, and the gap undermines Taylor's argument that "unproblematic" and "unchallenged" belief before 1500 gives way to a modern sensibility that sees belief merely as a choice among many, which Taylor argues is the central meaning of secularism (*SA*, 3).

For a historian, then, the issues raised in *A Secular Age* rest mainly with Taylor's account of secularity 3, which can be problematic in themselves but which are further compromised by evidence drawn frequently, but not exclusively, from accounts of lay affiliation and behavior (secularity 2) that impinge on Taylor's account of the conditions of belief (secularity 3). (Issues raised in Taylor's account of secularity 1 may be important, but they pertain largely to his account of modernity and not to his account of belief from the Middle Ages to the eighteenth century.) It would be unfair, of course, to criticize *A Secular Age* because it gives short shrift to secularity 2, since the book is primarily about conditions of belief (secularity 3). But it is not unfair to point up ways in which Taylor's account of secularity 3 is historically unsatisfactory and inaccurate, both in itself and in light of lay behavior. Too much of *A Secular Age* seems to assume that secularity 3 is the foundation for, yet remarkably different from, secularity 2. The critique that follows argues that Taylor's account of secularity 3 is, in itself, incomplete and is further compromised by evidence about behavior among ordinary people and views that would, in Taylor's scheme, most likely fall under secularity 2.

Before we begin, one observation about *A Secular Age* as a book: its complicated, prolix account of secularism's rise deflates causal linearity and produces too much confusion in readers, as Christopher Insole complains. Most reviewers see this as one of Taylor's goals—complicating rather than simplifying our understanding of the relationship between religion and secularity. Taylor succeeds, too well. *A Secular Age* glosses so many different and possible explanations for secularity so discursively that it would be nearly impossible to say that Taylor has missed something important, though the reader may have. It is difficult to find clear answers to too many points. Arguments in *A Secular Age* roll over each other at a dizzying pace. If one is interested in a particular topic, the extended discussions, such as Taylor's discussion of deism, can be captivating. But too often readers are forced to digest accounts and link arguments themselves. As a result, Taylor's rolling stone counterintuitively gathers too much moss, meaning puzzlement for readers and, certainly in my case, for critics as well. The book should have been half its size, even a third, because fewer pages would almost inevitably have forced more focused arguments and clearer expositions.

So how does Taylor assess the "conditions of belief" that constitute secularity 3 and the ways they changed from the Middle Ages to the late eighteenth century? He employs the concept of the "social imaginary," which he outlined in preliminary fashion in his 2004 *Modern Social Imaginaries*: "My basic hypothesis is that central to Western modernity is a new conception of the moral order of society. This was at first an idea in the minds of some influential thinkers, but it later came to shape the social imaginary of large strata, and then eventually whole societies" (2). The approach outlined in *Modern Social Imaginaries* thus is largely top-down, with a new "social imaginary" emerging through intellectual discourse that subsequently shapes influential groups and, ultimately, the whole of Western society.

A Secular Age seems to take a somewhat different tack to the operation of the social imaginary. Answering the question, "What is a 'social imaginary'?" Taylor differentiates between the "social imaginary" and "social theory" in the following way: "I speak of 'imaginary' (i) because I'm talking about the way ordinary people 'imagine' their social surroundings," while "(ii) theory is often the possession of a small minority, . . . what is interesting in the social imaginary is that it is shared by large groups of people, if not the whole society" (*SA*, 171–172). Taylor reinforced the point (I believe) in his keynote address at the 2008 Yale conference: "What we're talking about here is not simply ideas. I mean, people keep saying I'm writing about ideas. This is not an idea; this is a way of experiencing the world, which is so different [from ideas] that it's hard for us to get our minds around it, and if we aren't aware that the ways of experiencing the world have changed over history, we have no hope of understanding religion."[2]

Yet in the end, and somewhat strangely, Taylor's approach to "experiencing the world" in *A Secular Age* falls back on the approach outlined in *Modern Social Imaginaries,* an approach that stresses "ideas" and theory more than experience and ordinary people. True, *A Secular Age* invokes some social history, references to politics, asides on personalities, as well as glosses on artistic expression and some nods to music. Who else evokes Peggy Lee singing "Is That All There Is?" to nail the essential meaning of secularity?[3] But social patterns, race, politics, gender, ethnicity, national identity, art, and music are not the prime movers of change in recasting belief across the centuries, even if they evoke and reflect belief and unbelief, and certainly Taylor seldom invokes the experiences of ordinary people in recounting the transformation of social imaginaries before and after 1500.

Granted that *A Secular Age* often is more intellectual history than the history of mentalities, at least as they might appear from a broader social perspective, historians might inevitably gripe about Taylor's selection of major figures. Where is Pierre Bayle, whose sophistication in the early modern intellectual discourse on religion would seem to have fit Taylor's agenda so wonderfully?[4] Others might contest Taylor's description of interrelationships among the major figures he treats and their effects on thought and society, or the pace at which Taylor jumps from one figure to another. But they will not be unfamiliar with the chain of argument. In this regard, *A Secular Age* is not dissimilar to Mark Lilla's *The Stillborn God: Religion, Politics, and the Modern West,* published almost simultaneously with *A Secular Age,* in which "great" thinkers largely articulate the means through which people shape, accommodate, and disrupt the world between the Middle Ages and modern times.[5]

2 Charles Taylor, Keynote address, "Varieties of Secularism in *A Secular Age,*" Yale University, April 5, 2008, transcript.

3 *SA,* 311, 507. The second reference to Peggy Lee is written as though Taylor had not already made the point two hundred pages earlier.

4 See Elisabeth Labrousse, *Bayle,* trans. Denys Potts (Oxford: Oxford University Press, 1983); Thomas M. Lennon and Michael Hickson, "Pierre Bayle," *Stanford Encyclopedia of Philosophy,* fall 2008 ed., ed. Edward N. Zalta: http://plato.stanford.edu/archives/fall2008/entries/bayle/.

5 Mark Lilla, *The Stillborn God: Religion, Politics, and the Modern West* (New York: Knopf, 2007).

Taylor's account of shifts in conditions of belief in *A Secular Age* stresses two principal and deeply historical dichotomies. The first is the divide, at about 1500, between a Western capacity for religious belief that Taylor terms "axiomatic" or given and the pattern that develops after 1500, in which religious belief increasingly is a matter of choice, producing a fairly stark division between "belief" and "unbelief" and with the easy availability of choice compromising the impact of belief. True, Taylor is at enormous pains to dissect the complicated nature of both belief and unbelief both before and after 1500. For example, he notes the seeming anomaly of an increasing movement toward belief as optional along with a religious renewal that opened many new mechanisms meant to deepen belief—renewed Catholic emphasis on preaching, Purgatory, and devotional practice and Protestant emphasis on personal discipline and doctrinal purity (*SA,* 61–84, 143). But the "fact" of axiomatic Christian belief before 1500 and its deep problems after 1500 stands at the heart of Taylor's argument in both *Modern Social Imaginaries* and *A Secular Age.*

It could be said, as several commentators did at the Yale conference, that one can make too much of Taylor's emphasis on 1500 as the essential turning point in the breakdown of axiomatic Western religious belief and commitment. After all, Taylor discusses movements before 1500 that introduce the themes characteristic of modernity, such as the "voluntarism" of a figure like the thirteenth-century Franciscan philosopher and theologian Duns Scotus, which previewed the modern emphasis on individuality above collectivity. In addition, Taylor describes modern secularity's uneven emergence after 1500 and rightly notes the ways that a still significant sense of transcendence pulls believers together in the twentieth and twenty-first centuries despite the centrifugal thrust of modernity.

The problem, however, rests with Taylor's repeated emphasis in *A Secular Age* of the importance of 1500 as the critical divide between axiomatic belief and the modern conception that belief is a matter of choice. Taylor first broaches the importance of 1500 as marking the fundamental rupture that will result in "modernity" at page 13. As he observes, "Belief in God isn't quite the same thing in 1500 and 2000." He stresses the point sharply on page 25: "One way to put the question that I want to answer [in this book] is this: why was it virtually impossible not to believe in God in, say, 1500 in our Western society, while in 2000 many of us find this [not believing in God] not only easy but even inescapable?" Taylor references this divide at several other points in different ways, all meant, one assumes, to give it stress: "the outlook of European peasants in 1500" (26); "what happened between 1500 and 2000?" (26); "In the enchanted world of 500 years ago" (40); "before the climacteric of the early 1500s" (64). Of course, nothing is the same in 2000 as it was in 1500 or, for that matter, as it was in 01. Times change, so does God, and the question here is not so much one of change itself but whether or not 1500 marks the point of tilt that reshaped Western attitudes toward belief, as Taylor argues.[6]

Choosing 1500 as the fulcrum of change from axiomatic belief to mere choice obviously raises the issue of the Protestant Reformation, and Taylor's handling of it is telling. On the one hand, Taylor treats the Reformation as part of a broader "reform" that involves "a drive to make over the whole society to higher standards" (*SA*, 63). This "reform," running from the late medieval to the early modern period and highly variegated and richly influential, leads simultaneously to both greater devotional practice and "disenchanting" the world, meaning removing "the world of spirits, demons, and moral forces which our ancestors lived in" (26). On the other hand, Taylor also sees the Protestant Reformation as important in itself and "central to the story that I want to tell," since it involves "the abolition of the enchanted cosmos, and the eventual creation of a humanist alternative to faith" (77). But which Reformation? *A Secular Age* never provides a detailed account of different and similar roles that Lutheran, Calvinist, and Anabaptist movements, for example, might have played in forwarding or retarding the development of the "reform" that undermined the axiomatic religion of previous centuries.

Rather, the chapters entitled "The Bulwarks of Belief" and "The Rise of the Disciplinary Society," which constitute the heart of the discussion of the century surrounding 1500, consider their subjects broadly, and often abstractly. Taylor references Lucretius and Epicureanism, Erasmus, Augustine, *Hamlet*, Origin, Nicholas of Cusa, Montaigne, Thomas à Kempis, Luther, the Brethren of the Common Life, Saint Francis, Anselm, Gregory of Nyssa, New England Puritans, Arminianism, Charles Borromeo, William Perkins,

---

6 Here I have quoted only references to the divide at 1500 that use the year; there are many more that reference the divide with reference to other events in which the divide at about 1500 is assumed.

Philip Stubbes, Justus Lipsius, William Stoughton, Grotius, and Descartes, as well as modern historians and intellectuals including Natalie Davis, Mikhail Bakhtin, Victor Turner, Walter Benjamin, Mircea Eliade, Philippe Ariès, Jean Delumeau, Peter Burke, Louis Dupré and Philip Gorski (my colleagues, so I'm glad they're mentioned), Max Weber, Marc Raeff, and Norbert Elias.

But evidence "about the way ordinary people 'imagine' their social surroundings" seldom is offered. For example, a lengthy section on the enchanted world before 1500 brings forth discussion of what Taylor believes this world must have been like, as well as evocations of "porousness" and its contrast with the "bounded self" or the "buffered self," but no evidence drawn from the behavior of common people themselves. Similarly, a reasonably long discussion of Carnival, or the "feasts of misrule," brings forth rich interpretative commentary from terrific scholars and intellectuals—Natalie Zemon Davis, Mikhail Bakhtin, and Victor Turner—but no evidence from revelers themselves.

Even when secondary sources would provide detailed information on the experience of common people, Taylor prefers summary abstraction. Pierre Chaunu's *Le temps des Réformes* and Jean Delumeau's *Le peur en Occident* and *Le péché et la peur* are particularly strong on the mentalities of sin and fear, with abundant detail of real human experience to make them persuasive and lively.[7] But Taylor uses them largely to make abstract and general points. The dislike of descending to the particular and local is especially noticeable in the use Taylor makes, or does not make, of Eamon Duffy's *The Stripping of the Altars: Traditional Religion in England 1400–1580*.[8] Duffy offers a scrupulously detailed account of both healthy pre-Reformation English Roman Catholicism and its destruction by vigorous, and indeed often vicious, Protestant reformers. Yet Taylor seldom employs specific details of Duffy's remarkable account.

Taylor asks about people and places in gauging reaction to abolishing the pre-1500 Christian regime amid his discussion of change in sixteenth- and seventeenth-century social imaginaries: "Did people react with a visceral re-

7 Pierre Chaunu, *Le temps des Réformes* (Paris: Fayard, 1975); Jean Delumeau, *Le peur en Occident* (Paris: Fayard, 1978); Jean Delumeau, *Le péché et la peur* (Paris: Fayard, 1983).

8 Eamon Duffy, *The Stripping of the Altars: Traditional Religion in England 1400–1580* (New Haven: Yale University Press, 1992).

fusal of this destructive act? Or did they follow the reformers in channeling that energy into a new direction, a new register? This was undoubtedly crucial for the fate of the Reformation in many places" (*SA*, 70). But again, the discussions that follow seldom focus on specific people or places, and the people Taylor discusses usually are intellectuals and theologians, with reaction among ordinary people described in broad swaths rather than illustrated through specific examples drawn from distinct places in particular times.

Studies of ordinary people thrust up behavior that belies Taylor's assertion that belief was axiomatic in Europe before 1500. Taylor describes how "disbelief is hard in the enchanted world," and he argues that the principal reason is that "God figures in this world as the dominant spirit, and moreover, as the only thing that guarantees that in this awe-inspiring and frightening field of forces, good will triumph." In *A Secular Age*, "going against God is not an option in the enchanted world" and epitomized the lack of choice in that world. Modern choice came primarily from the success of "reform" that "opened the way to the kind of disengagement from cosmos and God which made exclusive humanism [of the modern age] a possibility" (41). In short, the primary cause for unbelief to falter before about 1500 was the inability to conceive of the choice.

A Secular Age elides the Church's necessary resort to force and authority to sustain Christian belief in the centuries before 1500 and only occasionally acknowledges just how physically dangerous religious doubt, much less unbelief, could be in the age of enchantment. After the formal Christianization of the Roman Empire and well into the early modern period, unbelief and behaviors seemingly supportive of unbelief became criminal. Paganism and heresy, not just atheism, brought gruesome punishment and death. Long before Luther or Calvin, Church and government tortured, burned, and executed critics and reformers. Clerical scandal, hypocrisy, greed, lust for power, and the simple manipulation of religion and Church for money were serious matters, not only because they violated Church and secular law but because they fostered doubt about belief and stimulated private criticism of the Church, whether within monasteries and convents or in the parishes. The complaints of Erasmus and Luther, and later Calvin, were not dangerous because they were unprecedented. Instead, Church authorities feared the complaints because the criticisms plumbed long-standing popular derision of Church hypocrisy, ranging from venality and lust to simple stupidity, that in turn cast doubt on the elemental truth of Christianity, which was the only authorized religion.[9]

Taylor comes closest to acknowledging the variability of religious belief in discussing the enchantment of the world before 1500—the world filled with design, purpose, and hierarchy. While Catholicism symbolized much of this world, enchantment also took other forms, some Christian (or seemingly so), some non-Christian, and some eclectic or syncretistic in ways that historians can understand but that "believers" cared little about except that they believed in them. These other forms of enchantment, reconstructed by historians who specialize in "popular religion" or "lived religion," represent both verification and challenge to Taylor's argument about the power of enchantment, the difficulty being, in part, that the God in whom it was "virtually impossible not to believe" may not have been the same God for everyone, or nearly the same, and that even the ubiquity of wide-ranging and varied enchantments could be questioned.[10]

Yet if *A Secular Age* vacillates between focusing on "conditions of belief" and "belief in God" and refers to "magic" as belief, only Christian belief re-

9 See Ramsay MacMullen, *Christianizing the Roman Empire*, A.D. 100–400 (New Haven: Yale University Press, 1984); Ronald C. Finucane, *Miracles and Pilgrims: Popular Beliefs in Medieval England* (Totowa, N.J.: Rowman and Littlefield, 1977); John Raymond Shinners, *Medieval Popular Religion, 1000–1500: A Reader* (Orchard Park, N.Y.: Broadview, 1997); Gábor Klaniczay, *The Uses of Supernatural Power: The Transformation of Popular Religion in Medieval and Early-Modern Europe*, trans. Susan Singerman (Princeton: Princeton University Press, 1990); Bernard Hamilton, *Religion in the Medieval West*, 2nd ed. (New York: Oxford University Press, 2003); Jean-Claude Schmitt, *The Holy Greyhound: Guinefort, Healer of Children since the Thirteenth Century* (Cambridge: Cambridge University Press, 1983); André Vauchez, *The Laity in the Middle Ages: Religious Beliefs and Devotional Practices*, trans. Margery J. Schneider (Notre Dame, Ind.: University of Notre Dame Press, 1993); Malcolm Barber, *The Cathars* (New York: Pearson Education, 2000).

10 See Keith Thomas, *Religion and the Decline of Magic* (New York: Scribner's, 1971); G. E. Aylmer, "Unbelief in Seventeenth-Century England," in *Puritans and Revolutionaries*, ed. D. Pennington and Keith Thomas (Oxford: Oxford University Press, 1978), 22–46; Ellen Badone, ed., *Religious Orthodoxy and Popular Faith in European Society* (Princeton: Princeton University Press, 1990); Yves-Marie Bercé, *Fête et révolte: Des mentalités populaires du XVIe au XVIIIe siècle* (Paris: Hachette, 1976); John Bossy, "Blood and Baptism: Kinship, Community and Christianity in Western Europe from the Fourteenth to the Seventeenth Century," in *Sanctity and Secularity: The Church and the World*, ed. Derek Baker (Oxford: Oxford University Press, 1973), 129–144; Theo Brown, *The Fate of the Dead: A Study in Folk Eschatology in the West Country after the Reformation* (Totowa, N.J.: Rowman and Littlefield, 1987); William A. Christian, Jr., *Local Religion in Sixteenth-Century Spain* (Princeton: Princeton University Press, 1981); Lucien Febvre, *The Problem of Unbelief in the Sixteenth Century: The Religion of Rabelais*, trans. Beatrice Gottlieb (Cambridge, Mass.: Harvard University Press, 1982); Carlo Ginzburg, *The Cheese and the Worms: The Cosmology of a Sixteenth-Century Italian Miller*, trans. John Tedeschi and Anne Tedeschi (Baltimore: Johns Hopkins University Press, 1981).

ceives systematic treatment. Neither through evidence nor through explication does Taylor suggest that by "belief" he takes non-Christian magic (or other non-Christian forms of belief) to be the "belief" or "faith" whose axiomatic character is lamentably erased by a growing modernity. The term "magic" does not appear in the index. Discussions of magic are handled even more abstractly than discussions of the "conditions of belief" and never probe specific magical practices. Magic is destroyed as the "age of enchantment" wanes, but discussion of the "deep theological objection [that] arose to the 'white magic' of the church" is as brief as the discussion of white magic itself (*SA*, 72).

Yet the Christian belief that is the centerpiece of faith before 1500 proved far more contingent, fluid, problematic, and variable than *A Secular Age* acknowledges or probes—characteristics also likely tied to the origins of modern secularism. A wide variety of literature demonstrates that the Church needed the support of secular authorities to sustain even a tentative, if also powerful, hold on the religious commitment of ordinary people before 1500. Rather than belief being axiomatic, as Taylor argues, it was contingent and threatened from inside as well as outside. Edward Peters's *Heresy and Authority in Medieval Europe* demonstrates the extraordinary threat that all forms of Christianity faced from a wide variety of challenges throughout the medieval period.[11] Heresy appeared in dizzying forms, shifting among the Cathars, Waldensians, a variety of unorthodox devotional practices, intellectual heresies, then to John Wycliff and Jan Hus. John Arnold's *Belief and Unbelief in Medieval Europe* is one of several books that describe the threats to Christianity of any and all kinds that stalked the medieval age. Arnold's argument is not that medieval Europeans were unbelievers. Rather, he demonstrates how the Church consistently had to struggle with at least nonbelief, if not unbelief, almost precisely because belief—and certainly not specific forms of belief, namely "orthodox" Christian forms—were far from axiomatic.[12]

Here is where evidence of secularity 2, with its emphasis on adherence to religious groups, crosses over to qualify assertions made about secularity 3, the conditions of belief. Of course, it could be said that the seeming chaos of medieval heresy and struggle to achieve Christian orthodoxy both represent

11 Edward Peters, *Heresy and Authority in Medieval Europe: Documents in Translation* (Philadelphia: University of Pennsylvania Press, 1980).

12 John Arnold, *Belief and Unbelief in Medieval Europe* (New York: Oxford University Press, 2005).

the triumph of belief nurtured in the conditions of the enchanted world. But in the real world of ordinary believers, where belief was not philosophical but faith in specific varieties of orthodoxy, heresy is not belief but paganism and blasphemy, not infrequently punishable by death. Medieval Christians (and non-Christians or partial Christians) were almost devastatingly accustomed to huge doubts about faith. They lived through them and, perhaps more to the point, died through them. How many lives were consumed by the Albigensian crusade to rid Languedoc of the Cathar heresy in the early thirteenth century? Medieval Christians knew that faith was not axiomatic, if only because so many needed to be killed to make it so.[13]

Gerald Strauss's *Luther's House of Learning* illustrates how the struggle to create an axiomatic faith continued, rather than began, with the Reformation. Strauss emphasizes Luther's failure to instill consistently held Lutheran beliefs and promote regular Lutheran practice among ordinary Germans of the later sixteenth century. Strauss's argument has indeed been criticized for depending on exaggerations of lay religious sloth by self-interested Lutheran bishops. But notice the remarkable consistency among reports about lay religious ambivalence and indifference from the mid- and late medieval eras into the era of the Reformation with Strauss's description of lay indifference. Then move into the seventeenth and eighteenth centuries. The European laity did not need the American wilderness to elicit waves of spiritual indifference. A third of Antwerp's adults failed to claim any religion in 1584; in France, if 90 percent of adults took Easter communion, only 2 to 5 percent attended mass weekly; in Hertfordshire in 1572, a reformer complained that on Sunday, "a man may find the churches empty, saving the minister and two or four lame, and old folke: for the rest are gone to follow the Devil's daunce."[14]

Indeed, eighteenth-century evidence of variability in religious adherence and perhaps conditions of belief among ordinary people suggests intriguing relationships between the problems of faith even in preindustrial Europe. The evidence is the 1743 Yorkshire Church of England visitation that showed a distinct relationship between religious practice and, presumably, belief in

---

13 *A Secular Age* does not discuss the Albigensian crusade. See Barber, *The Cathars,* and Jonathan Sumption, *The Albigensian Crusade* (London: Faber, 1978).

14 Quotations are taken from my *Awash in a Sea of Faith: Christianizing the American People* (Cambridge, Mass.: Harvard University Press, 1990), 7–36.

village and urban settings. The smallest villages could report little, because they seldom had clergy; midsized villages reported the most vigorous attendance and participation, because the parishes were healthy enough to support both clergy and vigorous parish activity; but long before industrialization, Yorkshire's largest parishes already were reporting disastrous religious participation: between 2 and 10 percent of adults were taking Easter communion, and Dissenters could claim to sop up only the tiniest additional numbers. All of this suggests the complex contingency of religious expression in the historical past—here a lack of engagement in religious ceremony at least coming in two remarkably different physical settings, isolated villages and relatively dense urban settings.[15]

Evidence from the Carolina backwoods of colonial America before the revolution suggests how evidence about the experience of ordinary people impinges on our perceptions of conditions of belief. Writing in his journal on Sunday, January 25, 1767, the Reverend Charles Woodmason, an itinerant Church of England minister, described a wilderness spiritual cacophony so bewildering that it produced religious paralysis and personal arrogance simultaneously. As Woodmason described it, the settlers "complain'd of being eaten up by Itinerant Teachers, Preachers, and Imposters from New England and Pennsylvania—Baptists, New Lights, Presbyterians, Independents, and an hundred other Sects—So that one day You might hear this System of Doctrine—the next day another—next day another, retrograde to both." The result? As Woodmason frustratingly interjected, "Thus, by the Variety of Taylors who would pretend to know the best fashion in which Christ[']s Coat is to be worn[,] none will put it on."[16]

Woodmason's observations raise questions about the stark choice between belief and unbelief raised in *A Secular Age*. Woodmason observed religious bewilderment, fascination, repulsion, confusion, and a distanced evasion, including indifference, rather than unbelief or a choice between belief and unbelief, or atheism. As Woodmason put it, these Europeans in the Carolina backwoods "came to Sermon with Itching Ears only, not with any Disposition of heart, or Sentiment of Mind—Assemble out of Curiosity, not Devo-

15 Ibid., 35–36.

16 Charles Woodmason, *The Carolina Backcountry on the Eve of the American Revolution: The Journal and Other Writings of Charles Woodmason, Anglican Itinerant*, ed. Richard J. Hooker (Chapel Hill: University of North Carolina Press, 1953), 13.

tion, and seem so pleas'd with their native Ignorance, as to be offended at any Attempts to rouse them out of it."[17]

Hector St. John de Crèvecoeur's *Letters from an American Farmer* makes a parallel, if also different, point. Perhaps thinking of Woodmason's paralyzed backwoods settlers, or perhaps not (Crèvecoeur would not have known of Woodmason or his letters), Crèvecoeur went even farther than Woodmason in his famous chapter, "What Is an American," by describing not only the spiritual confusion of eighteenth-century Americans but the ultimate cultural effects of their sentiment: "Thus all sects are mixed, as well as all nations; thus religious indifference is imperceptibly disseminated from one end of the continent to another, which is at present one of the strongest characteristics of the Americans. Where this will reach no one can tell; perhaps it may leave a vacuum fit to receive other systems."[18] For Taylor, the "it" that produced what Crèvecoeur termed "a vacuum fit to receive other systems" was, most obviously, the choice between belief and unbelief that he believes best describes secularity and that *A Secular Age* traces to the reform that accelerated in the century surrounding 1500.

Yet Woodmason and Crèvecoeur point up different circumstances—not a choice between belief and unbelief, but an inconstancy of "belief" that is not at all clearly rooted in unbelief and not obviously stimulated or shaped by the causal actors and processes outlined in *Modern Social Imaginaries*—"influential thinkers" who articulate a "new conception of the moral order of society" that "shape[s] the social imaginary of large strata, and then eventually whole societies" (2). Writing about commonplace opinion in the eighteenth-century American backwoods, they again signal something else at work, namely that belief seldom was axiomatic, whether before or after 1500, even if its achievements and agonies, and the causes of both, might have changed substantially in Western society between 300 and 2000.

Were Woodmason and Crèvecoeur describing "unbelief" caused by the increasing articulation of social imaginaries after 1500 that increasingly made belief a choice rather than an axiomatic fact? *A Secular Age* makes it difficult to answer this and similar questions, because it so seldom inquires about the social imaginaries of ordinary people—the kind of evidence that customarily

17 Ibid.
18 Hector St. John de Crèvecoeur, *Letters from an American Farmer and Sketches of Eighteenth-Century America,* ed. Albert E. Stone (New York: Penguin, 1981), 76.

comes from secularity 2 but impinges on the believability of secularity 3—as opposed to the social imaginaries described and created by prominent thinkers. This problem is equally severe as it moves into the two great centuries of Western secularization, the nineteenth and the twentieth.

Taylor admits puzzlement about religious behavior among ordinary people. He dismisses "statistics for church/synagogue attendance in the U.S., or some regions of it," as approaching "those for Friday mosque attendance" in Muslim societies, because in the United States belief is essentially an option, meaning that the "conditions of belief" no longer make religion axiomatic (*SA*, 3). Much later, in discussing lay religious adherence in Europe and in America—low in Europe and remarkably high and rising in America—Taylor rightly argues that secularity emerged unevenly, "bumpy" as he puts it, and in a markedly nonlinear fashion (424, 436).

But after outlining the vagaries of modern trends, particularly why the twentieth-century United States "so flagrantly stand[s] out from other Atlantic countries" (meaning Europe, not Africa or South America) in its apparent religiosity, Taylor avers, "I would be crazy even to pretend for a minute that I could answer these questions. They are perhaps even unanswerable in the terms in which they are often put by sociologists" (*SA*, 425, 437). In fact, Taylor proceeds for almost half a chapter to work through a fair number of theories about "secularization" that essentially depend on readings of ordinary religious practice. But this discussion ends inconclusively, and Taylor returns to large-scale generalizations that focus on "Weber-style ideal types," Durkheim, and others that seem more compatible with his views on secularity 3, the conditions of belief.

It would have been particularly helpful if Taylor had probed rather than rejected a point made in Steve Bruce's *God Is Dead* that Taylor quotes at length. Bruce argued that the "endpoint" of modern secularization might "not be self-conscious irreligion," since "you have to care too much about religion to be irreligious." Instead, the endpoint "would be widespread indifference (what Weber called being religiously unmusical); no socially significant shared religion; and religious ideas being no more common than would be the case if all minds were wiped blank and people began from scratch to think about the world and their place in it."[19]

Taylor rejects Bruce's scenario as "implausible." He "cannot see the 'de-

19 Steve Bruce, *God Is Dead* (Oxford: Blackwell, 2002), 42, quoted in *SA*, 435.

mand for religion' just disappearing like that" (*SA*, 435). It is one of the places where Taylor's personal convictions come through vividly and shape his analysis. As he puts it several paragraphs later, "I am moved by the life of Francis of Assisi . . . and that has something to do with why this picture of the disappearance of independent religious aspiration seems to me so implausible" (436). God's existence and what Taylor terms "our situation (the perennial human situation?)" draws us toward an engagement with the religious question no matter the forces unleashed in the century surrounding 1500 (435).

In highly different ways, Taylor misses something important about ordinary religious practice—that indifference, born of many different causes, may be more important to difficulties faced by religion in many ages, including the ages Taylor insists were axiomatic for religion in the West, than unbelief and the formal expressions of irreligion that attract great thinkers. My sense, I hope not presumptuously, is that Taylor prefers to discuss the "conditions of belief" and their intellectual fathers—intellectuals substantially outnumber all other indexed subjects in *A Secular Age*—because he works out of the philosophical tradition. There's nothing wrong with that in itself. The problem is that the preference doesn't fit the historical problem.

Of course, belief, unbelief, and skepticism have been the stuff of philosophical argument for centuries. But at best, indifference receives little attention and even less analysis. It shows up mainly in accounts of ordinary beliefs, attitudes, and behavior and usually in brief discussions of lay absence from religious observance, whether formal, as in church or synagogue or mosque services, or informal, as in discussion of popular leisure or otherwise "secular" culture. Typically, absence, and certainly indifference, are noted, often with some alarm, but little dissected. The many studies of religious observance (or nonobservance, as it turned out) in London from the 1850s to the early 1900s note how few Londoners attended services or otherwise engaged religious institutions at all but said relatively little about the causes. A 1904 survey of one block in New York City interpreted both religious and secular behavior almost exclusively in ethnic and racial terms and skated across issues of noninvolvement in religion. This was a part of the nearly 100,000 religious surveys of New York City households conducted by the Reverend Walter Laidlaw, whose work was funded by John D. Rockefeller and used survey data punched onto large cards processed by Hollerith machines, first used experimentally in the 1890 Census. Most survey-takers sought to recover a religiously axiomatic past through a Christian sociology, convinced that the principal culprit of modern secularity was urbanization and industrialization rather than the reform that Taylor stretches from the medieval period to the late eighteenth century.[20]

Perhaps examining the history of religious renewal in the eighteenth and nineteenth centuries might clarify the issue. When the Anglican reformer Thomas Bray organized the Society for Promoting Christian Knowledge (SPCK) in 1696 and the Society for the Propagation of the Gospel in Foreign Parts (SPG) in 1701 (the SPG focused on British settlers in the American mainland colonies), he did so not to combat unbelief but mainly to confront lax practice and, to some extent, competition from Protestant dissenters, especially Quakers (whose institutions he used as models for his societies) but also Presbyterians and Baptists. Protestant reformers in nineteenth-century New York City focused on providing social assistance (including ending the consumption of alcoholic beverages) and on creating evangelical techniques to help Christianity appeal to the masses. True, a few nineteenth-century reformers worried about "freethinkers" like Abner Kneeland, Frances Wright, and Robert G. Ingersoll. But reformers and Christian proselytizers overwhelmingly took what historian Paul Boyer simply terms the environmental approach to morality and religion.[21] From the 1830s to the 1880s, an "awakening" metaphor that assumed residual religiosity and even Christianity in the people, not unbelief, won the day. As one Manhattan minister put it, "What New York City needs is a general waking up; something big enough and of sufficient importance to arouse the slumbering powers of the people."[22]

20 Richard Mudie-Smith, ed., *The Religious Life of London* (London: Hodder and Stoughton, 1904); Charles Booth, *Life and Labour of the People of London* (London: Macmillan, 1902); Great Britain, General Register Office, *The Religious Census of 1851, a calendar of the returns relating to Wales* (Cardiff: University of Wales Press, 1976); K. S. Inglis, "Patterns of Religious Worship in 1851," *Journal of Ecclesiastical History* 11 (1960); John A. Vickers, ed., *The Religious Census of Sussex, 1851* (Lewes: Sussex Record Society, 1989); Thomas Jesse Jones, *The Sociology of a New York City Block* (New York: [Columbia University Press], 1904); Jon Butler, "Protestant Success in the New American City, 1870–1920: The Anxious Secrets of Rev. Walter Laidlaw, Ph.D.," in *New Directions in American Religious History*, ed. Harry S. Stout and D. G. Hart (New York: Oxford University Press, 1997), 296–333; Fernand Boulard, *An Introduction to Religious Sociology: Pioneer Work in France*, trans. M. J. Jackson (London: Darton, Lonyman and Todd, 1960); W. S. F. Pickering, "Abraham Hume (1814–1884): A Forgotten Pioneer in Religious Sociology," *Archives de sociologie des religions* 33 (1972): 33–48.

21 Paul Boyer, *Urban Masses and Moral Order in America, 1820–1920* (Cambridge, Mass.: Harvard University Press, 1978),

22 Ibid, 166. See also Jon Butler, *Power, Authority, and the Origins of American Denominational Order: The English Churches in the Delaware Valley, 1680–1730* (Tuscaloosa: University of Alabama Press, 2009), 39–40.

Taylor's critique of secularization's "subtraction theory"—meaning that urbanization, industrialization, technology, and bureaucratization removed critically important foundations of traditional belief—can be telling. Secularization theory often carries an aura of inevitability because its instruments seem so obviously irrepressible; who can deny the power of the "-izations"? Secularization theory's impulse toward inevitability also implicitly lacks explanations for religion's power in modern times, notably in the late twentieth and early twenty-first centuries, when the world has been aflame with faith. Moreover, Taylor rightly observes that religion's eighteenth- and nineteenth-century "decline" proceeded erratically and that new religious expressions emerged in the same period, such as the Methodist movement in eighteenth-century England and what Taylor terms "new spiritual directions in older established churches, the Catholic Church for instance" (*SA*, 436).

Regrettably, Taylor persistently returns to the dichotomy between belief and unbelief that especially makes it difficult to understand complex behavior and attitudes among ordinary people, if not the behavior and attitudes of religious leaders and thinkers. This is illustrated in Taylor's description of religion's current state. His description of "the present scene" begins with an appreciation for a broad complexity in the general contemporary religious scene, namely that it is "different and unrecognizable to any earlier epoch," that it contains "unheard-of pluralism of outlooks, religious and non- and anti-religious," and that these exhibit "a great deal of mutual fragilization, and hence movement between different outlooks." But then readers are brought back from complexity to the dichotomous. "It is harder and harder to find a niche where either belief or unbelief go without saying," meaning without strenuous explanation. "And as a consequence," Taylor concludes, "the proportion of belief is smaller and that of unbelief is larger than ever before" (437).

Belief or unbelief. The difficulty is that the laity have seldom phrased their own views about religion in such dichotomous and essentially exclusive ways. Unbelief was not the problem exhibited in the 1743 Yorkshire visitation; unbelief did not explain why the percentage of Puritan church members in Boston dropped below 50 in 1649 at the death of Massachusetts governor John Winthrop (from which it would not rise until the twentieth century); and in the 1920s and 1930s, despite public fascination for figures such as H. L. Mencken and Clarence Darrow and the seductive power of Hollywood, secularity did not necessarily mean unbelief, nor was the inattention to religion so clearly set in motion by shifts in the social imaginary rooted in either the reform whose critical thrust into Western society emerged in the century surrounding 1500 or in the coming of the Protestant Reformation, at whose doorstep Taylor has laid "the abolition of the enchanted cosmos, and the eventual creation of a humanist alternative to faith" (SA, 77).[23]

Taylor does not ignore the now traditional secularization thesis entirely. He acknowledges that "urbanization, industrialization, migration, [and] the fracturing of earlier communities . . . had a negative effect on the previously existing religious forms" (SA, 436). He constructs, confusingly, a "three-storey dwelling" as a metaphor for the "mainline secularization thesis." The first floor "represents the factual claim that religious belief and practice have declined," the "storey above" describes complications in "the place of religion today," and the basement houses "some claims about how to explain these changes" (431). Taylor writes that he comes "closest to agreement with the mainline [secularization] thesis on the ground floor; as to the basement, there is some convergence: factors like urbanization, migration, etc., did count." But, he argues, "the way they counted was not by bringing about an atrophy of independent religious motivation. On the contrary, this was and is evident in the creation of new forms, replacing those disrupted or rendered unviable by these 'secularizing' agents" (437).

To explain the dramatic shift from "some élite unbelief (the eighteenth century) to that of mass secularization," Taylor offers what he describes as "an outrageously potted history of the last two-and-some-centuries" (SA, 437). What is potted is not so much Taylor's brevity but his employment of "Weber-style ideal types" that assume effects in the laity, society, and culture without examining means. Taylor describes an "'ancien regime' matrix" —a "pre-modern" culture with "hierarchical complementarity" (438)—and a strenuous "Age of Mobilization" centered in the eighteenth and nineteenth centuries in which "people are persuaded, pushed, dragooned, or bullied into new forms of society, church, [and] association" (445). Generalizations at the highest levels depict broad cultural changes shifting elite to mass unbelief across Europe and America.

23 Darrett B. Rutman, *Winthrop's Boston: Portrait of a Puritan Town, 1630–1649* (Chapel Hill: University of North Carolina Press, 1965), 142–143, 195–196, 274–279; Beth Wenger, "Synagogues and the 'Spiritual Depression' in the 1930s," in *Perspectives on American Religion and Culture*, ed. Peter Williams (Malden, Mass.: Blackwell, 1999), 124–139; Robert T. Handy, "The American Religious Depression, 1925–1935," *Church History* 29 (1960): 3–16.

Some problems in Taylor's account of the shift from elite to mass secularization could be assigned to meandering arguments and confusing sentences. Here, at its middle, *A Secular Age* leans too often on obtuse jargon and winding syntax: "I will call this kind of link between religion and the state 'neo-Durkheimian,' contrasting on the one hand to the 'paleo-Durkheimian' mode of 'baroque' Catholic societies, and on the other to more recent forms in which the spiritual dimension of existence is quite unhooked from the political" (*SA*, 455).

But the main problem is an incomplete history, especially Taylor's resistance to insights from traditional secularization theory in his own account of shifting social imaginaries among actual believers. Fairly recent discussions of religion's modern fate have shown subtle and sometimes unexpectedly paradoxical relationships among these and the rise or fall of religion in modern times. Steve Bruce, Roy Wallis, Callum Brown, and Hugh McLeod have shown the clear importance of context, or environment, in assessing the relationship among urbanization, industrialization, and technology in thinking about either the rise or fall of religious conviction in nineteenth- and twentieth-century Europe.[24] Taylor to the contrary, there is a not-irrelevant reason that the Italian sociologist Sabino Acquaviva could entitle his study of the modern religious crisis *The Decline of the Sacred in Industrial Society*.[25] Yet *A Secular Age* comes up strangely short precisely when it arrives at the nineteenth century and the triumph of secularization. This is a historical mistake for at least two reasons.

First, the modern urban, industrial, technological, and bureaucratic age reshaped the conditions under which religion operated in ways that extend substantially beyond the premodern conditioning laid out in the first third of *A Secular Age* or in the minimal account of their influence Taylor offers later. This new environment reshaped the institutional structure of every organized religion as well as the intellectual environment in which religion competed. The confrontation with cities challenged every aspect of nineteenth-century European and American religion, from ecclesiology to theology. The rise of industrialism combined with the rapidly falling death rate and the rural migration to cities shattered traditional patterns of church attendance, religious instruction, and relations between clergy and laity.

24 Steve Bruce, ed., *Religion and Modernization: Sociologists and Historians Debate the Secularization Thesis* (Oxford: Clarendon, 1992).

25 Sabino S. Acquaviva, *The Decline of the Sacred in Industrial Society* (Oxford: Blackwell, 1979).

The rapidly rising anonymity of urban life recast the authority as well as the powerlessness of the clergy. Poverty hardly was invented in the nineteenth and twentieth centuries. But it came to have a new hold on individuals and society and brutally confronted traditional understandings of Christian charity. In cities impoverishment flourished rampantly without even a pretense of relief from rural face-to-face culture. Taylor's minimal and sometimes frankly glum acknowledgment of these developments appears to derive from his concern about the limitations and exclusivity of secularization theory but in turn reduces the effectiveness of his probe into secularity.[26]

The nineteenth century, and then the twentieth, reshaped the techniques of religion and, potentially, even religious belief. These changes include but extend beyond the emphasis on mobilization and the search for a highly individual "authenticity" that Taylor argues distinguishes religion as it survives as one among many choices of the social imaginary—and ultimate truth. The rise of science stimulated Biblical literalism as well as fundamentalism—they are not necessarily the same things—in part as a defense against challenges to the simple accuracy of the Christian scriptures: from geology and astronomy in particular; then, of course, from Darwin's theory of evolution; and finally from the higher Biblical criticism. The eighteenth-century American theologian Jonathan Edwards did not need to think about Biblical literalism or fundamentalism, if only because he had so little need to defend the Bible against such criticisms.[27]

Especially in the United States (whose religious activity sometimes seems to baffle Taylor), organized religion and persistent and even transformed belief distinguished far more of the twentieth century than historians often have acknowledged. Here I might part company with Taylor—although the complexity of his book makes me unclear whether the same point is not embedded there in some fashion I missed—by stressing the newness of this religious "persistence." Historians have missed the boat on this modern American religiosity so frequently that it appears as a kind of jack-in-the-box

26 For the United States, see Boyer, *Urban Masses and Moral Order in America.*

27 Paul Allen Carter, *The Spiritual Crisis of the Gilded Age* (DeKalb: Northern Illinois University Press, 1971), is exceptionally useful on nineteenth-century scientific challenges to religion. On literalism, both religious and legal, see Vincent Crapanzano, *Serving the Word: Literalism in America from the Pulpit to the Bench* (New York: New Press, 2000).

subject; in all but the very most recently published U.S. history texts, religion pops up seriously in the twentieth century only when Jerry Falwell comes on the scene (Martin Luther King's appearance is a different matter, as are accounts of the 1925 Scopes trial on the teaching of evolution as representing the death of "fundamentalism" in America). But this absence or fitful appearance of religion would be a surprise to mid- and late-twentieth-century American worshippers from many backgrounds, who have a strong sense of their own persistence and even their own creativity in engaging a vivid faith that is as much the faith of "authenticity," as Taylor describes it, as the faith of Jesus.[28]

Second, it strikes me that the nineteenth century especially, as well as the twentieth, remade nonreligious behavior in significant yet often unexplored ways linked not so much to the earlier heritage of disenchantment explored in *A Secular Age* but through new and independent means. The nonbelief—or, what I think is more important, the simple indifference to religion—of "modern" America and Europe (and they too are not the same) is not the nonbelief, or indifference, of the late early modern period, meaning the years between 1500 and 1800.

This new nonreligiousness is far more variegated, far more self-confident, far less inclined even to argue (the new "atheism" literature of the past several years to the contrary)—in short, far less obsessed with religion as even an artifact than any religious doubt or nonbelief in the period from 1500 to roughly 1800 or 1850. Much of it is centered in adolescent culture, but it quickly extends into the adult world at all levels. True, religion can be found embedded within it at almost all levels—professional sports, for example, where aggressive "Christian athlete" movements coexist with athletic worlds that are remarkably indifferent to religion, whether for athletes or fans or both. And perhaps that's the point—that the presence in modern times of choice to believe, as well as choice about what to believe, is the modern representation of long difficulties and complexities of belief itself, certainly in the West.

My point is simple, and perhaps crude. The disquieted history in *A Secular Age* stems not from its lack of learning and certainly not from a lack of

---

28 Jon Butler, "Jack-in-the-Box Faith? The Religion Problem in Modern American History," *Journal of American History* 90, 4 (2004): 1357–1378.

exposition. Rather, it reflects too much segregation of Taylor's secularity 2 from secularity 3 and slights centuries-old, not just modern, issues of "belief" among the ordinary people who have been the objects of attention from organized religion across centuries and whose lives, Taylor feels, so much stand in need of a "fullness" that secularity cannot provide.

9

When Was Disenchantment?
History and the Secular Age

JONATHAN SHEEHAN

It is a very old story, told over and again. We can find it in the Garden, when Adam stepped out of his shameless state into one of knowledge punished, ejected from his garden and forced "to till the ground from which he was made" (Genesis 3:22). We can find it in Hesiod's *Works and Days,* in the shift from the "golden generation of mortal people" who "lived as if they were gods" to the second generation of silver, who "lived for only a poor short time."[1] In Ovid, we see a time "when Man yet new / No rule but uncorrupted reason knew," and we could look further afield as well, tracing the ages when the harmonious relation between man, nature, and the gods collapsed into labor on the world and the self.[2] No more could man presume undivided relationships to anything. Rather, the work of reflection, and the knowledge of sin, possessed his very soul.

When did this golden age end? Even to ask the question is peculiar for the historian, who presumably puts store in chronology, period, and the movement of peoples, ideas, and events in differentiated time. Chronological time,

[1] Hesiod, *The Works and Days,* trans. Richmond Lattimore (Ann Arbor: University of Michigan Press, 1959), lines 110, 133; pp. 31, 33.

[2] Ovid, *Metamorphoses,* bk. 1, as translated by John Dryden, *Examen Poeticum: Being the Third Part of Miscellany Poems* (London, 1693), 8.

for historians, not only interrupts what Charles Taylor might call "higher times" (*SA,* 55) but also offers the stage on which argument is conducted. To say that the golden age ended (whenever that might be) is to say that it existed, and this is an argument that no historian would bother to make. But the issue is not just the hoary distinction between myth and history, as if the latter begins only where the former ends. It is also one of temporal function. Chronology gives force to the historical counterexample, allows the empirical to bear some argumentative weight: no, it was not *then,* because then things were otherwise.

The question is more sensible from the perspective of Hesiod, Ovid, and the Genesis authors, though. The chronological vagueness of the golden age is what makes it effective as an exhortation, as a form of exemplary life that frames our own, fallen and tarnished. But this exemplarity also demands some temporal link to historically identifiable human beings. Hesiod knew he stood in the "fifth generation," those who bore the traces of their golden ancestors, but on whom the gods "lay sore trouble."[3] Generations of men similarly link Adam to us. The Bible repeatedly provides this kind of information. The Genesis authors describe their book as "the book of the generations of Adam" (5:1), and their detailed descriptions of paternities and life-spans fueled centuries of research—the great chronologies of the Church father Eusebius are only one example—from Biblical times well into the modern day.[4] Without these connections, the laments of the ancient authors would have no purchase: they might as well be about aliens, or animals. The hortatory value of these stories thus requires two orientations, one that universalizes the figure (of the golden age, or the Garden) and another that locates it along the slide of human generations. The "before" and "after" are crucially important, but only as *internal* marks of distinction, scratches in the surface of history whose precise locations are essentially irrelevant.

I start with this perhaps obvious point in order to draw out what seems to me the fundamental issue of framing built into the history of the "secular." I am not a theoretician, and will let others gnaw on the philosophical concepts of the secular, secularism, secularity, and so on. Nor do I want to try to

---

3 Hesiod, *Works and Days,* line 175, p. 39.

4 On Eusebius and chronology, see Anthony Grafton and Megan Williams, *Christianity and the Transformation of the Book: Origen, Eusebius, and the Library of Caesarea* (Cambridge, Mass.: Harvard University Press, 2006).

rehearse the many virtues of this wide-ranging and powerfully articulated book. Rather, I want to ask the questions I am trained to ask, those of the historian. On the one hand, if we do live in "a secular age," when did it start? Or, to put it somewhat differently, when did the prior age—that age of enchantment—end? And, on the other, does it *matter* when it started? That is, what is the value of the postulated "before" for understanding the "after" that we presumably inhabit? How you answer these questions, it seems to me, has basic implications for the "secular," which, if nothing else, is always understood as a kind of present living in the historical shadow (or shedding the traces) of a more or less religious past. What Hans Blumenberg called the "scene of theology's self-interpretation"—that idea that an "intangible core content" of religion renders "theoretical service" to even the "most up-to-date human interest"—is on my mind here, since the legitimacy of the secular is usually both challenged and reinforced in reference to what came before.[5] Taylor's book, it seems to me, offers an opportunity to examine more closely the function of the historical in imagining a secular age. How this imaginative relationship is forged, I suggest, shapes the entire project of describing the secular as a "modern" condition, an "age" in which we live. As such, then, and also because it is my bailiwick, I want to keep our focus on a specific historical frame, the early modern, the period that presumably inaugurated the secular, whatever its forms.

When Was Reform?

I hope to ask this question not pedantically, in hopes of defining a chronological moment, whether 1517 or 1548. Rather, I want to ask how the question *applies* to thinking about the secular and its relationship to that temporal space historians like me call early modernity. Insofar as we live in a secular age, the laboratory for its production regularly falls into this period, one that—roughly speaking—encompasses those things we colloquially know as Renaissance, Reformation, and Enlightenment. Before the early modern, there was something like "enchantment." After came something like the "secular." Obvious enough, apparently. But it is worth specifying (temporar-

---

5 Hans Blumenberg, *The Legitimacy of the Modern Age,* trans. Robert M. Wallace (Cambridge: MIT Press, 1983), 6.

ily, as we will see) this laboratory of the secular, because it allows us to focus attention on the process by which enchantment meets its demise.

There is a historical hinge in time, one across which Taylor and many historians work, and one that articulates between two radically different conceptual, political, and social fields. On the one side, there is "a world we have lost, one in which spiritual forces impinged on porous agents, in which the social was grounded in the sacred and secular time in higher time." On the other side is us: "All this has been dismantled and replaced by something quite different in the transformation we often roughly call disenchantment" (*SA*, 61). The French historian Lucien Febvre famously described the hinge this way:

> *In the past,* in the sixteenth century . . . Christianity was the very air one breathed in what we call Europe and what was then Christendom. It was the atmosphere in which a man lived out his entire life—not just his intellectual life, but his private life in a multitude of activities, his public life in a variety of occupations. . . . It all happened somehow automatically, inevitably, independently of any express wish to be a believer, to be a Catholic, to accept one's religion, or to practice it. . . . *Today* we make a choice to be a Christian or not. There was no choice in the sixteenth century.[6]

The early modern period marks this hinge between "in the past" and "today," the period when what the great historian of early modern Christianity John Bossy called "traditional Christianity" gave way to something new.[7] Before disenchantment, traditional Christianity took a wholly foreign (to us) form, one that fully integrated the religious and the social. The most ordinary institutions of life reflected this integration. The appointment of godparents, for example, was carefully orchestrated by the Church. Their function was far more than doctrinal. Rather, they worked as a socially charged practice. They knit the Christian community into a whole bigger than that of the individual family. Through your godparents, your life was bound to people outside your blood kin. This artificial kinship was as powerful an institu-

6 Lucien Febvre, *The Problem of Unbelief in the Sixteenth Century: The Religion of Rabelais* (Cambridge, Mass.: Harvard University Press, 1982), 336 (my italics).

7 John Bossy, *Christianity in the West, 1400–1700* (Oxford: Oxford University Press, 1985), vii.

tion as that of the family. You could not marry the children of your godparents in the medieval Christian world, any more than you could marry your brother. The religious bond forged at baptism, when the godparents assumed their responsibilities, created a "Christian kindred" that extended from the person to the Christian world *in toto*.[8] In a sense, Christianity worked as a tool for the production of these extrafamilial kinship structures. Its institutions—marriage, baptism, communion—blended "religion" and "society" so seamlessly that the distinction made little sense. Even the dead were incorporated into this Christian community. As corpses in the grave, they remained kin to the living, cared for by those who said masses for their souls and relieved them of years spent in purgatorial pain. From birth to death and beyond, traditional Christianity constituted the very fabric of social life.

The sociality of Christian experience did not just remain on the surface of the human being. Rather, it saturated his inner life too. The deadly sins were personal failings. But envy, anger, and pride were above all offenses against charity. They offended against the communal and social bonds that forged a Christian whole out of unique men and women. For that reason, penance was not an individual practice but rather a form of community reconciliation. Sin was a "social matter to be redeemed by acts as visible and social as the Passion of Christ."[9] Obviously, this would work in both directions, as the historian David Sabean has argued: "A fission in the community could be seen as having . . . mystical consequences."[10] A battle about a stolen cow was a legal matter. It was also one with consequences for the community's relationship with God, since dissent and discontent always invited divine displeasure. Community grievances were thus apt to be resolved by religious means. Denial of the Eucharist was both a civil and a religious punishment. In a deep sense, then, community and religious discord were isomorphic. Imbalances demanded redress on both sides of what we now understand as the "social" and the "religious" spheres of life.

Between this past and our today lies what Taylor (but not only he) calls disenchantment. This former world was lost at the hands of "reform," that "drive to make over the whole society to higher standards . . . crucial to the

8 Ibid., 15.

9 Ibid., 45.

10 David Sabean, *Power in the Blood: Popular Culture and Village Discourse in Early Modern Germany* (Cambridge: Cambridge University Press, 1984), 54.

destruction of the old enchanted cosmos" (*SA, 63*). Among its many potent effects, reform pushed Christianity toward "excarnation," pushed Christianity away from corporeal practices to mental states, to doctrinal propositions to which one can assent or not. This newly powerful doctrinal core of Christianity is, many historians assert, essential to this side of the hinge, essential to the "Christian" as it emerges out of the early modern period. This is not just a Protestant shift. Indeed, the "confessionalization" thesis points to the convergent evolutions of Catholicism and Protestantism in the early modern period. As Christianity splintered in the wake of the European Reformation and each group produced a confession (the Lutheran Confession of Augsburg, the Catholic Tridentine Confession, and so on), the content of these confessions came to define the very essence of the religious lives of their adherents. Catechisms, and "typographical tyranny" more generally, helped, as Bossy has it, to "reduc[e] Christianity to whatever could be taught and learnt," a reduction that deflated the "sense of the Church as a *communitas*."[11] Once Christianity became the sum of its doctrines, the Church's particular sphere of competence in the social order disappeared. In its place arose a newly invigorated state, an "early modern authority" able to "regularize the very intimacy of the religious and moral lives of their subjects, and to supervise them by officials and spies." On our side of the divide, we find a "modern equality not so much of rights as of their loss," in the words of German historian Wolfgang Reinhard.[12]

I specify a consensus here among early modern historians to raise two general points. First, and most obviously, the consensus describes what is called modernization, and often secularization. Reinhard's seminal 1977 article "Counter-Reformation as Modernization" made this explicit, but he was not alone in seeing this move out of traditional religion as fundamental to the "modern" and "secular" world we inhabit.[13] The change was, needless to say, hardly a simple one. As Reinhard's great comrade in arms, Heinz Schilling, puts it, "Europe was 'programmed' to secularization," but this program was encoded in religious and secular institutions alike. The "energies, dispo-

---

11 Bossy, *Christianity in the West*, 120.

12 Wolfgang Reinhard, "Reformation, Counter-Reformation, and the Early Modern State," *Catholic Historical Review* 75 (July 1989): 404, 402.

13 Wolfgang Reinhard, "Gegenreformation als Modernisierung?: Prolegomena zu einer Theorie des konfessionellen Zeitalters," *Archiv für Reformationsgeschichte* 68 (1977): 226–252.

sitions, and paradigms of the religious and ecclesiastical system" were, in this account, essential to the emergence of a "modern state completely independent of ecclesiastical-religious forces."[14] At the end of the day, though, the formation of late sixteenth-century "Church-states" entailed real shifts in the social and economic institutions of early modern Europe. The actual secularization of Church lands, nearly complete across much of Europe by 1800, is only the clearest example, but one could also chart, as many have, the emergence of a full range of state institutions (schools, poorhouses, charitable organizations) that displaced in complicated ways the authority of the Church to administer the physical, social, and spiritual life of its adherents.

Second, and more importantly, this modernization frame makes these stories liable to interrogation by the historian. Counterexamples can be posed that gain argumentative traction. On our side of the hinge, we might look at the ways that Christians relocated or reinvented corporeal practices (practices of prayer, eighteenth-century religious camp meetings, later Pentacostal glossolalia, and so on) and wonder how these "fit" into the modernization story. We might examine those people identified most closely with "reform" and consider what it means that they resisted excarnation. John Calvin—to whom the name "reform" is bound more tightly than most—was highly reluctant to excarnate the Eucharist, for example. The *Institutes of the Christian Religion* held that the "Lord's body was once and for all so sacrificed . . . by feeding [we] feel in ourselves the workings of that unique sacrifice." The body of Christ did not and could not become fully symbolic for Calvin: we must still taste "that sacred blood," he thought, must make it part of our *own* bodies.[15] How does this need for the body correlate with Calvin's love of doctrinal purity?

We might look at the other side of the hinge as well. We might look, for example, at more ostensibly secular institutions (e.g., the law) to see how

14 Heinz Schilling, "Confessionalization: Historical and Scholarly Perspectives of a Comparative and Interdisciplinary Program," in *Confessionalization in Europe, 1555–1700: Essays in Honor and Memory of Bodo Nischan,* ed. John M. Headley et al. (Burlington, Vt.: Ashgate, 2004), 28. See also his *Religion, Political Culture, and the Emergence of Early Modern Society: Essays in German and Dutch History* (Leiden: E. J. Brill, 1992). More recently, see Philip Gorski, *The Disciplinary Revolution: Calvinism and the Rise of the State in Early Modern Europe* (Chicago: University of Chicago Press, 2003). For a review of confessionalization literature, see Thomas A. Brady, "Confessionalization: The Career of a Concept," in *Confessionalization in Europe, 1555–1700,* ed. Headley et al.

15 Calvin, *Institutes of the Christian Religion,* trans. Ford Lewis Battles (Louisville: Westminster John Knox, 1960), 2: 1361.

they push back against a concept of "traditional Christianity." We might also wonder whether village materialists like the famous Menocchio were not more common in the medieval world than the textual record allows us to see.[16] The virtual monopoly on the historical record held by elites and clerics almost certainly obscures variant strains of irreligion, not to mention the mundane phenomenal lives of hundreds of millions of Europeans. Festival times might have been "higher times," but the content of the "higher" is hard to assess. Christian, certainly, but also pagan, and stoutly materialist and vitalist worlds jostled together, as suspicious authorities repeatedly discovered. Was it "just so obvious that God is there, acting in the cosmos" for those who cursed the priests for stealing their crops or who refused to submit to clerically organized marriage (*SA, 26*)? It is hard to tell without much real access to the mental worlds of premodern humans. Inquisitions and other forms of clerical oversight consistently revealed enormous wellsprings of heterodox (anticlerical, non-Christian, astrological) sentiments, but even these records must be taken with a grain of salt.[17] An institution designed to discover heterodoxy tends to find it, and so it is quite difficult to generalize about traditional Christianity in any historically secure way. But these heteronomies were part and parcel of the premodern world.

My goal here is *not* to build a historical argument against the "traditional religion" consensus. All of the historians I mentioned above would admit the plurality and variety of the early modern cultural archive, and their arguments, to varying degrees, try to take this plurality into account. These historians, in other words, would be *responsive* to the countervailing historical example. The question, however, is whether and how such examples might matter to a construction like *Taylor's* "secular age." Jon Butler's excellent contribution to this volume poses just this challenge to Taylor, but my question is more basic: can historical examples such as those above (or Butler's) irritate or otherwise deflect the "secular age" concept in any way?

My sense is that they cannot, largely because of the nature of the hinge and the attendant temporality invoked by this secular age. "Who needs all

---

16 Carlo Ginzburg, *The Cheese and the Worms: The Cosmos of a Sixteenth-Century Miller*, trans. John Tedeschi and Anne Tedeschi (New York: Penguin, 1982).

17 For some efforts to assess these questions in Spain and England, see Henry Kamen, *The Phoenix and the Flame: Catalonia and the Counter Reformation* (New Haven: Yale University Press, 1993), and Keith Thomas, *Religion and the Decline of Magic* (New York: Scribner's, 1971).

this detail, this history?" Taylor rhetorically begins his book, only to insist that indeed "our past is sedimented in our present" (*SA*, 28–29). The temptation, for the historian, is to take up the argument on historical grounds, to ask whether Taylor's picture of absolutism really matches the empirical record (127), for example, or whether he gets John Toland right (231), or whether the "sense of mystery" really fades in the late seventeenth century (223), and so on. But empirical objections are not really the point. For the story of the "secular age" is not a history. Rather, it documents a set of contrastive categories: from a "move from a society where belief in God is unchallenged . . . to one in which it is understood to be one option among others" (3). *Before*, "people lived naively within a theistic construal" (14). *Now* they are reflective in their belief. *Before*, the self was "porous," open to the influences of demonic and angelic forces alike. *Now* it is buffered. *Before*, religion was incarnated in bodily practices. *Now* it has been removed from the corporeal, the ritual, and the practical. And so on. This is, as Butler points out, a kind of subtle romanticism. It is also, as Simon During has noted, a version of conjectural history, a history built around a mobile, at times heuristic distinction between yesterday and today.[18]

Conjectural history brings with it a complicated temporal argument. In the heyday of its production, the Enlightenment, it deployed a set of labile chronologies, which slipped along at different rates depending on the culture, people, or nation. In this way, empirical questions—was it really true that all or even most people in medieval Europe believed in extrahuman subjects? What kind of data set would give us good information about this? What percentage translates into "most"?—were (and are) put aside as irrelevant. One of the most important conjectural writers, Jean-Jacques Rousseau, was honest about this. "Let us therefore begin by setting aside all the facts," he famously began his *Discourse on the Origins of Inequality* (1755). His inquiries "ought not be taken for historical truths, but only for hypothetical or conditional reasonings, better suited to elucidate the Nature of things than to show their genuine origins."[19] Not that Rousseau really did set aside all facts. The *Discourse* is filled with factual claims about early man. But these facts do *phil-*

18 See During's post at www.ssrc.org/blogs/immanent_frame/2007/11/30/the-truth/. See also his chapter in this volume.

19 Jean-Jacques Rousseau, *The Discourses and Other Early Political Writings*, ed. and trans. Victor Gourevitch (Cambridge: Cambridge University Press, 1997), 132.

osophical rather than historical work. Rousseau's anti-empirical stance was principled. The conjecture solved an essential problem, that "the Mankind of one age is not the Mankind of another age."[20] To peel the layers of civilization away from modern man and reveal his prior state was, historically speaking, impossible. The inability to access in empirical terms a past whose loss is complete moves the ball out of the historical court. It is, Rousseau wrote, "up to Philosophy" to make good where history necessarily fails.[21]

Taylor's philosophical history of the secular age could argue a similar proposition, I think, that as a "modern social imaginary," the secular disallows any real apprehension of a traditional past. There would simply be no reliable way to apprehend the reality of the prior state, and so the facticity of "enchantment" takes on philosophical rather than historical import. In that case, though, our opening question—when was reform?—*does not matter.* In fact, even the question "Was there reform?" has less a historical meaning than a heuristic one. Reform is the stipulated agent that transforms the lost state ("traditional religion") into the present one. It is Rousseau's "spirit of Society" that "changes and corrupts all our natural inclinations."[22] As such, it can float free of historical empiricities and instead become a generalized logic embedded in the very structures of modern human existence. And in fact, this is exactly how it works in Taylor's book. At times he embodies reform in specific people (Calvin, Luther, and so on), and at times he offers approximate chronologies, ranging from the eleventh to the eighteenth century.[23] In truth, though, reform is not a historically specifiable process. Instead it is a structural element built into the religions of what he and others have called the "axial age." In this age—roughly 500 BCE, the age of Moses, Buddha, Plato, Confucius, Zoroaster, and others—"were born the fundamental categories within which we still think today," Karl Jaspers wrote, the categories by which man "discovered within himself the origin from which to raise himself above his own self and the world."[24] What Taylor calls the "axial revolu-

---

20 Ibid., 186.

21 Ibid., 160.

22 Ibid., 188.

23 For the longue-durée history of reform, see the quick history of the medieval Church, *SA*, 242ff. For a social historian's critique of this, see Butler's chapter in this volume.

24 Karl Jaspers, *The Origin and Goal of History* (New Haven: Yale University Press, 1953), 2, 3. See also Marcel Gauchet, *The Disenchantment of the World: A Political History of Religion*, trans. Oscar Burge (Princeton: Princeton University Press, 1997), to which Taylor provides a critical forward.

tion . . . reache[d] its logical conclusion," and that logic was the logic of re-form. It was this logic that broke the intimate connection between society and religious life and in turn generated the "individuated religion of devotion" that is so integral to our secular age (*SA*, 146). As such, then, reform is hardly contingently historical. It is instead the unfolding of the logic of axial religion.

What Was Religion?

For the suspicious historian, this sounds like a free lunch. The argument is given the power of historical fact, however construed, while inoculated against historical critique. But (and this is important) no one need be subjected unwillingly to the guild demands that I, as a historian, am supposed to shoulder. The story of the "secular age" need not be a historical one. And certainly the *phenomenology* of the secular is the ostensible goal here, a quest to discover "our *sense* of things . . . [how] the universe is spontaneously imagined, and therefore experienced" (*SA*, 325). If the framework looks Weberian, then the inspiration is far more Jamesian. William James famously defined religion along phenomenological lines, as "*the feelings, acts, and experiences of individual men in their solitude, so far as they apprehend themselves to stand in relation to whatever they may consider divine.*"[25] James's *Varieties of Religious Experience* was, in a sense, a jeremiad against the idea that religion was a "mere survival" of some earlier state. The facticity of religion—its reality for the human mind—is not tied to any objective religious institutions, but rather to a set of inner states, "our very experience itself," as James puts it, the place where reality and experience "are one." This inner state is a "*full* fact . . . it is the one thing that fills up the measure of our concrete actuality." As such, then, religion dwells in the place of fullness, where experience really happens. "By being religious, we establish ourselves in possession of ultimate reality at the only point at which reality is given to us to guard," as James soaringly wrote.[26] Taylor too gives religion its home in the inner world of believers, in the "place of fullness," where "life is fuller, richer, deeper, more

25 William James, *The Varieties of Religious Experience* (Cambridge, Mass.: Harvard University Press, 1985), 34.

26 Ibid., 390, 393, 394–395.

worthwhile," and to which the believer orients him- or herself "morally and spiritually" (*SA*, 5–6).

How does this bear on the secular age? We might argue—following Taylor still—that "experience" is the condition under which religion exists in the secular age. We cannot experience religion, the argument might go, except as an internal orientation to what we perceive as the divine. In this sense, then, the Jamesian position would be both a description and a symptom of modern secularity. This "religion" would, in this account, go hand in hand with "disenchantment," seen now not as a historical event but rather as secular sensibility, that "historical sense" that we have become secular by "overcoming and rising out of earlier modes of belief" (*SA*, 268). Disenchantment is "a description of our age" (ibid.), in this account, not because there really ever *was* anything like Bossy's "traditional religion," but because our very social imaginary (in Taylor's terms) depends on the sense that a "whole way of understanding things has fallen away" (324). What Taylor calls the "buffered self," the self able to stand alone in the world and free from the spiritual powers of demons and angels, is, then, what James would call a "sick soul."[27] That is, a soul for whom "from the bottom of every fountain of pleasure . . . something bitter rises up,"[28] the "spiritually unstable" soul, beset by a "sense of malaise, emptiness, a need for meaning" (*SA*, 302). To fight against this malaise, we postulate a specific relation to traditional religion, one of loss: "In closing ourselves to the enchanted world, we have been cut off from a great source of life and meaning" (315). Inasmuch as religion exists as an inner state of experience, its content is linked to a loss of meaning that must be recovered in some new way (34).

Now, stipulating this for the moment, it is clear that we have a very ambivalent relationship to the historical at work here. The novelty of Taylor's secular dispensation is hardly under dispute: it is "the fruit of new inventions, newly constructed self-understandings and related practices" (*SA*, 22), "this kind of secularity is modern . . . it comes about very recently in the history of mankind" (194), and so on. As such, then, "religion" too should be a historically contingent fact (or attitude, or practice, or imaginary). But since all of these attributes are characterized by their relation not to a *real* past but to one

---

27 James, *Varieties*, lectures 6 and 7; see also *VR*, chap. 2.
28 James, *Varieties*, 116.

imaginatively figured as a scene of loss, the historicity of religion (and indeed, of the secular as well) is difficult to pin down. It exists in historical time; it is recent in the history of mankind. And yet its constitution is a contrastive one. It is what comes *after*. As such, modern humans resemble Hesiod's "fifth generation," the Iron Age men whose golden ancestors serve as exhortation and as reminder of what was lost. Put crudely, the mark of before and after is *internal* to this secular age and disconnected to the *external* flow of time, events, and peoples.

So it is perhaps not surprising that the historical argument often proves elusive, punctuated by curious leaps in time, narrative disjunctions, reiterations, and circumscriptions. This is not helped by what I, when first reading the book, thought of as Taylor's frequent shifts into an anthropological register. It was difficult, for instance, to assess the *kind* of argument offered by statements like these:

> We all see our lives . . . as having a certain moral/spiritual shape. Somewhere, in some activity, or condition, lies a fullness, a richness . . . we often experience this as deeply moving, as inspiring. (*SA*, 5)

> Whether something like [a common human religious capacity] is an inescapable dimension of human life, or whether humans can eventually quite put it behind them, we can . . . leave open (although obviously the present writer has strong hunches on both of these issues). (147)

> I am taking it as axiomatic that everyone, and hence all philosophical positions, accept some definition of greatness and fullness in human life. (547)

These arguments resemble anthropological claims: they seem to argue that the structure of man entails something like a notion of "fullness," whose expression can take different forms at different times. This reading would presumably help us understand some opening bids in Taylor's book, in particular his argument that the desire to "reach fullness" is present not just in believers (Christian, Buddhist, others) but in nonbelievers as well (*SA*, 8). Only what supplies the spiritual and moral shape of our lives distinguishes between believers and nonbelievers. Believers find this shape in a "beyond," a transcendent something. Nonbelievers look downwards, to society, law, human relations, the here-and-now. As a constant, fullness defines the very possibilities of ethical, political, and social life: the "swirling debate between belief and unbelief . . . can . . . be seen as a debate about what real fullness consists in," as Taylor has it (600). The source, not the fact of this constant, distinguishes between the various subject positions enabled in a secular age.

But what kind of constant is this? It is not, I think, an anthropological one, not least because it is quite difficult to see whether premodern man had any need or experience of "fullness." Rather, it looks suspiciously—and I use the word again reflexively, to indicate my own sense of just how integral this accusation is to the modern human sciences—like a theological one. That is, the concept of "fullness" is *not* neutral in respect to belief. Rather, it contains an integral asymmetry with regard to what I will call the "indifferent" and Simon During calls the "mundane."[29] One could argue that the unbeliever makes very little use of the idea of fullness at all. It simply does not govern his or her phenomenal life the way it supposedly does that of the believer. Milking cows, eating lunch, even working long hours writing can all be done easily in ignorance of fullness. Of course, if forced to answer the question "What is fullness?" no doubt believers and unbelievers alike could and would come up with answers. But the *question* need not be posed in the first place. From where, after all, does the compulsion to ask and answer the question derive?

One can imagine a Kantian compulsion here, where "fullness"—like "causality," for example—is essential to the very structure of cognition. Analogy might be set up to Kant's critique of teleology, which stipulates both the necessity of a theology and the impossibility that its concepts will be adequate to reality. Our cognitive experience of the world, as he puts it, "drives

29 See During's post at www.ssrc.org/blogs/immanent_frame/2007/11/10/the-mundane-against-the-secular and his chapter in this volume. Note that indifference itself has a religious valence in the early modern period. Things "indifferent" are, roughly speaking, things that may be included or excluded from the practices of religion without harm to the believer's salvation. A history of how this religious notion of indifference relates to the problem of the "indifferent" human being (anathema, as Butler points out, to early modern divines) is to my mind an important desideratum in the study of early modern religion, and might tell much about the vocabularies of the "nonreligious" before the secular.

us to seek a theology, but it cannot produce one." We experience the world "as reason inexorably demands," as imbued with purpose, and thus we cannot help but "subordinate the ends that are only conditional to an unconditioned, supreme end."[30] In this sense, the question would have to be asked even to exist as a human. But as for Kant, where this "supreme end" turns out to be a legislative sovereign that is omniscient, omnipotent, omnibenevolent, and so on—in other words, God as understood by millennia of Christian thought—for Taylor too there is a remarkable convergence between "fullness" and the Christian religious imagination, with its insistence on a call from beyond, its insistence that ethical and social life demands transcendence, and its focus on the primal loss of a synthesis of man and God. In a sense, then, to be fully human is to engage with the Christian question. And Taylor knows this. The argument that "God is still a reference point for unbelievers" because even atheists need to define their rationality against him confirms it (*SA*, 268). It says that "fullness" demands transcendence, at least as referent. As Taylor concludes, "Modes of fullness recognized by exclusive humanisms, and others that remain within the immanent frame, are . . . responding to transcendent reality, but misrecognizing it" (768). Real recognition comes only from the sphere of religion. And not just any religion, I suspect, but one most powerfully expressed in the Romantic and Catholic writers that Taylor finds so compelling.

This raises some eyebrows. Historians are trained to detect exactly this kind of conceptual sleight of hand, as they are constitutionally suspicious that the gnome of theology is at work behind sober description. Smuggling theology into scholarship is, after all, one of the cardinal sins in the modern human sciences, and no accusation is more common than the performance of theology under the guise of pure science. But things change if you recognize that this is *not smuggling*. Theology is not being trafficked via some black market. It is the market. It is hardly appropriate, in the final analysis, to claim that there is some *secret* project here, one that "bare reason" can expose and demystify.[31] Suspicion is no longer on the table. For this reason, the final and

---

30 Kant, *Critique of the Power of Judgment*, trans. Paul Guyer and Eric Matthews (Cambridge: Cambridge University Press, 2000), 307, 310.

31 See Ronald A. Kuipers, "The New Atheism and the Spiritual Landscape of the West: A Conversation with Charles Taylor," *The Other Journal*, June 12, 2008: www.theotherjournal.com/article .php?id=375.

most moving chapters of the book, when Taylor lays out his own theological vision, are certainly ones I am happy that he included. In them, the temporal and historical architecture of the argument begins to snap into focus:

> None of us could ever grasp alone everything that is involved in our alienation from God and his action to bring us back. But there are a great many of us, scattered through history, who have had some powerful sense of some facet of this drama. Together we can live it more fully than any one of us could alone. Instead of reaching immediately for the weapons of polemic, we might better listen for a voice we could never have assumed ourselves, whose tone might have been forever unknown to us if we hadn't strained to understand it. (*SA*, 754)

Here a vision not of the past but of the *future,* a prophetic moment in a text that turns the experience of loss and disenchantment into a faith in a coming future and coming community, the "us" of the vision. It is a future where depth and profundity reinvigorate and moderate our shallow, violent, and overrationalized secular age, a future prophesied by Taylor's admired authors, Bede Griffiths, Gerard Manley Hopkins, Charles Péguy, Paul Claudel, Ivan Illich—Catholics to a man. "What was religion?" is not the question on the table. Rather, it is "What will religion become?"

What Is Apologetics?

We have come some distance, but it is still not quite clear why the secular age needs a history, and what its relation is to the future temporality of theology. It *does* demand such a history, however, at least if Taylor's book, rich with historical events and people, is any indication. I suggest that one way to think through these convolutions is to return with some attention to that primal site of the secular, the early modern period, a time when theology and history were knotted in tight and complex ways.

A short excursus, then, on the Neapolitan historian and man of letters Giambattista Vico. In 1744 he published the final edition of his *New Science*. It was a book profoundly in dialogue with the religious and historical scholarship of the previous age, when theological controversy was the motor of scholarly inquiry. From the work of legal scholars like John Selden and Hugo Grotius to that of antiquarians like Gerhard Vossius and Athanasius Kircher, the past lived on not as an archaic remnant but as normatively binding on the present, given significance by the transtemporal power of the theological. The history of Christ's death and the early Church were not past but present. They drove polemical conflicts between Christians, whether about the nature of the atonement, the taking of the sacraments, the uses of prayer, the governance and physical appearance of the Church, and so on.[32] The famous bishop of Armagh, James Ussher, was only one of many who put chronology to theological ends. His *Annals of the World,* for example, tried to reduce the "diversity" of chronologies to one "common and known account," so that the Christian story might be given a place in the history of the world.[33] Here the historical and the theological functioned as part of the same intellectual system.

Vico too started his book with a chronology. His "Chronological Table" listed in parallel columns the ancient histories of the Hebrews, the Chaldeans, the Scythians, the Phoenicians, the Egyptians, the Greeks, and the Romans. These were mapped onto "years of the world," set into the general flow of time from the Flood (1656 years after creation) to the Carthaginian wars (ca. 200 BCE).[34] Unlike other chronologists, though, Vico had no interest in offering the single history of mankind. On his map, the streams of humanity did not flow into one grand river. On the contrary, his chronology was *destructive.* It broke the history of humanity apart. The Hebrews neither learned from nor taught their sacred mysteries to the Egyptians. Orpheus was not the founder of Greek poetry; Lycurgus was not the founder of Greek law; no one person invented language, customs, or institutions. These diverse chronologies were a "no-man's-land," Vico commented, if they were taken to be real histories. Reducing them to "scientific principles"—offering a synthetic his-

32 On this, see my "The Altars of the Idols: Religion, Sacrifice, and the Early Modern Polity," *Journal of the History of Ideas* 67 (October 2006): 648–674, and "Sacred and Profane: Idolatry, Antiquarianism, and the Polemics of Distinction in the Seventeenth Century," *Past and Present* 192 (August 2006): 37–66. See also Debora Kuller Shuger, *The Renaissance Bible: Scholarship, Sacrifice, and Subjectivity* (Berkeley: University of California Press, 1995), and Ramie Targoff, *Common Prayer: The Language of Public Devotion in Early Modern England* (Chicago: University of Chicago Press, 2001).

33 James Ussher, "Epistle to the Reader," in *The Annals of the World Deduced from the Origin of Time, and Continued to the Beginning of the Emperour Vespasians Reign* (London, 1658), unpaginated.

34 Giambattista Vico, *The New Science,* trans. Thomas Goddard Bergin and Max Harold Fisch (Ithaca: Cornell University Press, 1961), 28.

tory of mankind that derived from some common constants in the human mind—was the goal of Vico's *New Science.*[35]

The work operated, then, with what I would call a convergent pluralism. "There must in the nature of human institutions be a mental language common to all nations, which uniformly grasps the substance of things feasible in human social life and expresses it with as many diverse modifications as these same things may have diverse aspects."[36]

The chronological table served, in other words, to show the parallel development of human institutions in different human societies at different times. The book itself made a sharp distinction between the "gentiles" and the "Hebrews"—the latter interested Vico very little, since God had given them their social and legal institutions directly. While he conceded the basic truth of sacred history, the evidence of the *gentes,* the gentile nations, was far more compelling to him. All began in the universal flood, he stipulated, the moment when the collective clock of human development was reset. Out of the flood, two species of man emerged: the giants, gentiles all, and "men of normal stature," the Hebrews. The act of historical imagination that Vico demanded was exactly the inverse of Hesiod's. How, he asked, did the Greeks, the Romans, the Egyptians, indeed nearly all the peoples of the ancient world, emerge from the "first men, stupid, insensate, and horrible beasts"?[37]

Vico's answer to this question was at once simple and deeply complicated. Simply (and piously) put: "Divine providence initiated the process by which the fierce and violent were brought from their outlaw state to humanity . . . by awaking in them a confused idea of divinity." Religion, in this sense, stood at the origin of the commonwealth. But this proposition—common enough in the early modern period—got peculiar treatment by Vico. If human institutions had their distant origin in "providence," the *manner* by which society, law, and political life came into being had little connection to anything recognizably Christian. Indeed, gentile institutions had their origins in nothing more or less natural than bolts of lightning and explosions of thunder, which led these bestial humans to "picture . . . the sky to themselves as a great animated body."[38] From this initial mistake, ancient men—each in his own way

35 Ibid., 58, 59.
36 Ibid., 67.
37 Ibid., 69.
38 Ibid., 70, 118.

—fabulated divine mythologies, mythologies that were *true* insofar as they began the process of social and institutional development. From these initial confused perceptions of the gods came principles of authority and natural law. From them too came an original poetic speech, aimed at interpreting the augurs and divination. From them too came a system of morality and its institutions (marriage, patriarchy, and so on), given social form out of an improper fear of the gods. And from them too came those social and political institutions common to all peoples: law, political systems of governance, contracts, and property.

All of this—and to detail each transformation would take pages—illuminated what Vico called a "rational civil theology of divine providence" (*una teologia civile ragionata della provvedenza divina*), a phrase that captured nicely the ambiguities of the project. On the one hand, this science would show what providence had "wrought in history . . . without human discernment or counsel . . . often against the designs of men." On the other hand, it was founded on the proposition that "the world of human society certainly has been made by men, and . . . its principles are therefore to be found within the modifications of our own human mind."[39] Vico walked a fine line vis-à-vis Christianity. The operations of providence were undeniable for him. They were what allowed the chaotic world of human beings to organize itself into stable institutions, and, even better, explained the parallel tracks of human societies long separated from one another. But at the end of the day, humans themselves determined these institutions and their specific forms. They did not follow any prescriptive divine plan, nor did they take their lead from an authoritative religious tradition. Egyptian law did not look like Roman law, after all, and the difference was not founded in religious design but emerged out of the different properties of these human societies and the people who make them up. The "civil theology" that Saint Augustine condemned as the "vanities and obscenities" of a hideous paganism, Vico reclaimed as a positive project.[40] Indeed, this human origin made it, in Vico's mind, uniquely available to human comprehension.

Vico was unusual. Just how unusual is apparent when we contrast him with his near contemporary, the French Jesuit missionary Joseph-François

39 Ibid., 102, 96.

40 Augustine, *The City of God Against the Pagans,* trans. R. W. Dyson (Cambridge: Cambridge University Press, 1998), 256. (VI.8).

Lafitau. Lafitau's *Customs of the American Indians, Compared with the Customs of Primitive Times* (1724)—written after six years spent among the Iroquois on the St. Lawrence River—sought to explain a similar problem, namely where do human social institutions come from and why are they so uniform? His years among the native Americans convinced him that there must be a "certain uniformity" in human cultures and myths, and his book documented the startling resemblances of modern tribal social institutions to those of ancient Greeks and Romans, separated by long centuries and thousands of miles. But unlike the Italian, he was resolute that this uniformity was explicable only if the peoples of the world "all came from the same stock."[41] Or, put another way, he saw the uniformity of customs—between Greeks, Romans, and native Americans—as proof that humans began in the same place, in the comfortable womb of the Biblical story.

Vico would have none of this. For him, a "rational civil theology" was just that: a theology that proceeded out of the *ratio* and *civitas* of human beings in their contingent histories. Even if shaped by providential forces, humanity had plural centers and plural lines of development. Those generations of men between Adam and modern man were broken by the force of a historical event—the Flood—and then reshaped by contingent forces operating across local chronologies. Time was heterogeneous and effective in distinguishing between peoples, who nevertheless were constrained by qualities inherent in the human mind. This was not quite "history" as we would understand it now, but clearly the historical framing of the project reshaped the relationship between religion and what we would now call the secular. No longer did the latter require an infusion of legitimacy from a therapeutic God. A responsible ethics, politics, and law were conceivable in total ignorance of Christianity.

This detour through the early modern helps—or at least, it helps me—to understand why the historical has such a tenacious hold on the "secular age." The presence of the historical frame sets the present not only into genealogical but also into moral, ethical, and spiritual relation with its past. For Lafitau, proper assessment of the human requires acknowledgment of the divine and

---

41 Joseph-François Lafitau, *Customs of the American Indians Compared with the Customs of Primitive Times,* trans. and ed. William N. Fenton and Elizabeth L. Moore (Toronto: Champlain Society, 1974), 1: 35, 37. On Lafitau, see Anthony Pagden, *The Fall of Natural Man: The American Indian and the Origins of Comparative Ethnology* (Cambridge: Cambridge University Press, 1982), chap. 8.

its workings in human history. For all of his genius in collecting rare bits of information about the New World, he fit comfortably into an age where the historical frame actively affirmed a pressing theological position. His histories—like hundreds of similar ones told in the early modern period by both Protestants and Catholics—ensured that human practices of life would always find their roots not just in a providential bolt of lightning but also in the active care of a Christian God. It also *proved* this active care by the data of diverse human experience.

There is a name in the Christian tradition for this combination of theological argument and historical framework. The name is *apologetics,* and in fact its history is one of the stories that Taylor recounts in his book. It is a history whose modern center lies in the period between 1600 and 1750, a century and a half during which Christians synthesized theological practice and the demands for an autonomous reason, insisting with ever more sophistication that Christianity *was* the religion of reasonable people. In the aftermath of the bloody religious and civil wars that followed the Reformation, the prime real estate lay exactly in the middle. It lay in that space of reasonableness between the extremes of atheism and heterodoxy, on one side, and ossified religious tradition, on the other. Here was the space that many people called "moderate," repudiating the "extremes" (and the nature of these extremes was highly labile) as unreasonable, enthusiastic, improper, tyrannical, and so on.[42]

In the tradition I know best, Protestant apologetics, historical thinkers from Hugo Grotius to John Locke triangulated their moderation between Catholicism and the specters of Spinozist and Hobbesian materialism, balancing "reason" in the space of equidistant tension. Early modern apologetics—unlike, perhaps, those of Tertullian—were not simple mixtures of credos and ad hominem attacks on nonbelievers. They were instead sophisticated affirmations of reasonability that wielded historical and philosophical arguments to establish their claims to the balanced middle. In so doing, they showed, or tried to show, how modern religion (that is, Christianity) might universalize its particular history into one applicable to the whole human race. Idolatry, for example, was a plague that affected all peoples—as history

---

42 Ethan Shagan is currently preparing for publication a full-length study of aggressive uses of moderation in the English tradition, tentatively entitled *The Golden Bridle: Moderation and Violence in Early Modern England* (Cambridge: Cambridge University Press, forthcoming).

demonstrated—but its overcoming lay only in the transcendent truths of Christ. That Christians themselves could be idolaters was unquestionable. But this was a superstitious deviance from the true message, whose therapeutic power returned man to a state of real insight. This was a daring high-wire act. Against atheists and Catholics alike, apologetics narrated the history of Church corruption and yet promised a future Christianity in harmony with reason and human freedom. It assigned the historical Church responsibility for many modern evils, and also revealed its Christian core as the cure for a civilization plagued by greed, violence, and tyranny.

Here, then, we are close to the essence of the thing. The historical cannot be let go, because it ensures that the (religious) past might always exert its claim over the secular age. If the "secular" and the reform that produces it are integral to religion, if they represent the dynamic of religion's own unfolding, then the secular is incipient *ab ovo*. It is incipient in religion, and from the moment (as Jaspers has it) when "man, as we know him today, came into being."[43] The past stipulated as religious, as enchanted, thus can assert its power over the present and determine its various forms. This asserted relationship between past and present is, of course, a choice. Vico's history of social and political institutions, by contrast, *loosened* their dependence on the Christian God and opened the space for a responsible ethical and moral praxis distinct from Christian content. His divine providence did not let Christianity press itself into the social world; rather, it offered nothing more than an impetus toward organization, differently institutionalized in different human societies. But apologetics work quite differently. Their goal is to ensure that Christianity is preserved as a history whose presence the present can ignore only at the price of its own inauthenticity.

The work of apologetics—its double temporal index, the Christianity-to-come and the Christianity-that-was—structures Taylor's work in important ways. The notion of fullness suddenly makes a great deal of sense, for example. Fullness is not just a theological first principle. It is also the balancing counterconcept of disenchantment. These go hand in hand. Because the drive to fullness is necessarily incomplete, the experience of the world is deeply structured by loss and self-alienation. The future-oriented temporality

43 Jaspers, *Origin and Goal*, 1.

of fullness—that drive toward a time of reconciliation—depends on the past inscribed into the modern and secular age as disenchanting. These are not, it must be said, *descriptive* but rather *prescriptive* assessments. The sphere of indifference or the mundane is not only conceptually excluded. It is also morally proscribed, as a form of inauthentic participation in the world, not reflective enough, unaware of the real situation that humans (or at least modern Western humans) find themselves in.

This kind of proscription fits the practice of apologetics, historical and modern. As for those apologetes of the seventeenth century, the goal is to colonize zones of intellectual responsibility. Take, for example, that ostensibly descriptive category (so general that the Social Science Research Council has used it for the title of its blog) the "immanent frame," that "sensed context in which we develop our beliefs" in the secular age. This immanent frame has different varieties, Taylor wants to argue, but its essential geography is split into "open" and "closed" forms, where the latter roughly entails atheism and the rejection of transcendence and the former some interest in the transcendent, however construed (*SA,* 555). This may look like a neutral distinction, but it is actually highly asymmetrical. It does not take a sharp-eyed reader, for example, to discover the deep moral peril of the closed universe, the capitalism, the greed, the totalitarian nationalism, the libertine individualism that ensue. "A lofty humanism posits high standards of self-worth," Taylor writes, but "by this very token it encourages force, despotism, tutelage, ultimately contempt" (697).

The asymmetry sharpens, moreover, when Taylor positions the common culture of modernity between the "extreme" poles of "orthodox religion" and "materialist atheism." The poles are ideal types against which we, in the modern Latin West, define our senses of meaning and fullness, and the "cross-pressure" between them "defines the whole culture," as he puts it (*SA,* 598). Note, however, how these two sets of distinctions map. To be "closed" is (roughly) to stand at the "extreme" pole of atheism, after all, but to be "open" is *not* to stand with the orthodox. No reader, in fact, feels him- or herself put into the camp of the "orthodox," whose existence is more a phantom than a reality in this book. This is not a work written for or against the "orthodox," whoever they may be. Instead, the "orthodox"—like the figure of the "Catholic" for early modern Protestants—has more a disciplinary than a descriptive value. It stands at a point *beyond* identification, and thus ensures that the "open" form of modern experience and intellectual participation in the world remains the normative one.

This is just how apologetics work. The historical and descriptive undergoes constant transmutation into the normative and prescriptive. Between the so-called extremes (already loaded against the "materialist" and the "indifferent") lies a territory that is most consonant with the nature of human striving, experience, and insight. This territory is, no surprise, also consonant with Christianity. Indeed, Christianity provides its original map, insofar as it is open to both transcendence and immanence, and mixes them in the original figure of its tradition, Christ himself. Nor does Christianity just offer moral resources for this territory, ways of valorizing openness, fullness, and transcendence. It also governs its historical development. "Modern civilization," Taylor wants to argue, "is in some way the historical creation of 'corrupted' Christianity" (*SA*, 741). As in the seventeenth century, the balancing act is delicate, since this critique begins with the very object that is later to be salvaged. But the balancing act is essential to the apologetic enterprise, for it is through this careful arrangement of forces that Christianity comes to occupy all of the available sites of intellectual responsibility. Christianity gets to possess the past, for example, as the original author of the secular age, and yet disavow a substantial responsibility for it. The monstrosities of the modern are, as Lafitau wrote nearly three hundred years ago, signs of the "most pitiable wandering of the mind and the greatest disorders of the heart," signs of man's limited ability to recognize the transcendent.[44] Christianity also gets to possess the future, as the resource available for the overcoming of the secular age, a Christianity-to-come. As such, Christianity is both the history and the future of the West, both the origin of the secular and the means of its renovation. It dwells in the sphere of reason yet promises incarnated passion. It critiques our past and offers a future unlike the one in which we live.

A Few Modest Alternatives

Clearly, for this materialist historian, the arguments here are highly provocative and at times frustrating. But I wonder now, at the end of the day, whether

44 Lafitau, *Customs*, 30.

the frame of our questions did not determine these reactions. It is remarkable, for example, how exactly aligned Taylor's book is with even such a fierce critic of Christianity as Gil Anidjar. When Anidjar argues that "secularism . . . serves mostly, and certainly it has *historically* served, one particular religion [Christianity]"—or that "Christianity invented the distinction between religious and secular"—it seems to me that he buys into exactly the frame that Taylor would like to establish.[45] He is, in other words, ensuring the Christian claim to the secular, to its inner workings, to its history, and, by default, to its future. It seems to me, in fact, that the "secular" as a concept may in fact invite exactly such an analysis. Just as the "atheist" cannot really function without the Christian referent—and the recent apologias for atheism miss how deflating this dependent relationship is, I think, miss how vulnerable it makes them to easy equations with modern fundamentalism, both so "rigid" and "immoderate"—so might the secular too demand an overengagement with the Christian question.[46] And it does so by excluding even the minimal areas of life that historically have been conducted in indifference to the "religious," however imagined, and nesting them inside a history of Christianity's self-formation.

It seems to me, as a historian of early modern Europe, that one might turn exactly to the premodern periods to explore not the *anti*-Christian but the *alternatives* to the Christian, the resources and archives on which people drew to understand and experience their lives and which they mobilized alongside, against, and within their understandings of Christ, his Church, and his salvation. We might begin with a writer like Vico, whose conjectural history of society, morality, law, and politics was written entirely without reference to the "secular." It was written, instead, with an open sense of the fragile institutions that human beings have created over time. It was written not to oppose Christian stories of mankind but to parallel them, to set up other possibilities, to see the forms that human thought can take not in terms of "Christian" and "secular" but as something different. It is not an accident —and here is a second alternative—that Vico was such a careful student of the law. Beating the bounds of the village was only one way, in medieval Europe, of determining the boundaries of community. Another was the more

45 Gil Anidjar, "Secularism," *Critical Inquiry* 33 (Autumn 2006): 65, 62.

46 For a history of the atheist as a figure of Christian orthodoxy, see Alan Kors, *Atheism in France, 1650–1729* (Princeton: Princeton University Press, 1990).

conflictual resource of the law courts, whose records document a relentlessly mundane set of decisions made with no reference to any transcendence, even of the law itself. Medieval law was hardly "secular," of course, not least because canon law and ecclesiastical courts were so fundamental to the entire business. But it was heterogeneous and differentiated in its functions and practices, and offered resources to plaintiffs and defendants to make claims fully indifferent to the Christian.[47] Even in the modern period, this heterogeneity is fundamental. Take—and here is a third alternative—the question of mystery. At the very moment that, as Taylor puts it, "the sense of mystery fades" in the late seventeenth century, it is also rehabilitated. Relocated, perhaps, but the affirmation of the mysterious workings of order was essential to Enlightenment understanding of the world. "Impenetrable mysteries surround us on all sides," wrote Jean-Jacques Rousseau in 1762, and even that epitome of Enlightenment naturalism the Comte de Buffon insisted that animal generation was "a mystery whose depths it seems impermissible for us to probe."[48] Mystery was an effective part of a materialist analytics of nature, one that was neither "secular" nor "religious" in any meaningful way.

I suggest these, at the end, to indicate that the concept (or experience) of "secular" does *not* exhaust the resources of the nonreligious. To indicate this is not to insist that only "bare reason" is an acceptable part of academic analysis. But it is to insist that any phenomenology or history needs to open itself to the variety of alternative resources that human beings have used to create and navigate their world. A history of these—a research program into the ways that alternatives to the secular have been written into the historical record—seems an important step in mapping this variety. And it is one, I would hope, that might open up new possibilities for imagining human life, past and present.

47 One recent work that shows this heterogeneity beautifully is Alan Harding, *Medieval Law and the Foundations of the State* (Oxford: Oxford University Press, 2002). Thanks to Ethan Shagan for discussion on this point.

48 Jean-Jacques Rousseau, *Emile, or Education,* trans. Allan Bloom (New York: Basic Books, 1979), 268; Georges-Louis Leclerc, comte de Buffon, "Histoire générale des animaux," in *Oeuvres philosophiques de Buffon,* ed. Jean Piveteau (Paris: Presses Universitaires de France, 1954), 233. On mystery and Enlightenment order, see Jonathan Sheehan and Dror Wahrman, *Invisible Hands: Self-Organization in the Eighteenth Century* (Chicago: University of Chicago Press, forthcoming).

10

The Civilizational, Spatial, and Sexual Powers of the Secular

Nilüfer Göle

A Secular Age can be read as an attempt to give us an alternative narrative of secularism. The author, without letting himself be intimidated by the prevalent critiques and the decline of master narratives in the social sciences, undertakes the task of reflecting on a longue-durée history of secularity in Latin Christendom. His work proposes an alternative to the understanding of secularity as an outcome of modernity, locating its origins in the religious transformations that occurred throughout the history of Western Christianity. Against the dominant thesis of dualistic and simplistic oppositions between religion and secularity that are framed in consecutive and alternating historical phases, such as secularization, the triumph of religion, and post-secularism, Taylor engages a complex reading of the interconnections between and recompositions of the religious-secular divide which end up, according to him, in mutual "fragilization" in the present stage. He opens up new ways of reading the religious and the antireligious as contemporary with each other, and hence distances himself from a linear sociological thesis of secularity and modernity. The uncoupling of the two permits him to speak of Western secularity in its own terms without making a claim for a universal ideal model. He acknowledges the "multiple modernities" and different patterns of secularism in other parts of the world, but he makes it explicit from the very beginning that his scope is limited and he is interested in what is unique in the experience of the West. It is inappropriate to regard his approach as ethnocentric; however, as I argue here, an introspective reading of Western secularity can lose sight of the cultural powers of the secular. As the authors of the introduction to this volume point out, the notion of the West becomes too limited if the "internal" history of secularity in Latin Christendom is thought to be unrelated to the processes by which colonialism developed. It is therefore a matter of recognizing not the plurality of historical trajectories and patterns of secularity but the enlargement of the notion of the West and a cross-cultural and cross-civilizational approach. Western secularity cannot be separated from its claim for a higher form of civilization, its impact in shaping and stigmatizing a certain understanding of religion (as backward), its role in spreading models of secular governance to different parts of the world, and, last but not least, its permeation of material culture in norms of sexuality and private-public distinctions. I will try to illuminate such blind spots in an inwardly West-looking narrative of the secular, which can be regarded as the civilizational, sexual, and spatial powers of the secular.

The civilizing missions of the secular are manifested in the shaping of non-Western historical processes by means of colonialism and Orientalism. We cannot therefore complete the picture of secularity unless we posit it in terms of interdependence between the West and its Oriental other or colonized counterpart. Critiques of European inwardness do not simply suggest a historical genealogy of secularity in different historical contexts or stress a plurality of secularisms. Limiting the narration of secularity to Latin Christendom dismisses the civilizational powers of Western modernity, which are inseparable from sexual and spatial politics. Although Taylor acknowledges the importance and correspondence of the disciplinary revolution and secularity, he does not link it with the civilizational claim of the West, namely its claim of superiority in mundane life, norms of sexuality, and cultural habitus.

Further, the location of secularity in a series of developments in Latin Christendom and hence the comprehension of secularity as a perspective that grew within religion —specifically within Christianity—remain a genealogical reading, without offering a key for uncoupling Christianity and secularity. Consequently, in privileging the long-term connections between secularity and Christianity, current transformations of European secularity as it encounters other religions, in particular Islam, are kept oddly outside the picture.

Bringing Islam into our readings of European secularity is not an unproblematic move; it requires a criticism of the universalistic underpinnings of the secular and its equation with the European experience. In fact, secularism as a universal, value-free, culturally disembodied phenomenon is scrutinized and criticized by many in the social sciences. The particular link between secularism and Christianity is explored by philosophical and historical approaches other than Taylor's, which offer a critique of universalist claims of the secular. Marcel Gauchet, for instance, depicted the ways secularism is transformed from within Christianity. His approach to secularism, critical of universalist claims, opened up a realm of plurality in the societal sphere.[1] The neutrality claims of secularism have also been criticized by Etienne Balibar, who illustrated the Catholic underpinnings of secularism, which he named "catho-laïcité."[2] Talal Asad's work on the formations of the secular offers a radical twist on and criticism of the universal claims of the secular underlying the power of the European states in their relation with Muslim migration.[3] Non-Western forms of secularism, including different models of secular authoritarianism or pluralism, such as Turkish and Indian, are also subject to new comparative research and attention, bringing to the academic agenda the multiple workings of the secular in non-Western contexts.

How does a Muslim experience of secularity transform and question our understanding of the secular age? How can one go beyond the limits of the local, particular qualifications and religious boundaries and address critiques of the "common" knowledge of secularism? The question is, who has access to the "universal"—what kind of agencies are considered to be bound by a particular culture and locality and what kind are considered to bear a universal significance? In other words, the taxonomies between the universal and the particular are not power-free, autonomous domains of knowledge.[4] Critiques of secularity therefore necessitate bringing into the picture those

---

1 Marcel Gauchet, *La religion dans la démocratie: Parcours de la laïcité* (Paris: Gallimard, 1998).

2 Etienne Balibar, "Dissonances within Laïcité," *Constellations* 11, 3 (September 2004): 353–367.

3 Talal Asad, *Formations of the Secular: Christianity, Islam, Modernity* (Stanford: Stanford University Press, 2003).

4 Talal Asad, *Genealogies of Religion* (Baltimore: Johns Hopkins University Press, 1993).

voices, practices, and experiences that are classified as particularistic, religious, traditional, that are not in conformity with the universal norms of secular modernity. My suggestion for reading the secular in relation to Islam is drawn not from totally outside Islam but, on the contrary, from close encounters, confrontations, and copenetrations of Islam and secularity. I focus on the interdependence of the two, rather than setting apart a particular tradition that is supposed to be authentically different from or immune to the "secular age," and propose a reading of secularity by means of a displacement of the perspective toward Islam.

One cannot but be reminded of the fact that the renewal of interest in secularism owes much empirically to the introduction of Islam into the picture.[5] Religious claims of Muslims living in Europe invigorated the debates on secularism. As a result, European secularity and religious Islam can no longer be thought of as separate from and indifferent to each other; the two are becoming closely interrelated and mutually transformed in the present day. Some aspects of (Western) secularism come to our attention only if we bring into the picture European Muslim perspectives. In other words, the contemporary powers of the secular are not working in mono-civilizational terms; they have become a matter of inter-civilizational conversation.

The headscarf debate illustrates the ways in which secularity is debated in inter-civilizational terms. This debate has occupied a central place mainly in two countries, Turkey and France, two secular republics that have radically different historical trajectories and patterns of secularism.[6] The Turkish heri-

---

5 The notions "secular," "secularism," "laïcité," and "secularization" concern different meanings and historical processes. Talal Asad refers to "secular" as an epistemic category and to "secularism" as a political doctrine, and searches for the connections between the two. Secularity is linked to Charles Taylor's notion of the "immanent frame"; namely, it provides an unformulated background to our thinking that makes us believe that the secular order is given, and therefore it appears to us as natural. French "laïcité" and Turkish "laiklik" are mainly approached as particular forms of political secularism that are assertive and exclusionary practices of the religious. "Secularization" refers to a long-term societal process through which the domain of religion is withdrawn from the realm of everyday life, changing practices of art, sexuality, and rationality. Secularization and modernization were thought to be inseparable and universal formations—an equation that today is open to increasing criticism. For a very elaborate approach to the variety of theories, historical meanings, and Western/non-Western trajectories of secularity, see Philip S. Gorski and Ateş Altinordu, "After Secularization?" *Annual Review of Sociology* 34 (March 29, 2008): 55–85.

6 For a comparison of secularism in France and Turkey, see Jean-Paul Burdy and Jean Marcou, ed., "Laïcité(s) en France et en Turquie," CEMOTI (Cahiers d'études sur la méditerranée orientale et le monde turco-iranien) 19 (1995).

tage of political authoritarianism and the role of the army in secular politics bear a different weight from the legacy of individual freedom and liberties that has shaped the history of France. The place of Islam is not symmetrical at all in the two cases: Turkey is a Muslim-majority country, whereas France is a Muslim-migrant one. Historical (repressed) memories are also very different: the transition from the multiethnic and multireligious Ottoman Empire to a Turkish Sunni majority in the building of a nation-state created a heavy legacy of the loss of cosmopolitanism and acts of ethnic cleansing; in France, it is the unacknowledged legacy of the colonial past that underpins the present relations of French society with its Muslim migrants. French and Turkish patterns of laïcité are compared and contrasted mainly as state secularisms. The varying degrees of tolerance for religious plurality and the nations' respective tendencies for exclusionary, assertive, if not authoritarian politics of laïcité are treated comparatively in the recent literature.[7]

Turkish secularism is often depicted as an authoritarian derivative of French laïcité, measured in terms of its gaps, inconsistencies, and deficiencies with regard to the ideal model of French secularism. Seyla Benhabib's way of interpreting Jacques Derrida's notion of iteration is useful here in going beyond such reductionism, because in the process of repeating a term or a concept, we never simply produce a replica of the original usage; every iteration transforms the original meaning and adds new meanings to it.[8] As such, the French notion of laïcité becomes laiklik in Turkish. The use of the same notion with a slight change of accent points to a process of iteration in which the workings of the secular power go beyond imitations and add new meanings, discourses, images, and practices.

By coupling the incomparable—Turkish and French secularism—one is invited to engage in an interdependent mirror reading of the two instead of measuring the gap between them or the deficiencies of the former in the

---

7 Nilüfer Göle, "Authoritarian Secularism and Islamic Participation: The Case of Turkey," in *Civil Society in the Middle East*, vol. II, ed. A. Richard Norton(Leiden: E. J. Brill, 1996); Elizabeth Shakman Hurd, *The Politics of Secularism in International Relations* (Princeton: Princeton University Press, 2008); Ahmet T. Kuru, *Secularism and State Policies toward Religion: United States, France, and Turkey* (Cambridge: Cambridge University Press, 2009).

8 Seyla Benhabib, "Democratic Iterations: The Local, the National and the Global," in *Another Cosmopolitanism: Hospitality, Sovereignty and Democratic Iterations*, ed. Jeremy Waldron, Bonnie Honig, and Will Kymlicka (Oxford: Oxford University Press, 2006).

ideal image called "French exceptionalism." Following the questions raised by Taylor, one can go beyond the political level of comparing state secularisms and understand the ways that (voluntary) secularism takes place at the level of presentation of the ("civilized") self and the phenomenology of everyday modern life. The headscarf debate draws into our view the importance of space, material culture, bodily habitus, gender, and sexuality–the implicit powers of European secularity.

The Refashioning of Secularity: The Headscarf Debate

During the headscarf debate that occupied the forefront of the French public scene in 2003 and 2004, one often heard the phrase "Secularism cannot be reduced to a piece of cloth."[9] This expression conveyed the resentment and apprehension of those who were witnessing a debate that had started with the religious claims of some female Muslim migrant students to cover their heads while attending public schools. Progressively it has been transformed into a more general debate on the meanings of French laïcité, an issue that was thought to be confined to regulations in the public schools but that later included hospitals and prisons and ended up as a debate on the secular values and foundations of the public sphere in general.

For many, secularism cannot be "reduced" to the headscarf issue because the claims over the headscarf appear to be a minor, trivial issue compared with the long-term historical heritage, philosophical definitions, and juridical underpinnings of French laïcité as a shared social value. Many feared that opening secularism to a public debate would mean giving up cultural singularity, referred to as "French exceptionalism." Secularism is understood as a

---

9 *"On ne peut reduire la laïcité à un bout de tissu."* The first debate on the Islamic headscarf took place in 1989, in Creil (a little town close to Paris), when three young female students came to school wearing scarves and were refused entry by the school authorities. See Françoise Gaspard and Farhad Khosrokhavar, *Le foulard et la république* (Paris: La Découverte, 1995). During the first debate, a regulation was issued by the minister of education, François Bayrou (called the *circulaire Bayrou*), that banned students from wearing "ostentatious" religious signs in public schools. The word "ostentatious" reappeared ten years later, in the fall 2003 debate. But the decision of whether to exclude the girls was then left to the interpretation of the school authorities.

The public debate on the same issue that took place in fall 2003, in a much more passionate, widely shared, and long-lasting way, ended in the passage of legislation on March 15, 2004, that banned the Islamic headscarf, along with other religious signs, from the public schools. A semantic shift occurred between the two debates, from "headscarf affair" to "Islamic veiling," indicating a move toward a more religious designation and the presentation of Muslims in France.

principle of the French republic that guarantees the "neutrality" of the public sphere, in which citizens are expected to bracket their ethnic, religious, or class origins. The public school represents the pillar of secular republicanism, a place where, ideally speaking, "particularistic" identities, whether they stem from regional, cultural, religious, or ethnic differences, are to be replaced by a common language, memory, and education. Both instructors and students are expected to be distanced from their traditional, particularistic differences in entering the classroom and to embrace French secular values of citizenship, prerequisites for freedom, critical thinking, and dialogue. The way Islam appeared in the public schools—namely, gendered and covered, which made religious-ethnic difference visible—disrupted the republican picture of French secularism. It meant the French republic had failed to integrate its migrants and accommodate Muslim difference. Finally, the phrase "Secularism cannot be reduced to a piece of cloth" conveyed the commitment and determination of the French not to yield secularism to new religious claims, especially not to girls who, by adopting the headscarf, contest not only the secular neutrality of the public schools but also gender equality.

For more than two years the headscarf debate occupied a central place in the public arena and fueled the collective passions of French society in defense of secularism. Commissions were created, with politicians, feminists, experts on Islam, historians, legislators, and spokespersons of migrant communities, to investigate the state of secularism in France.[10] The public, the commissions, the media, and the government all converged in the view that

10 The Stasi Commission, named for its head, then the minister of education, was to examine the application of the principle of secularism in the republic. The status of the commission and the role it played in the public debate require particular attention. It indicated the presence of the state and its way of intervention by nominating a sort of "enlightened public," the members of which are called "the wise people" (les sages). Among the members were public servants, experts on Islam, historians, sociologists, businessmen, representatives of nongovernmental associations, and interfaith personalities. After five months of intensive work and a series of semiprivate hearings, the commission published a report, "Laïcité et République" (December 11, 2003), and presented its recommendations, which had been adopted almost unanimously (one member, the historian and specialist in French secularism Jean Bobérot, dissented). The commission served by and large to legitimate the law to ban the headscarf for the enforcement of secularism. But the report acknowledged changes in the sociological makeup of France caused by migration and by the presence of Muslims and advised an opening up (to a certain extent) of the interpretation of secularism to a multicultural reality. It proposed, for instance, that the calendar be changed to include a major vacation for each monotheistic religion in France. However, such propositions were dismissed both by the public at large and by the lawmakers. For a discussion of the report's presentation of a pluralistic opening in the interpretation of French laïcité, see Immanuel Wallerstein, "Render unto Caesar?: The Dilemmas of a Multicultural World," Sociology of Religion 46, 2 (Summer 2005): 121–133.

French secularism was endangered and that a new law was required (enacted on March 15, 2004) to prohibit any sign or clothing that indicated a student's religious affiliation in public schools. The law banned all religious signs that were to be considered "conspicuous," such as Christian crosses and Jewish yarmulkes as well as the Islamic headscarf. Although the law mentioned all "conspicuous signs" without singling out the headscarf, everyone agreed that it was mainly designed to discourage Muslim girls from wearing head-scarves.[11]

John Bowen's book *Why the French Don't like Headscarves* attempts to answer this puzzling question and meticulously details the various debates that led to the lawmaking process and the ban. He argues that secularism is not a fixed, well-defined legal and cultural framework but a "narrative" framework that permits public figures—politicians, journalists, and public intellectuals—to debate what laïcité should be and how Muslims ought to act.[12] His work helps us understand the power of the secular discourses and the fear of political Islam in contemporary French society. He calls for acknowledgment of the importance of the multicultural challenges to French society and the need for the republic to develop a better acceptance of migrants and their religious signs without stigmatizing or excluding them. The confinement of the analysis to the national scale stresses not only French singularity but also the role of the state. The public sphere is taken to be a given entity granted by French republicanism, not a secular space that is transformed and trans-gressed by Muslims. Bowen's analysis is in line with the politics of integration and accommodation of differences. In a way he argues that the potentialities of French singularity can also work for migrants, as they give up some of the troublesome differences of Islam to become part of the republic.

In her book on the politics of the veil, Joan W. Scott engages a more argumentative and critical approach in regard to the French notion of laïcité that works as an exclusionary force for Muslim migrants from the public sphere. She argues that the new version of French laïcité, hardened and framed in

11 The ban has been enforced in the public schools without major opposition from Muslim girls. This leads many to think that the headscarf is no longer an issue in French society and the new legislation helped to resolve it. I think we need to pursue a closer investigation of the consequences of the law on the educational choices of Muslim girls and whether it leads to silence or helps to express their perceptions of self, religion, and French citizenship.

12 John R. Bowen, *Why the French Don't like Headscarves* (Princeton: Princeton University Press, 2007).

opposition to Islam, became "an ideological tool in an anti-Muslim campaign."[13] She criticizes the proponents of the headscarf ban in the schools, for whom "integration is a prerequisite for education," which is at odds with the French historical tradition that the school produces integration by means of shared experience of education, where some commonality is created.[14] In her view, banning headscarves in public schools makes the point clear that only one notion of personhood is possible and assimilation is the only route to membership in the nation. Thus, one cannot be both Muslim and French.[15] The notion of personhood includes that of womanhood as well in setting the model of citizenship. Scott acknowledges the realm of sexuality as a battleground between secular and Islamic conceptions of selfhood and points to the contradictions in Western feminism, which she calls the "psychology of denial." She criticizes the universal claims of French secularism and feminism that represent them as superior and "natural," and attempts to open up a space for recognition of religious and cultural differences.

The expression "Secularism is not to be reduced to a piece of cloth" was revealed to be false and true at the same time. False, because the debates on secularism became a matter of clothing, body, and gender. True, because by enacting a law, French society at large expressed its determination to maintain and reinforce the principles of republican secularism. But on the whole, the headscarf debate and the law signified a turning point for French secularism, leading to a critical review of its own understanding and self-presentation in its encounter with Islam. Islam became an active factor in redefining French self-presentation. By the same token, the defense of women's rights and gender equality were placed as core values of republican secularism. The debate also reconfigured the feminist field in France: the majority of French feminists defended the headscarf ban and aligned with republican values, while a minority stood up against the exclusion of girls from the schools (defending "one school for all"). The novelty was that new faces of migrant women appeared in public, voicing the struggle of young secular Muslim women for gender equality and secularism against their own oppressive communities in the *banlieues* (the movement of *"ni putes ni soumises,"* "neither prostitutes nor submissives"). In distinction from these "acceptable"

13 Joan Wallach Scott, *The Politics of the Veil*, (Princeton: Princeton University Press, 2007), 97.
14 Ibid., 102.
15 Ibid., 135.

voices of migrant women, a "subaltern" movement of French migrants emerged and took a critical stand against the republican legacy of secular feminism and the colonial past. They labeled themselves autochthones of the republic (*"les indigènes de la république"*). Thus, the Islamic headscarf debate (although there was more consensus than debate) calls for rethinking secularism from a new perspective.[16] The headscarf became a central marker in changing and reshaping perceptions and definitions of secularism, feminism, and the colonial legacy in France.

The headscarf became such a powerful marker because it condensed in one single icon the multilayered realm of conflict around gender, space, and intercultural issues (and, more precisely, civilisational issues, to the extent that the cultural difference is external to the Western model of enlightenment). The symbol draws attention to a strong visual aspect of the Islamic religion, both in ways in which it is personalized and embodied and in ways it is communicated and perceived. The notion of "conspicuous" that is used in the wording of the French law illustrates the importance of the visual aspect and the intercultural discord in the creation of a public. The notion also conveys ambiguity in terms of intersubjective communication: where to draw the boundaries between a conspicuous and a discreet sign (for instance, crosses and the hands of Fatima are allowed if they are small enough, but Jewish yarmulkes and Sikh turbans are not)—that is, which religious signs and clothing are to be considered conspicuous, and according to whose gaze? A religious sign that is familiar to a given community and therefore "invisible" to their eye can become noticeable, "conspicuous," and disturbing in the eyes of the members of a different religion.[17] The personal meanings attached to signs and clothing may differ from its public perceptions; similarly, public connotations of religious signs can impinge on self-perceptions. The ambiguities and discussions around the notion of "conspicuous" attest to the

16 Emmanuel Terray qualified the debate as a "collective hysteria" to the extent that it became contagious, meaning that all positions went in the same direction, in favor of legislation to ban the headscarf. See Emmanuel Terray, "L'hystérie politique," in *Le Foulard islamique en questions,* ed. C. Nordmann (Paris: Editions Amsterdam, 2004), 103–118.

17 For instance, classrooms were secularized in France a long time ago (by what is known as the Jules Ferry laws); however, in Germany the presence of a Christian cross on classroom walls became an issue when it became "visible" in a multireligious migrant country. For a comparative analysis of the debates, see Schirin Amir Moazami, "Discourses and Counter Discourses: The Islamic Headscarf in the French and German Public Spheres," doctoral diss., European University Institut, Florence, 2004.

importance of the visual, symbolic, and communicative aspects in debating the different meanings and powers of the secular.

As an outcome of this confrontational encounter, both French secularism and the Islamic headscarf, in different ways, ceased to be a monocultural issue. The making of a law guaranteed that the Islamic headscarf is imprinted in the French collective memory; it became an intrinsic part of French history, a "French possession."[18] On the other hand, as the Islamic headscarf entered the public realm of European societies, it ceased to be an exclusively Muslim issue, limited to a Muslim-majority country or to a region. Thereby it signifies that European Muslims as a minority group living in a secular (and Christian) environment face a set of new issues (interfaith relations, modes of gender sociability, dietary habits, and construction of mosques, use of cemeteries, and so on) that are not raised in a similar fashion, if at all, in national Muslim-majority contexts. Muslim migrants are called to (re)think about their religion and faith from the vantage point of their experiences as European citizens. Similarly, European secularism is refashioned in confrontation with issues raised by Muslims. Accounts of secularism limited to genealogies of the Christian religion and Christendom fall short of grasping the contemporary forms of intercultural intercourse.

The Civilizing Mission of the Secular: Turkish Gendered Laiklik

Turkish secularism hints at the ways in which the power of the secular works as part of a "civilizing mission" that operates at the level of everyday life practices and changes material culture, corporal appearances, spatial divisions, and gender sociability. Although Turkish secularism, laiklik, is mainly seen in its political and authoritarian aspects, it provides us with one of the most resourceful historical examples of how the modern secular is indigenized and acted out in changing Muslim definitions of self, ethics, and aesthetics. The Kemalist reforms exemplify the formations of the secular Muslim, namely Muslim habitations and iterations of the secular in a noncolonial context that is characterized by voluntary and authoritarian adaptations of the secular.[19]

18 Sidi Mohammed Barkat, "La loi contre le droit," in *Le Foulard islamique en questions,* ed. C. Nordmann, 28–37.

19 However, one should not think that the historical genealogy of the secular in Turkey starts with Atatürk republicanism; some aspects of the secular are part of the Ottoman state tradition and

The gendered dimension of secularism has been an intrinsic feature of Turkish modernization from its very beginnings in the Ottoman period, when different literary and political currents of thought were in favor of education of girls, free love, gender sociability, and the visibility of women in public as against the religious and traditional morals of society, which confined women to interior spaces and established roles and imposed gender segregation and polygamy. Turkish laiklik meant that the republican state had a strong will to endorse a public sphere where religion would be absent and women would be present. The reforms of the republic, whether they provided legal rights (with the abolition of the Sharia law and the adoption of a civil family code), political rights (women's right to vote and eligibility), educational rights (coeducation), or European clothing habits (taking off the veil, but also banning the fez for men), all underpinned the Turkish way of equating secularism and the "civilized" person, embodied by women's rights and visibility from the very beginning of the republic.

The powers of the secular can be traced in its capacity to develop a set of disciplinary practices, both corporal and spatial, that are inseparable from the formations of the secular self. Secularism is about state politics, lawmaking, and constitutional principles, but foremost it permeates and establishes the rhythm of a phenomenology of everyday life practices.[20] Secularism is not a "neutral," power-free space and a set of abstract principles; it is embodied in people's agencies and imaginaries. The powers of the secular can be traced in its capacity to develop a set of disciplinary practices, both corporal and spatial, that are inseparable from the formations of the secular self. Turkish laiklik illustrates well the didactic aspect of secularism: secularism as a learning process, as inhabiting a new space and learning new body techniques, forms a habitus of a secular way of life (considered to be a higher form of life, because of its equation with Western civilization). Ernest Gellner has referred to Turkish secularism as a "didactic secularism" in the sense that it was imposed by state authoritarianism. But it is also didactic in the sense that it becomes a learned practice, a habitus to be performed by new elites, men and

---

Islamic historical legacy. In order to locate the origins of Turkish republican ideology in the Ottoman past and to correct dualistic representations of the secular and the religious, see Şükrü Hanioğlu, *A Brief History of the Late Ottoman Empire* (Princeton: Princeton University Press, 2008).

20 José Casanova, *Public Religions in the Modern World* (Chicago: University of Chicago Press, 1994).

women who owe their status to the republican schools (that is, secular elites have been formed by means of the state monopoly over the educational system and the adoption of the Latin script in 1928). Secularism designates a habitus in the sense that it is a set of performative techniques and discursive practices (including speaking and writing in modern Turkish, from which Arabic and Persian influences have been eliminated) that are learned and interiorized; but it also designates a "colonized" lifeworld in the sense that it frames these realms in reference to Western notions of truth, ethics, and aesthetics.

The republic created its own secular elites but also its own secular spaces —schools, but also opera and ballet houses, concert halls, ballrooms (mainly in Ankara, the capital city, which seeks to distinguish itself from the cosmopolitan Istanbul), all the landmarks of a new way of life, women's visibility in public life, and social mixing of men and women. Learning how to inhabit these new spaces—husband and wife walking hand in hand; man and woman shaking hands, dancing at balls, and dining together—characterizes acquiring a new habitus required by secular modernity. The modern secular life becomes a sign of prestige through its performative everyday practices, pictorial representations, and material culture.

The emergence of Islam in the post-1980 period addresses a challenge to the hegemonic control of the secular over public spaces and personal habitus. Muslim students' desire to wear headscarves on university campuses meant that the secular was transgressed by the gendered religious. The Turkish and French headscarf debates, in spite of the differences, have some commonalities to the extent that in both cases gender equality and secular spaces framed the debate. The ban, both in Turkey[21] and France, revealed the unwritten secular laws and social imaginaries that governed the "public" spaces. Spaces such as schools, universities, hospitals, pools, and the parliament became controversial once the secular rules had been broken by the transgression caused by religious signs and pious practices. The secular background picture of the public sphere came to the forefront both in Turkey and in France. In both

---

21 Turkey's ban on headscarves at universities dates back to the 1980s but was significantly tightened after February 28, 1997, when army generals with public support ousted a government they deemed too Islamist. The ruling Justice and Development Party (AK Party) attempted to lift the ban, a move that was cited as evidence when a closure case was filed against the party on grounds that it had become a focal point of "antisecular activities."

cases secularism endorsed a role of "assimilation" of Muslims into the Western lifeworld, a civilizing mission, and compulsory learning of the disciplinary practices of the secular in the public spaces. And in both cases religious visibility and femininity defied the hegemony of the secular over definitions of self, sexuality, and space.

Secular and Islamic: Spatial Transgressions

The threshold for the tolerable is framed differently in the French and Turkish contexts. When and how does a religious sign cease to be "discreet" and acceptable and catche the eye, thus turning into a "conspicuous" sign that is troubling for public order? When does the headscarf cease to be perceived as a symbol of "authentic faith" and become a political symbol that provokes a public debate? The head covering of the peasant, the working-class migrant woman, or the grandmother is considered as a symbol of either faith or tradition and therefore is acceptable and invisible, whereas the young woman's headscarf unsettles the secular divisions between pious and traditional, public and modern, and becomes "conspicuous"—that is, visible to the public eye. It provokes powerful emotions of the secular, anger and aversion to the extent that the temporal comfort (religion as a relic from the past) and spatial separations (personal and public) between secular and religious disappear. Today's covered women, as compared with women in the past, who were segregated in private, are both pious and public. They become visible in leaving the traditional interior spaces reserved for women and entering public spaces such as schools, universities, and parliament, namely the spaces reserved for the secular elite. Women's move represents a spatial transgression for both the religious and the secular. Women who are proponents of the headscarf distance themselves from secular models of feminist emancipation but also seek autonomy from male interpretations of Islamic precepts. They represent a rupture of the frame both with secular female self-definitions and religious male prescriptions.[22] They want to have access to secular education, follow new life trajectories that are not in conformity with traditional gender roles, and yet fashion and assert a new pious self. The frontiers between the

22 Erving Goffman, *Frame Analysis: An Essay on the Organization of Experience* (New York: Harper and Row, 1974).

[256]

traditional and the pious are unsettled, as is that between the secular and the public.

The symbol of veiling needs to be readjusted, given its meanings in the past and its contemporary appropriations by new profiles of Muslim women. The symbol of veiling is undergoing a change to the extent that it is adopted by Muslim women who are overtly and assertively pious and public. The veiling is in the process of being changed from a sign of stigma and inferiority[23] into a sign of empowerment, in some cases by means of access to political power; a sign of distinction and prestige, by means of acquisition of social and cultural capital; and a sign of new aesthetics for Muslim women, by means of fashion production.[24] It is certainly a challenge to secular conceptions of female emancipation, but also to male Islam, which identifies the veil with submission to its own authority. But at the same time, the transformation of the veil from a symbol of faith, religion, and stigma into a sign of power, prestige, and aesthetics calls for a composition of the religious and secular divide in new ways.

One can depict this process in the Turkish context as the formation of Islamic counterelites, which in many ways mirror the republican secular elites.[25] The making of the elites follows similar paths: access (especially for girls) to education (both secular and religious); the unveiling and reveiling of women; the disciplinary practices of the secular versus religious habitus; transgression of gender roles from the interior/private realm to the exterior/ public domain. Muslim women cover their bodies yet become visible to the public eye, and hence unsettle the religious norms of modesty and the secular definitions of the feminist self. They are searching for ways to combine piousness and publicness, Muslim and modern at the same time (either by double assertion or by double negation, or neither/nor), and hence transforming the meanings of both.

Islam becomes a source of capital for the ascension of those social groups and social classes that were deprived of social and cultural recognition in the past. Their entry into the spaces reserved for the secular middle classes (uni-

23 Erving Goffman, *Stigma: Notes on the Management of Spoiled Identity* (New York: Touchstone, 1963), and Nilüfer Göle, "The Voluntary Adoption of Islamic Stigma Symbols," *Social Research* 70, 3 (Fall 2003): 809–828.

24 Alexandru Balesescu, *Paris Chic, Tehran Thrills* (Bucharest: Zeta Books, 2007).

25 Nilüfer Göle, "Secularism and Islamism: The Making of the Elites and Counter-elites," *Middle East Journal* 51, 1 (1977): 46–58.

versities, parliament, and leisure and consumption places of distinction such as beaches, concert halls, and commercial malls) disturb the unwritten laws that exclude the religious. The refusal to lift the ban on the headscarf in Turkish universities and the French lawmaking process to ban the headscarf in the public schools both illustrate the sensorial, emotional, and visceral aspects of the secular imaginaries. In spite of the fact that new legislation in Turkey to lift the ban on wearing the headscarf in the universities was formulated not in terms of freedom of religious faith but in the name of equal access of all to higher education and lack of discrimination, and that it therefore was in conformity with European norms and dress codes, it provoked fear and anger among secular women, the public, the media, and the establishment.[26] Ending the ban is feared to provide a first step that will pave the way for the escalation of Muslim claims and the spread of the headscarf beyond the universities to public schools and parliament and among public servants and professionals. The same fear of the escalation of Islamic claims and visibility from public schools to hospitals and to public life in general was expressed in France. The Islamic visibilities in public provoked secular anxieties and mobilized feminist agencies. The headscarf ban revealed the implicit secular norms and imaginaries of the public spaces that were taken for granted as the background picture.

In a similar fashion, public demonstrations in Turkey against the legislation to lift the headscarf ban signaled the transformation of Turkish secularism from state politics to street politics. The form of secularism that has been implemented as a principle of the republican state has been widely considered as a "top-down" ideology, foreign in its roots (inspired by French laïcité) and destined to disappear if not backed up by the army's power. But in the past three decades, secularism came to be expressed in women's groups and associations advocating the defense of a "modern secular way of life."[27] Public demonstrations during the summers of 2007 and 2008 involved millions and spread from one city to another. The abundance of national flags and the

---

26 Seyla Benhabib, "The Return of Political Theology under Conditions of Globalization," unpublished paper, Istanbul Seminars, Reset-Istanbul Bilgi University, 2008.

27 The Association for the Support of a Modern Lifestyle, (in Turkish, Çağdaş Yaşamı Destekleme Derneği) was created in 1989 by leading intellectual and professional women and became a fervent defender of secularism and gender equality. The association played a crucial role against lifting the ban on wearing an Islamic headscarf in the universities.

slogans that were widely used in these demonstrations signified the state-oriented and nationalist features of Turkish secularism. But they also meant a new secular protest movement in the streets. The secular formed a mise-en-scène by numbers, by masses getting together, by symbols (oversized flags acquiring a new popularity), by photographs and the sayings of Atatürk, but also by new modes of secular clothing for women (in tune with the colors of the Turkish flag: red and white miniskirts, ties, and caps), accompanied by music and slogans. Secularism was performed in the public collectively and visually; the numbers mattered, to display that secularism was not in the hands of a minority; a new market of icons and clothing attempted to create a secular fashion; and the use of Atatürk's pictures, deeds, and words provided a frame for commemorating Turkish secularism.[28] In many similar ways secularism was mirroring and competing with Islam to create a repertoire of action. One can speak of a two-way transgression; while the religious broke the rules and moved into secular spaces of the republic, the secular descended from state to street politics.

In both France and Turkey, cultural confrontations and emotional tensions between secular and religious groups are unfolding in the realm of the actions of everyday life, involving a tacit process of mirroring and competing with each other. Both for the secular and for the religious, visual signs, gendered performances, and spatial divisions become the battleground for self-distinction and discipline.

European Secularity and Islamic Self

The powers of both secularism and Islam cease to be bound to given national state formations, distinctive civilizations, but become part of a cross-civilizational and transnational European public. The European public sphere cannot be thought of as the extension and addition of national publics, as a national public written large; genealogical, historical readings of its formation do not capture the present-day encounters between different language communities, cultural codes, ethnicities, and religions. On the other hand, readings of Islam confined to the national politics of migration or, in an opposite

28 For the commemoration of the republican heritage, see Esra Özyürek, *The Nostalgia for the Modern: State Secularism and Everyday Politics in Turkey* (Raleigh: Duke University Press, 2006).

move, linked to global jihadist movements do not render the ways in which Islam becomes European.

The negative aspects of geographical and cultural displacements are often highlighted in the case of migration and the politicization of Islam. Conditions of migration are depicted in terms of economic precariousness, cultural alienation, and personal frustration caused by deficiencies of integration, leading to inward-looking communities, particularly ghettolike suburbs, which are taken to be the home of insecurity and the political radicalization of Islam. Islam is under the impact of dynamics of social mobility and modernity to the extent that it is no longer exclusively a reference for those groups who are attached to a place, to a territory, and to traditions. Olivier Roy points to the "de-territorialization" of Muslims, those who follow a global trajectory in their strategies and formations of neofundamentalism.[29] But there is another aspect of social mobility that is often neglected in approaches to Islam yet is crucial to understanding the formation of new Muslim subjectivities. Social mobility is not only deracinating and alienating; it also opens up a realm for the elaboration of improvisations, adaptations, and inventions of subjectivities and a sense of belonging.

Concomitant with the move into modern life spaces, religion and traditions cease to be prearranged entities; Islam no longer appears as a norm that is taken for granted, transmitted from one generation to another, socially embedded and institutionalized, but on the contrary faces discontinuities in its transmission and claims of authority. Islam, a binding force among those who belonged to a locality, to a particular confession, and to a nation-state, becomes a reference going beyond the local frontiers, providing an imaginary bond between Muslims, and enabling Muslim self-fashioning.

In exploring the literary genealogies of Renaissance self-fashioning, Stephen Greenblatt draws on the sociological work of Daniel Lerner to remind us of the positive and complex relations between mobility and the elaboration of modern personality.[30] Greenblatt argues that a person's identity, while determined by external circumstances, is subject to improvisations and hence remains partly fashionable. He views this form of mental mobility and agility (which Lerner calls "empathy," namely the capacity to project oneself into

29 Olivier Roy, *Globalized Islam: The Search for a New Ummah* (London: Hurst, 2004).

30 Daniel Lerner, *The Passing of Traditional Society: Modernizing the Middle East* (Glencoe, Ill.: Free Press, 1958). This book was subject to criticism for the outmoded duplication of binary categories of Western modernity and the traditional Middle East.

another person's situation) as characteristic of the rise of modern individuals. However, Lerner's notion of empathy, as an act of "imaginative generosity," disinterested and exempt from the exercise of Western power, is incomplete. For Greenblatt, modern individuation is not boundless, and the fashioning of the self takes place through mechanisms of "discipline, restraint and a partial suppression of the personality."[31]

We can speak of Islam as providing the mechanisms of discipline, restraint, and empowerment for a new self-fashioning of Muslims; they adapt and improvise their faith under new conditions of social mobility and cultural displacement. There is an element of "invention" (of traditions) in the self-fashioning process that is not separated from disciplinary practices of self-restraint (control of sexuality, mind, and self, called "nefs" in Islam). The notion of self-fashioning helps us move beyond the category of "identity" that remains equated with authenticity and emancipation. The notion of self-fashioning is helpful in conveying the visual and corporal aspects of personal identity; additionally, self-fashioning resonates with the disciplinary powers of both the secular and the religious idioms. The headscarf expresses the self-fashioning of Muslim girls with disciplinary categories of Islam, but for them faith is not a prearranged category and enters into the domain of improvisation, adaptation, and invention. It is a sign of self-restraint (*hijab* means modest behavior and dress) and self-fashioning, including, in literal terms, the production of Islamic fashion.

The "faith" cannot be taken for granted, as if the Islamic faith were carried in the luggage of the migrants as they arrive from villages and small towns in their home countries. Social mobility, on the contrary, means distancing oneself from one's country of origin and living under conditions of displacement in which the ties with the traditional, institutional forms of religiosity are cut off. Social groups that are undergoing social mobility are those that distance themselves from the family background, local authorities, and institutionalized traditions in which Islam was a prearranged norm. Piety is established not as a once-and-for-all category, handed down from one generation to another, or carried from the hometown, but in movement, in improvisation, and in acquisition through religious knowledge and self-fashioning. Islam becomes part of "disembedded," imagined forms of horizontal solidar-

31 Stephen Greenblatt, *Renaissance Self-Fashioning: From More to Shakespeare* (Chicago: University of Chicago Press. 1980). See also Jürgen Pieters, *Moments of Negotiation: The New Historicism of Stephen Greenblatt* (Amsterdam: Amsterdam University Press, 2001).

ity. Charles Taylor describes social disembeddedness as a condition for a different kind of social imaginary—that is, "horizontal forms of social imaginary in which people grasp themselves and great number of others as existing and acting simultaneously" (VR, 83).

In contexts of migration, Islam becomes part of an "intellectual learning" endeavor rather than learning by recitation and imitation from previous generations. Contemporary actors in Islam very often make the distinction between those who are Muslim by tradition and those who are Muslim by education, valorizing the second. Acquiring religious knowledge means learning how to interpret the Quran; achieving fluency in the Arabic language, but also engaging in collective prayers and conversations as a bond-making practice (sohbet); and building a community of believers. The acquisition of Islamic knowledge combines religious norms of virtue and disciplinary practices of body; praying, dietary habits, and sexual modesty become practices that require continuous surveillance and rigorous application in a secular environment.[32] Learning Islam by attending seminars and youth institutions but also by means of performative practices requires an alternative space—an alternative to both secular hegemonic and traditional religious "counterpublics."[33] Pious Muslims have to deal on an everyday basis with the incongruities between their faith and their secular public lives. In a Muslim-minority context, everything that is considered "natural"—for instance, the ritual of the ablution before prayer—necessitates a particular reserved "space," and the purification ritual becomes a complicated matter in its absence and disturbing in its visibility in public restrooms. Similarly, praying five times a day in a society organized according to secular time and in working spaces with instrumental rationality brings forth the question of praying rooms; use of secular spaces for religious observance will also bring conspicuous, disturbing visibility. While praying, a Muslim woman covers her hair; if she does so in a workplace, she becomes instantly visible, recognizable as a "Muslim." There are therefore strategies for visibility as well as for dissimulation of

32 Jeannette Jouili inquired in France and Germany how Muslim women learned to be pious Muslims, in acquiring religious knowledge, cultivating bodily disciplines, and surveying their minds and bodies. Jeanette S. Jouili, "Devenir pieuse: Femmes musulmanes en France et en Allemange entre réforme de soi et quête de reconnaissance," doctoral diss., Ecole des Hautes Etudes en Sciences Sociales, Paris, 2007.

33 For an elaboration of the notions of space, publicness, and counterpublics in the cultural politics of displaying differences, see Michael Warner, Publics and Counterpublics, (Cambridge, Mass.: Zone, 2002).

faith. The Islamic covering is one distinctive representation of piety that creates immediate recognition for male and female citizens. But there are pious Muslim women who do not adopt the veil but for whom the relation to a secular way of life—modes of address with non-Muslim men, dating, and alcohol consumption—becomes fuzzy in the absence of a clear-cut frontier, a visible religious marker.[34]

The public sphere becomes the site where the importance of the visual is played out. Especially where issues of Islamic religion and gender are in question, the gaze and spatial conventions acquire a greater salience in mediating power relations. When Muslim women cross the borders between inside and outside, the arousal of multiple senses—sight, smell, touch, and voice—and desires requires the preservation of decency and control of public morality. The visibility of Muslim women in public life means crossing and transgressing the interior, intimate, secret, gendered space, forbidden to foreign males' gaze *(mahrem)*. Veiling suggests the importance of the ocular (avoiding the gaze, casting down one's eyes). The notion of sexual modesty *(edep)* underpins the Muslim self-fashioning. Such Islamic behavior—the aesthetics of *edep*, the valorization of the *mahrem* with retained body exposure and self-protection, controlled gender sociability, and gender-differentiated modes of address—enact ways of being Muslim in secular publics. These behaviors are not alien to Muslim memory and culture. They are rooted in past traditions and memory, in the religious habitus. But they are not simple conventions that have always been there and that are unconsciously handed down from generation to generation. The habitus provides, in Pierre Bourdieu's terms, a source of improvisations; it allows for a process of continual correction and adjustment.[35] Islamic public performances reinvent religious traditions, correct and improvise them in counterdistinction to secular norms and disciplinary practices.

We can speak of what Victor Turner calls "performative reflexivity," "a condition in which a sociocultural group, or its most perceptive members, acting representatively, turn, bend, or reflect back upon themselves, upon the relations, actions, symbols, meanings, and codes, roles, statuses, social structures, ethical and legal rules, and other sociocultural components which

---

34 Jouili, "Devenir pieuse."

35 Craig Calhoun, "Habitus, Field, and Capital: The Question of Historical Specificity," in *Bourdieu: Critical Perspectives,* ed. Craig Calhoun, Edward LiPuma, and Moishe Postone (Chicago: University of Chicago Press, 1993), 61–89.

make up their public 'selves.'"[36] Islamic performance has a reflexive character to the extent that the codes and symbols embedded in the religious culture are critically appropriated and distanced from the traditional culture. It also has a reflexive feature in being engaged with a series of issues that are raised when one is a Muslim in a secular and Christian-majority society, ranging from spaces for practicing faith to public modes of self-presentation, sociability of men and women to competition with secular definitions of liberty and femininity. Muslims enter into common spaces of everyday life experience with Europeans that in turn calls for mutual transformations and reflexivity—a reflexivity that is translated not only in discursive terms but also in the transformation of the material culture.

One can suggest that European Islam is following similar dynamics to what Charles Taylor calls the post-Durkheimian situation, in which faith is not connected, or is only weakly connected, to a national political identity. But as the author argues, the human aspiration to religion does not disappear, and does not become a trivialized and utterly privatized spirituality. Similarly, Islam offers a sense of "believing," yet without "belonging" either to a national community or to an institutionalized religion. Islam becomes personally pious and publicly visible, disembedded from its institutionalized forms but more voluntary and mental; it is learned, performed, and imagined socially. Hence Islam is shaped by the secular age. As Taylor argues, religious and antireligious people in modernity have more assumptions in common than they often realize. But in distinction from what Charles Taylor calls the "expressive revolution," in which the ethic of authenticity is accompanied by a sexual revolution and undercuts the close connections of religious faith with a certain sexual morality, Islamic habitus brings forth alternative notions of self, morality, and piousness. That is why the discord with Islam is carried at the forefront by secular feminists, by those who are committed to the imperatives of the expressive revolution and sexual revolution, the cultural legacies of the 1968 movement. The Islamic presence in Europe defies the secular norms of individuality, gender equality, and sexuality. Mono-civilizational readings of both the secular and the religious fail to account for this ongoing process of mutual transformation.

36 Victor Turner, *The Anthropology of Performance* (New York: PAJ, 1986), 24.

II

A Secular Age: Dawn or Twilight?

José Casanova

Charles Taylor's *A Secular Age* offers the best analytical, phenomenological, and genealogical account we have of our modern, secular condition. By "best" I mean that it is simultaneously the most comprehensive, nuanced, and complex account I know. Analytically, it explains with distinct clarity the structural interlocking constellation of the cosmic, social, and moral orders that constitute the self-sufficient immanent frame within which we are constrained to live and experience our lives, secular as well as religious. All three orders—the cosmic, the social, and the moral—are understood as purely immanent secular orders, devoid of transcendence, and thus functioning *etsi Deus non daretur*. It is this phenomenological experience that, according to Taylor, constitutes our age paradigmatically as a secular one, irrespective of the extent to which people living in this age may still hold religious or theistic beliefs. Indeed, Taylor's primary interest is not to offer a sociological account of secularity in terms of standard theories of secularization, which measure the changing (mostly falling) rates of religious beliefs and practices in modern contemporary societies.

Taylor is primarily interested in offering a phenomenological account of the secular "conditions" of belief and of the "preontological" context of understanding, in order to explain the change from a Christian society around 1500 CE in which belief in God was unchallenged and unproblematic, indeed "naive" and taken for granted, to a post-Christian society today in which belief in God not only is no longer axiomatic but becomes increasingly problematic, so that even those who adopt an "engaged" standpoint as believers are forced to adopt simultaneously a "disengaged" standpoint, in which they experience reflectively their own belief as an option among many others— one, moreover, requiring a explicit justification. Secularity, by contrast, tends to become increasingly the default option, which can be naively experienced as natural and thus no longer in need of justification.

This phenomenological experience, as merely immanent, is what in turn serves to ground the phenomenological experience of exclusive humanism as the positive self-sufficient and self-limiting affirmation of human flourishing and as the critical rejection of transcendence beyond human flourishing as self-denial and self-defeating. Moreover, intrinsic to this phenomenological experience is a modern "stadial consciousness," inherited from the Enlightenment, which understands this anthropocentric change in the conditions of belief as a process of maturation and growth, as a "coming of age," and as progressive emancipation. Modern unbelief is not simply a condition of absence of belief, nor merely indifference. It is a historical condition that requires the perfect tense, "a condition of 'having overcome' the irrationality of belief" (*SA,* 269). As Taylor indicates, precisely "the superiority of our present outlook over other earlier forms of understanding is part of what defines the advance of the present stage over all earlier ones" (289). This historical consciousness turns the very idea of going back to a surpassed condition into an unthinkable intellectual regression. It is, in his words, "the ratchet at the end of the anthropocentric shift, which makes it (near) impossible to go back on it. This powerful understanding of an inescapable impersonal order, uniting social imaginary, epistemic ethic, and historical consciousness, becomes one of the (in a sense unrecognized) *idées forces* of the modern age" (289–290).

For that very reason, all analytical and phenomenological accounts of modernity are irremediably also grand narratives, indeed are always embedded in some genealogical account. Taylor's account is in this respect no different, and thus fully within the historical consciousness of modernity. Actually, it is the richness and complexity of his genealogical account, in obvious opposition to the postmodern illusion of being able to free ourselves from grand narratives, that make Taylor's analysis of secular modernity so compelling. Taylor's account is superior precisely insofar as it is able to integrate successfully the valid insights of most of the competing genealogical accounts.

One may group the genealogical accounts of modernity into four basic types: (1) the triumphant secularist and anthropocentric progressive stories of enlightenment and emancipation of the secular spheres from religious institutions and norms; (2) the inverse negative philosophies of history, counter-Enlightenment narratives, and mainly Catholic traditionalist defenses of a lost normative age; (3) the positive, mainly Protestant postmillennial identifications of Western modernity and Christian civilization that tend to interpret secular modernity as a process of internal secularization and progressive institutionalization of Christian principles and norms; and (4) their opposite, Nietzschean-derived critical genealogies of modernity, which question the legitimacy of the modern secular age and its disciplinary and civilizing project precisely because of its bastard Christian lineage. Taylor acknowledges and incorporates the valid insights of each of those accounts but faults them for their partial, one-sided focus and unidirectional teleology. His complex account, by contrast, is full of zigzags, unexpected turns, and unintended results.

Secularist genealogies of modernity, which derive from the Enlightenment critique of religion in all its cognitive, ideologico-political, and moral-aesthetic dimensions, are versions of what Taylor calls "subtraction theories." They are problematic not so much in their self-assertive humanist claims and positive evaluation of the progressive achievements of "our" secular age, which Taylor repeatedly acknowledges, but precisely insofar as secularist accounts are blind to the Christian roots of the entire process of secularization, to the repeated Christian dynamics of disciplinary inner-worldly transformation, and to the Christian moral energies that have fed much of the process of modern reform. Taylor challenges secularist prejudices that tend to understand the secular as merely the space left behind when this-worldly reality is emptied of religion or to view unbelief as resulting simply from the progress of science and rational inquiry. Similarly, he argues that exclusive humanism could not simply result from the disenchantment of the cosmos and the distancing of a deist God from a mechanistically run universe. Its moral sources, benevolence, and universal concern had to be created, discovered, or at least relocated and refashioned from its Christian roots in agape. Modern progressive philosophies of history are precisely problematic in viewing secular modernity as the last triumphant episode in a universal story of human development and secularization, while failing to recognize the particular contingent historical origins of the process in Latin Christendom.

Yet Taylor also wants to distinguish his account from all Catholic intellectual deviation stories and from all Protestant identifications of modernity as Christian. Intellectual deviation stories can clarify some of the theological connections between the critique of "realism" and the rise of nominalism, possibilism, voluntarism, and their connections with the rise of mechanistic science, ontic dualism, and modern instrumental reason—in brief, with the whole process of "disenchantment." But such a genealogy, anchored as it is in intellectual history, leaves out the entire reform master narrative, which is so central to Taylor's account. Reform also begins within Latin Christendom and is identified with "the thrust to complete the Axial revolution" and to end "the balance and complementarity between pre- and post-Axial elements in all higher civilizations." For Taylor, "Reform not only disenchants, but disciplines and re-orders life and society" (SA, 774).

In turn, the sanguine identification of Protestant Christianity and modern civilization, which one finds in German versions of Kulturprotestantismus and in British colonial civilizing projects, and which still lives on in contemporary versions of the American civil religion and of imperial manifest destiny, rightly direct attention to the close connection between Christian reformation, demanding "that everyone be a real, 100 percent Christian," and all modern processes of disciplinary and civilizing reform. Yet, while acknowledging the "invaluable gains," Taylor's narrative pays equal attention to the grievous losses, the Christian self-mutilation, and the homogenizing conformity that accompanies the triumph of secularity and of the immanent frame. Taylor warns us to be equally wary of all narratives of simple, cost-free suppression and supersession, whether narrated by Christians in the form of "God's pedagogy" or by protagonists of the Enlightenment in the form of the "ascent of man." Taylor's account has "no place for unproblematic breaks with a past which is simply left behind us" (772).

There are also clear affinities between Taylor's account and the neo-Nietzschean critiques of modernity, which Taylor calls "immanent counter-Enlightenment" and which can be interpreted as a revolt against the allegiance to the moral order and the affirmation of ordinary life that exclusive humanism inherited from the Christian tradition. It is, in Taylor's words, "the revolt from within unbelief, as it were, against the primacy of life" (*SA*, 372). Taylor can empathize with the rebellion against the exclusive humanism of modern culture. But insofar as the proponents of exclusive humanism reject any ontically grounded understanding of transcendence, they actually serve to reinforce further the immanent frame that Taylor aims precisely to destabilize.

Nieztschean-derived genealogical accounts of Western modernity that question the legitimacy of modernity precisely because of its association with Christianity tend to provoke in turn passionate defenses of the legitimacy of the modern secular age and its exclusive humanism, as in Blumenberg's thesis of human non-Christian self-assertion. Those in turn provoke the spirited defense of Christian apologists, who see the superiority of Christianity and Christian civilization precisely in its virtuous association with secular modernity, which in turn provokes the anti-modern critiques of Christian or Aristotelian traditionalists, and so on in circular fashion.[1] It is one of the virtues of Taylor's complex genealogical account that it is able to cut through the whole debate, indeed to transcend it, recognizing valid insights and uncritical blindness in each of the positions. This is the case not only because, as Robert Bellah points out in Chapter 1, Taylor's account is devoid of polemic and is generous hermeneutically in trying to understand all possible positions and to see virtue in all of them.

More importantly, he sees in the polemic responses and relations to one another an illustration of the kind of destabilization that is built into the contingent historical process of secularization he is trying to reconstruct in all its complexity. Such recognition may help, or so Taylor hopes, change our picture of modern culture. "Instead of seeing it as the scene of a two-sided battle, between 'tradition,' especially religious tradition, and secular humanism, we might rather see it as a kind of free-for-all, the scene of a three-cornered —perhaps ultimately, a four cornered—battle" (*SA*, 374). Taylor's own position in this battle and ultimately the thrust behind his compelling account of the modern immanent frame is to show the destabilizing cracks and the ungrounded and unreflexive certainty of exclusive humanism, in the hope of

---

1 Cf. Karl Löwith, Hans Blumenberg, Ernst Troeltsch, Talcott Parsons, Alisdair McIntyre, and John Milbank.

creating some openings for transcendence beyond human flourishing. The masterful account of the contemporary taken-for-granted conditions of un-belief developed in the first parts of the book (Parts I–IV) has the function precisely of creating an open space for the exploration of the contemporary "conditions of belief" in the final part of the book, where Taylor wants to destabilize the immanent frame and the unquiet frontiers of modernity by looking at its intrinsic cross-pressures and dilemmas and by illuminating the possibilities of conversion. If the first sections of the book reveal the analyti-cal, hermeneutic, and narrative gifts of a philosopher who can help us as few others can to understand our secular social imaginaries, the final part reveals the romantic soul of Christian love, the will to belief that accompanies the hope for eternity, and the utopian thirst for incarnated divinization and tran-scendence beyond mere human flourishing.

Let me reiterate, therefore, the beginning paragraph of this chapter and address the critical interrogation of the title. Taylor's *A Secular Age* offers the best analytical, phenomenological, and genealogical account we have of "our" modern, secular condition. But how is Taylor to be remembered: as the definitive philosopher of the immanent frame and of exclusive human-ism at the moment of its definitive triumph, or rather as the prophet of a dawning postsecular age? Clearly he aims to destabilize the immanent frame that shapes so much of our social imaginary. But is he able to offer such a de-finitive account only because his philosophical vision stands at the twilight of an age already anticipating a new dawn?

Ultimately, the crucial question one must pose is, who are the "we" of "our" secular age? Taylor makes clear in the very first paragraph of the book that he has in mind "the 'we' who live in the West, or perhaps Northwest, or otherwise put, the North Atlantic world—although secularity extends also partially, and in different ways, beyond this world" (*SA,* 1). Such an opening raises in my view two important questions, which I would like to explore as critical interrogations directed at Taylor's account. Both derive, no doubt, from my professional sociological bias, but they are nonetheless unavoidable as fundamental questions. Given Taylor's unitary phenomenological account of "our" contemporary "condition of belief," or rather unbelief, how is one to account sociologically for the radical bifurcation in the religious situation today between Western societies on both sides of the North Atlantic—that is, between the radical secularity of European societies, which indeed appears to match perfectly Taylor's phenomenological account, and the still predominant condition of religious belief among the immense majority of ordinary people that one finds in the United States?

The question of the relation between the two patently different phenomenological and sociological accounts can also be reframed inversely, so that one may ask, given the overwhelming sociological empirical evidence of the persistent and widespread condition of religious belief in the United States, is Taylor's phenomenological account of the uniform condition of unbelief across the North Atlantic world credible? In other words, who are the "we" of Taylor's phenomenological account? Does it exclude the immense majority of the population of the United States, who appear to live within the same immanent frame as modern Europeans yet are unlikely to recognize as their own the condition of exclusive humanism so clearly depicted by Taylor? No doubt there is an important and vocal minority of "secular humanists" in the United States. But the overwhelming majority of Americans are likely to view themselves as "religious" humanists rather than as secular ones. I do not think we are dealing here merely with a question of semantics. What is at stake is the very credibility of the transformation in the conditions of belief that anchors Taylor's entire narrative, from a condition around 1500 when belief in God was basically axiomatic to the current condition in the year 2000 when unbelief appears to be rather the default, almost natural condition. Except in the United States, of course, where historians and sociologists of religion never tire of pointing out that the immense majority of the population appears to live "awash in a sea of faith," as captured in the suggestive title of Jon Butler's history of American religion.[2] So how does one account for the old nagging question of American exceptionalism, and how does it affect our narratives of secular modernity?

Taylor is well aware of the problem, to the point where one may be tempted to argue that his more sociological "narratives of secularization" in Part IV are introduced precisely in order to counter possible critiques. He actually offers some important clues for what could be turned into a convincing sociological explanation of American exceptionalism. First of all, an important part of the explanation must certainly be the crucial historical fact that

2 Jon Butler, *Awash in a Sea of Faith: Christianizing the American People* (Cambridge, Mass.: Harvard University Press, 1990).

there was no United States in 1500, and therefore the people in the United States did not have to overcome either the established ecclesiastical institutions or the paleo-Durkheimian conditions of belief of the old European ancient regimes in any of its two main forms: in the unitary form of pre-Reformation medieval Christendom or in its post-Reformation Westphalian arrangement of territorialized confessional absolutist states.

Second, an important corollary of this primary fact must be the fact that the United States was born as a brand-new modern secular republic and that its very foundation coincides with "the age of mobilization," in the sense that religious mobilization and political mobilization are simultaneous and co-foundational in the Christian secular republic, so that the American Enlightenment and the American civil religion are for all practical purposes devoid of the kind of anti-Christian animus that occupies such a central place in Taylor's genealogical account of exclusive humanism. Indeed, one might ask whether the very term "neo-Durkheimian dispensation" is appropriate in a case like the United States, when there is not a previous stage of paleo-Durkheimian dispensation, of which it is supposed to be a transformed mutation—that is, when the very Christianization of the American people is the historical outcome of the religious-political mobilization that accompanies all the Great Awakenings and all the sociohistorical transformations of American democracy.

Third, one has to take into account the fact that what Taylor calls "the age of authenticity," which in his account emerges around 1960, after the exhaustion of "the age of mobilization" (1800–1950), in the case of the United States, at least in the religious sphere, should be dated much earlier. The age of authenticity, no doubt, owes much to the romantic reaction that Taylor has so persistently and distinctly illuminated for us throughout his work and that became democratized throughout the North American world with the countercultural movement and youth rebellions of the 1960s. One could legitimately argue that it constitutes possibly the turning point in the radical secularization of modern Western societies, certainly Western European ones. Yet in the case of the United States, in the sphere of religion, the age of authenticity may be said to have been already present and operative during the Second Great Awakening, certainly in the Burned Over District of upstate New York and in the myriad of utopian communities and radical spiritual experiments in all directions, which once again Butler has appropriately and suggestively characterized as the "spiritual hothouse" of antebellum America.[3]

But, one may further ask, if the stage theory of "paleo-," "neo-," and "post-" Durkheimian social orders does not fit so neatly the historical experience of the United States, could this constitute an almost insuperable impediment to the widespread acceptance of a stadial historical consciousness that views unbelief as the quasi-natural developmental result of a kind of secular coming of age and of adult maturation? Moreover, without the stadial consciousness of the superiority of unbelief, perhaps one also lacks the ratchet effect of the anthropocentric shift to exclusive humanism, so that what Taylor calls the nova and even supernova effects of the age of authenticity have always been operative in the United States, but only to multiply to the nth degree the myriad options of belief rather than those of unbelief.

One could turn the European theories of American exceptionalism upside-down and view the historical process of secularization of Latin Christendom not as the general rule but rather as the one truly exceptional process, unlikely to be reproduced anywhere else in the world with the same sequential arrangement and the corresponding stadial consciousness. It does not mean that one has to accept the now emerging theories of European exceptionalism, promoted by Peter Berger and Grace Davie, according to which secularity is a singular European phenomenon unknown in the rest of the world, other than among Westernized elites, so that the global condition is rather one of desecularization of the world and religious revival. There are plenty of indications of secularity in Japanese and Chinese cultures, for instance. What they lack, however, is precisely the stadial consciousness, and without it, one may ask, can the immanent frame of the secular modern order have the same phenomenological effect in the conditions of belief and unbelief in non-Western societies? Without a stadial consciousness, can "this powerful understanding of an inescapable impersonal order, uniting social imaginary, epistemic ethic, and historical consciousness, become one of the (in a sense unrecognized) *idées forces* of the modern age" also in non-Western societies (*SA*, 289–290)? Or will it rather be recognized for what it obviously is, namely a particular Western Christian process of secularization without the same force in non-Christian societies, which did not undergo a similar

3 Ibid.

process of historical development but instead always confronted Western secular modernity from their first encounter with European colonialism as "the other"?

I would like to look at the possible ways in which this decentering of the Western European experience, this provincializing of Europe that accompanies our global age, may serve also to destabilize even further Taylor's secular age, without necessarily opening new paths to novel forms of transcendence. This question is particularly justified as Taylor places the whole process of Western secularization as a radicalization of the great disembedding of the individual from the sacred cosmos and from society initiated by the axial revolutions. In the context of a general theory of "religious" evolution, one may understand this process as a redrawing of boundaries between sacred and profane, transcendence and immanence, and religious and secular. It should be obvious that these three dichotomous classificatory schemes do not fit neatly within one another. The sacred tends to be immanent in preaxial societies, transcendence does not need to be religious in some axial civilizations, and obviously much secular reality (the nation, citizenship, inalienable rights to life and freedom) can be sacred in the modern secular age, while individualized and privatized religiosity may lose its public sacred character.

Sacred and profane, following Durkheim, would be a general dichotomous classificatory scheme of all reality, characteristic of all preaxial human societies, encompassing within one single order what later will be distinguished as three separate realms: the cosmic, the social, and the moral. All reality—what we later will learn to distinguish as the gods or spirits, nature and cosmic forces, humans and other animal species, and the political, social, and moral orders—is integrated into a single order of things according precisely to the dichotomous classificatory system of sacred and profane. The entire system, moreover, is an immanent "this-worldly" one, if one is allowed to use anachronistically another dichotomous category that will only emerge precisely with the axial revolutions. What defines the axial revolutions is precisely the introduction of a new classificatory scheme that results from the emergence of "transcendence," of an order of being beyond the entire this-worldly reality, which now can serve as a transcendent principle to evaluate, regulate, and possibly transform this-worldly reality. As in the case of the Platonic world of "ideas," or the Confucian reformulation of the Chinese *tao*, transcendence is not necessarily "religious," nor does all "religion" need to become transcendent, if we are allowed once again to use anachronistically another dichotomous classificatory category, "religious/secular," which will only emerge with modernity.

To return to Taylor's analysis, what all axial revolutions introduce is transcendent paths, individual and collective, of salvation, redemption, or moral perfection "beyond human flourishing." Not all axial paths entail a refashioning or transformation of the world or the social order; in some cases, indeed, as in Buddhism, it may entail a radical devaluation and rejection of all reality and a flight from this world, switching now to a Weberian language. But all of them, in Taylor's analysis, will entail some refashioning of "the self," who is now "called" to live (or perhaps to deny herself) according to some transcendent norm beyond human flourishing. In the case of the radical transcendent monotheism introduced by the prophets in ancient Israel, the axial revolution entails a radical desacralization of all cosmic, natural, and social reality, of all creatures, gods, and idols, for the sake of the exclusive sacralization of Yahweh, the transcendent creator God.

The religious/secular dichotomy is a particular medieval Christian version of the more general axial dichotomous classification of transcendent and immanent orders of reality. Unique to the medieval system of Latin Christendom is the institutionalization of an ecclesiastical-sacramental system of mediation, the Church, between the transcendent City of God and the immanent City of Man. The Church can play this role precisely because it partakes of both realities. As *ecclesia invisibilis,* "the communion of the saints," the Christian Church is a "spiritual" reality, part of the eternal transcendent City of God. As *ecclesia visibilis,* the Christian Church is in the saeculum, a "temporal" reality, and thus part of the immanent City of Man. The modern Western process of secularization that culminates in "a secular age" is a particular historical dynamic that makes sense only as a response and reaction to the medieval Latin Christian system of classification of all reality into "spiritual" and "temporal," "religious" and "secular." It ends with the establishment of the secular immanent frame as the single reality, within which religion and spirituality will have to find its place. But it begins—and this is the crucial point of Taylor's master reform narrative—as a process of internal secular reform within Latin Christendom, as an attempt to "spiritualize" the temporal and to bring the religious life out of the monasteries into the saeculum, and thus, literally, to secularize the religious. The process of spiritualization of temporal-secular reality entails also a process of interiorization of religion, and thus a certain deritualization, desacralization, or demagicization of religion, which in the particular case of Christianity takes naturally the form of desacramentalizing and deecclesializing religion.

The repeated attempts at Christian reform of the saeculum, that is, to Christianize the immanent City of Man, began with the papal revolution and continued with the emergence of the spiritual orders of mendicant and preaching friars bent on Christianizing the growing medieval towns and cities and with the emergence of lay Christian communities of brothers and sisters, brotherhoods and sisterhoods, committed to a life of Christian perfection in the saeculum, in the world. These medieval movements of Christian reform already established the basic patterns of secularization which would later be radicalized by the accumulative processes of secularization brought by the Protestant Reformation and all subsequent modern civilizing and reform processes, which ushered in the modern revolution.

The general dynamic of secularization follows a consistent effort to bridge the gap, ultimately to eliminate altogether the dichotomous division, between the religious and the secular. But this basic pattern of secularization takes two different historical paths. The Protestant path, which will be radicalized in Anglo-Saxon societies, and particularly in the United States, takes the form of breaking the boundaries, "the monastery walls," between the religious and the secular, making the religious secular and the secular religious. It takes also a form of radical desacramentalization which will assume an extreme form with the radical sects in their attempt to dismantle all ecclesiastical institutions and to turn the ecclesia into a secular association of visible "saints." The Latin-Catholic path, by contrast, will take the form of laicization, and is basically marked by a civil-ecclesiastical and laic-clerical antagonistic dynamic. Thus the central role attained by anticlericalism in the process. It maintains rigidly the boundaries between the religious and the secular, but pushes those boundaries into the margins, containing, privatizing, and marginalizing everything religious. When it breaks the monastery walls, it will be not to bring the religious into the secular world but to laicize them, dissolving and emptying their religious content and making the religious persons, monks and nuns, civil and laic before forcing them into the world. This could well serve as the basic metaphor for all subtraction narratives of secular modernity.

Even within Western secular modernity one can find, therefore, two very different patterns of secularization, one could even say two different types of modernity. This would be the basic underlying reality behind the different European and American patterns of secularization, although one could also discern, following David Martin's analysis, a multiplicity of patterns within a common frame of secularization of the various types of ancient regimes, which emerged in Europe out of the dissolution of the medieval system of Latin Christendom and the formation of the Westphalian system of territorial states. According to Taylor's analysis, however, all of them can be viewed as variables within the same basic post-Christian pattern of Western secularization. All of them are embedded within a common immanent frame and within the same secular age.

It just happened, of course, as we are only now becoming increasingly aware, that this particular historical pattern of Western Christian secularization became globalized through the very particular historical process of European colonial expansion. As a result the immanent frame became in a certain sense globalized, at least in terms of certain crucial aspects of the cosmic order through the globalization of science and technology, certain crucial aspects of the institutional social order of the state, the market, and the public sphere, and certain crucial aspects of the moral order through the globalization of individual human rights. But the process of European colonial expansion encountered other postaxial civilizations with very different social imaginaries, which often had their own established patterns of reform in accordance with their own particular axial civilizational principles and norms. The outcomes that will result from these long historical dynamics of intercivilizational encounters, conflicts, borrowings, accommodations, and *aggiornamentos* are likely to change from place to place, from time to time, and from civilization to civilization.

As a critical comment to Taylor's genealogical account, one could argue with Peter van der Veer that the very pattern of Western secularization cannot be fully understood if one ignores the crucial significance of the colonial encounter in European developments.[4] Indeed, the best of postcolonial analysis has shown how every master reform narrative and every genealogical

4 Peter van der Veer, *Imperial Encounters: Religion and Modernity in India and Britain* (Princeton: Princeton University Press, 2001).

account of Western secular modernity needs to take account of those colonial and inter-civilizational encounters. Any comprehensive narrative of the modern civilizing process must take into account the Western European encounter with other civilizations. The very category of "civilization" in the singular only emerges out of these inter-civilizational encounters.

Moreover, this is even more the case when one attempts a genealogical reconstruction of the unique modern secular category of "religion," which has now also become globalized. The modern secular invention of the "world religions" and the disciplinary institutionalization of the scientific study of religion are intimately connected with this globalization of religion. One should be careful, however, to avoid making an essentialized secular modernity the dynamic causal force of everything, including religion, as some genealogies of the secular are now prone to do. One must simply recognize that there are no bounded histories within nation-states, within civilizations, or within religions. Even much of the master reform process of medieval Christianity and the renaissance and recovery of the memory of classical civilization as a now integral part of the collective European past are not fully intelligible without taking into account the Christian-European encounter with Islam and the many civilizational borrowings it acquired through such an encounter.

Furthermore, Christian missions always accompanied European colonialism. Even in the case of French republican colonialism, *l'état laïque* and *l'église catolique,* which were constantly at loggerheads at home, worked hand in hand in *la mission civilatrice* in the French colonies, whether in Muslim Algiers, in preaxial Madagascar, or in Buddhist Vietnam. In any case, even without looking at any particular outcome of the colonial encounter between Western Christian and post-Christian secular modernity and other civilizations, one can confidently say that generally the outcome is unlikely to have been simply the emptying of the non-Western and the superimposition of modern Western secular patterns and social imaginaries. Nor was it possible to simply reject the colonial encounter and preserve one's own civilizational patterns and social imaginaries, unaffected by Western secular modernity. The modern secular immanent frame may become globalized, but this will always happen as an interactive, dynamic interlocking, transforming and refashioning preexisting non-Western civilizational patterns and social imaginaries with Western modern secular ones. Moreover, in the same way "our" modern secular age is fundamentally and inevitably post-Christian. The emerging multiple modernities in the different postaxial civilizational areas are likely to be post-Hindu, or post-Confucian, or post-Muslim; that is, they will also be a modern refashioning and transformation of already existing civilizational patterns and social imaginaries.

We can finally, after this long detour, pose again the question, how is the process of globalization likely to affect "our" and Taylor's secular age? If, as I pointed out, globalization entails a certain decentering, provincializing, and historicizing of Europe and of European secular modernity, even in relation to the different pattern of American modernity within the same immanent frame, then it is unlikely that "our" secular age will simply become the common global secular age of all humanity, or that "our" secular age will become absolutely unaffected by this process of globalization and by the encounter with the emerging non-Western and in many respects nonsecular modernities. We are entering here the realm of social scientific forecasting, and we all know how dismal and inaccurate the record of the social sciences is in this respect. I certainly will not claim any special powers of futuristic vision. But certainly one can project into our global futures, all respect for historical contingency notwithstanding, some patterns already visible in the global present.

One likely effect, staying now within Taylor's analysis, is the further expansion of what he describes as the nova and supernova effects, so that all religions of the world, old and new, preaxial, axial, and postaxial, become available for individual appropriation anytime and anywhere, thus multiplying the options of conversion, cross-pressures, and individual search for transcendence. But as long as those paths remain individual and thus private and "invisible," in Thomas Luckmann's sense of the term,[5] they will serve to enrich our existing globalized spiritual and religious supermarket, but they are unlikely to shake up our immanent frame or fundamentally challenge exclusive humanism. It is worth pointing out, however, in this context the significantly different patterns of reception of "other" religions one finds in radically secular and religiously homogeneous Europe and in the highly religious and pluralistic United States. In Europe, the only visible collective dynamic is the

5 Thomas Luckmann, *The Invisible Religion: Transformation of Symbols in Industrial Society* (New York: MacMillan, 1967). Originally published as *Das Problem der Religion in der modernen Gesellschaft* (Freiburg, 1963).

massive conversion to secularity, either in the form of the movement from Christian affiliation to disaffiliation—that is, the unchurching of the European population—or from belief to unbelief—that is, the growth in the surveys of the categories of "no religion" and "atheist."

Taylor's description of the nova and supernova effects of the age of authenticity seems indeed hardly applicable to contemporary European societies, which, I would argue, basically remain extremely homogeneous, both in their forms of religiosity and in their forms of secularity, at least when compared with the already highly religious and extremely pluralistic and dynamic denominational system in the United States. The results from the recent Pew survey of American religiosity, based on a rather large representative sample, reveal: (1) the absolute, practically unchanged persistence of theistic belief (over 90 percent of the American population); (2) the increasingly dynamic fluency of religious denominational affiliation and the high level of conversions (practically one third of all Americans claim a different religious affiliation as adults from the one they had as children); and (3) a relatively significant weakening of religious denominational affiliation (those with "no religion" have doubled in the past decade, from 9 percent to 18 percent of the American population). But one should be careful in interpreting the change as evidence that the process of secularization is finally also taking place in the United States, since a majority of those without religion also fall within the category of "spiritual, not religious," and this can hardly be interpreted as evidence of conversion to outright secularity or to exclusive humanism.

Similar evidence emerges from the radically different patterns of incorporation of non-Western immigrant religions in post-Christian secular Europe and in Christian secular America. I would venture to say that there is no religion anywhere in the world that has not taken root at least individually, but also most likely communally, somewhere in the United States. Non-Western immigrant religions—Islam, Hinduism, Buddhism—are taking root and becoming American religions in the same way as Catholicism and Judaism eventually became, after much resistance, incorporated into Protestant Christian America, and into the denominational system as American religious denominations. Although such evidence may serve to put into question the extent to which the religious situation in the United States fits into Taylor's vision of a secular age, in itself this burgeoning religious pluralism is unlikely to fundamentally challenge the immanent frame.

The more relevant question, to which at this point one can only offer a tentative speculative answer, is whether the already apparent emergence of multiple and successful non-Western modernities beyond the single case of Japan, signaled by the rise of China and India as global economic, political, and sociocultural powers, is likely to shake at least the stadial consciousness of Western secular modernity. We do not know whether the destabilization of the secular stadial consciousness is likely to be accompanied by the emergence of a global postsecular age, in which the particularism and exceptionalism of Western secular modernity become increasingly visible. Undoubtedly it will force Europeans to come to terms with—that is, to become for the first time reflexively aware of—their post-Christian secularity. As is already happening with the rather hostile reception of Islam in Europe, this is likely to be accompanied by the reflexive reaffirmation and reformulation of European Christian and secular identities. But to speak of a postsecular Europe may be a bit premature.

However, one could speculate, if within non-Western civilizations new modern forms (post-Hindu, post-Buddhist, post-Confucian, post-Muslim) of postaxial transcendence beyond simple human flourishing were to become widely and globally available, then we would be compelled to speak of a global postsecular age. But it is futile to try to prophesy the possible forms and contents of such postsecular social imaginaries. In any case, the new global age is likely to be characterized by the increasing loosening of territorial civilizational boundaries and by the spread of what could be called global denominationalism.

If such a future comes to pass, then Taylor is likely to be recognized as the last philosopher of secular modernity and as the visionary prophet of the dawn of a postsecular age, as somebody who helped to make our own secular age reflexively available for us and in doing so helped to shake and destabilize even further our secular social imaginary and to open wider cracks in our secular immanent frame. I doubt, however, that the new postsecular paths of transcendence that may become available to us ordinary humans would be able to satiate Taylor's personal thirst for transcendent eternity and divine incarnation.

12

Can Secularism Be Other-wise?

SABA MAHMOOD

Given the extensive commentary and discussion that has followed the publication of *A Secular Age*, any further reflection on this work seems to risk repetition and redundancy. To avoid this, I will focus for the most part on three issues that I think have received little attention so far. These are: (1) the normative thrust of Taylor's account of secularism in Euro-Atlantic Christian societies; (2) the relationship of this largely subjectivist account to political secularism; and (3) the place accorded to religious difference in Taylor's vision for reshaping contemporary Christianity in Western liberal societies.

A number of commentators have noted the erudition of Taylor's book and the timely intervention it enacts in current debates about the proper place accorded to religion in theorizations of the secular. In my view, one of the greatest virtues of the book lies in its authoritative dismantling of the idea that religion and secularism are antithetical worldviews, forever locked in an epistemological battle and a fundamental disagreement about what constitutes the public good in modern societies. One of the basic premises of *A Secular Age*, broadly echoed in scholarly literature on the topic, is that mod-

I would like to thank Charles Hirschkind and Judith Butler for their comments on this essay.

ern secularism is ineluctably tied to a concomitant notion of religiosity that is enabled not simply by shifts within theology and religious doctrine but, more importantly, by a series of epistemological and institutional transformations in the fields of law, politics, and aesthetics. Taking this premise as its point of departure, Taylor's book focuses on the kind of religious subjectivity secularism makes possible in modern Christian societies. Not unlike his earlier book *Sources of the Self, A Secular Age* provides a rich account of this subjectivity, its experiential and phenomenological dimensions. This learned account makes it difficult, if not impossible, to sustain the banal but persistent claim that contemporary secularism is under duress from incursions made by religion into the public sphere, that secularism's purity needs to be restored from the sullying presence of obdurate religious presumptions and practices so as to make liberal societies more rational, democratic, and "truly" secular. The firm and easy divide between religion and secularism that such claims posit is challenged by Taylor's account, forcing readers to countenance the necessarily religious (that is, Christian) character of secular modernity in Western liberal societies.

Insomuch as Taylor's largely phenomenological account of modern religiosity privileges belief, it appears at first glance to follow the work of a range of scholars who have argued that modernity has changed religion from a set of practices (rites, rituals, liturgies) to a set of beliefs in a set of propositions (about transcendence, causality, cosmology) to which an individual gives assent. Transformed from a set of lived norms, practices, and conventions, religion comes to acquire an objectlike quality, whose relative truth an individual cognitively ponders as one among many competing truth claims.[1] Taylor links this well-known narrative about the modern transformation of religion to a particular construction of the self, the "buffered self," which he describes as "essentially . . . aware of the possibility of disengagement" from one's natural and social surroundings (*SA,* 42). This anthropocentric self, Taylor argues, is responsible for the uniquely European notion of "civilization" and "civility" (301). It is easy, at first flush, to read Taylor's emphasis on belief (as the locus of modern religion) in cognitivist terms, an account that overlooks the importance of practices and norms that ground and structure this

---

1 See, for example, Talal Asad, *Genealogies of Religion* (Baltimore: Johns Hopkins University Press, 1993); Wilfred Cantwell Smith, *The Meaning and End of Religion* (Minneapolis: Augsburg Fortress, 1991).

seemingly ephemeral disenchanted self. But this impression fades quickly as one progresses more deeply into the book. There emerges instead a thick and robust account of the attitudes, conventions, and sensibilities that undergird this "buffered self," a self whose values and judgments derive from, and are rooted in, the resources of the Christian tradition (particularly post-Reformation Christian tradition). In Taylor's account, it seems to me, belief is less a cognitivist stance than a deep, almost unconscious enmeshment in a thick texture of Christian norms, values, and practices. So extensive is the force wielded by these norms that even atheists and nonbelievers cannot escape it, despite their denials and/or denunciations of Christianity's transcendental truth claims. Many Christian attitudes, concepts, and practices have been absorbed, Taylor shows repeatedly, by nonbelievers (poets, literary figures, philosophers, and public figures) in "North Atlantic" (Taylor's term) societies, such that to tell a story of secularism is to simultaneously render its Christian underpinnings visible.[2] The buffered self—the secular self par excellence, in Taylor's account—is a distinctly Christian achievement. For an anthropologist reading this account, Christianity appears to take on a cultural dimension—culture understood as an all-encompassing web of meanings within which the inhabitants of "the North Atlantic"reside, some more capable of self-reflection on their state of enmeshment than others.[3]

Christianity's Empirical Claims

From the beginning of the book, Taylor delimits the empirical scope of his account to what he at times calls "Latin Christendom" and at times "the North Atlantic civilization." He defines his object of analysis on the first page of the book:

2 One of the many examples Taylor provides of this transmutation of Christian ethos to nontheistic contexts is in post-Romantic poetics. It expresses, he argues, both a subjectivist and an experiential account of what it means to be human, while retaining a recognition of the importance and place for the "action of God," otherwise captured in "a theological language and honed by tradition" (SA, 757). Also see chap. 10.

3 Here Taylor's debt to the Romantic tradition is clear, inasmuch as romanticism provides both a descriptive and a normative account of the role that culture, community, language, and tradition play in the constitution of the modern subject. The idea of culture as a "web of meaning" was popularized by the anthropologist Clifford Geertz, a notion indebted to the work of Talcott Parsons, on which Geertz expanded. For a critical analysis of the career of this notion of culture in the human sciences, see David Scott, "Culture in Political Theory," *Political Theory* 31, 1 (2003): 92–115.

What does it mean to say that we live in a secular age? Almost everyone would agree that in some sense we do: I mean the 'we' who live in the West, or perhaps North Atlantic West, or otherwise put, the North Atlantic world—although secularity extends also practically, and in different ways, beyond this world. And the judgment of secularity seems hard to resist when we compare these societies with anything else in human history: that is, almost all other contemporary societies (e.g., Islamic countries, India, Africa), on one hand; and with the rest of human history, Atlantic or otherwise, on the other. (*SA*, 1)

In this opening paragraph Taylor delineates his object of study: a coherent religious tradition, coextensive with a spatial geography, whose historical unfolding can be plotted without accounting for non-Christian religious traditions that have coexisted within that very space of "Latin Christendom." On the surface, this kind of analysis seems plausible, in fact necessary, given the long history of scholarly neglect of Christianity's contribution to the making of secular modernity. However, on closer examination, doubts surface about the neat boundary Taylor draws around his object of study. Some have argued that not only is the space of "Latin Christendom" not as homogenous as Taylor paints but, more importantly, it is impossible to understand its historical trajectory without Christianity's encounters with its "others."[4] These others are both internal to the geospatial boundary of the North Atlantic (Judaism in Europe marked the outer limits of Euro-Christian civilization well into the twentieth century) *and* external as Christianity encountered numerous other religious traditions in the course of its missionary and colonizing projects (across Latin America, Australia, Africa, Asia, and the Middle East). These encounters did not simply leave Christianity untouched but transformed it from within, a transformation that should be internal to any self-understanding of Christianity. Omission of this story is akin to the omission of the history of slavery and colonialism from accounts of post-Enlightenment modernity—an omission that enables both a progressivist no-

---

4 Both Wendy Brown and José Casanova make this point in passing in their contributions to this volume.

tion of history and normative claims about who is qualified to be "modern" or "civilized."

The boundary Taylor draws around Latin Christendom is difficult, if not impossible, to sustain for both historical and conceptual reasons. To begin with, the genealogy of ancient and modern Christianity is deeply intertwined with histories and traditions that cannot simply be cordoned off as the outside of Latin Christianity: consider a figure such as Augustine of Hippo, who hailed from a geospatial imaginary that precedes the emergence of an entity called "Europe" but who is central to many of the formative minds of Latin Christendom. Or consider the fact that many key institutions of Latin Christendom owe their genesis to Eastern Orthodox and Oriental Orthodox Christianity—such as the practice of collective monasticism developed by Coptic Christians in Egypt.[5] When we begin to think of Christianity's encounter with non-Christian traditions, even prior to the development of colonialism, it becomes more difficult to sustain the autochthonous narrative Taylor weaves. Not only did the discovery of and subsequent knowledge produced on other religious traditions serve as the mirror against which European Christianity fashioned itself, but the very concept of "religion"—its conceptual contours, its classificatory system and attendant calculus of inferior and superior civilizations—was crafted within the crucible of this encounter. When Hugo Grotius (1583–1645), for example, authored his apologetic *De Veritate Religiones Christianae,* one of the first Protestant texts of this genre, his discussion of "pagan religions," Judaism, and Islam was crucial to his rhetorical and argumentative securing of Christianity's truth and superiority (closely related to his conception of "historical consciousness"). Immensely popular at the time, this text was initially distributed to the Dutch sailors traveling to the Far East and was later used extensively in missionary work well into the nineteenth century. It was translated into a number of languages, including Arabic, Persian, and Chinese, all of which were spoken in lands where European missionaries sought converts. No understanding of Western Christianity would be complete, I am suggesting, without taking into account how seminal figures such as Grotius formulated their self-conception in dialogue

---

5 Similarly, how would one account for the indebtedness of someone like Thomas Aquinas to a series of Islamic philosophers whose ideas and contributions were incorporated into and imbibed by mainstream Christianity?

with other religious traditions, a self-conception moreover that was increasingly shaped by Christianity's enmeshment in an imperial world order.

Taylor's demarcation of a selfsame Latin Christian identity becomes even harder to sustain when we enter into the modern period so central to Taylor's argument, a period that marks the zenith of colonial power and an unprecedented expansion of Christian missionary work around the world. During this period (1858–1914), there was hardly a corner of the globe where Christian missions did not establish some kind of a presence aimed at the conversion of non-Christian natives. Importantly, these missions did not simply pave the way for colonial rule (as is often noted) but played a crucial role in shaping and redefining modern Christianity to fit the requirements of an emergent liberal social and political order in Europe. Missionary activity was not pursued by a marginal population, but exercised the imagination of key political and religious figures in Britain, France, Holland, Belgium, Italy, and later North America. The question of how missionary work was to be conducted, what role it was to play in creating a new geopolitical order, and its relationship to European societies was hotly debated among the protagonists of Taylor's story. Missionary work, I want to emphasize, was important to developments within Christianity and to many of the central ideas and institutions of Latin Christendom.

For example, some have argued that key ideas within the pietist movement (such as the emphasis on personal conversion, witnessing, close fellowship in society/church community) were sharpened and defined through missionary work, the responsibility ordinary Europeans came to feel to bring the gospel to the "heathens" and those living in ignorance of Christ's truth.[6] Similarly, the emphasis that nineteenth-century colonial missions placed on education, the imperative to educate all of "Christ's children," had far-reaching effects on the shape secular education took within Europe. Gauri Viswanathan, for example, has copiously documented how the standoff between the evangelicals and the utilitarians in nineteenth-century colonial India eventually resulted in the banishment of the Bible from Indian schools, replacing it with English literature (in Matthew Arnold's sense). This colonial

---

6 See Stephen Neill, *A History of Christian Missions* (London: Penguin, 1994), especially 194–198.

policy was eventually adopted in Britain itself and set the standard for secular education in British public schools.[7] Later in the century, the development of "muscular Christianity" in British schools once again linked the colony and the metropole in a pattern that was repeated over the course of the twentieth century.[8] Within the clerical establishment, the dramatic increase in the number of women serving in foreign missions, Roman Catholic and Protestant alike, fundamentally transformed gendered notions of what it meant to serve God and Christ in much of the Western Christian world. It has been argued, in fact, that one of the largest impacts of missionary work on Christianity was women's entry into the clergy, which serves as an important precursor to current debates about women's ordination in the Catholic Church.[9]

While it is common within academic literature to acknowledge the influence Christian colonial missions had on non-Christian "local traditions," the reverse process is rarely studied, its force and extent seldom acknowledged. This lacuna is a reflection of the asymmetry of power that structures the scholarship on colonial missions, an asymmetry that Taylor assimilates into his empirical claim without adequate reflection. Missionary work in regions colonized by European powers was not simply an extension of a stable Christian essence into foreign traditions and cultures but transformative of Western Christianity itself. Missionary work was a significant nexus through which long-standing tensions between Roman Catholicism, Eastern and Oriental Orthodox churches, and Protestantism were negotiated. Consider, for example, the strict theological and doctrinal distinctions the Roman Catholic Church drew with Eastern Orthodox churches for centuries and its ceaseless efforts to win converts through missionary activity among the Maronites, the Syrian Orthodox, the Copts, the Ethiopians, and the Greek and Armenian Orthodox in the Middle East. Faced, however, with resistance to its efforts at

7 Gauri Viswanathan, *Masks of Conquest: Literary Study and British Rule in India* (New York: Columbia University Press, 1989). Viswanathan shows that secular utilitarians (such as Thomas Macaulay) and Christian evangelicals were united in their support for the Anglicization of the public school curriculum in India, against Orientalists, who supported the teaching of indigenous languages (Sanskrit, Persian, etc.).

8 See Peter van der Veer's *Imperial Encounters: Religion and Modernity in India and Britain* (Princeton: Princeton University Press, 2001).

9 Neill notes that by the early twentieth century, women in foreign missions outnumbered men (*A History of Christian Missions,* 218). On this point, for a discussion of Protestant missions sent from England, see Rhonda Semple, *Missionary Women: Gender, Professionalism, and the Victorian Idea of Christian Missions* (Rochester: Boydell, 2003).

Romanization and the rise in conversions to Protestantism, the Roman Catholic Church finally decided to make good with members of the Uniate Churches. This was not simply a politic decision but required transformations and accommodations in the Church's doctrinal positions and administrative organization.[10] Through these brief examples one can see how what Taylor calls "Latin Christianity" is in fact indelibly connected to its "non-Latinate" partners, constantly engaged in a practice of accommodation and reaction, a process that is as wholly constitutive of "North Atlantic" history as it is of intra- and interdenominational struggles.[11]

Christianity's Universalism

To ask *A Secular Age* to take account of the various ways in which Western Christianity is linked with its non-Western others is not simply to make Taylor's narrative more inclusive, more copious, but to question if indeed Taylor misidentifies the very object of which he speaks. It might be argued in response that no book can possibly do justice to such a complicated history. Taylor is, after all, a scholar of Euro-Atlantic and Christianity history, not of European colonialism. If one desires to tell such a story, it would have to be undertaken by someone who commands this archive and inhabits its particular set of problematizations. Such a response, however, ignores how the constitution of an empirical object is itself constituted by a prior conceptual and ideological delimitation and not simply a given that a scholar discovers. Given the historical developments I have traced, to represent Latin Christendom as simply an empirical field is to fail to acknowledge the immense ideological force the "empirical history" of Christianity commands in securing what constitutes as the properly religious and the secular in the analytical domain. To secure secularism as a uniquely Christian (or, for that matter, Western) achievement is not simply a documentary exercise. Rather, it is to engage in a

---

10 See Neill, *A History of Christian Missions*, chap. 11, and Heather Sharkey, *American Evangelicals in Egypt* (Princeton: Princeton University Press, 2008), chap. 2.

11 The development of liberation theology in Latin America through the 1960s and 1970s is a more recent example in this vein: a movement that built on and extended various aspects of Jesuit theology and practice, challenging the Vatican to rethink its position on poverty and social justice. Similarly, the current rebellion of Anglican bishops in Africa to the position of the Archbishop of Canterbury, Rowan Williams, on ordaining gay ministers is illustrative of the fact that it is impossible to treat Western Christianity as if it is autonomous of developments in other parts of the world.

practice through which the "North Atlantic" has historically secured its exceptionality—the simultaneous uniqueness *and* universality of its religious forms and the superiority of its civilization. To inhabit this founding gesture uncritically (as Taylor does), by which the West consolidates its epistemic and historical privilege, is not simply to describe a discursive structure but to write from within its concepts and ambitions—one might say even to further its aims and strengthen its presuppositions. The fact that Taylor sometimes inhabits this discourse ironically (evident in his acknowledgment of other possible accounts one could give of secularism) does not undermine the force of this discourse but only makes it more palatable to a postimperial audience.

The problem of how to reconcile the particularity of Christianity with its universal and transhistorical claims has long exercised modern European philosophers and historians. This was the preoccupation not only of Christian apologists but of a range of Enlightenment thinkers who acknowledged that Christianity was one among many religious forms embraced by humanity. They remained convinced nonetheless that only Christianity was capable of transcending its historicity and addressing the modern human condition.[12] For thinkers as disparate as Locke, Hume, and Kant, what enabled Christianity to rise above its particularity was its singularity, its unique ability to capture and embody universal principles and truths in a manner that other religions could not because they remained mired in their cultural and doctrinal particularities.

Tomoko Masuzawa, in her book *The Invention of World Religions,* traces the transmutation of this argument into the discourse of "world religions" dedicated to the scientific study of religion, *Religionswissenschaft,* when it first emerged in the mid-nineteenth century.[13] While this discourse has been instituted in the academic disciplines of comparative religions, history of religions, and religious studies more broadly, many of its presuppositions and founding assumptions continue to inform popular discussions about religion

---

12 See David Hume, "The Natural History of Religion," in *Dialogues and Natural History of Natural Religion,* ed. J. C. A. Gaskin (Oxford: Oxford University Press, 1999), 134–196. Also see John Locke, *The Reasonableness of Christianity as Delivered in the Scriptures* (Oxford: Oxford University Press, 1999). Marcel Gauchet's book *The Disechantment of the World: A Political History of Religion* (Princeton: Princeton University Press, 1997) represents a contemporary secularized version of this argument.

13 Tomoko Masuzawa, *The Invention of World Religions* (Chicago: Chicago University Press, 2005).

today. The commitment of this body of knowledge to religious diversity not-withstanding, Masuzawa shows that it has been able to retain the structural superiority of Christianity over other religious traditions. This has been made possible largely by two important analytical assumptions internal to this tradition of scholarship. First, key transformations within Christian history have come to serve as the entelechy through which the adequacy, inadequacy, or development of other religious traditions has been measured. Second, a developmentalist notion of history posits a linear progress of mankind from "primitivism" to "civilization," wherein each stage of human development is assumed to correspond to a particular model of religion. In this narrative, if "primitive religion" is a sign of the "infancy of mankind," then Western European Christianity signals the most refined and highest achievement of human history. As Masuzawa points out, this progressivist account when it first emerged allowed liberal Christians to recognize the achievements of other religious traditions while retaining Christianity's "exclusive claim to universal truth."[14]

It is clear that Taylor's political sympathies are far from colonial and his account not as triumphalist as other developmentalist accounts tend to be. He is critical of Christianity's overidentification with its civilizational mission, of its obsession with rules and codes at the cost of its ethical and affective values (SA, 737–744). Despite these qualifications, A Secular Age makes liberal use of many terms and concepts that are germane to the account I have traced above. These include, for example, Taylor's reliance on the typology of religion organized around Karl Jasper's notion of the axial age, on "primitive religion" as a generic category that amasses a variety of beliefs and prac-

---

14 Ibid., 119. At times Masuzawa's argument seems to augment Taylor's account—particularly in the emphasis Taylor places on the sense of disengagement produced by the recognition among Christians that theirs was one among many religious traditions in the modern world. But what is missing from Taylor is an analysis of the field of power within which this recognition operated, the conditions of Euro-Christianity's ascendance to global domination, which was transformative of the conceptual and practical world of both Christians and non-Christians. Importantly, the condition of emergence for the "buffered self" that Taylor tracks was not only an epistemological shift but also civilizational, in that the self-reflection induced by encounters with others was taken as a sign of the superiority and uniqueness of Western European Christianity. History had a singular trajectory, in which the so-called primitive religions did not even qualify as contenders. Is it possible to think *with* Taylor's conception of the buffered self, which no doubt captures something quite important about modern secular sensibility, while remaining attentive to the relations of power that provided the structural conditions for the emergence of this peculiar self-conception?

tices that supposedly belong to the "past" of mankind, and on a progressivist notion of history. Perhaps what is most surprising is Taylor's consistent movement (or slippage?) throughout the book from the particularity of Christianity to its universal transcendence. Even in the opening paragraph of the book, which I quote above, the text oscillates between recognizing that the secular age exceeds the borders of the North Atlantic and the judgment that secularity *is* what makes the North Atlantic singular and distinct from "all other contemporary societies (e.g. Islamic countries, India, Africa) . . . and with the rest of human history, Atlantic or otherwise." The "rest of human history" sometimes operates to mark a temporal distinction from the "premodern" and sometimes a civilizational one between "us" and "them."[15] There is little doubt that Christian secularism has its particularities—it would be banal to say otherwise. But historical accounts of this particularity are saturated with Christianity's claims to civilizational superiority as well as universal transcendence that have been secured through a long history of global power and concomitant patterns of analytical thought. The pressing question that I am left with on reading Taylor's account is, how might the story of Christian secularism be told otherwise? How would one fold in decades of critical scholarship produced on the concepts and categories germane to the discourse of "world religion" so as not to rehearse the assumptions of power that have secured the great divide between "us" and "them?"[16] How would an

15 It is worth pointing out that in his diagnosis of what ails North Atlantic Christianity and in his prescriptions to solve the problem, Taylor draws on an older vocabulary from the "anthropology of religion" that has deep roots in the emergence of the discourse of "world religions." In the mid-nineteenth century, when the study of "primitive and prehistoric" religions was assigned to the discipline of anthropology, it was the discipline of "comparative religion" (and later religious studies) that took upon itself the task of studying the "great historical religions" of the world (which included Christianity, Buddhism, Islam). This division of labor was accompanied by a typology of religion ("primitive" versus "axial"/"historical" religions, great versus little traditions, and so on) and attendant analytical paraphernalia that have been largely discarded in anthropology but continue to hold sway in the disciplines of comparative religion and religious studies. Anthropologists Victor Turner and Stanley Tambiah, whose work Taylor draws on, belong to this older tradition within anthropology. For two different moments in anthropological critiques of how the discipline's conceptual apparatus facilitated colonial projects, see Talal Asad, *Anthropology and the Colonial Encounter* (London: Prometheus, 1973), and George Stocking, *Victorian Anthropology* (New York: Free Press, 1987).

16 I want to be clear that I am quite sympathetic to exploring conceptual and historical distinctions that might exist across time, space, and social formations. These differences, however, are no more "civilizational" than they are "cultural." These are ideological terms that neither describe nor analyze the formations of which they speak. Furthermore, the modern condition links "us" and "them" through a variety of global structures of governance, capital, and law that cannot be accounted for by tired old tropes of civilizational and cultural distinction.

author as extraordinary and humane as Taylor cleave apart the normative from the descriptive so as to render the colonial aspects of Christianity's history contingent rather than necessary to such accounts?

Political Secularism

I would like to push Taylor's argument in a direction that might open up ways of addressing these questions. Secularism until recently was primarily understood as a political doctrine of state neutrality toward religion (encapsulated in the principle of Church and state separation). Recent scholarship has come to analyze secularism as a formation that exceeds this rather limited understanding and focuses on transformations wrought in the domain of ethics, aesthetics, and epistemology. It is important to point out that these transformations are not neutral in relation to the exercise of politics but are transformative of it. While Taylor's book provides a culturalist and phenomenological account of the subjectivity characteristic of modern liberal secularism, it remains indifferent to questions of political secularism. By political secularism, following Talal Asad, I do not simply mean the principle of state neutrality toward religion but the sovereign prerogative of the state to regulate religious life through a variety of disciplinary practices that are political as well as ethical.[17] Importantly, these disciplines of subjectivity are undertaken not simply by state but also by nonstate (civic and cultural) institutions that authorize normative models of religious subjectivity and practice. Notably, these models are often unstable and mutually contradictory; the enforcement of one over the other is an exercise of power rather than simply cultural assimilation. Taylor's important articulation of the buffered self belongs to this field of contestation and power, an account of which seems to be crucially missing from *A Secular Age*.

To provide such an account is consequential for how one might think analytically and critically about the normative thrust of modern political secularism (and its cultural entailments).[18] Taylor's argument, for example, that the buffered self is *the* authoritative model in the secular age crucially depends

17 Talal Asad, *Formations of the Secular* (Palo Alto: Stanford University Press, 2003).

18 Taylor has written about the question of political secularism in "The Secular Imperative," in *Secularism and Its Critics*, ed. Rajeev Bhargava (Oxford: Oxford University Press, 1998), 31–53. In this article, while Taylor analyzes the relationship between secularism and democracy, his main focus is on the principle of state neutrality toward religion.

on other, competing conceptions of the self (theistic and nontheistic), which he often marks as "nonsecular" or "premodern." Their contemporaniety with the buffered self in Taylor's account is often denied by relegating it either to a geospatial location of the "non-West" or to a temporal past. This exercise in defining what *is* secular and what *is not* is a normative exercise and not simply a descriptive one. This definition, Taylor's intentions notwithstanding, belongs, crucially, to the operation of modern secular power through which certain religious subjectivities are authorized and others made the object of reform and subject to the "civility" of secular norms and conventions. Unruly subjects (such as the fundamentalist, the evangelical, the religious extremist) are crucially formed by operations of secular power even as they challenge many aspects of this operation. The "otherness" of these subjectivities is not only a product of their unruly actions but also an effect of how secular power establishes its claim to truth and normativity.[19] Is it possible to make the work of secular power visible in Taylor's account? What are the mechanisms, institutions, and strategies of modern governance through which an authoritative definition of secular religiosity is secured in modern liberal societies? What is the relationship between the culturalist account Taylor provides of the buffered self and the regulatory reach and scope of political secularism? How would one think *critically* about peoples and places described as "nonsecular" while acknowledging the empirical and historical specificity of Western European secularism? How would one locate and demarcate ethically and responsibly that very specificity if it turns out to be defined in part by that which it excludes?

Finally, I would submit that to think critically about political secularism and its cultural entailments is also to render visible the relationship between Western and non-Western traditions of secularism. There is no doubt that many ideas and concepts that are now integral to the practices and institutions of modern governance are indebted to developments within European Christianity.[20] These conceptions and practices of governance have become globalized, however, in a manner that makes it difficult to trace a simple story

19 One cannot inhabit the label "nonsecular" indifferently in our age but must bear the consequences of such an inhabitation. On this point, see my "Secularism, Hermeneutics, Empire," *Public Culture* 18, 2 (2006): 323–347.

20 To acknowledge the Western origin of such conceptions is not to concede the claim of Europe's civlizational superiority but to recognize the transformative role that European capitalism and

of Christian origins. The modern nation-state, for example, with its juridical, executive, and administrative functions, enfolds a variety of conceptions of the self, agency, privacy, publicity, religion, and ethics that have become globalized. The history of this transformation belongs less to the Christianization of non-Western societies and more to their secularization under modern rule.[21] How would *A Secular Age* account for these globalized practices of law and governance that exceed the Christian narrative of secularism? Are there conceptions of the self, agency, and accountability that modern secularism makes possible which link "us" and "them" indelibly (if messily) across putatively civilizational divides? If so, how would one parse out the cultural from the political in such an account?

Christian Reform and Religious Difference

Beyond providing an account of Christianity's unique production of modern secularity, in the last section of his book Taylor outlines a prescriptive vision for what Christianity should strive to become in the current age, what resources from the past it should draw on to renew itself and speak to the needs of secular Christians. Taylor's vision is built upon the diagnosis that Christianity has become corrupted over time, tripped up in its project of reform, rule-obsessed and overidentified with its civilizational mission (*SA,* 742–743).[22] Contemporary Christianity should recreate itself, Taylor argues, by recuperating its old commitments to agape, spiritual renewal, and a quest for meaning beyond the immanent goods of this world. The tools for this recuperation that he provides are both ideational and practical, but, importantly, all of them emanate from what he describes as a Christian attitude and philosophical stance. Taylor speaks compellingly to fellow Christians, crying out for

---

colonialism played in non-European societies. For example, many aspects of Taylor's buffered self can be found in non-Western societies, carried historically through a complex movement not only of ideas but, more importantly, of law, political structures, and capital.

21 Taylor himself recognizes this in an earlier article: "The inescapability of secularism flows from the nature of the modern state." "The Secular Imperative," 38. In other words, he recognizes the necessarily secular character of the modern nation-state. Also see the chapter "Modern Social Imaginary" in *SA.*

22 Here Taylor agrees with Ivan Illich's diagnosis of the fall of Christianity but amends it with his own prescriptions of what should be done to make Christianity whole again (742ff).

greater understanding across different points of view internal to Christianity (what Taylor calls different "itineraries to God"):

> Christians today . . . have to climb out of an age in which Hell and the wrath of God are often very faintly felt, if they are understood at all. But they live in a world where objectification and excarnation reign, where death undermines meaning, and so on. We have to struggle to recover a sense of what the Incarnation can mean. . . . None of us could ever grasp alone everything that is involved in our alienation from God and his action to bring us back. But there are a great many of us . . . who have had some powerful sense of some facet of this drama. Together we can live it more fully than any one of us could alone. Instead of reaching immediately for the weapons of polemic, we might better listen for a voice which we could never have assumed ourselves, whose tone might have been forever unknown to us if we hadn't strained to understand it. We will find that we have to extend this courtesy even to people who would never have extended it to us (like Jonathan Edwards)—in that respect, perhaps we have made some modest headway towards truth in the last couple of centuries, although we can certainly find precedents in the whole of Christianity. Our faith is not the acme of Christianity, but nor is it a degenerate version; it should rather be open to conversations that range over the whole of the last 20 centuries and even in some ways before. (754)

Many academics are disturbed by Taylor's partisan call to Christian reform. In a moment of intense global struggle fought in the name of religion, to root a call for greater tolerance in Christian ethics and to limit it to a Christian audience is to reinscribe a divide that needs to be overcome. For these critics, a true language of tolerance would need to be necessarily nontheistic. For others, to combine the project of academic analysis with religious reform is to commit a category mistake.

In a keynote address delivered at Yale University, Taylor responded to his critics by stating that while it is inevitable that a text carries the traces of the position its author occupies (in Taylor's case, his Catholic faith), this does not mean that the analysis and solutions he offers are not relevant to those out-side of this position.[23] He argues in this lecture that his larger aim in author-ing *A Secular Age* was to forge conversations across differences of belief and unbelief, across religious traditions, one might say, so that a better, more tol-erant world can be realized than the one we currently live in. Drawing on his recent experience as the cochair of the Quebec government's Commission on Accommodation Practices Related to Cultural Differences (established by Quebec premier Jean Charest in 2007), Taylor gives the example of Islamo-phobia expressed by many Canadians in the course of the commission's hear-ings.[24] Such testimonies seem to have reinscribed for Taylor the need to forge ways of communicating across religious difference. Such a practice, he ar-gues in his keynote address, is a further elaboration of the Christian value of reconciliation and captures the spirit of what he termed the "communion of saints" in *A Secular Age*—a spirit that he defines not simply as a "communion of perfected persons" but a "communion of whole itineraries towards God" (*SA*, 754).

Even though this expanded vision of interreligious dialogue is not pres-ent in *A Secular Age*, I want to briefly comment on what I think is the more generous interpretation that Taylor's keynote address provides of the last sec-tion of his book. Given that the current geopolitical conflict has taken reli-gious dimensions, it is important for voices from within religious traditions to find new ways of cohabitation and mutual accommodation across prac-tices of difference. Given the power Christianity commands in our world to-day, Taylor's expansion of his message is an important one to engage with, regardless of one's beliefs. Let me start with Taylor's call to be attentive to "a voice which we could never have assumed ourselves, whose tone might have been forever unknown to us if we hadn't strained to understand it. We will find that we have to extend this courtesy even to people who would never have extended it to us." Is it possible to extend this call not just to be open to voices that are Christian (such as Jonathan Edwards, whom Taylor cites) but

23 Charles Taylor, "Varieties of Secularism in a Secular Age," Keynote address, Yale University, April 5, 2008, transcript, 8.

24 The mandate of the commission was to find ways of identifying and combating practices of discrimination that might result from widely practiced cultural norms across lines of ethnic, racial, or religious difference. For a full explanation of this mandate, see www.accommodements.qc.ca/commission/mandat-en.html.

also to those that cut across religious truths, across limits of secular tolerance, across differences of political and ethical projects? As Taylor's own experience on the Quebec commission testifies, to grasp the nettle of tolerance
these days is to deal with what has come to be glossed as "fundamentalism"
—particularly "Islamic fundamentalism"—a highly reductive trope that tells
us more about limits to liberal tolerance than about the social formation
such a label purports to describe. The figure of the "Muslim fundamentalist"
marks the limit of the discourse of tolerance for many. How would such a
figure be accommodated and addressed in Taylor's call to reach across difference—how would it fit (or not) in Taylor's typology of the "secular" and
"nonsecular"? If indeed, as Wendy Brown has argued persuasively, the discourse of tolerance is also a discourse of power, how does one contend with
the power of secularism to define and delimit who becomes worthy of "our"
engagement?[25]

In closing, let me return to the chimera of interreligious dialogue that
haunts Taylor's remarks in the last section of his book. It is indeed the case
that any invitation to dialogue emanates from a commitment to its own positions and perspectives. This pertains not only to religious dialogue but to any
dialogue that claims to reach beyond its limits—otherwise it would be meaningless to converse across difference. Any such endeavor must translate values, principles, and concepts across differences. As Taylor must know from
his service on the Quebec commission, the possibility of communication is
limited by the relations of power in which a communicative act unfolds. Certain differences are more legible than others, and their legibility depends not
on one's ability to speak or translate but on the ability to hear, on the conditions that limit what can be heard and understood. Given this intractability of
power, how would one think about the Christian structure of Taylor's call for
conversation across religious difference? By this structure I do not mean simply the language and metaphors internal to Taylor's call, but the structure of
global power that Christianity occupies in modern history. If the task of contemporary Christianity is to become open to others, would it not need to begin with an internal accounting of how this historical privilege structures
the possibility of communication across difference? Given the simultaneous

25 Wendy Brown, *Regulating Aversion: Tolerance in the Age of Identity and Empire* (Princeton: Princeton University Press, 2006).

claim to the singularity and universality of Christianity that is part of the history of Christian secularism, would it not be necessary to address this history internally before any reconciliation could be reached with others? Christianity's historical relationship to its others, to put it another way, would have to become internal to Christianity's current preoccupations in order to embark on what is truly a worthy project of intrareligious dialogue. The prescriptive vision of *A Secular Age* is severely compromised, it turns out, by the historical demarcation of "Latin Christendom" which remains ideologically impervious to its others. How would one imagine embarking on a dialogue when the other is not even acknowledged in political, existential, or epistemological terms? It seems that by delineating an account of Christian secularism that remains blind to the normative assumptions and power of Western Christianity, Taylor's invitation to interreligious dialogue sidesteps the greatest challenge of our time.

Afterword: Apologia pro Libro suo

Charles Taylor

Master Narratives

My book lays out, unashamedly, a master narrative. The adverb bespeaks the view I hold, that we can't avoid such narratives. The attempt to escape them only means that we operate by an unacknowledged, hence unexamined and uncriticized, narrative. That's because we (modern Westerners) can't help understanding ourselves in these terms.

I'm not claiming this for all human beings at all times. Some other kind of global sense of the context of our lives is always there; but in other times and civilizations, this context might be defined by myths, say. And these will often have narrative form but not in the same way as ours. Our narratives deal with how we have become what we are; how we have put aside and moved away from earlier ways of being. There are many stories we tell or have told to us that give form to this sense of becoming. They even may have radically different normative import. But they try to capture the same sense that our society has evolved from earlier, less "developed" forms, so that different life possibilities are often identified by the place they occupy in the narrative. This idea is "medieval," that is, "progressive"; this person is "ahead of her time," and so on.

The stories are not all of progress or advance. A standard "reactionary" view is that contemporary society is in some way fallen; that our departure from an earlier understanding of order has only given more place to chaos, to disorder, to a loss of meaning, discipline, or whatever. But these are master narratives of the same form, relating how we have become what we are.

I've tried to give a master narrative of secularity. And one of the central ideas of the book is that one only understands what secularity is through the narrative. The aim is to criticize, and perhaps replace, a widespread understanding of secularity as the inevitable by-product of modernization, however this is understood. Generally it is seen as consisting of processes like economic growth, industrialization, social and geographical mobility, urbanization, the development of science and technology, the advance of instrumental reason, and the like. Various tellings of the story of how we have become carry this sense of secularity as an inevitable consequence. To challenge this, you have to tell another story. Hence the length of the book.

But the book could have been—in a sense, should have been—longer. A master narrative convinces if it offers a better alternative reading of what happened than the one it is trying to displace. But to see how the reading is better, you need to look again at the detail. So ideally, a book like this would look at a great many facets of our history, a great many more circumscribed stories that are part of the big narrative. There should have been lots more chapters, describing regions and times that I have left relatively neglected. Above all, I have neglected the way in which Western understandings of religion were informed through the precolonial and then the colonial encounter with other parts of the world, as Peter van der Veer has strongly argued.

Master narratives of modernity take many forms. One that is very common I find unhelpful. This is the kind that deals in "subtraction stories." A subtraction story is one that identifies a certain essential tendency or character which holds everywhere and always of human beings. The name I'm using here comes from a very common type of such a story. On this construal, the essential character was always there, but previously it was impeded by factors that have since been removed. Once these are subtracted, the essential character emerges in full force. An example of this, one of the cruder versions, is the picture of human agents as essentially individuals operating by instrumental reason. In the past, this tendency was held in by illusory religious or metaphysical views or by tight community mores. The rise of modernity has set these aside, and human agents now operate fully by their intrinsic nature. A more sophisticated view would see the essential character as lying in the ability to reason universally by principles, and the liberated individual would also have the capacity and the desire to act on universalizable maxims, taking account of others' point of view.

But the view may also be structured differently. We may identify a universal tendency in human action. This was inhibited in the past by ignorance, or by blind custom, or by authoritarian commands. But it eventually works its way to center stage and comes to take its proper place in human life. Adam Smith's supposition that there is a universal tendency to "truck and barter," but that this is held in check in earlier social forms, is an example of this. This is less a "subtraction story" than it is a "breakthrough story," but there is essential similarity between the two, in that they posit a ubiquitous character or tendency.

Alternatively, there are views that see humans as shaped by a variety of cultures, so that they have quite different practices, outlooks, goals. These cultures are "constructed" over time, but by long processes which no one oversees or controls (hence the misleading element in the word "construction"). A narrative of modernity that starts from this understanding will never be satisfied with a subtraction story. Modernity is defined not just by our "losing" an earlier world, but by the kind of human culture that we have constructed. It is this kind of account that I am trying to give.

Everyone can agree that one of the big differences between us and our ancestors of five hundred years ago is that they lived in an "enchanted" world and we do not, or at the least much less so. We might think of this as our having "lost" a number of beliefs and the practices that they made possible. Essentially we become modern by breaking out of "superstition" and becoming more scientific and technological in our stance toward our world. But I want to accentuate something different. The "enchanted" world was one in which spirits and forces defined by their meanings (the kind of forces given off by love potions or relics) played a big role. Leaving this kind of world was not just a matter of dropping certain beliefs. One can see this if one reflects that the "beliefs" themselves are rather strange for us, and the spirits not just invisible personal beings but often embodied forces.

But more, the enchanted world was one in which these forces could cross a porous boundary and shape our lives, psychic and physical. One of the big differences between us and them is that we live with a much firmer sense of the boundary between self and other. We are "buffered" selves. We have changed. We sometimes find it hard to be frightened the way they were, and indeed, we tend to invoke the uncanny things they feared with a pleasurable frisson, sitting through films about witches and sorcerers. They would have found this incomprehensible.

Here you see the difference between a subtraction story and one that thinks not only of loss but of remaking. In the subtraction story, there can be no epistemic loss involved in the transition; we have just shucked off some false beliefs, some fears of imagined objects. Looked at my way, the process of disenchantment involves a change in sensibility; one is open to different things. One has lost a way in which people used to experience the world.

It is this sense of loss that underlies many attempts in our day to "reenchant" the world. This idea is invoked in Akeel Bilgrami's chapter. It ought to be clear that what would be regained here is not what we have "lost." People are talking of quite other ways of recovering an analogue of the original sensibility: in the sense of the forces moving through nature in the poems of Hölderlin or Wordsworth, or in the contact with spirits of the dead that Courtney Bender studies.

Disenchantment in my use (and partly in Weber's) really translates Weber's term *Entzauberung*, where the key kernel concept is *Zauber*, magic. In a sense, moderns constructed their own concept of magic from and through the process of disenchantment. Carried out first under reforming Christian auspices, the condemned practices all involved using spiritual force against or at least independently of our relation to God. The worst examples were things like saying a black mass for the dead to kill off your enemy, or using the host as a love charm. But in the more exigent modes of reform, the distinction between white and black magic tended to disappear, and all independent recourse to forces independent of God was seen as culpable. The category "magic" was constituted through this rejection, and this distinction was then handed on to the post-Enlightenment anthropology, as with Frazer in his distinction between "magic" and "religion."[1]

The process of disenchantment, involving a change in us, can be seen as

---

1 Peter van der Veer shows how a not-dissimilar category, *"wu,"* which can be translated as either "shamansism" or "magic," emerging out of a parallel process of supposedly rational reform, was developed in modern China, that is, as a category for what was rejected as inferior, not really religion. See his "Secularism's Magic," in *Rethinking Secularism*, ed. Craig Calhoun, Mark Juergensmeyer, and Jonathan VanAntwerpen (forthcoming, 2010).

a loss of a certain sensibility, which is really an impoverishment (as against simply the shedding of irrational feelings). And there have been frequent attempts to "reenchant" the world, or at least admonitions and invitations to do so. In a sense, the Romantic movement can be seen as engaged in such a project. Think of Novalis's "magic realism"; think of the depiction of the Newtonian universe as a dead one, shorn of the life it used to have (Schiller's "The Gods of Greece"). But it is clear that the poetry of Wordsworth, or of Novalis, or that of Rilke, can't come close to the original experience of porous selves. The experience it evokes is more fragile, often evanescent, subject to doubt. It is also one that draws on an ontology which is highly undetermined, and must remain so.[2]

But disenchantment covers just part of the story I wanted to tell. It points to one facet. The fuller story, in a nutshell, goes something like this.

The Story

How did this secular age come about? And what exactly is this age whose development I'm trying to explain? There are all sorts of ways of describing it: separation of religion from public life, decline of religious belief and practice. But while I'll touch on these, I'm interested in another facet of our age: belief in God, or in the transcendent in any form, is contested; it is an option among many; it is therefore fragile; for some people in some milieus very difficult, even "weird." Five hundred years ago in our civilization, it wasn't so. Unbelief was off the map for most people, close to inconceivable. But that description also applies to the whole of human history outside the modern West.

What had to happen for this kind of secular climate to come about? (1) There had to develop a culture that marks a clear division between the "natural" and the "supernatural," and (2) it had to come to seem possible to live entirely within the natural. Point 1 was something striven for, but point 2 came about at first quite inadvertently.

It came about as the by-product of an attempt to make over the lives of Christians, and their social order, so as to make them conform thoroughly to the demands of the gospel. I am talking not of a particular, revolutionary

2 See *SA*, chap. 10.

moment but of a long, ascending series of attempts to establish a Christian order, of which the Reformation is a key phase. These attempts show a progressive impatience with older modes of postaxial religion in which certain collective, ritualistic forms of earlier religions uneasily coexisted with the demands of individual devotion and ethical reform which came from the "higher" revelations. In Latin Christendom, the attempt was to recover and impose on everyone a more individually committed and Christocentric religion of devotion and action, and to repress or even abolish older, supposedly "magical" or "superstitious" forms of collective ritual practice.

Allied with a neo-Stoic outlook, this became the charter for a series of attempts to establish new forms of social order, drawing on new disciplines (Foucault enters the story here), which helped to reduce violence and disorder and create populations of relatively pacific and productive artisans and peasants, who were more and more induced/forced into the new forms of devotional practice and moral behavior, be this in Protestant England, Holland, or later the American colonies, or in Counter-Reformation France, or in the Germany of the *Polizeistaat*.

My hypothesis is that this new creation of a civilized, "polite" order succeeded beyond what its originators could have hoped for, and that this in turn led to a new reading of what a Christian order might be, one that was seen more and more in "immanent" terms (the polite, civilized order is the Christian order). This version of Christianity was shorn of much of its "transcendent" content and was thus open to a new departure, in which the understanding of good order (what I call the "modern moral order") could be embraced outside of the original theological, providential framework, and in certain cases even against it (as with Voltaire, Gibbon, and, in another way, Hume).

Disbelief in God arises in close symbiosis with this belief in a moral order of rights-bearing individuals, who are destined (by God or nature) to act for mutual benefit; an order that thus rejects the earlier honor ethic which exalted the warrior, as it also tends to occlude any transcendent horizon. (We see one good formulation of this notion of order in Locke's *Second Treatise*.) This understanding of order has profoundly shaped the forms of social imaginary that dominate in the modern West: the market economy, the public sphere, the sovereign "people."

This is the key entry point to modern secularity, because this understanding of order was and is hotly contested, and this from a host of directions. Some saw it as insufficiently inspiring and uplifting; others, as poisoned by forms of discipline that repress and crush the spontaneous or the emotional in us; others, as rejecting true human sympathy and generosity in condemning "enthusiasm." But others again rejected it because it turned its back on violence, and hence heroism, and hence greatness—because it leveled us all in a demeaning equality. We find some of this latter kind of reaction in Tocqueville, for instance, but most famously in Nietzsche.

Nietzsche brings me to the key point here: that all these various forms of reaction can be taken in different directions. They can be the basis either for a return to faith or for the invention of new forms of secular, even atheist, outlook. The original connection of unbelief with the modern moral order sets the framework within which there has been a kind of "nova" effect, the multiplication of a greater and greater variety of different spiritual options, from the most reductive atheist materialism to the most unreconstructed orthodoxy, through all possible variations and combinations in between. Very remarkable are the positions that I describe as "immanent counter-Enlightenment," those of which Nietzsche is a paradigm example, who refuse all transcendence but fiercely turn against the "morality" implicit in the modern understanding of order.

Modern secularity therefore must be understood as this field of increasingly multiform contestation, in which every position is rendered uneasy and questionable because it can be challenged from many angles. These challenges have intensified in the past half-century in the West because of the spread of what one might call a "culture of authenticity," in which individuals and groups are encouraged to define and express their own particular identities. I want to argue that we are moving toward a sort of "fragmentation" of the spiritual, in which its previous connection with whole societies, be this in the older medieval form of sacred monarchies or in the modern form of "civil religion," is being strained to breaking point. We are entering a "post-Durkheimian" age.

We end up living in what I want to call an "immanent frame." This understanding draws on the sharp distinction between "natural" and "supernatural" that became dominant in Latin Christendom. The sense of the immanent frame is that of living in impersonal orders, cosmic, social, and ethical orders which can be fully explained in their own terms and don't need to be conceived as dependent on anything outside, on the "supernatural" or the "transcendent." This frame can be lived as "closed" but also as "open" to a beyond, and the tension between these two spins runs through the multiplying gamut of mutually cross-pressured positions that I call the nova.

To put this baldly (and even put at exhausting length in the book), this kind of account runs into misunderstandings. Some react like Jon Butler and speak of an explanation based on "ideas." Some similar criticism is afoot in Wendy Brown's contribution. I recognize that there is always a gap between aspiration and execution, but it should be clear that this is not what I am trying to do at all. The central target that I am trying to track is the change in the conditions of belief, which I call "secularity 3." The crucial features concern whether an issue arises about belief, and if so, in what terms and in what context?

Now, changes of this kind cannot be defined in terms of ideas or beliefs alone. The "conditions" in this sense are a matter of *experience*, the way these matters present themselves even prior to any articulation or reflection. Thus, as I argued above, disenchantment to me is not a matter of changing theory but rather of a transformation of sensibility. One of the big differences between, say, a Quebecois today and his French ancestors of five centuries ago lies not merely in different *beliefs* about spirits of the woods or the healing power of relics but in our inability to conjure up the experience of woods and relics as charged, to sense the charge inherent in these objects rather than seeing it as a *theory* we have formed about their power.

Further, the sense that we live in an "immanent frame" is also much more than a question of beliefs. This frame is part of our background understanding. It belongs to our "cosmic imaginary," and even more to our "social imaginary."

What Is a "Social Imaginary"?

What I'm trying to get at with this term is something much broader and deeper than the intellectual schemes people may entertain when they think about social reality in a disengaged mode. I am thinking rather of the ways in which they imagine their social existence, how they fit together with others, how things go on between them and their fellows, the expectations that are normally met, and the deeper normative notions and images that underlie these expectations.

I want to speak of "social imaginary" here, rather than social theory, because there are important differences between the two. There are, in fact, several differences. I speak of "imaginary" (1) because I'm talking about the way ordinary people "imagine" their social surroundings, and this is often not expressed in theoretical terms but carried in images, stories, legends, etc. But it is also the case that (2) theory is often the possession of a small minority, whereas what is interesting in the social imaginary is that it is shared by large groups of people, if not the whole society. Which leads to a third difference: (3) the social imaginary is that common understanding which makes possible common practices and a widely shared sense of legitimacy.

It very often happens that what starts off as theories held by a few people may come to infiltrate the social imaginary, first of elites, perhaps, and then of the whole society. This is what has happened, *grosso modo,* to the theories of Grotius and Locke, although the transformations have been many along the way, and the ultimate forms are rather varied.

Our social imaginary at any given time is complex. It incorporates a sense of the normal expectations that we have of each other, the kind of common understanding that enables us to carry out the collective practices which make up our social life. This incorporates some sense of how we all fit together in carrying out the common practice. This understanding is both factual and "normative"; that is, we have a sense of how things usually go, but this is interwoven with an idea of how they ought to go, of what missteps would invalidate the practice. Take our practice of choosing governments through general elections. Part of the background understanding that makes sense of the act of voting for each one of us is our awareness of the whole action, involving all citizens, each choosing individually but from among the same alternatives, and the compounding of these microchoices into one binding, collective decision. Essential to our understanding of what is involved in this kind of macrodecision is our ability to identify what would constitute a foul: certain kinds of influence, buying votes, threats, and the like. This kind of macrodecision has, in other words, to meet certain norms if it is to be what it is meant to be. If a minority could force all others to conform to their orders, it would cease to be a democratic decision, for instance.

Now, implicit in this understanding of the norms is the ability to recognize ideal cases, for instance, an election in which each citizen exercised to the maximum his or her judgment autonomously, in which everyone was heard, etc. And beyond the ideal stands some notion of a moral or metaphysical order, in the context of which the norms and ideals make sense.

What I'm calling the social imaginary extends beyond the immediate background understanding that makes sense of our particular practices. This is not an arbitrary extension of the concept, because just as the practice without the understanding wouldn't make sense for us, and thus wouldn't be possible, so this understanding supposes, if it is to make sense. a wider grasp of our whole predicament, how we stand to each other, how we got to where we are, how we relate to other groups, and so forth.

This wider grasp has no clear limits. That's the very nature of what contemporary philosophers have described as the "background."[3] It is in fact that largely unstructured and inarticulate understanding of our whole situation, within which particular features of our world show up for us in the sense they have. It can never be adequately expressed in the form of explicit doctrines, because of its very unlimited and indefinite nature. That is another reason for speaking here of an "imaginary" and not a theory.

The relation between practices and the background understanding behind them is therefore not one-sided. If the understanding makes the practice possible, it is also true that it is the practice which largely carries the understanding. At any given time, we can speak of the "repertory" of collective actions at the disposal of a given group of society. These are the common actions that they know how to undertake, all the way from the general election, involving the whole society, to knowing how to strike up a polite but uninvolved conversation with a casual group in a reception hall. The discriminations we have to make to carry these off, knowing whom to speak to and when and how, carry an implicit map of social space, of what kinds of people we can associate with, in what ways, in what circumstances. Perhaps I don't initiate the conversation at all, if the members of the group are all socially superior to me, or outrank me in the bureaucracy, or consist entirely of women.

3 See the discussions in Hubert L. Dreyfus, *Being-in-the-World* (Cambridge: MIT Press, 1991), and John Searle, *The Construction of Social Reality* (New York: Free Press, 1995), drawing on the work of Heidegger, Wittgenstein, and Polanyi.

This implicit grasp of social space is unlike a theoretical description of this space, distinguishing different kinds of people and the norms connected to them. The understanding implicit in practice stands to social theory the way that my ability to get around a familiar environment stands to a (literal) map of this area. I may very well be able to orient myself without ever adopting the standpoint of overview that the map offers me. And similarly, for most of human history, and for most of social life, we function through the grasp we have on the common repertory, without benefit of theoretical overview. Humans operated with a social imaginary well before they ever got into the business of theorizing about themselves.[4]

Another example might help to make more palpable the width and depth of this implicit understanding. Let's say we organize a demonstration. This indicates that this act is already in our repertory. We know how to assemble, pick up banners, and march. We know that this is meant to remain within certain bounds, both spatially (don't invade certain spaces) and in the way it impinges on others (this side of a threshold of aggressivity—no violence). We understand the ritual.

The background understanding that makes this act possible for us is complex, but part of what makes sense of it is some picture of ourselves as speaking to others, to which we are related in a certain way—say, compatriots, or the human race. There is a speech act here, addresser and addressees, and some understanding of how they can stand in this relation to each other. There are public spaces; we are already in some kind of conversation with each other. Like all speech acts, it is addressed to a previously spoken word, in the prospect of a to-be-spoken word.[5]

---

4 The way in which the social imaginary extends well beyond what has been (or even can be) theorized is illustrated in Francis Fukuyama's interesting discussion of the economics of social trust. Some economies find it difficult to build large-scale nonstate enterprises because a climate of trust that extends wider than the family is absent or weak. The social imaginary in these societies marks discriminations—between kin and nonkin—for purposes of economic association, which have gone largely unremarked in the theories of the economy that we all share, including the people in those societies. And governments can be induced to adopt policies, legal changes, incentives, etc., on the assumption that forming enterprises of any scale is there in the repertory and just needs encouragement. But the sense of a sharp boundary of mutual reliability around the family may severely restrict the repertory, however much it might be theoretically demonstrated to people that they would be better off changing their way of doing business. The implicit map of social space has deep fissures, which are profoundly anchored in culture and imaginary, beyond the reach of correction by better theory. See Francis Fukuyama, *Trust* (New York; Free Press, 1995).

5 Mikhail Bakhtin, *Speech Genres and Other Late Essays* (Austin: University of Texas Press, 1986).

The mode of address says something about the footing we stand on with our addressees. The action is forceful; it is meant to impress, perhaps even to threaten certain consequences if our message is not heard. But it is also meant to persuade; it remains this side of violence. It figures the addressee as one who can be, must be, reasoned with.

The immediate sense of what we're doing—getting the message to the government and our fellow citizens that the cuts must stop, say—makes sense in a wider context, in which we see ourselves as standing in a continuing relation with others, in which it is appropriate to address them in this manner and not, say, by humble supplication, or by threats of armed insurrection. We can gesture quickly at all this by saying that this kind of demonstration has its normal place in a stable, ordered, democratic society.

This does not mean that there are not cases where we might do this—Manila 1985, Tiananmen 1989—where armed insurrection would be perfectly justified. But precisely the point of this act in those circumstances is to invite tyranny to open up to a democratic transition.

We can see here how the understanding of what we're doing right now (without which we couldn't be doing *this* action) makes the sense it does because of our grasp on the wider predicament: how we continuingly stand or have stood to others and to power. This in turn opens out wider perspectives on where we stand in space and time: our relation to other nations and peoples, e.g., to external models of democratic life we are trying to imitate or of tyranny we are trying to distance ourselves from; and also of where we stand in our history, in the narrative of our becoming, whereby we recognize this capacity to demonstrate peacefully as an achievement of democracy, hard-won by our ancestors, or something we aspire to become capable of through this common action.

This sense of standing internationally and in history can be invoked in the iconography of the demonstration itself, as in Tiananmen in 1989, with its references to the French Revolution and its "citation" of the American case through the Statue of Liberty.

The background that makes sense of any given act is thus wide and deep. It doesn't include everything in our world, but the relevant sense-giving features can't be circumscribed; and because of this we can say that sense-giving draws on our whole world, that is, our sense of our whole predicament in time and space, among others and in history.

An important part of this wider background is what I called above a sense of moral order. I mean by this more than just a grasp of the norms underlying our social practice, which are part of the immediate understanding that makes this practice possible. There also must be a sense, as I stated above, of what makes these norms realizable. This too is an essential part of the context of action. People don't demonstrate for the impossible, for the utopic[6]—or if they do, then this becomes, ipso facto, a rather different action. Part of what we're saying as we march on Tiananmen is that a (somewhat more) democratic society is possible for us, that we could bring it off in spite of the skepticism of our gerontocratic rulers.

Just what this confidence is based on—for instance, that we, like other human beings, can sustain a democratic order together, that this is within our human possibilities—will include the images of moral order through which we understand human life and history. It ought to be clear from the above that our images of moral order, although they make sense of some of our actions, are by no means necessarily tilted toward the status quo. They may also underlie revolutionary practice, as at Manila and Beijing, just as they may underwrite the established order.

What I tried to do in *A Secular Age* was sketch the changeover, the process in which the modern theory of moral order gradually infiltrated and transformed the social imaginary. In this process, what is originally just an idealization grows into a complex imaginary by being taken up and associated with social practices, in part traditional ones, though it is often transformed by the contact. This is crucial to what I called above the extension of the understanding of moral order. It couldn't have become the dominant view in our culture without this penetration/transformation of our imaginary.

We see transitions of this kind happening, for instance, in the great founding revolutions of our contemporary world, the American and the French. The transition was much smoother and less catastrophic in one case, because the idealization of popular sovereignty connected up relatively unproblem-

---

6 This doesn't mean that utopias don't deal in their own kind of possibility. They may describe far-off lands or remote future societies which can't be imitated today, which we may never be able to imitate. But the underlying idea is that these things are really possible in the sense that they lie in the bent of human nature. This is what the narrator of More's book thinks: the Utopians are living according to nature (see Bronislaw Baczko, *Les imaginaires sociaux* [Paris: Payot, 1984], 75). This is also what Plato thought; he provided one of the models for More's book, and for a host of other utopian writings.

atically with an existing practice of popular election of assemblies; whereas in the other case, the inability to "translate" the same principle into a stable and agreed set of practices was an immense source of conflict and uncertainty for more than a century. But in both of these great events there was some awareness of the historical primacy of theory, which is central to the modern idea of a "revolution," whereby we set out to remake our political life according to agreed principles. This "constructivism" has become a central feature of modern political culture.

What exactly is involved when a theory penetrates and transforms the social imaginary? Well, for the most part people take up, improvise, or are inducted into new practices. These are made sense of by the new outlook, the one first articulated in the theory; this outlook is the context that gives sense to the practices. And hence the new understanding comes to be accessible to the participants in a way it wasn't before. It begins to define the contours of their world, and can eventually come to count as the taken-for-granted shape of things, too obvious to mention.

But this process isn't just one-sided, a theory making over a social imaginary. The theory, in coming to make sense of the action, is "glossed," as it were, given a particular shape as the context of these practices. Rather like Kant's notion of an abstract category becoming "schematized" when it is applied to reality in space and time,[7] the theory is schematized in the dense sphere of common practice.

Nor need the process end here. The new practice, with the implicit understanding it generates, can be the basis for modifications of theory, which in turn can inflect practice, and so on.

We can think of this process as a "long march," during which new practices, or modifications of old ones, either developed through improvisation among certain groups and strata of the population (e.g., the public sphere among educated elites in the eighteenth century, trade unions among workers in the nineteenth) or launched by elites in such a way as to recruit a larger and larger base (e.g., the Jacobin organization of the "sections" in Paris). Alternatively, a set of practices in the course of their slow development and ramification gradually changed their meaning for people, and hence helped

---

7 Immanuel Kant, "Von dem Schematismus der reinen Verständnisbegriffe," in *Kritik der reinen Vernunft*, vol. III (Berlin; Walter de Gruyter, 1968), 133–139.

to constitute a new social imaginary (the "economy"). The result in all these cases was a profound transformation of the social imaginary in Western societies, and thus of the world in which we live.

Cross-Purposes

Perhaps one of the reasons why some readers see my account as giving primacy to "ideas" is that the modern social imaginary I talk about *did* as a matter of fact originate in theory. This is something exceptional in history. The earlier social imaginaries it displaced weren't like this. Take, for instance, the sense in many earlier societies that our people live by our distinctive law "since time out of mind." This is the kind of imaginary that later gives rise to theories, like that of "the Ancient Constitution."[8] But it didn't originate in a theory. This feature is distinctive of the modern idea of moral order. It provides part of the basis for the widespread sense among Westerners that their civilization is defined by "enlightenment," and for our "stadial" consciousness, the sense that our way of life has emerged out of an earlier series of stages of human societies.

Moreover, it is connected to what I called "the great disembedding," which gives primacy to the individual. It is not only true, as I argued above, that this theory only enters our imaginary by the spread of political practices that it informs, but it is also the case that our modern sense of the individual is informed by a host of extrapolitical practices, for instance, those by which individuals discipline themselves (and of course these are also connected to politics in their own way).

The historiography I'm trying to draw on here, admittedly as an incompetent amateur consumer rather than a professional producer, is akin to that of *mentalités* and focuses on social imaginaries. This awakens insuperable skepticism in the breast of many historians. There is an important warning here, which I don't want to ignore, not to overplay the hand. But I don't think it ought to stop a mapper of social imaginaries altogether in her tracks.

Jonathan Sheehan gives voice to this skepticism in a very forceful way in Chapter 9. All this is not really history, he declares; rather it is conjectural his-

---

8 J. G. A. Pocock, *The Ancient Constitution and Feudal Law,* 2nd ed. (Cambridge: Cambridge University Press, 1987).

tory, the kind of thing Jean-Jacques Rousseau practiced, grandly declaring at the outset: *"Commençons par écarter tous les faits."* Commenting on my account of disenchantment, Sheehan raises a series of "empirical questions": Was it really true that all or even most people in mediaeval Europe believed in extrahuman subjects? What kind of data would give us good information abut this? What percentage translates into "most"? Returning in a time machine with a set of questionnaires would settle this kind of question, but short of this, we are not entirely without means. One involves looking at certain practices of the time, such as "beating the bounds" of a parish to protect it against the damage that spirits and other forces could wreak on it, or ringing the *carillon de tonnerre* when a storm descended on the village.

One way of defining a social imaginary is as the kind of collective understanding that a group has to have in order to make sense of their practices. Sometimes you can get an insight into the social imaginary of a society at a given time if you have some knowledge of its practices. Of course, this can go wrong in all sorts of ways. You may badly misidentify the point of the practice in question. You may utterly fail to see the important differences of interpretation that some global imaginary allows. You may be unable to discern important movements of internal dissidence, people who are profoundly disaffected but have to go along with the practice anyway, so that you are unprepared for a radical overturn that occurs soon afterward. And so on. I've probably made all these mistakes and more, but my *intentions* are not those of Jean-Jacques.

Later in his chapter, Sheehan takes up my use of the term "fullness." I wanted to use this as something like a category term to capture the very different ways in which each of us (as I claim) sees life as capable of some fuller, higher, more genuine, more authentic, more intense . . . form. The list of adjectives is indefinitely long, because the positions we may adopt have no finite limit. Why do this? Because I think that it is valuable to try to grasp a position you find unfamiliar and even baffling through trying to bring into focus the understanding of fullness it involves. This is particularly the case if you want really to understand it, to be able to feel the power it has for its protagonists, as against simply dismissing it. And this kind of understanding is crucial for me, as I will explain in a minute.

But this term seems to have led to more misunderstanding than communication. A lot of readers saw it as applying only to religious conceptions of fullness. Sheehan does not attribute this to me, at first anyway, but many others have. I guess the term can be pronounced in a way that has a religious or metaphysical ring. But this doesn't have to be the case.

Take Sportin' Life in *Porgy and Bess:* "Methuseleh lived 900 years; / who calls that livin' / when no gal will give in / to no man what's 900 years." Who calls that living? Some living isn't the real thing. There is *real* living—living to the full, as you might call it. My claim is that analogous distinctions crop up in all life forms. This distinction and its analogues are a human universal.

Sheehan chides me once again. How can I say this without any factual evidence? It has to be an anthropological claim. And indeed it is a claim of (philosophical) anthropology. This seems to Sheehan illegitimate, so he redefines it as a "theological claim." He takes back his original perception that the category was meant to be universal. Or perhaps he detects some sharp practice here: what is put forward as universal is secretly hooked up to the theological, to draw in unwary humanists (you gotta watch these Catholics).

But is this kind of philosophical anthropology so impossible to reason about? Think of Wittgensteinian ways of exploring the limits of sense-making.

Someone says: "Then I was really living," or "That's what I call living to the full." Why believe that this is one way of marking a universal distinction?

Well, imagine that someone replies to the first remark: "I don't know what you're talking about. Now you're alive, then you were alive. What's the difference?"

How do we understand this? It could be (1) an expression of despair: I never have this experience of living fully; my life is just one thing after another. Your making this remark reminds us of this, as a lack.

Or (2) our interlocutor might be making a point, telling us that we shouldn't see full life as something that only comes some of the time, that we should try to live every moment, every "now," as full. There are many variants of this. A Nietzschean might say this, or a Buddhist.

Or (3) our interlocutor might be chiding us for thinking that there are higher and lower activities; we should be able to find the fullness of life in the most ordinary or banal contexts. This objection parallels (2), on the level of activities rather than moments or temporal segments.

Or (4) our interlocutor might be chiding us for using the adverb "really."

That's not the way to distinguish (what I'm calling) full life from the rest. He wants us to use his term—"higher," say.

All these replies suppose that something like fullness can be identified, that there is such a thing as really living, full living. Could we really understand the remark in another sense, (5): I don't have the faintest idea what you're talking about, as I might react to someone who distinguished some trees or birds that I can't distinguish? Someone who might say: I never thought of my life like this at all. And this would be an incomprehension that couldn't be cleared up by using some other word, like "higher" or "charged" or whatever. My claim is that we're at least approaching, if we haven't passed, the point of unintelligibility.

Doesn't that tell us something about human life? Fullness is not a category fundamental to *cognition* in the Kantian sense, as Sheehan suggests I might be saying, but to human life in its mutual intelligibility.

The argument that I'm putting forward is this: all human beings make something like this kind of distinction, and it's very important to me to have, if not this word, this, as it were, general category, because I think that part of what's involved in understanding other positions is understanding their notion of fullness (or "motivating intensity," as Michael Warner suggests we put it). We see again and again these shallow misunderstandings of others' positions: how a lot of people with strong faith think that people who are atheists must find the world totally meaningless; or how people thought during the 1960s that all these kids out there are getting high and having these various kinds of sexual experiences, have just embraced hedonism, they are just letting everything go. The new sense of intensity in the movement was ignored or passed over. You can go on and on and on about how people fail to understand other people because they aren't asking themselves the question— given that this is, as I think, something that crops up in all different human lives—what is *their* sense of "fullness" (or "motivating intensity")? So I think it was a very, very useful idea to try to introduce this notion of a general facet or dimension of the human condition where people strive for—have a sense of—what really, fully, authentically, living would be, and to feel that they either aren't there or they are there, or they're getting there, or they're losing it, or they'd like to get there, and so on. This is something that plays a role in people's lives.

Now that I'm on a roll in my complaints of misunderstanding, I'd like to mention one other thing, which my mode of writing has generated among many readers. A crucial part of the book deals with what I call the nova, the widening brace of mutually defined positions that people adopt on the spiritual-moral, or anti-spiritual-moral, plane. This calls for a certain amount of explanation of opposed positions: on one hand, some say this; on the other hand, some say that.

I find it hard to write this if I have to repeat at the start of every sentence "According to position A" or "According to position B." So once I get launched into a description of a given position, I drop these annoying reminders. Moreover, I try to give the position in the rhetorical terms that those who espouse it use. The unfortunate result is that I often find ascribed to me as my own conclusion one of the views I have been describing in laying out a crucial opposition. So Sheehan affirms: "As Taylor concludes, 'Modes of fullness recognized by exclusive humanisms, and others that remain within the immanent frame, are . . . responding to transcendent reality, but misrecognizing it'" (SA, 768). The enclosed quote is mine, indeed; it comes in attempt to lay out the assumptions underlying two views of the future. It describes the suppositions underlying one of those views.

Now it is quite true that most people will find themselves closer to one or the other set of assumptions here. In the interests of full disclosure (which I think is important in a book of this kind), I am happy to state where I personally stand. *But this is not the conclusion of the book.* To put it that way backs up Sheehan's hermeneutic of suspicion, that I am putting forward putatively universal terms of description that are subtly devised to weight the dice in favor of one position.

But this is not what I'm trying to do. If the book has a desired perlocutionary effect, it is rather this: I think what we badly need is a conversation between a host of different positions, religious, nonreligious, antireligious, humanistic, antihumanistic, and so on, in which we eschew mutual caricature and try to understand what "fullness" means for the other. What makes me impatient are the positions that are put forward as conversation-stoppers: I have a three-line argument which shows that your position is absurd or impossible or totally immoral. Of course, I have my own, theologically defined reasons for wanting this, but I also know that we can have a widely based "overlapping consensus" on the value of this conversation.

There are many things to be said in favor of such a conversation. But one that I think is of paramount importance is that it is an antidote to the tendency of some people in all positions to project evil onto other positions and call for their elimination for the sake of mankind. This tendency has risen to world-threatening force in many milieus, and it is all too easy for this total, potentially violent rejection to call forth equal and opposite modes of rejection from the positions it targets.

I think that it might help if I clarified more fully my own motivation in writing this book. My Catholic faith enters into the equation, but not in the way many people think it must. I want to pick up something that Philip Gorski said about the relation of certain Christians to Buddhism, like the undercurrent in a man's relation to his "attractive sister-in-law." I don't see it in those illicit terms. I'll tell you why. Let me come out of the closet and tell you what it means to be my kind of Catholic. I think that we have a calling to understand very different positions, particularly very different understandings of fullness. One important reason is that if one doesn't do that, one hobbles around on crutches. That is, you give yourself a sense that your position is right because of some caricature of the alternative you entertain, and you say, "Well, I mean, I can't be that kind of thing." Think of the pictures of Buddhism that have often circulated in Christendom: totally otherworldly, not interested in helping people, and so on. Who wants to accept that? "So I'm going to remain a Christian if the alternative is to be a Buddhist"—the problem is solved. We all need to get over those crutches by really coming to experience the power and attraction of quite different understandings of the world, atheist and theist. I happen to have been granted the possibility of having some deep sense—I'm sure I don't understand it very well—of the power of Buddhism. But I don't think this is something that, as it were, threatens or is against my Christian faith. On the contrary, I think it's something that I'm called on to do more of. And so one reason is that you don't live by what's powerful in your own faith unless you throw away the crutches that keep you from facing that, and the crutches are depreciating stories about others.

That's the first reason. And the second is, of course, that you can learn something from these other positions. But the third, and for my argument here the decisive, reason is that it's possible to build friendship across these boundaries based on a real mutual sense, a powerful sense, of what moves the other person. That's why I want very much to agree with Bill Connolly's whole approach. The relationships are agonistic in his sense because we're not in the business of trying to make some kind of middle, compromised solution or synthesis—no. We're in the business of friendship, which incorporates the kind of understanding where each can come to be moved by what moves the other.

Now, what has that got to do with Christianity? Everything, to me: that is what it's all about. It's all about reconciliation. It's all about reconciliation between human beings, and it doesn't simply mean within the Church, and it doesn't mean that it's conditioned on being within the Church. If you ever get to Chapter 20—and, you know, I don't blame you for dropping out before then—the invocation there of the communion of saints may help explain what I mean.

And in this context, let me say to Colin Jager, I plead guilty as charged: I'm a hopeless German romantic of the 1790s. I resonate with Herder's idea of humanity as the orchestra, in which all the differences between human beings could ultimately sound together in harmony.

Now, what does all this amount to? There's a certain amount of argument in the book, and the motivation partly comes from my faith position. Does this mean that the book's an apology? Well, I suppose that I'm offering reasons for a certain kind of Christian position. The first thing I'm trying to do is get this kind of conversation going across as many differences as I can, and I recognize that my sympathies are narrow, so I don't go as broad as I should, but I'd like to get this conversation going. And that means that I am critical of other ways of being Catholic today. I have inevitably addressed some things in the book to my coreligionaries; I have, obviously, great reservations about certain versions of Catholicism which come from relatively high places.

And so a big part of the intellectual agenda of the book is trying to explain the whole phenomenon of modern secularity and the nova of ever more varied positions in a way in which we could go on having a conversation about it that bridges these differences. But there's a practical extension of this, and that's what I've just been living for the last year in the Quebec commission on the practices of reasonable accommodation, where, as you know, great issues arose about religious difference, in particular targeting Islam—and Islamophobia naturally came into the debate. We tried to orchestrate some meetings—not just the usual kind of hearings, where sober mayors and secretaries of organizations come before you with a brief, but we had meetings in which a lot of people just came in off the street and started to talk, and some of it was pretty raw stuff and came pretty close to xenophobia, but others were there to answer these remarks. And in some cases people actually learned something—they learned something by being confronted with others and having to recognize that these others didn't match the caricatures that they had of them.

Now, I don't think that we're going to manage to get through this tremendous diversification of Western society with a decent society unless we not only have the right rules and the right principles and so on, but have enough people who have this kind of gut sense that there's something really valuable in that other person—and other view, etc.—and are willing to talk to them, because when the rubber hits the road and the going gets really tough, when certain media are, let's say, not behaving entirely responsibly in whipping up the wrong kinds of sentiments, it matters a lot. See—in politics you discover this—sometimes the small battalions really count. If there are enough people here and there who have enough meeting and understanding of the others, they can stand like firebreaks in a forest fire. We were in the business, in a certain sense, of trying to multiply those firebreaks, and so this particular political action I consider to be entirely in continuity with the conversations and exchanges that have animated the present volume. I value this tremendously—this kind of exchange. I value this personally. I value this in terms of my faith. I value this in terms of what I can discover. But I also value this because I see that it's something we really need in our present predicament. And so for all these reasons, the attempt of *A Secular Age*—to lay out a basis of conversation (and I'm sure it's very incomplete, and it needs to be changed, amended, etc.)—this is the kind of thing we have to be doing.

Contributors

Name Index

Subject Index

Contributors

ROBERT N. BELLAH, University of California, Berkeley

AKEEL BILGRAMI, Columbia University

WENDY BROWN, University of California, Berkeley

JON BUTLER, Yale University

CRAIG CALHOUN, Social Science Research Council and New York University

JOSÉ CASANOVA, Georgetown University

WILLIAM E. CONNOLLY, Johns Hopkins University

SIMON DURING, Johns Hopkins University

NILÜFER GÖLE, Ecole des Hautes Etudes, Paris

COLIN JAGER, Rutgers University

SABA MAHMOOD, University of California, Berkeley

JOHN MILBANK, University of Nottingham, United Kingdom

JONATHAN SHEEHAN, University of California, Berkeley

CHARLES TAYLOR, McGill University

JONATHAN VANANTWERPEN, Social Science Research Council and New York University

MICHAEL WARNER, Yale University

Name Index

Subject Index

Immanent Frame (blog), 1n1, 25n28, 107, 177n, 225n18, 230n29, 239

immanentism, 71

immanent materialism, 110, 131

immanent naturalism, 128–129, 131–134, 136, 138. *See also* naturalism; supernaturalism

incarnation, 19, 66, 79, 80, 81. *See also* excarnation

indifference, religious, 205–209, 215, 230n

intellectual deviation story, 71, 77–79

Islam, 70, 82; Bush administration on, 84; disembeddedness and, 261–262, 264; fundamentalism and, 298; gender and, 248–263; headscarf debate in France, 248–253; headscarf debate in Turkey, 253–256; Islamophobia, 320; Kemalist reforms, 253; Muslim migration, 245, 249n, 259, 260, 262; Muslim self-fashioning, 260–261, 263; neofundamentalism and, 260; pluralism and, 14, 134, 137; Quran, 67, 70, 262; secularism and, 84, 245–263; sexuality and, 248, 251, 256, 262–264; Turkish secularism (laiklik), 247, 253–259; Wahhabism, 62

and, 37–39, 47, 56; sovereign people and, 37–39, 46–47

Modern Social Imaginaries (Taylor), 43, 194, 197, 199, 207

monotheism, 62, 72

mundane (as philosophical and historical concept), 105, 113–125, 183, 230, 239; mundane transcendence, 131–133

Muslims. *See* Islam

n +1 (journal), 5

naturalism, 24, 75; immanent, 128–129, 131–134, 136, 138. *See also* supernaturalism

neoliberalism. *See* liberalism

New Left: Charles Taylor and, 105, 108

New Left Review, 33

New Republic, 6

New York Times Book Review, 4

9/11, 84

nova effect, 56, 175, 178–179, 279, 306–307, 318, 320; in Europe, 280; in the United States, 273

Judaism, 66, 69, 70; Marx on, 95–98

orthodoxy, radical. *See* radical orthodoxy

Latin Christendom. *See* Christianity

liberalism: Carl Schmitt on, 118; neoliberalism, 104, 121; Rousseau on, 74, 76

Lyrical Ballads (Wordsworth), 180

magic, 204, 303

materialism, 87–90, 102; immanence and, 109, 110, 131; Marx on, 165; mechanical materialism, 136–137

Middle Ages, 220–222, 224, 275–276

modernity: democracy and, 32, 37–47; early, 219–227, 232–240; economy and, 37–40; ethics and, 47–53; public sphere

paganism, 69, 202, 205

particularism, 42, 46, 49

personalism: in Christianity and Judaism, 55, 70–71; prayer and, 68

Phenomenology of Spirit, The (Hegel), 108, 116

pluralism: deep, 134, 137, 143; Islam and, 14, 134, 137; multidimensional, 136–137; religious difference and, 282, 295–299

Prelude, The (Wordsworth), 189–191

Protestant Reformation, 200, 205, 212, 222, 276, 305; as part of larger history of reform, 15–16; Protestant establishment, 150; as universal religion, 183.